Representations of "the Jew" have long been a topic of interest in Joyce studies; in *James Joyce, 'Ulysses', and the construction of Jewish identity* Neil R. Davison argues that Joyce's lifelong encounter with pseudo-scientific, religious, and political discourse about "the Jew" forms a unifying component of his career. Davison offers new biographical material to support the claim that "the Jew" was a dynamic aspect of Joyce's imagination from youth to adulthood, and presents a detailed reading of *Ulysses* to show how Joyce draws on Christian folklore, Dreyfus Affair propaganda, Sinn Fein politics, and theories of Jewish sexual perversion and financial conspiracy. Inscriptions of "the Jew" in *Ulysses* form an attack on the authority of the discourse of anti-Semitism and evince the realist narrative buried beneath the pyrotechnics of Joyce's writing. Throughout, Joyce confronts the controversy of "race", the psychology of internalized sterotype, and the contradictions of *fin-de-siècle* anti-Semitism.

JAMES JOYCE, *ULYSSES*, AND THE CONSTRUCTION OF JEWISH IDENTITY

JAMES JOYCE, *ULYSSES*, AND THE CONSTRUCTION OF JEWISH IDENTITY

Culture, Biography, and "The Jew"
in Modernist Europe

NEIL R. DAVISON

CAMBRIDGE
UNIVERSITY PRESS

Published by the Press Syndicate of the University of Cambridge
The Pitt Building, Trumpington Street, Cambridge CB2 1RP
40 West 20th Street, New York, NY 10011-4211, USA
10 Stamford Road, Oakleigh, Melbourne 3166, Australia

First published 1996

Printed in Great Britain at the University Press, Cambridge

A catalogue record for this book is available from the British Library

Library of Congress cataloguing in publication data

Davison, Neil R.
James Joyce, *Ulysses*, and the construction of Jewish identity / Neil R. Davison
p.   cm.
Includes bibliographical references and index.
ISBN 0 521 55181 1 (hardback)
1. Joyce, James, 1882–1941. Ulysses. 2. Joyce, James, 1882–1941 –
Religion. 3. Joyce, James, 1882–1941–Characters–Jews. 4. Jews
in literature. 5. Anti-Semitism–History–20th century. 6. Bloom,
Leopold (Fictitious character) 7. Stereotype (Psychology) in
literature. 8. Novelists, Irish–20th century–Biography.
I. Title.
PR6019.09U6363 1996
823'.912–dc20
95 – 7530
CIP

ISBN 0 521 55181 1 hardback

In the alien, therefore, man discovered the idea of humanity.
Hermann Cohen (1842–1918)

Contents

Acknowledgements

For their assistance in the many and varied tasks that helped to complete this project I would like to express my gratitude to the staffs of the Library of Congress, the National Library Dublin, the Archives of University College Dublin, the Georgetown University Library, McKeldon Library at the University of Maryland, the Catholic University Library, the Johns Hopkins University Library, *The Irish Times*, the archives of *The Times*, archives of the *Freeman's Journal*, the James Joyce Museum at Sandymount, and the International James Joyce Foundation. I am indebted to Ira Nadel, Ralph Joly, Marilyn Reizbaum, John Russell, Corinna Del Greco Lobner, Patrick McCarthy, Gerald Goldberg, and Morton Levitt for either their encouragement, discussions of, comments on, or readings of portions of this work. A special thanks to Sander Gilman for reading and recommending the manuscript for publication, and to Father Fergus O'Donoghue, SJ for his guidance and advice on the Jesuit research of the project. This book began as a Ph.D. thesis at the University of Maryland at College Park, and I am especially grateful to my director, Professor W. Milne Holton, as well as my second reader, Professor David Wyatt. I would also like to thank Professor Marshall Grossman for his comments on, and support of, my work from thesis to book. Thank you as well to Kevin Taylor and Josie Dixon at Cambridge University Press. My gratitude to my parents, brother and sister, and friends for their love and devotion, and for their support of my goals and aspirations.

Finally, I am most grateful to my wife Nadine, whose patience, kindness, intelligence, and untiring support made this work possible.

Abbreviations

CW   Joyce, James, *The Critical Writings*, eds., Ellsworth Mason and Richard Ellmann (Ithaca: Cornell University Press, 1989).

D   Joyce, James, *Dubliners*, eds., Robert Scholes and A. Walton Litz (New York: Viking Penguin, Inc., 1968).

JJII   Ellmann, Richard, *James Joyce*, revised edition (Oxford: Oxford University Press, 1982).

JJQ   *James Joyce Quarterly*, ed., Robert Spoo (Tulsa: University of Tulsa).

P   Joyce, James, *A Portrait of the Artist as a Young Man: Text, Criticism, and Notes*, ed., Chester G. Anderson (New York: The Viking Critical Library, 1968).

SH   Joyce, James, *Stephen Hero*, eds., Theodor Spencer, John J. Slocum, and Herbert Cahoon (New York: New Directions Publications, 1963).

U   Joyce, James, *Ulysses: The Corrected Texts*, eds., Hans Walter Gabler, Wolfhard Steppe, and Clause Melchor (New York: Random House, 1986).

Introduction

[In 1938] when a young Harvard student wrote to him to praise *Ulysses* but complain of Joyce's attitude toward his race, Joyce remarked, "I have written with the greatest sympathy about the Jews."[1]

Richard Ellmann, James Joyce

Sixteen years after the publication of *Ulysses*, James Joyce remained sensitive to the controversy of Leopold Bloom's "Jewishness." Nearly sixty years later, and despite an often undervalued wealth of argument on the subject, we ourselves are still contending with the "indeterminacies" of Bloom's Jewish identity, as well as with the role of "the Jew" in the novel. While *fin-de-siècle* discourse about "the Jew" informs Bloom's character throughout the text, within the framework of Judaic law, he cannot of course be considered *Halachically* Jewish.[2] A few readers of the novel, moreover, may continue to assert that – despite efforts on Joyce's part to the contrary – *Ulysses* perpetuates pernicious Jewish stereotypes. It is less arguable, however, that a multitude of European cultural markers of "Jewishness" are critical to Joyce's construction of Bloom's inner-life as well as to his subject position. In this manner, a study of the extrinsic forces that impacted on both Joyce and his work is central to an understanding of "the Jew" in *Ulysses*. But contextual analysis alone cannot evince the meanings of the text's representations of "the Jew"; Joyce's narrative experiments also play a decisive role in such an endeavor, and often render intricate portrayals of Bloom's plight as a marginal Jew. Bloom's "Jewishness," then, whatever we discover it to be, cuts across both form and content, becoming pivotal to the representational, narratological, and even historiographical aspects of the novel.

Like many complex social/textual issues, however, questions surrounding "the Jew" in *Ulysses* have met over the years with some devastating ironies. While Stuart Gilbert's work inaugurated the subject's study, which has steadily and quietly continued to this day, a recognition of the centrality of "Jewishness" in both Joyce's consciousness and the novel has yet to be achieved. Joyce scholars still often view discussions of "the Jew" as less crucial than those of other fields of interest, or even worse, regard it merely as anecdotal for the Joycean "insider." In the past, this lesser status has been enabled because, despite the movement in humanities from a liberal to a radical center, "the Jew" as a key point of cultural analysis has negligently remained a "specialized" endeavor. Moreover, in traditional Joyce studies, "the Jew" was and is too often investigated not through cultural discourse or political history, but as a mythic trope, a static element of hermeneutics. In his recent work, *Constructions of "the Jew" in English Literature and Society: Racial Representations, 1875–1945* (1993), Bryan Cheyette locates such a failure to address both "the Jew" and anti-Semitism at the center of contemporary literary studies:

Not unlike Michel Foucault's history of sexuality, 'literary anti-semitism' has been conceived as an open 'secret' or unacknowledged common place that, during intermittent 'storms of abuse' is also spoken about *'ad infinitum'*. This unhappy state of affairs has, furthermore, been unwittingly reinforced by influential studies of 'The Jew in English literature' which have defined Jewish literary representations as fixed 'stereotypes', 'myths' or 'images' that have remained essentially the same across centuries and are thus, in the words of Hannah Arendt, 'natural consequences of an eternal problem.' The privileged cultural realm of literature remains essentially unthreatened by the naturalized construction of an eternal mythic 'Jew'. The mythic 'Jew', that is, exists quite comfortably in the realm of 'culture' which is, supposedly, above and beyond the messy contingencies of history and the crude expediencies of politics.[3]

Due to the breadth of his project, Cheyette conducts a predominantly textual analysis of Joyce's "semitic discourse." As my work here demonstrates, however, grasping "the Jew" in *Ulysses* entails no less than weighing the cultural, biographical, political, intertextual, and textual into a combined approach toward a rereading of the novel.

Despite the inattention of the larger world of Joyce studies, however, a retrospect of work on "the Jew" in *Ulysses* could begin with the book's very first reviews. Valéry Larbaud, one of Joyce's earliest supporters, claimed Bloom was a Jew because of "symbolical, mystical and ethnological reasons. . .[and] not because of anti-Semitism."[4] Frank Budgen was also interested in the controversy of

Bloom as a Jew, and characterized him as "no stage Jew. . .[but] a product of three-hundred years of social and political emancipation."[5] (Budgen would have been more accurate in altering his phrase to *attempted* emancipation.) Writing under the pseudonym Lawrence K. Emery, A. J. Leventhal, a Trinity University lecturer and an acquaintance of Joyce, suggested Bloom's Jewishness as central among the novel's "themes" as early as 1923.[6] In 1963, he postulated that Stephen Dedalus' "silence, exile, and cunning," as a strategy for survival in the margins of society, also attaches to Bloom as a Jew:

Joyce's choice of these three unusual weapons has a special significance in regard to the relationship in *Ulysses* between Stephen and Bloom. Bloom more than a symbol of the eternal Jew is in exile in the Irish capital; Joyce has imposed exile on himself in many European capitals. "Cunning," if we omit the overtone of artistic craft in the case of Joyce, is a characteristic of all oppressed races – an astuteness in avoiding penal laws and in skirting the pitfalls created by prejudice and hate. This applies only partly to Joyce himself, though it covers the Irish at an earlier period of history, and almost wholly to Bloom as a stranger among Irish patriots unwilling to accept him as one of themselves.[7]

Leventhal saw Jewish silence in the face of Nazi persecution and Joyce's silence toward the political turmoil of the post-Parnell years as analogous. Accordingly, Joyce chose expatriation rather than the arguments of nationalist politics, "the songs" of the Celtic revival, or the sounds of armed rebellion.

In America, two of the earliest voices to demonstrate the value of "the Jew" in the novel were those of Marvin Magalaner and Morton Levitt. Magalaner's 1953 research on Joyce's anti-Semitic sources was revelatory.[8] Levitt, whose 1969 article "The Family of Bloom" was one of the first readings to foreground Bloom's struggle with Jewishness, continued his interest through several other pieces, and has recently explored Talmudic aspects of *Finnegans Wake*.[9] Stanley Sultan's work, *The Argument of Ulysses* (1965) established the text's anti-Semitic tropes as vital to the overall narrative development of the novel.[10] In addition, various articles have appeared over the years, all of which have added to our knowledge of Joyce's "Jewish sources," as well as continually shaped and reshaped our view of Bloom.[11] In his more casual essays, for example, Leslie Fielder has over the years remained particularly vocal about Bloom as a Jew and Joyce's sensibility as a "*Yiddisher Kopf.*"[12]

At present, *Ulysses* has also generated three book-length studies of its discourse on "the Jew." The first of these was Ralph Joly's *The Jewish Element in James Joyce's Ulysses* (1973), a Chapel Hill dissertation. Joly demonstrates how Judaic lore and ritual creates a textual structure as significant to the book as the influence of Homer's *Odyssey*. In her 1985 Wisconsin dissertation, *Joyce's Judaic Other: Texts and Contexts*, Marilyn Reizbaum explores Joyce's use of political and scientific sources to create Bloom's "Otherness" as a Jew. Reizbaum has, as well, maintained her interest in "Jewish Joyce" through several scholarly articles.[13] Collating such arguments and presenting new research, Ira Nadel published *Joyce and the Jews* in 1989, the only book on the subject to appear in print. Nadel's work is an excellent introduction to Joyce's relations with Jewish individuals and Judaic motifs, and offers key insights into Talmudic allusions in *Finnegans Wake*. As a study in "Culture and Texts," however, Nadel focuses mainly on social influences and makes no argument about Bloom's Jewishness as a central interpretative element of *Ulysses*.

Conversely, many extant textual analyses of "the Jew" in the novel too often highlight the same exact select passages. Because such discrete exegesis fails to explore the over-arching relevance of European anti-Semitic culture to the entire text, none have accomplished a comprehensive reading from this standpoint. Moreover, the failure (with the exception of Nadel) to examine the evolution of Joyce's lifelong encounter with ideas and programs about "the Jew" has only added to the subject's demotion in Joyce criticism. Explored in depth, however, Joyce's awareness of the cultural positions of such programs indeed forms a unifying component of his career.

In constructing Bloom, Joyce drew on a complex body of representations of "the Jew" that he had absorbed first as a Catholic child and adolescent, then as a disgruntled liberal Irishman, and finally as a "Europeanized," "modernist" author. On one level, Bloom is Joyce's construction of his era's assimilated Jew who was often marginal to both a dominant culture as well as to the culture of *Halachic* Judaism. But, *inter alia*, Bloom also reveals how Joyce, as a member of one disenfranchised group, imagines the racial or biological "nature" of a member of another. While a reader may respond to Bloom as an Irishman, Hungarian, or even "Everyman," Joyce appears always to have perceived him first as a Jew. This privileging of one of Bloom's many identities indicates that the converted, agnostic character embodied traits recognizable to Joyce as "Jewish." On occasion, Joyce in fact underscored his belief in "Jewish characteristics" with a bit of humor, a canard that ironically draws on the era's British convention of the "Jew joke" and "Scotch Joke":

A Scotchman and a Jew were traveling on a ship which foundered and sank. They spent three days together in a lifeboat. At the end of that time, the Jew said, "I'm a Jew." The Scotchman said, "I'm a hunchback."[14]

What were "Jewish traits" to Joyce and why did he become so obsessed with them? On what cultural assumptions does his construction of Jewish identity rely? How does *Ulysses* appropriate and subvert hegemony about "Jewishness" in Europe? Why did Jews become so pivotal to Joyce? How did he arrive at the conclusion that certain "Jewish traits" lend themselves to the empowerment of Otherness? How do those specific traits figure in Bloom's conflict? Such questions have prompted me to reinvestigate Joyce biography, intertextual relations among Joyce's work and a host of sources, and the position(s) of "the Jew" in nineteenth-century European culture.

Scholars have indeed recently been called to the task of re-evaluating Joycean biography.[15] A central target for this approach, of course, is Richard Ellmann's work. Revisionary renderings of Joyce's life, however, do not always question the accuracy of Ellmann's findings, but rather provoke the curious to look for other "Joyces" than the one discovered in those conclusions. This study also attempts to broaden the scope of how we perceive Joyce by reinvestigating key moments of his career and offering new research to support the idea that "the Jew" was a dynamic aspect of his imagination since childhood. In this manner, juxtaposition of historical event, religious and racial discourse, Joyce's progress as a thinker, and the work itself, opens many new insights. My inquiry into the evolution of "Joyce's Jew" indeed culminates in a rereading of *Ulysses*, in which Bloom's struggle for a Jewish identity becomes the crux of the character's dilemma, as well as an entrance into the text's evaluation of "Jewishness" and its positioning of the era's Jewish question.[16]

Critics often work under the assumption that Bloom sprung nearly full blown from Joyce's imagination around 1914, some time after his friendship with Italo Svevo. But this is not the case. As alluded to above, the task of decoding "the Jew" in *Ulysses* is inseparable from a recognition of the cultural and political forces that played on Joyce throughout his life. The interplay of those forces, issuing from the distinct environments of Dublin, Paris, Trieste, and Zurich, is precisely where one must begin to unravel Bloom, who, as the product of Joyce's long-running fascination with "the Jew," is on many levels a demythologizing of the central notions about "Jewishness" in Europe.

Joyce was of course born into the liberal nineteenth-century atmosphere in which the subject of "the Jew" pervaded Christian doctrine as well as cultural, scientific, and political discourse. Shortly after he became an apostate from Catholicism, he encountered fully the Continent's racialist/scientized discourse about biologically inherited "Jewish nature." By the time the thirty-two-year-old Joyce began to compose *Ulysses*, his knowledge of culturally sanctioned myths about "the Jew" had reached a boiling point. In manipulating Bloom's conflicts, Joyce acknowledged that such stereotypes were based in and fueled by the dominant ideologies of his world: pseudo-scientific racism, Christian theologies, Church politics, aggressive nationalism, liberal culture-worship, and imperialist economic doctrine.[17]

Nineteenth-century scholarly discussions of Judaism were, moreover, often set in the context of the broader "verities" of Orientalism. One result of this placement was a bifurcated vision of "the Jew." On one level, Judaism as religion found a new popularity as a means to study ancient "Hebraism," now cast as the foundation of one pole of "European culture." On another level, "the Jew" was positioned as an inferior racial type and economic subversive, untrustworthy as a citizen. More decisively than the first, the second representation drew its strength solely from stereotype and of course fostered prejudice in both the educated and working classes throughout Europe. But the first notion about Jews as "Hebraic" was presented as an "academically unbiased" aspect of the history of "Western culture." Drawing on the work of German Romantics, especially that of Heine, these arguments routinely proposed Hebraism, the ancient, opposing force to Hellenism, as one of the twin poles of Western consciousness – an idea that Matthew Arnold made palpable for the British reading public through his theories in *Culture and Anarchy: an Essay in Political and Social Criticism* (1869). Becoming central to Victorian discourse on "the Jew," however, such assertions ultimately helped to solidify the perception of Jews as the modern "Semitic people" subordinate to those of "Indo-European" descent.

Acutely aware of how the Irish had been cast as Other in British society, Joyce eventually perceived a similarity between the plight of his people and that of the Jews. Demonstrating his acceptance of the era's "science," however, Joyce believed to some extent that this bond was grounded in the parallel "nature" of the two peoples: "They were alike, he [once] declared, in being impulsive, given to fantasy, addicted to associative thinking, [and] wanting in rational discipline."[18] In the avant-garde circles he entered on the Continent, Joyce came to perceive assimilated Jewish intellectuals as his literati, and soon selected "the Jew" as his dominant trope of Otherness. By the latter years of his career, Joyce suggested through "Shem the Penman" in *Finnegans Wake* that the position of the Jew was analogous to that of the twentieth-century writer, the fragmented voice (re)defining itself through the word. This shared sense of difference was later echoed by Jacques Derrida in his discussion of Edmond Jabès: "The only thing that begins by reflecting itself is history. And this fold, this furrow, is the Jew...the situation of the Jew becomes exemplary of the situation of the poet, the man of speech and writing."[19] For Joyce, however, this connection began well before he created Bloom, and grew to mean more to him than merely a literary "fellowship of alienation."

Joyce's theory about an Irish–Jewish similarity also drew on nationalistic rhetoric he had encountered in childhood. Utilizing Irish histories that claimed an Hebraic ancestry for the Milesian Celts, Parnell-as-Moses images influenced Joyce's earliest political awareness. But by the composition of *Ulysses*, Jews to Joyce were not so much "legendary forefathers" as much as they were brothers in marginality. Both groups to him had suffered a discrediting at the hand of Western tradition: both had played crucial roles in the development of Europe, yet both were disempowered by cultures that portrayed them as "racially" inferior and thus destructive to "blood-based" political programs.[20]

Previous to these influences, however, Joyce's formative years had taught him that the Jews' deicidal guilt was a central precept of Christian theology. But having for the most part discarded those beliefs as an adult, he came to view "the Jew" of Europe – the modern, assimilated Jew – as a focal point of some of the more volatile social issues of his day. This liberal, "secular" Jew – dubbed "the non Jewish-Jew" by Isaac Deutscher in the 1950s – was the product of years of acculturation within what had become the centers of *fin-de-siècle* thought.[21] To Joyce, Bloom represented the urban, Westernized Jew, lost to Judaism but still somehow inwardly "Jewish." This sense of "Jewishness" was embodied for Joyce in such renowned contemporaries as Stefan Zweig, Otto Weininger, Theodor Herzl, and, closer to his own experience, Italo Svevo. In interrogating his own culture, Joyce took that "Jew" and transported him to Dublin; if that city was to be made an exemplum of the era, then "the Jew" would reside at the center of *Ulysses'* narrative.

As an adolescent, Joyce of course became obsessed with the paralyzing self-hate of his own ethnic Irish legacy. When he moved to the Continent and began socializing with Jews, he discovered a similar self-hatred in many of those with whom he became closely acquainted. Recognizing the parallel, Joyce soon displaced onto his "Jew" his ambivalence toward being an apostate, expatriated Irishman – indeed, toward his own "Irishness." This dynamic is central to understanding Joyce's need to construct the seemingly indefatigable ambiguity of Bloom's "Jewishness."[22] But although such projection is essential to stereotyping, "Joyce's Jew" is neither stereotypical nor consciously anti-Semitic. Bloom is more a mosaic of Jewish representation, made complex through both Joyce's projection and critical imagination. Rather than fixing "the Jew" as a static reality, *Ulysses* presents a spectrum of anti-Jewish myths for analysis – from "the Jew" of Christianity to that of racial degeneracy to that of nationalistic pariahism.

Indeed, by confronting the differing anti-Semitic arguments inscribed in *Ulysses*, one simultaneously confronts nineteenth-century Europe's most prevalent representations of "the Jew." For example, the notion that during the imperialist era Jewish banking dynasties lost status in the nation-state and social hatred of "the Jew" thus gained a new power – a notion Joyce represents in *Ulysses* – was later studied by Hannah Arendt in *The Origins of Totalitarianism* (1951).[23] The contemporary work of Sander Gilman explores many of the same Jewish stereotypes that surround Bloom, especially in those scenes where he is perceived as a Jew by non-Jews. Gilman demonstrates how psychological and physiognomic myths of "the Jew" formed cultural mythologies in European societies ranging from Vienna, to Paris, to London. In *Jewish Self-Hatred: Anti-Semitism and the Hidden Language of the Jews* (1986), Gilman illustrates how Jewish writers themselves, from Heine to Freud, encode in their language an internalized self-hatred of "the Jew" produced through the haunting sense of Otherness. Although he is not a writer, Bloom as a character expresses a similar self-abnegation, complicating it through his experience of both an Irish and Jewish identity. Another Gilman project, *The Jew's Body* (1991), also relates how "the Jew" of these myths appears most often as male.[24] This too is true for Joyce's "Jew"; while Joyce had a lifelong infatuation with "dark Jewish females," "the Jew" of his literary imagination was most often male. As products of his Catholic upbringing, Joyce's childhood images of "the Jew" relied on prototypes such as Judas, Caiaphas, and perhaps most importantly, Ahasuerus. But because Joyce admired many of the Jewish men he came to know as an adult, this "Jew" soon served as an object on to which he projected his own self-image as a male – one which he characterized as non-violent, bookish, and domestically minded. Joyce often perceived "the Jew" as the Christian male's binary opposite; thus Bloom's struggle for a Jewish identity is also a struggle for a "Jewish masculinity," which encompasses discourse about the "feminized Jew" Joyce encountered most prominently in the writings of the German psychobiologist, Weininger.

Despite the crucial role "the Jew" played in Joyce's psychology, however, some readers of *Ulysses* continue to question the relevance of calling Bloom a Jew in any sense of the term. One prominent example is the disturbing apathy toward Bloom found in Phillip Herring's *Joyce's Uncertainty Principle* (1987). Herring asserts that the "indeterminacy of identity" in characters such as Stephen, Molly, and "the man in the mackintosh" are "fascinating" examples of Joyce's use of "uncertainty."[25] In regard to the web of Bloom's Jewish identity, however, Herring claims that "the answer obviously depends on definitions about which there is no consensus and can never be," and thus concludes: "this is an example of indeterminacy of character I find unsolvable and not very interesting."[26] But while such a stance refuses to acknowledge Joyce's awareness of the intricacies of assimilated Jewish identity, Bloom's "Jewishness" does indeed present some daunting hurdles. Is Bloom, the uncircumcised, agnostic son of a Gentile mother, Jewish? Using such ambiguities in attempts to "universalize" the novel, there will always be those who maintain, evasively, that Bloom is neither Jewish nor Irish, but "the alienated outsider," a citizen of every country and none. But one cannot ignore the text's facts: Bloom's lineage is at least two- if not three-quarters Jewish, and the most poignant sense of continuity he expresses toward his existence revolves around his own Jewish identity as it relates to that of his father and his son.[27]

The answer to the question, then, resides not in *Halachic* law, nor in definitions of ethnicity, nor in Bloom's belief in God, or in Zionism, or in his doubts about being socially accepted as a Jew. Rather, Bloom's "Jewishness" can be measured by his desire to (re)attach himself to an identity that most empowers him as an adjusted male, a character who can get on with "living" – those essential aspects of humanity that Joyce himself always placed well above sectarian divisiveness. On June 16, the identity which Bloom discovers in every meeting and under every rock, is ultimately a Jewish one. That discovery becomes for Bloom, moreover, the moral core of his own *Yiddishkeit*, and in turn suggests the broader idea of a Joycean "*Menschlichkeit*." And there can be no doubt that Joyce knew the puzzle he was creating: it is not random that Bloom's non-Jewish quarter of blood is matrilineal, nor that he is the uncircumcised son of an immigrant convert who, in his final years, returned to practicing Judaism. Joyce drew on a range of experience and sources to construct Bloom as a representation of the assimilated or marginal Jew's "double binds": the struggle to straddle both a Jewish and nationalist identity; to believe oneself a Jew while often rejecting organized Judaism; to be legitimized as "European" and not continually cast as Other to Christian society; to occupy mercantile roles and not be condemned by the Left as a paradigm of bourgeois greed – Bloom is indeed backed into the very same corners the nineteenth-century created for "the Jew."

This cultural reading of Bloom may be one answer to the curiosity of why so many Jewish readers of the novel – readers who know quite well both the rubrics of Orthodox Jewish identity as well as Bloom's lack thereof – have for so long perceived the character as "Jewish." Perhaps the most notable utterance from this subject position was attributed in 1982 to David Ben-Gurion by Gerschom Scholem. While attending the Dublin symposium of the centennial of Joyce's birth, Scholem recalled a "conversation. . .in which Ben-Gurion said, 'Well, the rabbis might not say that Bloom was a Jew, but *I* do.'"[28] Secular Jews and Israeli political leaders alike, of course, may have self-serving reasons for viewing Bloom as a Jew. But even the sheer number of Jewish scholars of Joyce's work suggests that the play *Ulysses* offers with such concepts as matrilineal descent, race, religious knowledge, and Rabbinical edict does not end the discussion of Bloom's "Jewishness," but rather opens the ambiguities of ethnic identity in a manner that cuts to the core of our present explorations of racial, gender, religious, and nationalistic inclusions and exclusions.

Bloom is, moreover, not only a "Jewish character," but also one of the most deliberately complex literary constructs in all of fiction. Through the intricate portrayal of his quotidian life – his fears, desires, complacency, masturbatory obsessions, failures, "stream-thinking," ambivalence, confusion – Bloom becomes an uncompro-

mising depiction of how culture and social reality play on self-making
and self-perception. But Bloom's detailed interiority and his identity
as a Jew are not mutually exclusive. Aside from the many programs
about "the Jew" Joyce had encountered, Bloom's *petit-bourgeois*,
l'homme moyen sensuel profile was modeled in part on Joyce's perception
of some of his closest Jewish friends in Trieste and Zurich. Through
those relationships, Joyce became even more fascinated with the
ambiguities of assimilated and marginal Jewish identity, as well as
what he perceived as the "earthiness" of the "Jewish temperament."
Beginning with that awareness, Joyce went on to perform a small
miracle: in Bloom, one of the era's most prevalent stereotypes – "the
degenerate Jew" – has been transformed into the great paradigm of
complete characterization.

But perhaps foremost of the complexities that make Bloom so
fascinating is his struggle with his own Jewish identity. Here,
however, we do indeed confront a major obstacle, perhaps one often
avoided in reading *Ulysses*: elements of Bloom's "Jewishness" do issue
from the era's most popular racialist assumptions about "the Jew." As
disturbing as it may be, one can draw the conclusion from such
passages that Joyce himself acknowledged certain stereotypes of Jews.
But the pertinent question is not whether Joyce believed in stereotypes;
"racial essence" was a staple intellectual presumption of the era, and
Joyce did not escape it entirely. Rather, we should ask from what
cultural biases, specific sources, and intertextual play Joyce built his
"Jew," and in what ways has Bloom been constructed as an example
of self-doubt or self-abnegation produced through the imposition of
stereotype on consciousness. Avoiding a simplistic dogmatism toward
stereotype as either "the truth" of an essentialism or as absurdly
irrelevant, Joyce instead offers the *experience* of Bloom's identity-struggle,
set before the reader through Joycean minutia, and without a
preemptive morality.

A close reading of Bloom indeed reveals that such stereotypical
aspects of his personality become a kind of sounding board: after
recognizing them as such, he realizes which of his traits are products
of Jewish thought and tradition, and which stem from the anti-Semitic
depictions of "Jewishness" he has internalized through his marginality.
In the beginning of the narrative, Bloom initially senses that those
stereotypes are connected to the most troubling aspects of his
self-image. It is not that he must escape them to be content; he must
confront them to achieve a balanced psychological autonomy. In this

Bloom finally embodies Joyce's recognition of stereotype as social/ cultural myth and yet often as entrenched aspects of self-perception as well. As Joyce unfolds Bloom's juggling of identities, he emphasizes how difference can be accepted or rejected as a means to empowerment. Thus by the end of his day, Bloom has recognized himself as both Jewish and Irish in his own idiosyncratic and justifiable manner. It is not Otherness, but its by-products – social opprobrium, masochistic self-denial, overwhelming guilt, and the resultant self-abnegation – that perpetuate Bloom's intrapersonal conflicts.

Moreover, positioning Bloom's struggle to locate and accept his Jewish identity as an essential element of the narrative moves beyond questions of a "specialized social history" and into the controversies of Modernist aesthetics. As "decadent" or "indulgent" as he appears through his stream-of-consciousness, Bloom's psyche has of course been shaped and is haunted by culturally dominant markers of "the Jew." Thus through the "avant-garde" narrative techniques that Joyce believed would eclipse the nineteenth-century novel, *Ulysses* ironically divulges the social reality of Bloom's plight.

Within the context of this controversy, early Marxists attacked *Ulysses* for being a prime example of Modernist "subjectivist" writing. R. D. Charques, Karl Radek, Georg Lukàcs, (and later, even the young Terry Eagleton) claimed Joyce and his contemporaries "abandoned society and history to look at the isolated individual...in his or her social relationships in order to study inner thoughts and sensation."[29] Lukàcs, certainly the strongest and most influential of Marxist critics, made a whipping-boy of Joyce, accusing him of betraying the importance of plot, social history, and the common reader. In *The Historical Novel* (1962) Lukàcs noted that a central danger for the novelist was creating characters with "the lack of organic connection between personal fates and the historical problems of popular life, the essential social-historical contents of the period . . . the personal fates may come to life humanly and psychologically and may be socially typical in a certain sense, but they remain nevertheless private destinies, and the function of history becomes merely that of a background, a decorative stage."[30] This "backdrop" argument could be no less true of Bloom's struggle as an Irish-Jew. Nor does his conflict "remain a private destiny" – it represents the impact of the historical social ills of nationalistic societies on individual consciousness: religious hatreds, racism, xenophobia, and in the least, rigid lines of Otherness.

Theodor Adorno, always a Lukàcs' detractor from within the Marxist fold, defends *Ulysses* along these lines. Adorno rescues Joyce's technique by asserting that the avant-grade novel was the next step in refining realism – a "new" realism based in a "reflection [that] takes a stand against the lie of representation, actually against the narrator himself, who tries, as an extra-alert commentator on events, to correct his unavoidable way of proceeding."[31] Foremost of Joyce's maneuvers to complete this program, of course, was the interior monologue:

> The *monologue intérior*, the worldlessness of modern art that Lukàcs is so indignant about, is both the truth and the illusion of a free-floating subjectivity. The truth, because in a world that is everywhere atomistic, alienation rules human beings and because – as we may concede to Lukàcs – they thereby become shadows. But the free-floating subject is an illusion, because the social totality is objectively prior to the individual; the totality becomes consolidated and reproduces itself in and through alienation. The great avant-garde works of art cut through this illusion of subjectivity both by throwing the frailty of the individual into relief and by grasping the totality in the individual, who is a moment in the totality and yet can know nothing about it.[32]

Bloom's inner-voice indeed exposes his attempts to realize himself as a "free-floating subject," but his alienation from Dublin's "prior social totality" has of course rendered him a "shadow" in many ways. Joyce drew on his knowledge of anti-Jewish myths as well as on his perception of his assimilated Jewish friends to connect Bloom's alienation with two key dilemmas mediating his individuality and the totality within him: his subject position as a marginal Jew in a Christian, nationalistic culture, and the loss of his son as a missed opportunity to re-establish a sense of Judaism in his life. Bloom's conflicts, then, above those of Stephen or any other character in the text, provide the novel's claim to social realism.

In the culture-critique of present literary theory, "the Jew" in *Ulysses* has also become an entrance into Joyce's subversion of nineteenth-century liberalism. Working within the rhetoric of deconstruction, some critics posit Joyce's "Postmodern indeterminacy" as his refusal of "historical specificities" that stabilized such structures as bourgeois economic anti-Semitism or nationalistic "Jewish pariahism."[33] Other writers attempt to situate "the Jew" within the extrinsic liberal-humanistic discourses Joyce railed against in much of his prose. Seamus Deane explains that the decade of Joyce's birth introduced "an inventory of the forces which were to influence [his work'] such as: (a) Irish nationalism; (b) British liberalism; (c) the emergence of a specifically modern literature from the Romantic-Victorian climate; (d) the emergence of a mass audience; (e) the salience of modern Irish writing, led by Wilde, Shaw, Moore, and Yeats."[34] In this approach, Matthew Arnold's ideas – which influenced both Irish and Jewish questions of the era through theories of "Celticism" and "Hebraism and Hellenism" – are positioned as the centrifugal target of Joyce's sabotage of Victorian liberal culture.[35]

While these studies have much merit, they too often disregard the protean nature of actual anti-Semitism and its effects on living Jews, either of more marginal or normative identities. Scarcely the sole property of liberalism, destructive polemics about "the Jew" were prevalent from both the Left as well as from Joyce's avant-garde milieux on the Continent; Joyce lived through the Dreyfus Affair, and knew many Jews who suffered the effects of political anti-Semitic platforms. Thus despite our assault on the ideological bases of historical and fictional narratives, disregarding environment, occurrence, and *Zeitgeist* in lieu of Joyce's "indeterminate linguistical qualities" is limiting, if not indeed irresponsible. Moreover, Joyce himself viewed "the artist" as a marginalized "radical aristocrat," and although disturbing to him, Arnoldian liberalism was hardly his point of departure toward either "the Jew" or his cursory leftist-politics in Trieste. Rather, this study argues that while Joyce certainly takes Arnold's "Greek-Jewish" theories to task in *Ulysses*, within the larger Hebraic–Hellenistic context, Joyce's historical/political notions about the Jews were revised through his reading of Friedrich Nietzsche, whose influence in Dublin and throughout the Continent was far greater than that of Arnold. But even beyond specific arguments of influence, "Joyce's Jew" is, to say the least, much more multivalent and historiographically revisionary than any single-minded approach may argue.

A. J. Leventhal's previously quoted passage about Dedalus' "silence, exile, and cunning" – although perhaps at first seeming a bit pedestrian – in the final analysis proves useful to understanding Joyce's progressive fascination with the position of "the Jew" and the plight of European Jewry. As a literary construct, Leopold Bloom conflates discourse about "the Jew" Joyce had "silently" accepted in childhood; the "exilic" association he often felt with Jews as an adult; and finally, what he believed was one of the most enduring strengths the Jews possessed as an unterritoried people: the "cunning" ability to reshape themselves yet maintain their Jewish identities – and thus what Joyce saw as their essential humanity – in many varying forms. Delighted with Victor Bérard's *Les Phéniciens et L'Odyssée* (1902) as a kismet for his own "Jewish Ulysses," Joyce came to believe his creation had exposed the political naivete of Arnold's theory about the Greco-Hebraic synthesis of culture. Even more crucially, however, through particularizing Bloom as a marginal Jew, Joyce had discovered a glass through which he could reread the culture and politics of his own tumultuous era on a much more pervasive level.

CHAPTER I

Silence: family values

> I sometimes think that it was an heroic sacrifice on [the Jews']
> part when they refused to accept the Christian revelation. Look
> at them. They are better husbands then we are, better fathers
> and better sons.[1]

Joyce's comment from 1920 suggests an historical sense of Otherness
as well as a grave concern with traditional familial roles – both prime
aspects of Leopold Bloom's subjectivity – as essential traits in his
construction of "Jewish nature." While the statement stereotypes
Jews, it also indicates Joyce's fascination with one of many discourses
about "the Jew" that witnessed a renewed intensity during the
Modernist era. Leopold Bloom is, of course, Joyce's mature depiction
of his era's marginal Jew. Joyce's interest in "the Jew," however, was
established long before he ever wrote *Ulysses*; indeed, his curiosity
involved nearly a lifetime of notions surrounding the "mysterious
Other" first introduced into his imagination through Catholic
doctrine. The statement above, in fact, reveals how even as an adult,
Joyce on occasion still conceived "the Jew" within the context of the
Christian discourse he absorbed in Dublin.

As he was a devout child, Joyce as a youngster had to grapple with
contradictions between the Church's condemnation of the Jews and
its imperatives of charity and forgiveness. That incongruity sat at the
center of his earliest mental constructions of "the Jew"; but although
Joyce rose above Catholic stereotypes as an adult, he never lost
interest in the ambiguity of the representations that fostered those
earliest notions. Educated as a Catholic in an era that exacerbated
age-old Judeophobia through political, social, and pseudo-scientific
arguments, Joyce would ultimately employ "the Jew" to investigate
and censure the discourse of religious prejudice, chauvinistic nationalism, and biologically-based racism. Placing Christian myth and
political antagonism at the center of Bloom's struggle indeed became

for Joyce a means of exploring his ambivalence toward Irish culture, and finally toward rethinking Western culture in general.

Aside from the Christian discourse that formed a foundation of his earliest notions, Joyce also absorbed other representations of "the Jew" through the Home Rule arguments of his childhood. The first of these stemmed from his father's early involvement in the movement. When John Joyce joined the growing ranks of Parnellites in 1880, he inherited a fifty-year-old animus toward Benjamin Disraeli, who was often viewed as the personification of Victoria's *laissez-faire* policy toward the Irish. While Disraeli was a convert to Anglicanism, he was regularly castigated as a "callous Jew" by his political enemies. Another discourse about "the Jew" that passed through political rhetoric from father to son stemmed from popular similes about the "Irish as Hebrews" subjugated by the yoke of a "British-Egyptian" enslavement.[2] As Parnell-era demagoguery, such comparisons were reinforced by legends of the pre-Celtic and Celtic Irish as lost tribes of Israel. This Irish cultural-fantasy had been fostered much earlier by seventeenth-century Gaelic histories that, due to the influence of the Irish Renaissance, had undergone new translations during Joyce's youth. But perhaps more significant to such metaphors were published reactions from Home Rule leaders against a rise in Irish nationalist anti-Semitism. While this rhetoric also made use of the Irish-Jewish simile as a means of denouncing anti-Semitic activity, nationalist leaders often took the trope one step further by drawing comparisons between their own struggle and the persecution of living Jews in the modern world – an argument that left a lasting impression on James Joyce.

I   THE POPE, THE CHURCH, A NANNY, AND A MOTHER

While studies of Joyce's youth most often begin with his time at Clongowes Wood College, gaining insight into his initial notions about "the Jew" requires an even earlier point of inquiry. During his years before school, Joyce learned traditional Catholic positions toward "the Jew" from both his nursemaid, Elizabeth "Dante" Conway, and his mother, Mary Jane "May" Murray Joyce. Both of these women were devout Catholics and accepted the Church's position on nearly all matters of debate, both political and domestic. While May Joyce's role was perhaps less influential during this preschool period, it is certain that Conway spent a significant amount of time enlightening the eldest Joyce child on both religious matters and Catholic orthodoxy. An element of those essential "truths" for Conway was an acceptance of the Church's anti-Jewish arguments of the 1880s.

The general tenor of late nineteenth-century Christian anti-Jewishness was absorbed in Dublin – perhaps more than in London – because of its adamant ties to papal doctrine. Beginning in the 1870s, Catholic attitudes on the accursedness of Jews underwent a modern recycling. At the outset of the decade, Italian nationalist troops undertook to seal the unity of their country by seizing control of Rome itself. The action ended the ghettoization of Jews in the city; Rome's ghetto had been re-established by Pope Leo XII as one of the last of such in all of Europe. But while secular freedoms achieved by the Risorgimento inspired support from Italian Jews, complete Jewish emancipation in Italy provoked a new vigor in anti-Jewish rhetoric from the Pope. A reactionary anti-Jewishness – often drawing on the racialism of the era – soon spread throughout the Church.

Although Leo XIII was liberal on many matters of Catholic doctrine, his Papacy (1879–1903) witnessed a continued antagonism toward the Jews as a "sinful people" conspiring against the Christian world in collusion with both the Freemasons and the forces of socialism. Confronting rising nationalism throughout the Continent, the Pope encouraged Catholic nations to create cooperative atmospheres with new regimes, such as in the case of the late-century turmoil over France's Third Republic.[3] But despite such papal tolerance, influential factions of the Church fostered intense anti-Jewish campaigns that drew on the oldest Catholic discourse about "the Jew's" accursedness. Such arguments were promulgated in both Catholic and secular Italian publications throughout the *fin de siècle*, reaching a first pinnacle during Dreyfus. An Italian Jesuit journal, *Civilta Cattolica*, was an important vehicle of this propaganda, and its views often conformed to those of the Holy See.[4] Many of *Civilta's* earlier anti-Jewish theories were republished in 1891 in a pamphlet titled *Della Questione Ebraica in Europa*, which obtained widespread notoriety throughout the Continent. A few years later, *Civilta* joined other publications – including such popular French organs as *L'Univers* – to become central voices of Catholic anti-Dreyfusard arguments. Such journals accused the Jews of a world-conspiracy to destroy Christianity, and reintroduced the medieval myth of Jewish sacrifice of Christian children and the drinking of their blood during the Passover feast.

The accusation, long-recognized as one of the most noxious ends of Christian folklore, was indeed resuscitated during the era, resulting in devastating effects in rural communities throughout Europe. The impact was ubiquitous enough, however, to gain the attention of one of the twentieth-century's most urbane writers; during Joyce's most fervent religious period, rising anti-Jewishness in Ireland fostered a renewed belief in the crime in areas of extreme Catholic chauvinism, such as Limerick. The myth eventually played a wider role in the popularity of the fraudulent *Protocols of the Elders of Zion*, which saw its first editions in Russian in 1903 and produced an English version by 1920.[5] Even as late as 1911, fear of the "Jewish blood-sacrifice" held enough weight for a Russian Jew of Kiev, Mendel Beilis, to be arrested on the grounds of ritual murder.[6] Ellmann informs us that in 1919, Joyce accompanied one of his Zurich acquaintances, Ottocaro Weiss, to a protest meeting over a recent "false accusation of ritual murder."[7]

In *Ulysses*, Joyce would of course make a centerpiece of the recurring myth of "Jewish vampirism" in the "Ithaca" episode, in which Stephen sings some bars of "The Ballad of Little Harry Hughes."[8] The allusion marks Joyce's recognition of the cultural weight of one of the strangest and bloodiest myths of "the Jew" in Europe – a myth that certainly predates nineteenth-century racial theories. But in his use of discourse about "the Jew's" satanic nature, Joyce was also drawing on a well-established literary trope: Stephen's song is based on the folk-ballad "Sir Hugh, or The Jew's Daughter."[9] Mythologizing the actual legal case of Hugh of Lincoln in 1255 – in which eighteen English Jews were executed for ritual murder – the ballad saw many versions by the nineteenth century.[10] It had been of course memorialized in Chaucer's "Prioresse's Tale," as well as alluded to in Marlowe's *The Jew of Malta*, and Joyce studied *The Canterbury Tales*, along with *The Merchant of Venice*, as part of the curriculum at Belvedere.[11] But those lessons were not Joyce's first encounter with the myth of Jewish ritual murder. An earnest belief in the act was a century-old element of anti-Jewish folklore throughout the Catholic world – a prevalence Leslie Fiedler has associated with the story of Abraham and Isaac as an archetype in the Christian mind of Jewish blood-lust.[12] Sander Gilman further argures that the myth evinces a repugnance toward the rite of circumcision, which in turn galvanized the belief in "the blood-thirsty Jew."[13] Joyce's final

comment on the myth, however, is best understood through my
exegesis of the "Ithaca" episode appearing in the final chapter of this
work.

The decade into which Joyce was born also witnessed Russian
Orthodoxy's support of the legalized political persecution of Slavic
Jewry. The passing of Czar Alexander III's May Laws in 1882, two
months after Joyce's birth, instigated the increase of pogroms in Jewish
villages throughout Russia and Poland. Restrictive laws and repeated
brutality eventually caused a wave of Jewish immigration moving east
to west across Europe.[14] From 1881 to the beginning of the First World
War, in fact, some 120,000 Jews arrived in Great Britain alone, and
Dublin, and to a lesser degree Cork, received their share of those
immigrants.[15] During this period of widespread mobilization, fear of
more Jews entering economically depressed Dublin buttressed papal
anti-Jewishness in the minds of many Irish Catholics.

Added to these influences on the Catholicism ingested by Joyce's
mother, his nursemaid, and ultimately Joyce himself was the often
underestimated sway over Irish Catholicism from the nineteenth-
century Spanish Church. Historian Paul Blanshard asserts that "Irish
Catholicism has always acknowledged a great debt to Spain and a
great affinity with its outlook."[16] Given the history of Spanish
Catholicism's anti-Jewishness, the influence only supported the Irish
Catholic anti-Jewishness Joyce encountered as a young boy. In her
study, *How Catholics Look at Jews* (1974), Clair Bishop documents the
preconceptions about "the Jew" fostered by the Spanish and other
continental Churches throughout the nineteenth century. A study of
parochial educational techniques, Bishop's work relates the era's
most pervasive doctrinal Catholic representations of Jews. She
concludes that those educated in Catholic institutions during the
nineteenth century were typically taught these common assumptions:

1. That the Jews are collectively responsible for the Crucifixion and that
   they are a "deicide people."
2. That the Diaspora is the Jews' punishment for the Crucifixion and for
   their cry "His blood be upon us and upon our children."
3. That Jesus predicted the punishment of his people; that the Jews remain
   cursed by him and by God; and that Jerusalem, as a city, is particularly
   guilty.
4. That the Jewish people as a whole rejected Jesus during his lifetime
   because of their materialism.
5. That the Jewish people have put themselves beyond salvation and

consigned themselves to eternal damnation.
6. That the Jewish people have been unfaithful to their mission and are guilty of apostasy.
7. That Judaism was once the best religion, but then became ossified and ceased to exist with the coming of Jesus.
8. That the Jews are no longer the Chosen People, but have been superseded as such by the Christians.[17]

Given the scriptural basis of these, Joyce's earliest mental construct-ions of "the Jew" encompassed similar prejudices. Throughout the century, Christian educational texts often instructed children that any sympathy they may feel for the Jews was to remind them that, as the betrayers of Christ, Jews had brought persecution upon themselves. Such ideas regularly formed perceptions of "the Jew" in Irish Catholic children, and Joyce's earliest perception of living Jews was predisposed to this a priori notion of "the Jew" as betrayer and subversive.

Irish Catholicism itself also had undercurrents of anti-Jewishness that went beyond doctrinal condemnation. In corresponding with his bishops during the famine years, Dr. Paul Cullen – later Archbishop of Dublin – appropriated the representation of "the Jew" as financial conspirator:

The Landlords have raised their rents enormously, so that the graizers gain little. If the grass does not grow, the rents must be lowered. . .I think all the money of Ireland goes to the Jews of London. The land-lords and bankers live in London and live extravagantly – the Jews fatten on them – but intano [meanwhile] Ireland is starved.[18]

Cullen implies here that Catholic Ireland is being starved by Jews. While such an indictment may rely on scriptural notions about "the Jew," it also suggests a tacit belief in "the Jewish financial conspiracy" against the Christian nations of Europe.

Other publications in Dublin outside of the classroom represented Jews as clandestine in their efforts to destroy Papal authority. A prime example of this kind of text was the 1889 publication *The Pope and Ireland*, a book that may well have been found in the Joyce house-hold. In discussing the inauguration of Leo XIII, author Stephen McCormick asserts that:

among the line of successors of St. Peter, few Popes have been more maligned and misrepresented than Leo XIII, at present gloriously reigning. . .the enemies of the Church in Italy, France and England have been untiring in

their efforts to prejudice public opinion of him in every portion of the world
. . .a coterie of *Jews* [italics mine] and infidels have the management of the
cable dispatches sent from Rome. . .and some of the most malignant and
baseless misrepresentations. . .have been furnished to the reading world.[19]

Such popular reading – as well as Cullen's comments above – have
little to do with the Church's stance on Jewish blood-guilt. These
attitudes were more an expression of an Irish prejudice toward the
supposedly wealthy Jews of London, and Joyce would directly
confront such economic anti-Semitism later in life through his interest
in Arthur Griffith's Sinn Fein. But the main arena for encountering a
negative conception of "the Jew" based on scripture was parochial
learning itself, and Joyce's earliest, preschool religious instruction
included such traditional Catholic notions.

Before marrying, Mrs. Elizabeth Hearn, a Cork relative of John
Joyce, had been committed to becoming a nun and moving to
America. After her husband Conway deserted her and took with him
her inheritance, she returned to her zealous Catholicism as well as
becoming an ardent nationalist. She was a pious woman who added
color to her beliefs through popular superstitions. Her interpretation
of Church doctrine was unquestioning, such as her belief that an
unbaptized infant could not enter heaven.[20] As the principal religious
influence of Joyce's earliest years, "Dante" Conway not only sided
with the Church on most matters of debate, but is credited with
establishing in Joyce's mind what was to become a lifelong fear of
thunder as the angry voice of God.[21] Chester Anderson describes
Conway as "a bigoted Catholic and nationalist, [from whom] Joyce
learnt superstition and religious fear as well as the names of the
mountains of the moons – then monuments to the work of Jesuit
astronomers."[22] Even at a young age, Stanislaus Joyce found Conway's
religious ideas repulsively ignorant, but stated that his elder brother

assimilated her teaching and vivified it in his imagination. She had made
much of him from infancy, and, no doubt, in return for her care, he gave her
if not an affection at least respect.[23]

Raised in Cork, Conway attended school in that city throughout her
childhood. Ellmann states that as an adult, she was "well educated
and evidently a competent teacher."[24] One would initially assume
that Conway was educated at a Catholic institution. The first
Catholic educational facility founded at the outset of the repeal of the

Penal Laws was Nano Nagle's Cork Presentation School, expressly created for the education of poorer Catholic girls and boys.[25] But even by the 1830s such schools could not contend with the overwhelming amount of Catholic children, and the recently established National System's "model schools," which were ecumenical in design, absorbed the greater number of Catholic students during the middle decades of the century.[26] In attending a model school during these years, Conway would encounter the controversial set of primers entitled *Lessons on the Truth of Christianity*, by Richard Whately, Anglican Archbishop of Dublin and Church of Ireland representative of the first Irish School Board, formed in 1831. His books were used throughout the model schools until 1853, when Cullen, then Rector of the Irish College in Rome, condemned them as improper for Catholic youths.[27]

Whately's fourth book of lessons is strewn with traditional arguments over the controversy of why the Jews condemned Jesus. The concluding lesson, "Modern Jews," explains how the Jews came to be a persecuted people in the modern world. Before this lesson, the text reviews common precepts of New Testament theology, such as Jesus being "despised, and persecuted, and put to shameful death, by the Jews themselves, his own countrymen." The Jews are also accused of ignoring Jesus' message because they "had always been brought up in the notion that worldly prosperity was a sign of God's favor; such being the rewards promised in the Mosaic Law."[28] The suggestion to the child is thus to measure Christian spirituality against Jewish materialism; in *Ulysses*, Stephen's encounter with Bloom occurs, in part, within such a context.

The book concludes with instructions for the Christian youth's relations to contemporary Jews, makes a sympathetic acknowledgement of Jewish suffering, and implores the youth not to persecute Jews, but to focus his or her criticism on Christians who acknowledge Jesus as Lord yet don't attempt in any way to "copy the pattern of his life." A righteous Christian life is thus cast as the best antidote for the persistence of the Jews. And while the text incriminates Jews as deicidal, it does instruct the young to have a guarded charity for these intransigent people who are suffering because of their false beliefs.

Such assumptions formed Conway's perception of "the Jew," which undoubtedly became central to the teachings she passed on to Joyce. Throughout the childhood section of *My Brother's Keeper*, Stanislaus reiterates that Conway was the prime agent of religious

education for Joyce before he left for Clongowes in 1888.[29] But given
her adult orthodoxy, even at a young age Conway may have reacted
against the teachings of a Protestant text. Although mainstream
Catholic doctrine on the Jews concurs with the above assumptions,
Conway herself could well have formed opinions about Jews in
opposition to those of Whately's theories. Whether Conway's perception
of the Jews as an accursed nation became more stringent or perhaps
more lenient as a result of studying this text, however, can only be left
to speculation. In either case, the fact that Whately's primer
concludes with an entire chapter on "modern Jews" represents the
prevalence of "the Jew" as a subject of Christian discourse throughout
the nineteenth century.

The "Dante" of *A Portrait of the Artist as a Young Man*, Mrs. Riordan,
is remembered by Stephen as wearing "two brushes in her press" one
for Davitt and one for Parnell.[30] Her nationalism, however, becomes
no match for her allegiance to the Church. The scene in which Dante
is most vocal, of course, is the Christmas dinner argument with Simon
Dedalus and Mr. Casey over the Church's rejection of Parnell. This
altercation – which makes as great an impression on Stephen as the
actual argument made on the young Joyce – captures Conway's
loyalty to the Irish priesthood as well as her allegiance to the Church's
stance on all political matters.

Conway's teachings must have encouraged a depiction of "the
Jew" as sorrowful yet unredeemed and thus evil, and at the age of six
Joyce would have already found the complexity of such an imagined
disposition engaging. In any event, when he departed home to begin
his Jesuit education, the image of "the Jew" as guilty for betraying
Jesus was embedded in Joyce's young imagination. Through reinforcement from his Jesuit instructors, the belief appears to have
become somewhat ineluctable; curiously enough, it appears to have
contributed to Joyce's construction of Bloom's personality, in which a
humility and generalized guilt pervade. Moreover, before Joyce's
formal education, his mother added support to such assumptions.
May Joyce was educated with the same preconceptions as
Conway, and most likely knew few Jews in her years growing up in
Dublin.

While Joyce's maternal grandparents lived for a time near South
Circular Road – then the Jewish neighborhood of Dublin – it is
unlikely that May Murray knew many Jews well in her youth or

adulthood. Ira Nadel concludes that "Joyce's awareness of Irish Jewish life began in his youth since his grandfather and step-grandmother lived at 7 Clanbrassil Street. . .where Stephen attends a party" (see *P*, pp. 68–69).[31] Nadel reminds us that Upper Clanbrassil at the intersection of South Circular was the area with the largest Jewish population in Dublin in the last two decades of the century. But while the Murrays may have known some of their Jewish neighbors, the assumption that May – or even Joyce as a toddler – became sensitive to Jewish life in Dublin is tenuous at best; May's father, John Murray, only began renting a house at number 7 Clanbrassil the year his daughter married John Joyce. Moreover, among those living on Clanbrassil during the period before Joyce entered Clongowes, not one commonly Jewish name can be found.[32] While many of the Jewish residents would have changed their names, common Jewish names in other areas of the city during this period indicate that this was not as frequent a practice as one would first believe. Although John Joyce lodged at 15 Clanbrassil before his marriage, by the time the couple's first child was born, they had moved from that area.

In *A Portrait*, Joyce portrays Stephen as confused as to where the Jewish quarter of the city is actually located; when wandering toward nighttown, which is quite a distance northeast of Clanbrassil Street, he wonders if "he had strayed into the quarter of the jews" (*P*, p. 100).[33] His suspicions imply that he associates the Jewish quarter of the city with its seedier areas. Several years later, Stephen has apparently become no more aware of the Jewish section of the city; however, the narrator informs us that Davin and Stephen have entered the area north of Grantham Street in south central Dublin: "the two were walking toward Davin's room through the dark narrow streets of the poorer jews" (*P*, p. 181).[34]

May Joyce's involvement in the musical life of Dublin did, however, bring her in contact with the family of Marcus Bloom, an Irish-Jewish convert to Catholicism. A well-known Dublin dentist, Bloom had two daughters who were teachers at the Royal Irish Academy of Music, and who sang in a concert with May in 1888.[35] Like his fictional name-barer, "Max" Bloom converted to marry, and his son, Joseph, who was practicing dentistry in Dublin in 1904, is mentioned in the "Cyclops" episode (*U*12.1638). Although other Jewish families of Blooms may have been in Joyce's mind at the time, in 1921 he asked A. J. Leventhal if "the Blooms" still lived in the

South Circular Road area, and was pleased to be informed that they were no longer residents of the city.[36]

In any event, by the time she began to influence her son's religious beliefs, May Joyce had an entrenched orthodox Catholic world view. Stanislaus believes that later in life, May became for Joyce the embodiment of Catholic repression:

his mother became for him the woman who fears and with pitiful insistence, tries to hinder the adventures of his spirit. Above all, she became for him the Irish woman, the accomplice of the Irish Catholic church, which Joyce called the scullery-maid of Christianity. That is to say, she became the accomplice of a form of religion which is more Puritan than Catholic and a vigilant and pitiless enemy of free thought and joyful living, for the Catholic church in Ireland is a cross between English Puritanism and the most unenlightened features of Catholic doctrine.[37]

Stanislaus also relates that although his mother "had been the companion of his devotions when he was a religious boy. . .when Joyce had given up religion, she rarely reproached him, except for one bitter and painful altercation, for his change of heart." That argument was the antecedent of the confrontation between mother and son in the *Stephen Hero* manuscript.[38] During the discussion, Stephen asserts his opinion concerning the truth of the Gospel: "It's absurd: it's barnum. He comes into the world God knows how, walks on the water, gets out of his grave and goes up off the Hill of Howth. What drivel is this?" (*SH*, p. 133). The passage not only portrays Joyce's loss of faith, but is as well a testament to May's complete allegiance to orthodox interpretation of scripture. The scene captures a mind that insists Stephen's rebellion is a product of his "suffering from the pride of intellect" (*SH*, p. 134). In rejecting his mother's belief in the miracles of the Gospels, the adolescent Joyce also began to subvert the preconception of "the Jew" as an essentially cursed being, and his verbalizations of doubt were indeed welcomed by his disgruntled and anti-clerical father.

II PAPPY'S POLITICS

John Joyce's influence on his eldest son's earliest political biases are fictionalized in both *Stephen Hero* and *A Portrait*. As a once active Home Ruler and lifelong anti-cleric, the elder Joyce's attitudes toward "the Jew" may well have departed from those his Catholic upbringing would most readily suggest. In any event, the father's years in politics became the vehicle for his son's introduction to politically antagonistic representations of "the Jew." Even more confusing, positive allusions to Parnell as "Moses" and the Irish as metaphoric "Hebrews" first came to Joyce through his father as well. The complication led to Joyce's earliest recognition of a conspicuous ambiguity in Irish representations of "the Jew."

Until he entered public life in Dublin after 1875, John Joyce knew few if any actual Jews. Sunday's Well, the Cork suburb where he spent his youth, had no resident Jewish families during this period. John's childhood years in Cork (1849–65) coincided with the first diminishment of the Jewish population of Cork city since its initial growth in the eighteenth century.[39] Moreover, in early adolescence, John was already becoming anti-religious and anti-clerical, two attitudes he inherited from his father and which he would in turn pass on to his son. With his zeal for nationalism and growing mistrust of the clergy, the elder Joyce as a youth appears to have had little vested interest in anti-Jewish prejudice or Jews in general.

John Joyce entered Queen's College Cork in 1867, studied medicine, and passed all his first year course examinations. Following the policy of Trinity, Queen's had been graduating Jews from the time of its inception in 1845, and John may have met some Jewish students while attending the school.[40] On his twenty-first birthday, however, he was given his father's legacy of 315 pounds annually and several Cork properties, and he dropped out of university never to return. By 1874 he had moved to Dublin, the city with the largest Jewish population in Ireland. His ventures into Dublin public life over the next ten years increased his contact with both Irish Jews and representations of "the Jew."

Throughout the eighteenth and nineteenth centuries, Dublin had a small but thriving Jewish community. The city's first house of worship, the Marlborough Green Synagogue, was acquired sometime between 1746 and 1762.[41] Its successor, the Mary's Abbey Synagogue, was purchased in 1836 from the trustees of a sect of the Kirk of Scotland.[42] By the 1890s the Jews had built a much larger synagogue on Adelaide Road, which is mentioned in *Ulysses* (*U*10.412–13). The community had been established by "native" or ascendancy-like families of Polish and German extraction who had immigrated to Dublin during the eighteenth-century growth period. Jewish families from both England and Eastern Europe came to the city in large numbers during the period of 1820–70. By 1876, the small community had assimilated enough to enter local politics. In that year a Jewish merchant named Lewis Harris was appointed Lord Mayor, although he died just before he could be sworn into office.[43] (Not coincidentally, Bloom becomes Lord Mayor in the "Circe" episode, [U15.1363].) Later in the century, Jews fleeing the anti-Semitism of Russia and Eastern Europe arrived in the city.[44] This wave of immigration contributed to the Dublin community of Joyce's day – a community that included even Hungarian Jews, whose presence is embodied in the fictional Rudolph Virag. The majority of this population was able to keep at least an ethnic sense of Jewish identity while otherwise assimilating into Dublin life. Living in such a predominately Catholic environment, however, many intermarried and converted.

While the Jewish community in Joyce's lifetime grew in numbers, it remained small in comparison to other English-speaking populations such as in London or New York. The Jews of Dublin were of little consequence in the Catholic city during this era, and a youngster such as Joyce may have met few if any Jews during his entire childhood. Often speaking only a broken English, many of the newer Jewish Dubliners of Eastern European extraction found no welcome in liberal professions or in local politics. As immigrant merchants, however, they gained a foothold in the small business trade in areas such as the Grafton Street shops. The Joyce family was certainly aware of the south-side Jewish section of Dublin, which was often referred to as "little Jerusalem." But contact between unassimilated Jews and other Dubliners was minimal at best.[45] One exception to this during Joyce's youth was the Dublin tea merchant Marcus Tertius Moses, who John Joyce knew in Bray. But as Moses' grandfather had converted to Christianity in 1785, the Joyces may or may not have perceived their friend as solely a Jew; if they did, Moses becomes an early prototype for Leopold Bloom's "non-Jewish Jewishness."[46] Both the man and his business indeed endured in Joyce's memory: during one of the foci of "Wandering Rocks," the character of M'Coy – who is about to defend Bloom as an "allaroundman" – peers into "Marcus Tertius Moses' sombre office . . ." (U10.508).

Upon his arrival in Dublin, John Joyce became active in the City's musical life and sang in a concert in the Antient Concert Rooms that year.[47] Several Jewish families were involved in the Dublin music world during the second half of the century, among them the Levenstons. These two brothers, who were both accomplished violinists, taught music and played in many of the show orchestras around Dublin throughout the decades of the 1870s and 1880s. Other members of their family ran a dancing academy, which also offered piano-tuning and lessons. In *Ulysses*, as Bloom follows the progress of a blind stripling in "Lestrygonians," he remarks "There he goes into Frederick Street. Perhaps to Levenston's dancing academy piano" (*U*8.1139). While John's interaction with the Levenstons was minimal, he must have perceived them as artistic and enterprising, two attributes his eldest son would later build into Bloom. But Dublin's music community became less and less important to John during this period as his interest in Home Rule politics grew. And indeed, local Liberal party circles became his first encounter with the prevalence of secular stereotypes of "the Jew."

By the time John Joyce arrived in Dublin in 1874, Isaac Butt's Home Rule League had become a fully fledged parliamentary movement. Established four years earlier, the League had proposed parliamentary bills for Land Reform and Home Rule on several occasions.[48] By 1880, however, Butt had died, and the leadership of the movement had been assumed by the charismatic Charles Stewart Parnell. In that year John Joyce joined The United Liberal Club in Dublin and transformed himself into an enthusiastic Home Ruler. 1880 was also the year that Disraeli's Tory government called for a general election in which the Prime Minister was defeated. During that campaign, John assumed the position of Secretary for the Club in Dublin and aided in unseating the two incumbent Conservative members of the City Council.[49]

While Liberals argued with Home Rulers over the most beneficial type of Irish freedom, they were united in a distrust of Benjamin Disraeli. Raised to the peerage as Lord Beaconsfield in 1876, Disraeli had been viewed since O'Connell's heyday as a prime obstacle to the Irish cause. Both Gladstonian Whigs and Butt's party had continually confronted Disraeli's conservativism throughout the years leading up to John's years in politics. A repeated element of that opposition included insults of Disraeli as an "untrustworthy Jew" and a prime example of "Jewish opportunism." Through such rhetoric, John learned of the politically-charged stereotype of "the Jew" – devious, mercenary, and concerned only for himself, or at least only for other Jews.

While Disraeli was converted to the Anglican Church at thirteen, he never denied his Jewish roots. More importantly, his Liberal enemies continuously slandered him as a politician by reasoning that, because he was a "dirty Jew," he was a less than fair-minded or even honorable leader.[50] Liberal opposition to Disraeli as a "Jewish scoundrel" reached its first climax in his campaign for the Eastern Question beginning around 1875. Most disturbing to Gladstone and his constituency was Disraeli's interests in the Middle East and eventual purchase of the Suez Canal in 1876. The acquisition, funded by the most prominent English Jew of the era, Baron Lionel de Rothschild, was viewed by Disraeli's enemies as another example of his "Hebraic" brashness, as well as of how Jews colluded toward their own political empowerment. For Liberals, especially the Irish, the action was a "prelude to further imperial expansion by Britain in the area," and Disraeli was again cast as Victoria's imperialistic henchman.[51] In the larger public sphere, he also appeared as the embodiment of "the Jew's" megalomania and spiteful disregard for the Christian masses. Two examples of this hostility were evident in the widely read *The Times'* articles of Goldwin Smith in the 1870s and in Sir Richard Burton's *Lord Beaconsfield: a Sketch*, published in 1882.[52]

More directly relevant to John Joyce's politics were the earlier arguments against Disraeli from Daniel O'Connell. Disraeli's career as a parliamentarian was indeed launched through a public debate with "The Liberator." Campaigning at Taunton in 1834, Disraeli attacked the Whig alliance with the Irish leader "as a cynical compact with a man whom they despised, effected solely for the purpose of keeping themselves in power."[53] Reading of the speech in Dublin journals, O'Connell responded by publicly questioning Disraeli's commitment and character. In return, Disraeli called O'Connell an "incendiary and traitor." O'Connell's speech, made a few days later in Dublin, rebutted his challenger by continuing the name-calling:

Disraeli's name shows he is by descent a Jew. His father became a Convert. He is the better for that in this world, and I hope he will be the better for that in the next. I have the happiness of being acquainted with some Jewish families in London, and among them more accomplished ladies, or more humane, cordial, high-minded, or better educated gentlemen I have never met. It will not be supposed, therefore, that when I speak of Disraeli as a descendant of a Jew, that I mean to tarnish him on that account. They were once the chosen people of God. There were miscreants among them, however, also, and it must certainly have been from one of these that Disraeli descended. He possesses just the qualities of the impenitent thief who died upon the Cross, whose name, I verily believe, must have been Disraeli.[54]

Although he came to despise Disraeli, O'Connell was not an anti-Semite, and had supported the emancipation of British Jewry.[55] While his speech denies the "essential evil" of "the Jew," however, his left-handed praise of a people who are admirable *despite* their disbelief, as well as his aligning Disraeli with "the worst of his kind," nevertheless perpetuated the MP's image as a "suspect Jew." Moreover, O'Connell's biblical allusion links Disraeli's "Jewishness" with the crucifixion; the total effect of the speech was enough to stir even a dormant anti-Jewishness among Catholic liberals, in spite of O'Connell's sentiment about "respectable Jews." In a letter to *The Times* the following month, Disraeli challenged O'Connell to a duel. Although there was no response, Disraeli was arrested and bound over to keep the peace. The entire affair, however, had an effect O'Connell could not have foreseen: it brought Disraeli into the public eye as a young, flamboyant Conservative. In the next election of 1837, Disraeli won his first seat in Parliament and soon aligned himself with Peel's Conservative Party and the new Queen.

After rejecting O'Connell's programs, Disraeli later became an impediment to Gladstonian reforms and remained so until his death in 1881. During John Joyce's lifetime, Disraeli argued directly against Butt quite often. In 1874, on the occasion of debates over the Home Rule motion, Disraeli took the opportunity to present some of his sophistry:

The Irish have a strange passion for calling themselves a conquered people. He [Butt] failed to perceive when or where they had been conquered. It may be urged that they had been conquered by Cromwell. What of that? Had not Cromwell previously conquered England? Why should his eloquent and imaginative friends [the Irish members of the House of Commons] try to extract a peculiar grievance out of a common misfortune?[56]

Disraeli had summed up the Irish situation in 1844 as "a starving population, an absentee aristocracy, an alien Church, and in addition the weakest executive in the world."[57] Given this view, it is not surprising that his election address of 1880 warned his fellow Conservatives of the dangers of Home Rule. During the last year of his life Disraeli continued, now as Prime Minister, to rail against both Gladstone and Parnell. On January 7, 1880, he pointed to Gladstone's blindness to the growing dangers of the situation in Ireland. He characterized The Land Bill and Coercion Bill as Gladstone's carrot and stick policy to his constituents, and accused the MP of permitting the previous year's ineffectual trial of Parnell and his Land League associates, who in return, "launched a campaign of obstruction without precedent which. . .made the English House of Commons 'the laughing stock of Europe.'"[58] Ironically, James Joyce's adult opinion of Gladstone was closer to Disraeli's than one would imagine; Home-Rulers ultimately perceived Gladstone as more of an opportunist than a true believer in the Irish cause. But it was nonetheless Disraeli's policies that remained to them a primary symbol of the English refusal of Irish demands.

In addition to his political platform, Disraeli the novelist of course made Jewish pride and anti-Semitism central themes in many of his works, including his renowned trilogy, *Coningsby, Sybil*, and *Tancred* (1844–47). As early as his third novel, *Contarini Fleming* (1832), he colored his Conservatism with his Jewish roots, supporting his position as a Tory by suggesting he was "aristocratic" by birth:

Was then this mixed population of Saxons and Normans. . .of purer blood then he? Oh no, he was descended in a direct line from one of the oldest races in the world, from that rigidly separate and unmixed race who had developed a high civilization at a time when the inhabitants of England were going half naked and eating acorns in their woods.[59]

Such reverse racism was a well-known aspect of Disraeli's public image. His attitudes draw on the century's racialist assumptions by identifying "the Jew" as a separate "race," and his claim for the superior nature of "Jewishness" is as negligent as other claims of their essential inferiority. His comment, "all is race; there is no other truth," has indeed been offered as a catch-phrase of the era.[60]

Like many *fin-de-siècle* literati, however, James Joyce perceived Disraeli as an influential albeit amateurish novelist, and read him to some extent. He made reference to Disraeli's later work *Lothair* in a letter in 1905.[61] In the 1907 essay "The Shade of Parnell," though, Joyce's opinion of the leader was nothing short of scathing: "Today how flimsy seem the studied gibes, the greasy locks, and the stupid novels of Disraeli."[62] Disraeli as a politician would always remain to Joyce a symbol of Victoria's chauvinistic neglect of the Irish. In his essay on Irish history, "Ireland Isle of Saints and Sages" (1907), Joyce characterized the relationship between Queen and Prime Minister:

The Irish attitude and the Irish character were antipathetic to the queen, who was fed on the aristocratic and imperialistic theories of Benjamin

Disraeli, her favorite minister, and showed little or no interest in the Irish people, except for disparaging remarks, to which they naturally responded in a lively way.[63]

In an offhand manner, Joyce implies that Disraeli was more culpable than the Queen herself.

Joyce also has Bloom allude to Disraeli during the hallucinations of the "Circe" episode. As Bloom transmogrifies into "many historical personages" to prove his Messianic identity, he initially becomes Lord Beaconsfield (*U*15.1845). Later, as Elijah/Bloom, he quotes Disraeli's speech against Darwinism at the 1864 Oxford Diocesan Conference: "...the question is this: Is man an ape or an angel? I, my lord, am on the side of the angels." Bloom then remembers a quotation from Disraeli's speech to the House of Commons in 1849: "a man, always studying one subject, will view the general affairs of the world through the colored prism of his own atmosphere'(*U*15.2197–98).[64] Because of Bloom's desire to view himself as both a Jew and a fair-minded political thinker, he recalls Disraeli, a Jew who gained political power. But Bloom avoids, or is perhaps ignorant of, Disraeli's reputation as a Conservative, who would have found the "new Bloomusalem" childishly quixotic to say the least.[65] Joyce must have enjoyed this play with Disraeli's image; in addition to these allusions in Bloom's thoughts, there are at least six references to Disraeli in *Finnegans Wake*.[66] But Bloom's allusions to Disraeli indicate Joyce's understanding that the statesman's "Jewishness" had little to do with his politics. In his essays, Joyce never references Disraeli as a "Jew," but rather characterizes him simply as an adversary to Irish independence.

Nevertheless, before the rise of Parnell, Disraeli was often portrayed by liberals as a "mercenary, cunning Jew." After his death, however, memories of the Prime Minister became useful to the Irish imagination in an opposite manner. In 1910, the Home Ruler F. H. O'Donnell wrote that Disraeli's "cosmopolitan spirit never descended to the nadir of prejudice of the British Philistine. . .he had been known to speak of the island of sorrows with some of the sympathetic imagery appropriate to his own persecuted race."[67] But O'Donnell's words here are more suggestive of another type of rhetoric about Jews that existed simultaneously with Irish Liberal anti-Semitism. This discourse, which relied on the trope of the Jews and Irish as "brothers in sorrow," was another element of the Irish nationalist rhetoric that John Joyce passed on to his son.

Although this use of "the Jew" was quite opposite from popular arguments against Disraeli, it nonetheless appears at the center of Home Rule nationalism along side its counterpart. Most nationalists of the era, while often having no position on the actual Jews of Dublin or London, were in fact "pro-Hebraic." The basis of this attitude was their obsessive use of similes that compared their cause with ancient Hebraic heroism; isolated, persecuted, and shaped by one of the oldest Churches, the Irish had long metaphorized themselves a Christianized "chosen nation." Indeed, an admiration for "Bible Jews" and yet an ambivalence toward, or ignorance of, living Jews had a long history in Britain. One foundation of this schism was the popularity of Matthew Arnold's "Hebraism and Hellenism" from *Culture and Anarchy*, which Joyce later studied at University College Dublin. Seamus Deane reminds us that amongst the novelists most affected by Arnold's theories was George Eliot, who gives "wonderful expression to this view in *Middlemarch* (1871–72) in the characters of Dorothea (a Hebraist) and Ladislaw (a Hellenist) and also in *Daniel Deronda* (1876), in which Zionism becomes the great project for the establishment of a new and harmonious community."[68] In the second work, Eliot also inscribes a version of this duplicity surrounding "the Jew," of which Arnold often seems unaware:

the Meyricks and their extraordinary Jewish friends. . .caused some astonished questioning from minds to which the idea of live Jews, out of a book, suggested a difference deep enough to be almost zoological, as of a strange race in Pliny's *Natural History* that might sleep under the shade of its own ears.[69]

When Joyce read *Daniel Deronda* is unclear, but *Ulysses* would someday revise such representations of "the Jew" that rely on the tension between mythic traditions and political reality.[70]

Based to some extent on this mythological currency of "the admirable Hebrew," an empathy between the Irish and "the Jewish cause" appeared in many letters and speeches during the rise of Parnell. The argument can be found in the words of leaders such as Michael Davitt, Standish O'Grady, and, indeed, Parnell himself. Parnell's mother, surprisingly enough, was often rumored to have come from Jewish origins.[71] Several anti-Jewish outbursts in Ireland during the last two decades of the century occasioned adamant support for the Jews from both Davitt and Parnell, both of whose status fostered a greater Irish sympathy for the Jews on a political level. Such defenses often characterized Jews as a people suffering a persecution similar to that of the Irish; this "brothers in a common struggle" simile indeed obtained its most widespread popularity during Joyce's youth.

The legend that the Irish had descended from a lost tribe of Israel, however, had been a keynote of their political myth-making long before the rise of Home Rule Irish-Hebrew parallels. Inspired by the O'Neill uprising in the late seventeenth century, historians such as Geoffrey Keating, O'Sullivan Beare, and Peter Lombard drew on both annals and chronicles to remake Irish "lost tribe legends" into legitimized "history."[72] Their conclusions about the lineage and influences on the Celtic forefather, Milesius, implied that the Irish were somehow "chosen" like the Jews, and that they shared, through racial memory, an Hebraic sense of righteousness and commitment, as well as a privileged philological knowledge of the original tongues spoken before Babel.[73] This legendary status lent a much needed fuel to Irish pride both during and after the plantation years. In the eighteenth century, Charles Vallancey's linguistic theories about the Semitic origins of Gaelic served to perpetuate the legend.[74] Nineteenth-century Irish historians and philologists supported Vallancey's research well into Joyce's lifetime.[75] After Keating was translated from Gaelic around 1908, Joyce read his theories; aspects of his philology, and possibly those of Vallancey as well, are included in the "Ithaca" episode.[76] O'Sullivan Beare's portrait appears on the citizen's mythical belt of painted "seastones" in the "Cyclops" episode (*U*12.199). On occasion Joyce himself directly supported these theories; in "Ireland, Island of Saints and Sages," he states: "This language [Gaelic] is oriental in origin, and has been identified by many philologists with the ancient language of the Phoenicians."[77] But whether by 1914 he saw the theory as enchanting myth, historical possibility, or political rhetoric is again best realized through a rereading of *Ulysses*.

Joyce was also influenced early on through his father's politics to regard the myth of "Parnell the Irish Moses" as central to the leader's public image. As an outspoken Parnellite, the elder Joyce repeated the simile in his household quite often. Later on as a University College student, Joyce, of course, heard the Dublin barrister John Taylor's now famous use of the metaphor in a speech on Irish independence – a version which combined both the Irish-as-Hebrews and Parnell-as-Moses images. Passages of Taylor's speech are, of course, transcribed into the text of *Ulysses* (*U*7.828–70). Still later in life, Joyce himself more than once made use of the Parnell-as-Moses allusion: ". . .and, like another Moses, [Parnell] led a turbulent and unstable people from the house of shame to the verge of the promised land."[78] By 1911, the Abbey Theater staged the metaphor: with the premier of Lady Gregory's *The Deliverer* that year, the "Parnell as Moses" trope came full circle in its cultural currency.

Influenced by such uses of "the Jew" for their own political ends, Home Rule leadership often found itself supporting a newly-threatened Irish Jewry during Joyce's childhood. In the 1880s, the rise of racially-based Gaelic nationalism combined with the economic pressures of post-famine land-reform to create a hostile environment toward urban Jews in the larger Irish cities. Informed of a possible outbreak of violence against Jews in Cork in 1888, Parnell himself telegraphed the Lord Mayor, John O'Brien, and ordered him to put a quick end to the agitation. The Cork community had been outraged at the business practices of two immigrants named Katz, who were rumored to be German Jews. The men pretended to have set up a factory, advertising that by using foreign cabinet-makers and cheap American prison labor they could undersell other Cork furniture merchants. The Cork trade unions denounced them, and Liberal factions seized the opportunity to fortify their anti-Jewish appeals.

Following Parnell's lead, O'Brien responded to an article in *The Times* that had been overly critical of Cork Jews. The mayor condemned any actions against the Jews, who he characterized as "wanderers driven abroad by oppression, [and who] are in the very same position [as] the evicted Irish emigrants." Yet he ended his response on a note of incredulity as to why English Jews, with all their wealth and power, would allow their wayward brothers to come to a place as unprosperous as Ireland.[79] Parnell's instructions and the mayor's article were meant to combat anti-Jewish anger head on. In his piece, however, the mayor unintentionally invokes a prevalent stereotype of English Jewry by portraying London Jews as rich and influential. Thus, despite his intentions, O'Brien merely reinforced "the Jew" as an international financier whose allegiance was always first to other Jews.

Throughout his years in politics, John Joyce read other pieces supporting Irish Jewry, most prominent among them those written by the Land League's Michael Davitt. Indeed, Davitt wrote eloquently on several occasions for support of the Jews.[80] His articles again characterized Jews as sufferers, whose diaspora and persecution allied them to the Irish struggle for freedom. Later on in his career, Davitt researched the 1895 "Kishineff Affair" in Russo-Bessarabia, in which the charge of ritual murder again lead to the deaths of innocent Jews; the interest culminated in his study, *Within the Pale: the True Story of Anti-Semitic Persecutions in Russia* (1903). In "Nestor," Stephen's rebuttle to Deasy's anti-Semitism – "A merchant. . .is one who buys cheap and sells dear, jew or gentile, is he not?" (*U*2.359–60) – appears to draw on one of Davitt's passages:

Are not historical conditions and centuries of deliberate oppression in every land (Ireland honourably excepted) answerable for the Hebrew predilection to profit-seeking by other than the methods of immediate production? And are the Gentiles of the lofty moral school of critics so much above the doctrine and practice of the commercial greed of buying in the cheapest, and selling in the dearest, market?[81]

Both John and James Joyce read Davitt's letter to the *Freeman's Journal* of January 18, 1904, concerning the anti-Jewish riots that year in the city of Limerick. This episode – one of the more violent expressions of anti-Semitism in Irish history – involved the denunciation of Irish Jewry, the subsequent stoning of Limerick Jewish shopkeepers and their homes, and a two-year boycott of the city's Jewish-owned businesses. The incident has become over the years the most often referenced historical event in terms of "the Jew" in *Ulysses*.[82] Indeed, during the year it occurred, the Limerick affair and the anti-Jewish attitudes it represented was newsworthy throughout Ireland. The activities even occasioned comment about the Jewish presence in Ireland from the influential Standish O'Grady. In several editorials in his journal, the *All Ireland Review*, O'Grady denounced the persecution of Jews at the hands of the Irish, once again depicting both groups as "brothers in a common struggle."[83] In his *Freeman's Journal* piece, Davitt also attacked those who participated in the riots. Curious as to the atmosphere in Limerick, he later went to the city and visited the homes of some of the victims of the violence.[84] His article is one of the most moving appeals to issue from Irish Catholic ranks concerning Jewish relations:

There is not one atom of truth in the horrible allegation of ritual murder, here insinuated, against this persecuted race. . .I protest, as an Irishman and as a Christian, against the spirit of barbarous malignity being introduced

into Ireland, under the intended form of a material regard for our workers'
...The Jews have never done any injury to Ireland. Like our own race, they
have endured a persecution, the records of which will forever remain a
reproach to the 'Christian' nations of Europe. Ireland has no share in this
black record. Our country has this proud distinction – freely acknowledged
by Jewish writers – of never having resorted to this un-Christian and
barbarous treatment of an unfortunate people.[85]

Among other possibilities, this passage may well be a source for the
ironic comment made by Garrett Deasy at the close of the "Nestor"
episode.

   Notwithstanding this use of Davitt's words, however, it is puzzling
that Joyce did not include a direct allusion to the Limerick event in
Ulysses. Erwin Steinberg has pointed to Bloom's reference in "Cyclops"
to the persecution of Moroccan Jews, asserting that, as an Irish Jew, it
would appear Bloom should have more readily referred to the events
in Limerick.[86] Indeed, the fact that Bloom works for the *Freeman's
Journal* would seem to warrant at least a mention of the riots
somewhere in the text. Perhaps in "Cyclops," however, the omission
was a matter of Bloom's awareness of audience; because he has a stake
in his own identity as an Irishman while arguing with such an
aggressive bigot, Bloom may avoid mentioning the riots so as not to
enrage the already provoked citizen. But the absence of any allusion
to the incident throughout *Ulysses* remains a curiosity.

   After Parnell's death, John Joyce's rage at the Church's renunciation
of his "dead King" also became the vehicle for a slight altering of the
Hebraic simile. Viewing Parnell's 1890 "betrayal" as a prime example
of the clergy's myopia, John became even more soured on religion and
often incorporated anti-clerical insults into his remorse for the late
leader. The Dublin Rev. Hugh Price Hughes had led the first attacks
on Parnell, castigating him at the 1890 session of the National Liberal
Federation.[87] Afterwards, prominent members of the Catholic clergy
joined in the condemnation; Joyce's father felt his world turning
against him. To Irish Liberals, Parnell now became the Moses, who,
while absent from the foot of Sinai, was betrayed by the people he
sought to redeem. By Joyce's tenth year, his father's anti-clerical
outbursts had become a common sound throughout their household.
In recording his thoughts in Trieste in 1907 about his father's
home-life, Joyce included some of these favorite insults: "He calls the
prince of the church a tub of guts. He offers the pope's nose at the table.
He calls Canon Keon frosty face and Cardinal Logue a tub of guts."[88]

John's anti-clericism was also easily transferred into other aspects of Home Rule rhetoric. One such trope likened Parnell's ruin by his own colleagues to Judas' betrayal of Jesus. Aside from references to him as the "Moses of his people," in fact, Parnell's most popular appellation was "Christ the redeemer."[89] Michael Healy's opposition to Parnell, of course, became the subject of Joyce's first published work, "Et Tu, Healy" (1891), which exploited another, more Classical metaphor. But in his father's tirades, Joyce already recognized the parallel of the biblical and Classical that he would continue to draw on throughout his career. If, however, he chose the betrayal of Caesar as the metaphor best suited for his essay, we can be certain that the Judas–Jesus image was readily at his disposal as well. The betrayal of Jesus was in fact one of the elder Joyce's favorite biblical allusions, as in his often repeated admonition to his children, "I'll leave you all where Jesus left the Jews."[90] This expression also endured in Joyce's imagination: it appears in the "Wandering Rocks" episode (*U*10.697–98). Most significantly, however, John Joyce's anti-clericism further subverted the authority of the Church in his young son's eyes.

The very idea of betrayal became, of course, a preoccupation of Joyce's adult life. As apparent from all biographical reminiscences about him, Joyce was hypersensitive to signs of personal disloyalty. During his adolescence as well as his years on the Continent, Joyce concluded many friendships because he felt betrayed in ways others close to him often could not understand. And like many Irish thinkers, Joyce was obsessed with the "self-hating traitor" as one of the chief factors behind Irish nationalist failure, which, during his lifetime, of course reached its nadir in the Parnell affair.[91] An emphasis on Irish turncoats became commonplace in references to their own political foibles; a good example is the proverb, "Put an Irishman on the spit and you can always get another Irishman to baste him."[92] And Joyce had his own versions of the sentiment: "In Ireland, just at the right moment, an informer always appears" and "She has betrayed her heroes always in the hour of need and always without gaining recompense." Later on in life, he versified the viewpoint: "This lovely land that always sent / Her writers and artists to banishment / And in the spirit of Irish fun / Betrayed her own leaders, one by one."[93] Joyce's outrage at "Irish betrayal" indeed points to a type of learned ethnic self-hatred with which he would later become fascinated, and the preoccupation certainly had one of

its most poignant beginnings for him in his father's attack on those
who betrayed Parnell. But the concept of "betrayal" – indeed the
great paradigm of the gravity of all acts of betrayal – had been
engraved in Joyce's young mind through Catholic dogma concerning
Jewish deicide. Given the "Irish-Hebraic" context of Parnell's rise
and fall, very few Catholic Irishmen thought of their misfortune
without associating it to Judas' betrayal of Jesus; not surprisingly,
"the Jew" as untrustworthy and back-stabbing regained its currency
in the country's next major political movement, Griffith's Sinn Féin.

Joyce later used his father's bitterness over Parnell as raw material
for his sketch of both Simon Dedalus' and John Casey's fulminations
during the Christmas dinner scene in *A Portrait*. Although the elder
Dedalus expresses no anti-anti-Jewishness during that argument, as
John Joyce became more anti-clerical during a period when the
clergy was encouraging anti-Jewish thought, he must have found
fault with those attitudes and passed his anger on to his son. But Joyce
did not manifest his own apostasy until after twelve years of Jesuit
education. And during his time as a student of the Jesuits, Joyce in
fact encountered several new representations of "the Jew."

CHAPTER 2

Silence: Jesuit years – Clongowes and Belvedere

Except for his year with the Christian Brothers in 1892, Joyce's entire formal education was under the Jesuits. As an adult, he often acknowledged the debt he owed to the Society's discipline, and continued to call his thought patterns "Jesuit," claiming the Order taught him how to "arrange things in such a way that they become easy to survey and judge."[1] Oliver Gogarty characterized Joyce as an "inverted Jesuit" who failed to relinquish the Society's obsession with preciseness and pedantry.[2] Joyce learned Catholic doctrine in its most detailed form from the Jesuits, and so found a sophisticated reinforcement there for "the Jew" as the betrayer of Jesus. But Joyce's education emphasized as well the virtue of Old Testament patriarchs as a crucial element of Bible typology. During his years at Belvedere, Joyce also read Sir Walter Scott's *Ivanhoe*, which provided him with a new, secular representation of "the Jew." Undermining that image, however, were Jesuit arguments he encountered that connected the Church's long-running anti-Masonry campaign with a renewed animus against the Jews.

During the eighteenth century, the Society had lost its struggle for influence in Ireland with the suppression of the world-wide Order by Pope Clement XIV in 1773. Yet throughout the next century it grew to become a formidable force of Irish Catholic education. During a growth period from 1814 onward, the Jesuits established Dublin as a center of power, employing both members and lay teachers in institutions such as the College of Saint Francis Xavier or "Belvedere" and the older Clongowes Woods. While Joyce was an honor student at these two schools for some ten years, he ultimately betrayed his mentors during his adolescence. The Jesuits, nonetheless, had left their mark; even on the Continent Joyce maintained an interest in Catholic discourse, at times from the standpoint of subversion, at times with nostalgic admiration.

41

The Jesuits themselves had a history with the Jews; it was common knowledge in the Society that their beginnings were steeped in controversy surrounding their early efforts to recruit Jewish *conversos* of sixteenth-century Spain.[3] The result of those efforts was a reversal by the end of the century of the Society's fundamental pledge to welcome "New Christians" into the Order. After the second generalship, there was a continuous drive to exclude all Muslim and Jewish converts from any involvement whatsoever. In 1592, a command to all provincials disallowed any "New Christians" into the order. The edict was soon made the Society's fifty-second decree, and enforced for the next five centuries, not being rescinded until 1946 at the General Congregation XXIX.[4]

As part of the Catholic bourgeoisie of Dublin, the Joyce family was well aware of the history of the Society as an identifying mark of its organization. In Ireland, the Order's distinction of having no converts in its ranks was perceived as a superior purity. Moreover, after its suppression in the eighteenth century, the Society had worked to regain its foothold in Irish Catholicism. During O'Connell's era, the Jesuits began reconsolidating their power in Ireland. Beginning at Carlow College around 1803, Father Peter Kenny and his followers opened more schools and re-established the Society in Ireland as the principle purveyors of Catholic education. In 1814 Kenny managed the purchase of Castle Brown and its environs in Kildare, known as Silva de Clongow, and founded the school he respectfully named Clongowes Wood. By the following year, one hundred and ten boys were registered as students at the new school.[5] From that point onward, "The Pope's soldiers" triumphantly regained their power.[6] By the time James Joyce entered Clongowes, it was indeed revered as one of the finest boarding schools in the country.

I   OLD TESTAMENT IMAGES

When the six-year-old Joyce arrived at Clongowes, he was the youngest child in the Lower Line. He was also a sensitive, bright boy who was sickly, bullied more than once, and a favorite of the Rector of the school, Father John Conmee. His situation is fictionalized in the opening chapters of *A Portrait*, and has been subsequently supported by the research of both Kevin Sullivan's *Joyce Among the Jesuits* and Bruce Bradley's *James Joyce's Schooldays*.

But even with the aid of these sources, little is known about precisely what Joyce was taught at Clongowes. Outside of the general standards of the revised *Ratio Studiorum* of 1832, no record of the curriculum at the school has survived. Sullivan states further that Joyce "left no memoir whatever."[7] The revision of the *Ratio Studiorum* from its 1773 version contained few changes of any significance in the area of scriptural instruction. It did contain, however, "a new emphasis on the vernacular, the specific recognition of scientific subjects as such, and a removal of Cicero from his dominant position in language studies."[8] Even more problematic, during this period there was often a lack of attention paid to the precise standards of the *Ratio Studiorum*.[9]

Indeed, the few extant facts about Joyce's years at Clongowes reveal further inconsistencies with Jesuit standards. Before leaving for Christmas vacation in 1890, Joyce and the entire Lower Line took a grueling, yet somewhat atypical, Jesuit examination. Included in this test were "the first fourteen chapters of the *Maynooth Catechism,* which were to be learned verbatim, one hundred and fifty pages of the Bible history (Old Testament), and half as many pages again of *Darhbe's Catechism*."[10] Although the examination itself is unavailable, the large portion of the Old Testament Joyce was asked to learn is curious because direct Bible study – especially memorization – was antithetical to the most common Jesuit practices throughout the nineteenth century.[11] Research does indicate, however, that Joyce would have been tested rigidly on the Catechism. In agreement with Sullivan, Jesuit historian Robert Schwickerath states that extreme attention to the catechism was central to the lower lines of most Jesuit institutions. The emphasis contributed to Joyce's admiration of the catechetical form, as it is demonstrated in the "Ithaca" chapter of *Ulysses*. Later in life, Joyce in fact mentioned to Frank Budgen that "Ithaca was his favorite episode, 'It [he said] is the ugly duckling of the book.'"[12]

Jesuit proscriptions on Bible instruction, however, contradict Joyce's early, intense study of the Old Testament. The Jesuits did often teach prepared selections of the Old Testament so as to demonstrate the prefigurations of the coming of Christ. But these passages, usually excerpts about martyrs or Messianic prophets such as Isaiah, served as the *materia poetica* for the hermeneutics of biblical typology. Given the scope of his examination, however, when Joyce returned home that year images of Hebrew patriarchs were fresh in his mind. Learning Old Testament narrative provoked in Joyce a new respect for the commitment of the Jews, even if, as he already had been taught, their heroism was marred by their later deicide. Thus in turning away from Jesuit standards of Bible instruction, Joyce's teachers at Clongowes were instrumental in planting a more ambiguous perception of "the Jew" in his early imagination.

Beyond Joyce's earliest Jesuit curriculum, the major influence on him at Clongowes was the Rector himself, Father John Conmee. Conmee had made special arrangements with John Joyce to allow his sons to enter the school at a reduced tuition. He furthered his favors by permitting James and Stanislaus to attend Belvedere as "free-boys" in 1893; it was common practice to allow a few local youngsters to attend the school free of charge. Conmee was at that time Prefect of Studies at the College, and in 1904, he would become Provincial of the Jesuit Order of Ireland.[13] Conmee's reputation as Rector of Clongowes was one of peaceful overseer; he was thought of as an "Irish gentleman" with a lilting brogue and a forgiving temperament.[14] Bradley surmised that the scene in *A Portrait* in which Stephen protests being falsely accused by Father Dolan, accurately depicts the real event. (*P*, 1). Conmee is portrayed in that passage as a warm, paternal figure. He appears to have been to Joyce at this time an embodiment of the voice of righteous authority. Conmee's equitable use of power shaped Joyce's youthful respect for the temperance and intelligence of the "Jesuit mind"[15] Yet as the author of *Ulysses*, Joyce would depict the polite and genial Conmee in "Wandering Rocks" as a toadying hypocrite. Although his personal warmth remains in this portrait, Conmee's thoughts, in Stanley Sultan's words, reveal him as "a representative Jesuit priest, conscientious and diplomatic, with his calculation placed at the service of the Church. . .his many faults show him to be a weak vessel, but there is no indication that he is to be considered uniquely so and therefore unqualified to bear the 'Roman ensign'."[16] But in making the revered priest "embrace the values of the world" and succumb to the most base secular impulses, Joyce was also expressing an adult regret for having once regarded Conmee as a spiritually-minded, good father-figure.

Joyce's adult work indeed implies that Catholic patriarchy often blinded the earnest believer to injustices against women, Jews, freethinkers, and other marginal groups. But it is important to realize that, as a young boy, Joyce's respect for his superiors at Clongowes did not reveal the smallest hints of rebellion. The loyalty he felt toward the priests at Clongowes, moreover, served to buttress the

Jesuit discussions of Old Testament patriarchs as figures of exemplary virtue. This doubling of a living and textual patriarchy only added to Joyce's future interest in Judaism, the paternal religion of Christianity. Hebrew patriarchs were suggested to Joyce as the spiritual fathers who essentially had been outdone by the spiritual son. In Joyce's own secularized version, that scenario would find a lasting niche in his imagination. Stanislaus commented that his brother's temperament reveals that, as a boy, Joyce was always obedient to both paternal figures and the very concept of patriarchy: "The two dominant passions of my brother's life were to be love of father and of fatherland. . .both passions stemmed, I believe, from his ancient love of God."[17]

At Clongowes, Joyce was a devout child who ingested Catholic doctrinal representations of "the Jew" with little or no objection. At Belvedere, however, his unquestioning faith would begin to falter. Moreover, at that institution Joyce developed a relationship with a mentor who also had a predilection for Old Testament allusions. If Joyce's respect for Conmee prefigures his adult obsession with paternalism, his encounter with Father James Cullen at Belvedere again reinforced Old Testament Hebrews as the spiritual fathers of Christianity.

II PATRIARCHS AND ROMANTIC NOVELS

While not officially an instructor at Belvedere, James Aloysius Cullen, SJ was appointed Spiritual Father to the school as early as 1884.[18] During the next two decades, Cullen occupied that office and devoted time to his publication the *Irish Messenger of the Sacred Heart*, created to further his Temperance Campaign throughout Ireland.[19] The magazine itself may well have passed through the Joyce household in the hands of Conway or May Joyce. Promoting prayer and devotion as the key to abstinence, Cullen conducted a lifelong crusade to spread his message to the Dublin community. At Belvedere he was also Director of the Sodality Society, an office whose duties included both the instructing and private counseling of the students at large. In 1896, Joyce was elected Student Prefect of the Society, the most prestigious devotional position a student could aspire to at Belvedere.[20] In this capacity Joyce and Cullen had direct contact, both in private consultation and in larger groups; Cullen also compiled and printed the manual for Sodality in 1886.[21]

One such group event during which Joyce heard Cullen preach was a retreat in 1897 to commemorate the feast of Francis Xavier, the patron saint of the College. The retreat and sermons appear to have been the model for those of chapter III of *A Portrait*. Although Joyce indicated that Fr. Arnall's sermon was modeled on that of the actual Fr. Power, Bradley confirms Sullivan's belief that a regular teacher at Belvedere would never have been called on to preach on retreat, and that the model for Arnall had to be Cullen.[22] Like Stephen, Joyce experienced a period of piety as a result of this retreat. While there are no notes from Cullen's sermons available, it also appears that Joyce modeled the sermons in *A Portrait* at least partially on those of Cullen.[23] The bulk of the sermons of the actual retreat – as well as those of the novel – were of course based on the five meditations of The First Week from Ignatius' *Spiritual Exercises*, predominately those on Sin and Hell.[24] But interestingly enough, Cullen had another favorite source-book for his work at the school and this text was once again rife with Old Testament allusion.

The book Cullen kept on his desk at all times, and on which he may have drawn for his sermons, was *The Instruction of Youth in Christian Piety: taken out of the Sacred Scriptures and Holy Fathers*, by Rev. Charles Gobinet, DD.[25] This manual, which includes descriptions of suffering in Hell similar to those of the *Spiritual Exercises*, begins in a much more benign manner. The first lesson that a youth, given the generic name "Theotime," must learn is how a virtuous childhood plants the seeds of a virtuous adulthood. These opening chapters make use of examples taken exclusively from the Old Testament.

Chapter IX of this first section is subtitled "This Truth Confirmed by Remarkable Examples, taken out of the Sacred Scripture, of Those Who Having Been Virtuous in Their Youth, Continued so All Their Life." The initial examples that follow are of Joseph's bravery and lack of vindictiveness at the hands of his brothers' persecution, and of Tobias' allegiance to God when so many had begun to worship the golden calf of Jeroboam.[26] A final example is that of Eleazer's martyrdom. Here the text explains that when Eleazer was asked to renounce his religion by King Antiochus, persecutor of the Jews, "he [Eleazer] would rather die than consent to such a criminal action: upon which his torments were redoubled, and he suffered death with incredible patience" (p. 37). The lesson ends with an imperative: "Learn, dear Theotime, from this example, and the preceding, what virtue acquired in youth is able to do, when confirmed by a continual exercise of good actions; and labor to be such now, as you would wish to be the remainder of your life." The text continues to use the Hebrew patriarchs' courage and righteousness to direct the thoughts and actions of the Christian youth.

The last example here of Eleazer is typical of the Jesuit emphasis on martyrdom as a prefiguration of the passion of Jesus. The first two, however, and several subsequent narratives, seem only intended to portray the virtue of the Hebrew patriarchs in their own right and not only as prototypes of Jesus. Once again Joyce was encountering a use of the Old Testament somewhat unusual for Jesuit standards. Yet Cullen appears to have spoken of such passages to the students who visited him for consultation during his years at Belvedere. He may have offered the book to his more astute students, a group that would certainly include James Joyce. Joyce retained Cullen's emphasis on Old Testament figures for a long time, and the allusions may well have contributed to his adult admiration of the Jews; the quotation at the opening of the first chapter of this study in reference to the heroism of the Jewish refusal to accept Christ suggests such a lasting impression. Such a statement would have been heresy to many of Joyce's former Jesuit instructors. Ironically, however, the seeds of such an attitude were planted by those very same teachers.

Joyce's study of Hebrew patriarchs does not imply, however, that as a fifteen-year-old boy who had had no contact with Jews, he would have drawn parallels between Old Testament martyrs and the Jewish struggles of his own place and time. Regardless of this, though, Joyce's impression of the heroism of Hebraic figures was intensified at this time because of his simultaneous fascination with heroic figures from the Classical world; it was during this period that he read Charles Lamb's *The Adventures of Ulysses* and subsequently wrote his now lost essay, "My Favorite Hero."[27] The two bodies of representation, Hebraic and Classical – appearing in Joyce's imagination here as early as 1897 – of course became the germs of major motifs in *Ulysses*. While not yet conscious of their impact on his life's work, Joyce was being provided with analogues for his future obsessions with the concepts of betrayal, righteous indignation, and the return of the wayward, the marginal, and the persecuted. Moreover, even before Cullen's influence, Joyce was primed to respond to other positive representations of "the Jew"; sometime after his admission to Belvedere in 1893, he had read Sir Walter Scott's *Ivanhoe*.[28]

Ivanhoe was typical fare for the University College Dublin English curriculum that Joyce would soon encounter. In *A Portrait*, Cranly observes earnestly that Scott "writes something lovely. . .there is no writer that can touch Sir Walter Scott" (*P*, p. 228). Scott is also alluded to twice in the childhood stories of *Dubliners*. In the second piece, "An Encounter," the "old josser" mentions to the boys his reading of "all Sir Walter Scott's works and all Lord Lytton's works," so as to concur with their interest in "adventure." In the adjoining story, "Araby," Scott's *The Abbot* is found by the protagonist among the books belonging to the dead priest in the back drawing room.[29] Both of these references suggest Scott as a romantic adventure writer whom those with an "unsophisticated" taste would read. The appearance of *The Bride of Lammermoor* in the list of "gigantic" heroes in the "Cyclops" episode of *Ulysses* further implies Joyce's adult opinion of the overly romantic tenor of Scott's stories (*U*12.189–90). But regardless of his later facetious allusions to Scott, Joyce's youthful reading of *Ivanhoe* affected his earliest conception of "the Jew" and in many ways challenged what he had learned from the Jesuits. Although the novel form was considered improper extra-curricular reading for a student of the Jesuits, Joyce was tempted to read *Ivanhoe* because of a controversy surrounding the work that occurred about the time he entered the College.[30]

The incident at Belvedere concerning *Ivanhoe* was fairly innocent. It involved J. F. Byrne, who directly afterwards made friends with a new "frail looking lad named James Augustine Joyce."[31] Byrne's instructor, Father Fagan, had been fond of reading a passage of fiction to the class once or twice a week. He suggested that his students read novels to improve their vocabulary, and one of his recommendations was Scott's work. But when Byrne's older cousin discovered him reading the book, she was outraged. Byrne explained: "Father Fagan told us boys to read some good books, books like. . .'Like *Ivanhoe*,' she interrupted, 'a NOVEL – by Sir Walter Scott, whoever the wretch is. So Father Fagan, a Jesuit, tells you to read NOVELS. I'll see about that first thing in the morning.'"[32] The result of this innocuous affair was a reprimand from Father Fagan to his class, and an end to his in-class reading time. The incident occurred in February 1893; two months later, when Joyce entered Belvedere, Byrne must have mentioned the "forbidden" novel to his new friend.

The Byrne event also appears influential to the scene in "An Encounter" in which Leo Dillon has a copy of *The Apache Chief* taken from him by Father Butler. While *Ivanhoe* has been replaced with a hack, "dime-store" novel, the priest's anger at the discovery of his student "wasting his time" on such "rubbish" seems parallel to Byrne's cousin's reaction (*D*, p. 20). Her outrage appears as well to have been grounded in a distaste for the novel form rather than in the particular work. That a Jesuit-trained youngster of twelve years should be reading something as frivolous as a novel, and further that a Jesuit instructor had suggested such reading, was to her disgraceful.

Regardless of such parochial attitudes, by 1893 *Ivanhoe* had not only enjoyed nearly a century of popularity, but had spawned a plethora of spin-off books based to a great extent on the novel's Jewish characters.[33] Because of their aestheticized, safely-distant suffering, the Jewish characters in the novel generated an interest among liberal readers, and updated for the novel's wider Victorian audience the convention of the cowardly Jewish moneylender and his angelic daughter. Moreover, Scott's sympathetic portrayal of Isaac, the Jew of York, also crystallized for a growing secular readership the idea that "Jewish obsequiousness and vengefulness" was as much historically determined as it was a product of "God's curse."

When Joyce read *Ivanhoe*, we can be certain it affected his preconceptions of "the Jew" as well. The persecution of Isaac is integral to the novel's main plot of Ivanhoe's struggle to become a victorious champion of Richard I. The entire narrative maintains a discussion of disinheritance, a notion which, even in 1893, would have entranced the son of ex-Parnellite John Joyce. Moreover, as a young man Joyce would feel a certain pity for the character of Rebecca, the dark beauty and Jewish heroine of the novel.

Scott's Rebecca indeed seems an early source for Joyce's infatuation with the "oriental" looks of Jewish women. While Joyce's own fictional "Jew" would later be constructed as a male – indeed, would define a certain type of maleness – his passion for "the Jewess" grew throughout his adult life and ultimately manifested itself in at least two known extra-marital interests. His youthful encounter with Jewish characters such as Rebecca may have always shadowed that desire. Rebecca herself, in both her demeanor and dress (as well as her chambers in her father's house) is continuously described as "Eastern" and "Oriental."[34] Stirring his early erotic fantasies for the "Mediterranean dark lady," Joyce's reading of Rebecca also contributed to his later creation of Molly Bloom. Before he ever created Molly, however,

Joyce developed a passion for a young Jewish woman in Trieste named Amalia Popper, and of course from that infatuation constructed the fictional love-object of *Giacomo Joyce* (1914).[35]

Joyce's love poem displays a forbidden attraction toward Otherness by incorporating "the bifurcated female" with the "oriental darkness" of "the Jew." Vicki Mahaffey postulates that "Giacomo's lady is not only an incarnation of the 'double' women of Joyce's youthful dreams. . .she is also the subject of [his] first experiments with the protean inclusiveness of Bertha Rowen, Molly Bloom, and Ann Livia Plurabelle. . ."[36] Mahaffey also claims that Popper was always a central model for Molly. But prior to this, Scott's Rebecca becomes a direct antecedent for Joyce's creation of the "dark lady" in the poem. Before Joyce met the Triestine student, the character of Rebecca influenced the mysteriousness of the beauty of Mangan's sister and the other oriental tropes in "Araby." Joyce's adult retrospective awareness of his youthful response to Rebecca seems a stimulus as well for the creation in *A Portrait* of Stephen's search for a living Mercedes – another fantasy provoked by a work of popular fiction.

After bidding farewell in *Giacomo* to his love object, Joyce would no longer worship his "dark lady" from a distance, but envision her body and soul through the creation of Molly. Thus as an adult, Joyce imagined his dark heroine in *Ulysses* not only as a Gentile, but sexualized in a manner quite distant from Rebecca's maternal ministering. Joyce eventually contained the Otherness of his female subject to unleash fully his attraction while simultaneously lessening his fear of opposition. But this was not the case between his reading of Scott and his writing of *Giacomo*. Similarities in Scott's description of Rebecca and Joyce's investigation of his love for Popper reveal a direct influence.

Scott's Prince John describes Rebecca as "the very model of perfection whose charms drove frantic the wisest king that ever lived," and "the very bride of the Canticles" (p. 94). The Prince's admiration for Rebecca's "biblical" beauty define her allure as based in the exotic flavor of her "Jewishness":

The brilliancy of her eyes, the superb arch of her eyebrows, her well-formed aquiline nose, her teeth as white as pearl, and the profusion of her sable tresses, which, each arranged in its own little spiral of twisted curls, fell down upon as much of a lovely neck and bosom as a simarre of the richest Persian silk, exhibiting flowers in their natural colors embossed upon a purple ground, permitted to be visible – all these constituted a combination of loveliness which yielded not to the most beautiful of the maidens who surrounded her.(p. 94)

In *Giacomo*, Joyce describes his dark lady – based on a living Jewish woman – with similar attributes:

She walks before me along the corridor and as she walks a dark coil of her hair slowly uncoils and falls. Slowly uncoiling, falling hair. She does not know and she walks before me, simple and proud. So did she walk by Dante in simple pride and so, stainless of blood and violation, the daughter of Cenci, Beatrice, to her death. . .[37]

Joyce's passage emphasizes the same focal point – the ringlets of dark hair – as does Scott's description of Rebecca. Both writers may have also heard the echo of Milton's "her unadorned golden tresses wore / Dishevelled, but in wanton ringlets wav'd."[38] Joyce secularizes the tragedy of his subject by way of his allusion to Shelley's Beatrice in an analogous manner to the Prince's comparison of Rebecca and the beauties of the Bible.[39] Following Shakespeare's Jessica in *The Merchant of Venice* as well, both subjects are all the more challenging as the protected daughters of wealthy men.

  Even more vital to each lover's imaginative freedom, however, is his fascination with the "Jewishness" of the subject. As representations of the forbidden Other, both Rebecca and Amalia are enticing in a way Anglo-Norman or Celtic beauty could not be. Scott has Prince John's Prior remind him of this motivating enticement: "the Rose of Sharon. . .the Lily of the Valley. . .but your Grace must remember, she is still but a Jewess" (p. 94). After following his subject to the Jewish cemetery in Trieste, Joyce also reminds himself that his desire in part stems from an intrigue about Popper's Jewishness:

The tomb of her people and hers: black stone, silence without hope: and all is ready. Do not die!(p. 6)

and further, that as she belongs to the "disinherited," her fate is to wander – most poignantly away from him:

Ay. They love their country when they are quite sure which country it is.(p. 9)

This last remark, of course, ironically became part of J. J. O'Molloy's argument in the "Cyclops" about the presence of Jews in Ireland (*U*12.1630). And indeed, the speaker of *Giacomo* now begins to register his own confusion about the subject herself.

Recognizing his ambivalence, the persona of the poem becomes overwhelmed by his dark Jewish woman.[40] In his perception she has shifted from the Madonna to a "corpse and faithless whore, [who], like the ghost of May Dedalus in *Ulysses* appears to the man she haunts with a grey face and 'dank matted hair, and when she kisses Giacomo, 'her sighing breath comes through'."[41] In hopes of defeating his dreams of the enticing darkness, the speaker cries "I am lost! / – Nora! – " (p. 15). Joyce would, indeed, go on to create Molly out of the buried remnants of his "dark lady" coupled with the experience of his true intimacy with Nora Barnacle. But even while composing *Ulysses* in 1918, Joyce remained fascinated with dark women of Jewish backgrounds, as demonstrated in his brief liaison that year with Martha Fleischmann. In writing to her on one of several occasions, he revealed an element of his obsession with her "Jewishness": "I noticed the softness and regularity of your features . . . And I thought: a Jewess. If I am wrong, you must not be offended, Jesus Christ put on his human body: in the womb of a Jewish Woman."[42] Joyce was wrong; Fleischmann was from a Swiss Christian background. His attraction nonetheless was based on her dark "Jewish looks," such as those of Scott's Rebecca.

The character of Rebecca, however, was not the only aspect of Scott's novel to make an impact on Joyce's perceptions of "the Jew." After being disinherited by his father, Ivanhoe returns from the Holy Land in disguise to compete in a tournament. The armor he wears has been loaned to him by a Jewish associate of Isaac of York. Isaac undertook the favor because he was indebted to Ivanhoe after being aided by him in escaping from Cedric's Hall. In securing that escape and relieving Isaac from the Jew's obligatory ransom, Ivanhoe completes the first act of charity in the novel. Yet his action defies the Christian laws of the land. Ivanhoe, the disowned son, is thus further disinherited; he is now an outlaw who cavorts with "the demon Jew." At the climax of the novel Ivanhoe repeats his kindness by defending the honor of Rebecca, who has nursed him with her "Jewish healing arts" back from near death. In the last chapters she stands accused of being – like all of her "accursed race" – a sorceress who has enchanted the lecherous Brian de Bois-Guilbert. Ivanhoe is victorious in defending Rebecca's honor, and soon marries Lady Rowena and lives for a time in the glory of Richard's united England. The love marriage of a Saxon hero and a Jewish heroine, according to Scott, had been "realistically avoided."[43] The "high-minded," (Rebecca)

Scott explains, find "adequate recompense in the form of that peace which the world cannot give or take away"[44]; Thus while their portrayal is based in key secular assumptions about "the Jew," Scott's Jewish characters do not escape his romantic idealism.

At the close of the narrative, the truly disinherited characters, Isaac and Rebecca, leave for Grenada, "for less cruel are the cruelties of the Moors unto the race of Jacob than the cruelties of the Nazarenes of England" (p. 393). The plight of the wandering Jew, once only an apocryphal story for Joyce, was now fixed more securely in his future recognition of which injustices best portrayed the "nightmares of history." Indeed, the other characters' attitudes toward Isaac and Rebecca act throughout the novel as a barometer of Christian charity – such a marker of toleration would of course later play a pivotal role in Bloom's acceptance as an Irish Jew.[45] In understanding Rebecca and Isaac's oppression by the Christian powers, Joyce was also afforded one of his earliest opportunities outside of his knowledge of Irish history to identify with the notion of voluntary exile.

By his University College years, Joyce of course found Scott's heroics overdone, and had recognized the convention of a Jewish merchant and his angelic daughter who is "saved" by a Christian; he was examined on *The Merchant of Venice* in his third year at the university.[46] Nonetheless, Scott's depiction of a Jewish usurer acting out of kindness to a Christian knight offered a new complexity of image to the younger Joyce. The Jewish characters in the novel suggest how the disenfranchised can empower themselves by resisting the temptation to internalize stereotype. Joyce may well have made an historical link between Isaac's persecution and that of the Old Testament martyrs he had been learning about from the Jesuits.

Scott's fictional "history" appears to have made a mark on Joyce in a more generic manner as well. In the same vein that Georg Lukàcs credits Scott with inventing the classical form of the Historical Novel in English, Joyce reserved in his memory the type of character who can represent the class, ethnic, or institutional struggles of his day.[47] Yet, as mentioned in my introduction, Lukàcs read *Ulysses* as the opposite type of novel, one which replaces an objective sense of history with a "narrow and subjectivist attitude toward life."[48] But what Lukàcs overlooks about *Ulysses* is that Bloom's Jewish identity struggle, albeit mostly internalized and highly subjective, provides the novel with an historical objectivity "toward race, economics, and political and social division." Scott thus represents an early source for

Joyce's perception of "the Jew" as a cultural marker of political antagonism and prejudice.

As a young boy reading *Ivanhoe*, Joyce encountered a representation of "the Jew" that threatened the stability of the discourse he had absorbed earlier in life. The stereotypical "Jew" in Scott's book shifts from an "evil unbeliever" to one of history's most unfortunate victims. But all of this reading at Belvedere, both religious and secular, had to compete in Joyce's mind with another type of anti-Jewishness he absorbed from his Jesuit instructors. At his new school, Joyce was introduced to Church-based arguments that linked Freemasons and Jews in a co-conspiracy for world domination.

III   "WHAT'S THE BLOODY FREEMASON DOING"

In *Ulysses*, the perception of Bloom by his peers as a cowardly and subversive Jew is bolstered by their belief that he is also a Freemason.[49] Those characters who denounce Bloom as a Freemason often do so in the same breath as they insult him as a Jew. The title of this section is, in fact, taken from the very first comment the anti-Semitic citizen makes about Bloom in the "Cyclops" episode (*U*12.300). Other allusions to Bloom's suspected Freemasonry include Nosey Flynn's explanation of Bloom's "success" – "He's in the craft" (*U*8.960), as well as Bloom's satiric use of Masonic ritual hand signs in the "Circe" episode (*U*15.758, 2724).[50] This running commentary suggests that Joyce had learned the rhetoric connecting Jews and Freemasons from some earlier source. As one of the Dublin "in-jokes" of *Ulysses*, such references indeed draw on an entire body of assumptions concerning an alleged Masonic–Jewish collusion.

While the Irish Catholic Church had had a campaign against Freemasonry as an agent of Protestantism throughout the nineteenth century, during Joyce's childhood those arguments increasingly co-opted the anti-Semitism of the era. When he was named to the Holy See in 1879, three years before Joyce's birth, Leo XIII began a crusade that called for all Catholics to join the fight against Socialists, Freemasons, Jews, and a host of other enemies of the Church. The Pope himself had a particular fear of Freemasonry as a destructive element amongst Catholic populations. In 1884, as one of his eighty-six encyclicals, the *Humanus Genus* spoke of the Masonic heresy that was "working openly for the ruin of the holy Church with the object of depriving Christian peoples of all those blessings brought by the redeemer."[51]

Provoked by these Papal attitudes, Irish Jesuits on occasion asserted the Jewish–Freemasonry connection. Such arguments were easily absorbed by the Irish Catholic leadership because of their previously established fear of Freemasonry. During the Synod of Thurles in 1850, in fact, one edict passed into law commanded that "the Parish priests must let it be known that all incur the sentence of excommunication who become Freemasons."[52] While anti-Free-masonry was generally reinforced by the anti-Semitism of the 1890s, during the ensuing years in Dublin, Edward Cahill, SJ rose to the forefront of an anti-Mason/anti-Jewish movement in Ireland. Although Cahill, and his successor in the campaign Father Denis Fahy, are two extreme cases, the tenor of their thought was present in Dublin throughout the last decades of the century.[53]

Cahill was ordained a Jesuit priest in 1897 and spent twenty years at Mungret College, Limerick.[54] Throughout the 1880's, the College acquired more and more French Jesuit instructors, whose anti-Jewishness on the whole was much more vociferous than that of their Irish counterparts.[55] Mungret was the institution at which Cahill began his research for a series of books he would publish at Milltown Park in Dublin in the 1930s. The first of these was his 1929 *Freemasons and the Anti-Christian Movement*. But his most vehement attack on both the Masons and the Jews appears in his 1932 piece, *The Framework of a Christian State: an Introduction to Social Science*. Cahill's rhetoric represents a fanatical level of Jesuit anti-Jewishness:

The modern anti-Christian movement, which centres around Liberalism, owes much of its rapid progress to the secret society of the Free masons. . . Freemasonry is today the central enemy of the Church and of every Catholic government and Catholic institution in the world. It is closely associated with Modern Judaism (including the Rationalistic Jews, as well as those of Talmud and Cabala); and is largely under Jewish influence and guidance.[56]

He also emphasizes how Masons and Jews spread their message by way of taking control of the media:

The great capitalistic Press of the United States, England, Germany and France, is now almost entirely controlled by the great Jewish International financiers. Of the papers not directly owned by Jews, Jewish influence usually predominates in the management. Not only what is called the

Capitalistic Press, but even the Socialistic Press of the world, is in a large part
owned and controlled by Jewish financiers. . .What is said here of the Press
applies with equal or greater force to the Cinema; practically all of which
over the two continents of Europe and America is in the hands of the Jews."[57]

While Cahill's treatise does not represent the center of Irish Jesuit
thought, it certainly repeats popular accusations leveled against the
Jews in Britain and throughout the Continent. Rather than a product
of his own idiosyncratic hatreds, however, Cahill's diatribe represents
a fanaticism about Freemasonry and "the Jew" that was grown in the
soil of the Dublin Jesuit world as far back as the 1850s.[58]

One of the most influential Jesuits in Dublin during Joyce's
childhood, Father Tom Finlay, was also involved in the anti-Masonic
campaign of his day.[59] As Rector of Belvedere from 1883–88, Finlay's
influence dominated the school's halls, and remained a shaping force
throughout his lifetime, which ended in 1940.[60] After his tenure as
Rector, Finlay became a staple of the Dublin Jesuit community and
received a professorship of political economy at University College
during Joyce's years there.[61] In 1930 Finlay presided over the Jesuit
Colloquium on Spiritual Exercises held in the city. In that capacity
he praised the address of Cahill, whose speech once again accused the
press and the cinema of dishonoring Christ and climaxed in an attack
on "Naturalism – the spirit of irreligion and practical unbelief which
repudiates Christ, rejects Christian principles and ideas, [and]
practically recognizes no life but the temporal one in which we live."[62]

Although Finlay was not educated at Mungret, he did spend time
in Limerick at the older Jesuit school, The Crescent.[63] Early on in his
career, from 1871–73, he studied in Maria Laach, Germany, where
he encountered a more overt type of anti-Semitism among the
German clergy. Moreover, the clergy's general curiosity about the
Talmud during this period may have drawn Finlay to the writings of
the popular German Catholic scholar, August Rohling. Rohling had
published an edited version of a section of the Talmud, entitled *Der
Talmud Jude* (1871). Describing the Talmud as an unsophisticated
doctrine without a benevolent metaphysics, Rohling claimed it was
an evil guideline for Jewish anti-Christian activity. He further argued
that the specific passage he had translated in his book gave Jews the
moral imperative of ritual murder.[64] Later on in his career, Finlay
read a much more equitable review of the Talmud, entitled *The
Talmud: Selections From the Contents of That Ancient Book*. The book,
dated from the Hebrew Tammuz 5636 (1875), was a popular read for

students at St. Stanislaus College in Offlay (known as "Tullabeg"), where Finlay completed his theological studies in 1880.[65]

Finlay influenced the methods and frequency of discourse about Freemasons during his rectorship at Belvedere. His years at the school and beyond coincide with his involvement in campaigns against "economic and social monopolies among special interest groups."[66] That concern was made manifest in his rhetoric against the Freemasons. Finlay feared the growing popularity of Freemasonry in Dublin with an eye on institutions such as the Masonic Boy's School in Glasnevin. No one involved with that institution, though, either among its founders in 1867 or its faculty during Finlay's years, appears to have been Jewish.[67] Louis Hyman informs us, however, that beginning with wealthier Jews of eighteenth-century Dublin, "Freemasonry was an important sphere of contact between Jew and Gentile, and eight out of a community of some forty householders belonged to Lodge 206 of the Irish Constitution in Dublin in 1770–1, one rising to the high office of Prince Mason."[68] Indeed, during Joyce's youth some Dublin Jews rose to powerful positions in a few of the city's Masonic lodges; Finlay may have suspected a connection.[69]

Joyce not only attended the Finlay-influenced Belvedere, but sat in Finlay's courses in metaphysics and political economy during his years at University College.[70] Finlay founded two periodicals Joyce read at University College, *The Lyceum*, as well as its successor, *The New Ireland Review*. Finlay also developed the *Irish Homestead*, the Co-operative Movement's journal in which Joyce published the initial story of what was to become *Dubliners*. By way of these associations, Finlay's anti-Freemasonry became a ripe source for the anti-Masonic/anti-Jewish animus found in several references to Bloom throughout *Ulysses*.

IV "OF THE TRIBE OF SHYLOCK"

Joyce's years at Belvedere also coincide with John Joyce's continuing financial decline. During a recess in 1894, Joyce and his father went on a search for funds to the family's home town of Cork, where John sold the last remaining properties that he had inherited from his father. The trip of course became fictionalized as one of the earliest moments of Stephen Dedalus' self-righteous awakening in *A Portrait*. When Simon Dedalus takes Stephen to Queen's College, Stephen imagines his father's carelessness compared to the seriousness of the

other students and becomes ashamed. An embarrassment about his
father, however, was not the only regret Joyce experienced during his
trip to Cork. The very reason for the trip set in Joyce's mind a lasting
memory of his father's "betrayal" at the hands of a Dublin solicitor
named Reuben J. Dodd; what had occasioned the journey was
Dodd's demand for payment on several mortgage debts John had
incurred with him.[71]

Joyce internalized his father's anger toward Dodd and later
snubbed Dodd's son, who was a classmate at Belvedere.[72] Later on in
life Joyce reified those feelings by including in *Ulysses* the younger
Dodd's embarrassing plunge into the Liffey in 1911, which was
rumored to have been an attempt at suicide (*U*6.264–91). Joyce
altered the date of the younger Dodd's "swim" so the event could
become a joke shared by the mourners in the "Hades" episode.
On their way to the burial of Paddy Dignam, Bloom and his
companions see the elder Dodd and immediately begin to slander
him. Martin Cunningham is the first to point Dodd out: "Of the
tribe of Reuben" (*U*6.251). When the passengers recall the younger
Dodd's action, however, Joyce omits the name of the person who
rescued the drowning man. Bloom refers to him simply as "the
boatman," but Joyce may have known from his reading of an article
on the event in the *Irish Worker* of December 2, 1911, that the rescuer
of the younger Dodd was a dock-worker named Moses Goldin, in
all likelihood a Dublin Jew.[73] Perhaps Bloom avoids this bit of
information so he can share the joke and appear unoffended by
Cunningham's apparent allusion to Dodd's "Jewishness." On the
other hand, Joyce may have omitted the name because it would have
subverted his own anger against Dodd as a "Shylock."[74]

As a young man Joyce did not understand that his father's
vindictiveness was misdirected; it was John's own spendthrift nature
that had been ruining him for some years when Dodd moved to
collect his payment. But as an adult novelist, Joyce created from the
experience of Dodd's actions a fictional incident that has become a
controversial part of "the Jew" in *Ulysses*, primarily because of its
ambiguous use of an anti-Jewish insult. Much argument has transpired
over the years about the reader's confusion over Dodd as an actual
Jew versus the label used as merely a cultural pejorative.[75] Even
more, the question of Bloom's participation in the name-calling of
Dodd in "Hades" has been offered as Joyce's manipulation, or even
tacit belief in, the concept of Jewish self-hatred.

Curiously enough, however, the real Reuben J. Dodd was not Jewish.[76] His son, of course, would not have been enrolled at Belvedere if he had been. But in *Ulysses*, Dodd is insulted by both Cunningham and Simon Dedalus in an overtly anti-Jewish manner. Dedalus' remark – "the devil break the hasp of your back" (*U*6.251) – is a curse against Dodd as a "gombeen man" who ruins "good Irishmen" by exacting his payments unmercifully. It is unclear, however, whether Cunningham and the others believe Dodd is actually Jewish or if they merely imply he is "Jewish" as a derogation because of his "Jewish deeds." Bloom himself later thinks: "Now he's [Dodd] really what they call a dirty Jew" (*U*8.1158). Bloom's slander of Dodd appears to be at first ambiguous as well: he could be alluding to Dodd's unkempt appearance, his business practices, or indeed, his identity as a "Jew of the worst kind," the unscrupulous usurer. During Bloom's hallucinations in "Circe," this defaming of Dodd generates the phantom of "Reuben J. Dodd, [as] black-bearded Iscariot," and later "Antichrist, wandering Jew" (*U*15.1918, 2145). Thus whether Joyce intended the reader to perceive Dodd as actually being a Jew or not, in Bloom's imagination Dodd represents some central, negative myths about "the Jew."

Certainly one possible meaning of Dodd's appearance in *Ulysses*, however, directly corresponds to the role the actual Dodd played in the life of James Joyce. Dodd's unmerciful claims – and usury in general – was of course the social offense most associated with the Jews throughout the history of Europe, and the likelihood that John Joyce referred to Dodd as a "Shylock" is great. Hearing such a defamation, the thirteen-year-old Joyce, who had been learning of virtue and betrayal in the Old Testament, was apparently quite confused by the event. The slander would support the anti-Jewish discourse that he encountered from his Jesuit instructors. But when he later read Scott, he may have found a conflict between his father's prejudices and his new awareness of the history of Jewish persecution. Yet for years Joyce harbored support for his father's castigation of Dodd as a "gombeen man," likening Dodd to "the Jew" as a merciless creditor.

Later on in life, Joyce began to unravel the history of that stereotype and so rose above the memory of any anti-Jewish insult his father leveled against Dodd. Indeed, in the *Dubliners*' story "Grace," rewritten in 1906, a prototype for Dodd, the character of Mr. Harford, is called an "Irish Jew" by his "fellow-Catholics" because of his lending of money at "usurious interest," and not because he is actually a Jew; Harford is later spotted by Martin Cunningham in attendance at Father Purdon's retreat (*D*, pp. 150–74). The insult thus reveals more about the character who levels it than its target. In this manner, through the equivocal nature of Dodd's Jewish identity in *Ulysses*, Joyce reties a knot for his readers that he himself had already learned to untie.

Joyce's mature insights into the psychology of anti-Semitism and Jewish identity, however, began a long time after John Joyce sold his last remaining properties in Cork. Four years after that trip, Joyce graduated from Belvedere College, and that autumn entered University College Dublin. Having spent the past year reading voraciously to prepare himself for what he imagined was the cosmopolitan atmosphere at the university, Joyce ironically found his first year English lecturer, Father Joseph Darlington, quite boring.[77] By May of 1899 Joyce would refuse to sign a petition against W. B. Yeats' drama *The Countess Cathleen* as an "un-Irish" play, and thus set himself apart from many of his fellow Catholic students.

That initial moment of Joyce's rebellion also holds some revealing elements of his changing perception of "the Jew." During his undergraduate years, Joyce "excommunicated" himself from Catholicism, made references to "the Jew" in his writing, and was introduced to the first Jews he may have ever met. Shortly thereafter he left Dublin and soon "exiled" himself from his own country. The thoughts that provoked these grave decisions began for him in the turbulent year of 1898, the most volatile period of the Dreyfus Affair.

CHAPTER 3

Silence: university years – the Church, Dreyfus, and aesthetics

The year before he entered University College, Joyce had already begun separating himself from Catholicism; he apparently never took communion after Easter, 1897.[1] Joyce's apostasy was motivated by his desire for freedom of expression and sexuality, as well by his anger toward the Church's intrusion into nationalist politics.[2] By 1898, however, even his nostalgia for Parnell and liberalism had grown stale – finding his new identity as a secular artist more suitable, Joyce began to consider himself "apolitical." But if John Redmond's new Home Rule leadership left Joyce irresolute, he was soon to rebel against forces he felt certain were misdirected: the Church, the Literary Revival, the Gaelic League – the very fabric of Dublin nationalist culture in his day. At University College, Joyce discovered the focal point of his rebellion to be the Church's disruptive roles in Irish literary arts. During the ensuing years he became increasingly incensed with Yeats' "rabble-pandering" dramas as well as with the Celtic Revival in general. By graduation Joyce had left for Paris, ostensibly to attend medical school, but actually to discover Europe and become a "European poet." All of Joyce's pent-up anger toward the Church, however, exploded in the year of his matriculation, and that brief period also provoked his initial reevaluations of some key cultural positions of "the Jew."

Constantine Curran, Joyce's adolescent companion, believed his friend underwent an acute change in personality between Belvedere and their first year at University College. While Joyce's classmates at the school always thought of him as nothing short of gregarious, "from 1899 [onward] none of his University College friends failed to note aloofness and detachment as a special characteristic [on Joyce's part]."[3] What had happened to the amiable young man who had once been so pious and so "Irish"? The answer to that question lies in Joyce's reaction to the atmosphere at University College, as well as in his new reading and writing during this period. Joyce's expanding literary taste from 1897 onward evinces his growing obsession with the idea of "Europeanism." Subsequently, the essays he wrote during these years rationalize his revolt against the Church and its repressive culture – a stance that his companions at the university took as a rebellion against Ireland and all things Irish.

Throughout the year 1898–99, Joyce was also reading about the Dreyfus Affair in several Dublin journals. Discourse about "the Jew" in these articles affected his ill feelings toward the Church as well. The circumstances that led to Dreyfus' second trial in 1899 revealed actual traitors, led to anti-Semitic riots in both Paris and Algiers, and of course eventually inspired Émile Zola's involvement. In his then notorious open letter, *J'accuse* (1898), Zola declared Dreyfus' innocence and the French Offices of War's cover-up of vital facts in the case. Included in Joyce's reading about the Affair was a translation of the infamous letter. Joyce viewed the Church's anti-Dreyfusard position as another abuse of its institutional power – an abuse that perpetuated stereotypes of "the Jew" as conspirator against the Christian state. Joyce's curiosity, of course, would have had to compete with his nascent interest in avant-garde literature. But perceiving a connection between the "Europeanism" of those works and the news from Paris, Joyce's ire was raised; Europe was boiling over, and his provincial Catholic peers couldn't hear the kettle whistling.

Moreover, during his preparatory year Joyce experienced a disenchantment with University College itself. The institution, which at first appeared to offer him a new level of secular knowledge, remained a Jesuit school, staffed, in fact, by many ex-Belvederians. Joyce was frustrated with University College's identity as Trinity's "lesser counterpart for Catholics" and yet its desire to be molded on "proper English" universities. He found his matriculation English course boring and his instructor, Darlington, "harmless and rather pitiable."[4] The standard fare that his course offered – Goldsmith, Byron, Shelley, Newman, Tennyson – was old hat to Joyce. His interests for the moment lay rather in the radical aesthetics he could discuss with his new associates in the Literary and Historical Society of the College (the L&H). Joyce's presence in the Society's discussions grew quickly; by March of that first year he was nominated to the position of treasurer.[5] Although he lost the election, Joyce volunteered to read a paper that month and the members accepted his proposal unanimously. Their readiness to include him as a speaker is notable

because the honor usually went to a senior member. But their high
regard for the new student would soon be diminished entirely.

Whether Joyce, at the time he volunteered, had a subject for his
paper is unknown. His essay "Drama and Life" was not presented
until January 20, 1900. The gap between proposal and delivery was
the result of events that had transpired after the premier of Yeats' first
play for the new Irish Literary Theater, *The Countess Cathleen*. Before
the opening, many of the young men from Stephen's Green were
disturbed by a criticism of the play they had read in a pamphlet by F.
H. O'Donnell, entitled *Souls for Gold*. Distributed throughout Dublin,
the flyer attacked the play as heretical, claiming it was "nonsense!
. . .and unutterable profanity."[6] Hearing of the pamphlet's charges,
the elderly Cardinal Logue declared the play unfit for a Catholic
audience. The entire L&H decided to attend the publicized play, and
although Joyce went along, he did not join the others in their voiced
protests. Indeed, at the fall of the curtain Joyce was said to have
"clapped vigorously."[7] The morning after the play, he further defied
the pro-Church position of the L&H by refusing to sign their petition
against Yeats' work. The members shunned Joyce for the rest of the
summer, and a few maintained the grudge throughout the next year.

That May, Joyce entered for the Honors paper of the June
matriculation examination. While the University College *Calendar*
(1899) includes the option to change from Honors to Pass by notifying
the secretary with a "satisfactory reason" for the switch "at least one
fortnight before the examination," there is no evidence that Joyce
exercised this option. Rather, he sat for the Honors examination.[8]
Kevin Sullivan was in error, however, when he drew the subject
matter for this exam from the 1900 *Calendar*, as the scope of exams at
the University was presented in the publication *prior* to the test date,
in this case in the 1899 *Calendar*.[9] As Joyce's name does not appear in
the "Honors in English" category in the 1900 *Calendar*, yet is
mentioned in the list of those who matriculated, his answers on this
section must have been judged to deserve only a "Pass." Joyce's
expectations for his new life at University College had been all but
dashed during that first year, and his poor performance reflected that
disappointment.

Directly after the controversy over Yeats' play, and armed with
both his incipient awareness of the Dreyfus Affair and his own
burgeoning aesthetic, Joyce began to write a series of essays. That
September he was impelled to draft a piece on a painting he had

viewed at the Royal Hibernian Academy – a curious decision considering his lack of enthusiasm for the visual arts. By choosing Mihály Munkácsy's *Ecce Homo* as his subject, however, Joyce was addressing one of the most iconographically anti-Jewish scenes of the Gospels. Yet any discussion of the deicidal aspect of the tableau is conspicuously absent from Joyce's critique, and the essay is obviously a furthering of what was now an open antagonism to the Church.

Joyce's thoughts about "the Jew" during this period were also expanded through his ongoing relationship with John Francis Byrne. A companion since Belvedere, Byrne had been the only member of the L&H who supported Joyce during *The Countess Cathleen* controversy. While at University College, Byrne had come in contact with the Dublin Jewish community through his chess game, as several Jews in Dublin were avid players. By 1902, Byrne developed an interest in Dublin Jewry and in Jewish history in general, and through this, Joyce was introduced to some of the first Jewish Dubliners he ever met.

By the time of his graduation from the university, Joyce had dubbed the Irish "the most belated race in Europe."[10] The epithet suggests that as early as 1902 Joyce was measuring "Irishness" against a continental standard. A sampling of the artists he saw as important – Ibsen, Hauptmann, Strindberg, D'Annunzio, Verlaine, Rimbaud, Mallarmé – demonstrate that by his graduation, Joyce's identity as a middle-class Catholic Dubliner had become a burden. He would prefer now to have been a continental "modern," more comfortable in the intelligentsia of Paris or Vienna – a kind of Stefan Zweig with a brogue.[11] By mid-life, Joyce recognized his desire to reinvent himself in this manner and mentioned to his friend, Heinrich Straumann, that "the Jewish intelligentsia had always interested him in particular."[12] But Joyce's years at University College, in which he discovered his new definitions for Irish art and his own "Irishness," represent the tacit beginnings of his conscious interest in "the Jew."

I   1898–99: THE DREYFUS SCANDAL GROWS

During the winter of 1898, Dreyfus' original 1894 conviction was publicly challenged in France. From that point until the summer of the following year the press in Britain and throughout the Continent helped to make the ongoing events into an international scandal. That coverage included continuous reports of anti-Semitic speeches and incidents that were at the center of the Affair. Colonel Marie-Georges Picquart, the discoverer of Dreyfus' innocence in 1896, had single-handedly undertaken to save the honor of the French military. By June of 1899, the *Cour de Cassation* ordered a retrial for the imprisoned former captain. Through a copious journalistic effort, however, Europe at large was made to perceive the unfolding events as more to do with French Jewry than with the procedures of a French court martial.

During his stay in Paris in 1902, Joyce would experience at first hand the Affair's effects on Parisian life. In 1898, however, he had been reading about the court martial of Major Waslin-Esterhazy. Esterhazy had been charged as the author of a newly discovered copy of the treasonous *bordereau* – a counterfeit of which had been determined to have been written by Dreyfus and used to convict him four years earlier.[13] Esterhazy was indicted after Picquart found evidence that suggested the letter had been originally written in the Colonel's hand. After Esterhazy was acquitted by a court martial that convened for a mere two days, Joyce would read a translation of Zola's letter, *J'accuse*, published in *The London Times* on January 14. The piece was one installment of a then daily column in the paper alternately titled "The Dreyfus Case" or "The Esterhazy–Dreyfus Affair."

The original of Zola's letter had been published in George Clemenceau's paper *L'Aurore* on January 13. Its charges were duly supported by a growing contingent calling themselves "the Dreyfusards." The group was composed of Dreyfus family members, Socialists such as Jean Jaurès, and writers such as Bernard Lazare, Charles Péguy, and, of course, Zola himself. While most of these names would not be meaningful to Joyce until years later, in 1898 his curiosity was piqued by Zola's dominating presence in the group. Zola's *J'Accuse* indicted the French Office of War and its Royalist sympathizers; the Catholic Church, as traditional ally of the Army, was also implicated by the Dreyfusards as a major force supporting the conspiracy. Engaged in his own rebellion against Irish Catholicism, Joyce was now discovering corroborating accusations from abroad.

Throughout the year, Joyce also read of the Affair in other Dublin periodicals. He obtained all of the basic information concerning Dreyfus in his family's favorite morning daily, the *Freeman's Journal*. As a Dublin-oriented paper, however, the *Freeman's Journal* never devoted a great amount of space to international news – unless of

course it was related to Irish nationalism. But Joyce at this time was
also reading Arthur Griffith's *United Irishman*. Although Griffith
despised the influence of the Church, he used anti-Dreyfusard
arguments – including an unabashed anti-Semitism – to further his
nationalistic agenda. The most significant publication for Joyce's
reading of detailed accounts of the Affair, however, was *The London
Times*. Throughout the year 1898–99, *The Times* was the best source
of consistent reporting about the Affair available in Dublin, the
paper's second largest circulation center.[14] Joyce also may have
occasionally scanned the pages of the *Irish Times*. While this paper
was the chief organ of Unionist politics in Dublin, its international
news was more complete than other city papers because it ran
wire-stories, and even clipped others, from *The Times*.[15] But as he was
never vehemently anti-English, Joyce was more inclined to read the
London paper than the pages of the Unionist journal.

Almost a century old by Joyce's adolescence, the *Freeman's Journal
and National Press* was the main voice of parliamentary nationalism in
Dublin. While the majority of the paper was devoted to Irish concerns
and Dublin classifieds, the editors did reserve a page or so each issue
for international news. During the year 1898, brief articles on the
Affair were to be found daily on this page. But factual errors in several
pieces indicate that the paper either procured erroneous information
or manipulated facts to excite its nationalist readers. For example, on
January 13, Joyce read about Esterhazy's controversial acquittal:

The Dreyfus case is far from being finished and several sensational
developments are likely to follow the acquittal. . .Two young lawyers who
quarrelled violently about Dreyfus. . .have arranged to fight a duel. M. Zola
is preparing a novel on the case of the ex-captain. . .[16]

Although it is uncertain how the reporter knew that Zola was
"planning to write a novel" on the Affair, such information could not
have failed to gain Joyce's attention. His interest piqued, he would
find in *The Times* a more accurate account.

Perhaps more important than the frequency or accuracy of *The
Times*' articles, however, was their continuous discussion of the role of
anti-Semitism in the Affair. As a case in point, *The Times* on January
13, 1898 presented the argument that the innocent verdict for
Esterhazy was inspired not by the facts in the case, but by a particularly
"French" anti-Semitism. The article, however, also charges the Jews
with bringing much of the persecution upon themselves:

It is, however, but fair to say that the Jews have not too much right to complain of the animosity displayed against them. Some of them have forgotten that for more than a century they have enjoyed the benefits of citizenship, equality and liberty, they owe it to the Christians, and especially to Catholics . . . Now, when 15 years ago the persecution of Catholics broke out. . .many Jews applauded, and not a single voice was raised among them to protest against that anti-Clericism which has sown the seed of anti-Semitism. The acclamations bestowed last night on Major Esterhazy are simply the outcome of that racial hatred directed against the Jews, which is ever ready to cover French soil with victims and ruin.[17]

The passage invokes a well-worn rationalization of prejudice: the persecuted group brings hatred upon themselves. Joyce had heard similar arguments about the Irish from pro-British sources in Dublin; in this case, three key points were recognizable to him: Catholic persecution, anti-Clericism, and racial hatred. But the fourth term, "anti-Semitism," introduced a new element into the equation.

An article in *The Times* a few days later contained a translation of the Parisian Socialist manifesto on Dreyfus' guilt, in which they claim to have no position whatsoever in the matter. Their statement insinuates, however, that "Jewish Capitalists" supported Dreyfus in an attempt to exonerate the Jews from accusations of parasitism: "after the scandals which have discredited them, [Jewish capitalists] have to preserve their share of the booty and rehabilitate themselves If they could prove the existence of a Judicial error . . . they would attempt to wash away in this fountain all the spots of Israel.[18] Although the socialists claim no prejudice against Dreyfus, the piece implies that they nonetheless possess their own brand of anti-Semitism. The Left in France often portrayed French Jewry as the most self-serving element of the bourgeoisie. They maintained this anti-Jewish program, however, while still being at odds with the Church. And a position that was at once anti-Semitic and anti-Catholic surely interested Joyce. While Joyce was aware that socialists and Irish liberals often shared an adamant anti-clericism, leftist anti-Jewishness was a new concept for him.

Most relevant to Dublin was *The Times*' series of articles entitled "The Roman Catholic Church and the Dreyfus Case." Running during the first weeks of September 1899, the series' appearance coincides, interestingly enough, with Joyce's composition of his "Ecce Homo" essay. Considering *The Times*' conservative viewpoint, Joyce must have had reservations against siding with a British paper's

anti-Catholic propaganda. Yet in offering the Church's challenge to
Parisian Jewry, the articles stand as another portrayal of the Church's
abuse of power. In reviewing the relationship between Catholic
publications and the Affair, one of the articles claims that

> there is scarcely a paper amongst those which claim to be supporters of the
> Catholic idea in France which has not contributed to the creation of the
> great myth of the syndicate of treason – the cosmopolitan conspiracy of Jews,
> Protestants, Freemasons and Atheists; there is scarcely one which has not
> helped to inflame to a white heat the racial and religious passions of a people
> naturally prone to gusts of unreasoning fury and suspicion.[19]

In feeding Joyce's anger against the Church, such charges also
affected his perception of "the Jew." Coupled with the anti-Masonic/
anti-Jewish discourse he had encountered in his youth, Joyce began to
suspect such anti-Jewishness with a keener eye. And as these articles
sparked Joyce's curiosity about Jews and Irish culture, his reading of
Griffith's *United Irishman* provided him with an example of anti-Semitism
at the heart of Sinn Féin nationalism.

Seizing the events of 1898 as an opportunity to further the racialist
tenor it used to incite anti-English sentiment, the *United Irishmen*
began in that year as well to use anti-Jewish propaganda to provoke
its Irish audience.[20] In his front page editorials, Griffith often
appropriated and reversed English discourse about Irish racial
degeneracy by stereotyping the English as a megalomaniacal,
unscrupulous race. Although he preached economic independence
and was adamantly anti-Socialist, Griffith first mounted an attack
on Jews in his paper by using the Affair as a vehicle to cast aspersions
against Irish Jews. Griffith wanted Sinn Féin to be a cause for those
who were "racy of the soil." The phrase itself had been a rallying cry
of Irish nationalism since Thomas Davis' Young Ireland movement.
But Griffith's sense of racial purity was entirely xenophobic, and
drew on the discourse of "the Other" for strength. Indeed, Griffith
denied persons born in England the right to take part in any Irish
affairs.[21] During the initial years of his paper's popularity, Griffith
used his "Foreign Notes" column to express his anti-Dreyfusard
opinions and ultimately to invoke the rhetoric of international
anti-Semitism. "The Jew's" supposed unscrupulous huckstering was
to Griffith another sign of a "Jewish nationalism" that was undermining the economic future of independence. During and after
Dreyfus' second trial, Griffith characterized the Affair as absolutely

not a religious controversy, but as evidence of "the Jew's" mercenary "nature":

For the Jews, of course, it is of supreme importance to secure the whitewashing of a Jew Officer who had been admitted too deeply into the military secrets of France, and they are spending millions to effect their object. No Jew is admitted to any rank in Austria, Germany, or Russia, and so the Jews feel that to be excluded from high rank in France would be a stunning blow to their ambition. And I would insist that the exclusion of Jews in Germany, Russia, and Austria has nothing to do with religious beliefs. It is rather a question of Patriotism. The Jew has at heart no country but the Promised Land. He forms a nation apart wherever he goes. He may be a German citizen today, and a British subject tomorrow. He is always a Jew Nationalist bound by the most solemn obligations and the fiercest hopes to the achievement of National Restoration and Revenge. Touch a Jew in Warsaw, and collections will be made to protect him in Moorish Synagogues on the edge of the Sahara and in Chinese Synagogues on the Yellow River. The French Army has sent a Jew to a convict settlement. So, woe to the French Army if the Jews can manage it.[22]

Notice that Griffith "insists" that European discrimination against the Jews has "nothing to do with religion." Notice, as well, that he avoids addressing both the controversy of Dreyfus' conviction on circumstantial evidence and what had already been established – through Picquart's case against Esterhazy – as Dreyfus' undeniable innocence. Such a tendentious refusal to acknowledge the continuity of prejudice against Jews in Europe indeed became a focus for Joyce when he began to compose *Ulysses*.

Throughout the year, Griffith continued his defamation by coopting long-running Continental arguments against "the Jew." In November, the front page of *Irishman* contained popular *fin-de-siècle* theories of Jewish world conspiracy:

No manly action is to be expected from unhappy France, so long as the present conspiracy of Jews and Huguenots governs . . . Every Frenchman knows that Germany is disposed to help against England in many questions, as in South Africa, for instance. To make such a German alliance impossible, the Anglo-Jewish Conspiracy, working in combination with the Huguenots and the Freemasons, are concocting an infamous plan, which aside from assailing Catholic Religion, is certain to make the gulf of hate between France and Germany wider than ever.[23]

Griffith's anti-clericism is undermined here by his allusion to the Jewish–Freemason conspiracy, which was of course traditionally fostered by the Church. But more importantly, this rhetoric was offered to his readership as a lesson in the inherent treachery of "the Jew," a treachery that for the anti-Semite moves beyond even the most common xenophobia.

Although he decreased such arguments after the Dreyfus controversy faded from public consciousness, in 1904 Griffith defended Father Creagh, the instigator of the anti-Jewish riots in Limerick:

In all countries and in all Christian ages he ['the Jew'] has been a usurer and a grinder of the poor. The influence he has recently acquired in this country is a matter of the most serious concern to the people. In Dublin half the labourer population is locked in his toils. Father Creagh deserves the thanks of the Irish people for preventing the poor of Limerick being placed in a similar predicament. The Jew in Ireland is in every respect an economic evil. He produces no wealth himself – he draws it from others – he is the most successful seller of foreign goods, he is an unfair competitor with the ratepaying Irish shopkeeper, and he remains among us, ever and always an alien.[24]

Joyce later cannibalized such rhetoric for the accusations hurled against Bloom by the citizen in the "Cyclops" episode, such as "coming over here to Ireland filling the country with bugs," or "Swindling the peasants. . .and the poor of Ireland" (*U*12.1141, 1150).

Yet although he supported racial Gaelicism, Griffith's central concern was not Irish Jewry. His platform focused opposition on Redmond's Home Rule and the spirit of Parnell, and promised to re-establish both an Irish Parliament and a free Irish Constitution – a plan modeled on the accomplishments of Hungary's Francis Deak and his "dual monarchy" system. Yet even as late as 1906, Griffith's paper continued to utilize the most popular stereotypes of Jews to stimulate feelings of "us against them." While in Rome, for example, Joyce obtained *United Irishman* from his brother, and read a running allegorical piece entitled "Ireland at Auction," in which Ireland represented by a "woman with child" is swindled by buyers and auctioneers, including one simply called "the Jew."[25] By this period, Joyce expressed an unchecked anger toward the racialist failures of Griffith's program.

In reading Griffith's anti-Semitic arguments during his University College years, Joyce recognized how a very familiar Christian animus had found a new source of life.[26] Yet Griffith himself was publicly both anti-clerical and anti-Church, and claimed Sinn Féin's economic anti-Semitism was based on "the Jew" as a pariah, who could never achieve a deep allegiance to any culture into which he attempted to assimilate. Ironically, however, much of Griffith's aspersions against Jewry can be viewed as recycled Church rhetoric about Jewish accursedness, the baseness of their practice of usury, and their subversive "natures" as those who refuse(d) the divinity of Jesus. Dreyfus had merely afforded him a platform from which to chant such hypnotic hatreds.

While at University College Joyce also read the popular university magazine, *The New Ireland Review*. This publication replaced the *Lyceum* in 1894 as the principal university periodical.[27] In 1898 it was the competitor of the University's literary journal, *St. Stephen's*, the magazine that rejected both Joyce's and Francis Skeffington's work in 1901. On a few but significant occasions, *The Review* took a position on Dreyfus. The article entitled "The Zola-Dreyfus Mystery" in the May, 1898 issue is a good example of the journal's use of the Affair to voice its own liberal Catholic viewpoint. Even if he read this piece, however, Joyce had already seen *The Times'* article in which both a translation of *J'accuse* as well as news of Zola's indictment for libel appear. *The Review*'s article discusses the facts concerning Dreyfus, Esterhazy, and Zola, and passes judgment on the recent verdict of innocence for Esterhazy:

And the public went away shrugging its shoulders, quite satisfied that as the man was too corrupt a thing to get a fair hearing, the only course was to look upon him as the craftily selected scape-goat of an able and unscrupulous faction – those clever scheming Jews. They forgot that if to be a Jew is to be a scoundrel, [then] Esterhazy was quite as well qualified for the Ile du Diable as was Dreyfus.[28]

The passage makes reference to Esterhazy's absurd self-defense – that as he was of such a disreputable character, the jury would have a natural prejudice against him. The piece also relates his counsel's argument that a mysterious and powerful "Jewish Syndicate" had framed Esterhazy by imitating his handwriting. But the article fails to mention that this same "Jewish Syndicate" was also the prime target of the Church supported anti-Dreyfusards, whose rhetoric included charges against Freemasons, Protestants, atheists, and Jews as co-conspirators. The article rather posits that the central factor of the entire Affair was an indigenous "French anti-Semitism." Given the Church's involvement in the Affair as related in *The Times'* articles, the lacuna in *The Review*'s argument becomes even more conspicuous.

The Review itself would later become one of the journals that supported the Abbey and its "Celtic" writers. By 1899 , Joyce was already expressing his contempt for both.[29]

Joyce's knowledge of Dreyfus was thus gained from several sources whose agendas were all quite different. While the controversies of the Affair were confusing, the Church's role in the scandal served only to galvanize his rebellion. Directly after reading about Dreyfus, Joyce experienced the scandal raised over Yeats' *The Countess Cathleen*, and his belief in himself as a "voice of reform" trapped in a wilderness of provincial minds was futher reinforced.

The seeds of Joyce's anger had of course been planted years before, as far back as 1891 and Parnell's fall. During this year at University College, however, his apostasy was being reinforced by his reading of avant-garde literature issuing from the Continent. After obtaining Arthur Symon's *Symbolist Movement in Literature,* Joyce quickly consumed Verlaine, Rimbaud, Villiers de L'Isle Adam, and, of course, more Ibsen. He began, as well, to champion James Clarence Mangan, who had been shunned as a licentious, melancholy Celt by the mass of Anglo-Irish literary enthusiasts. Joyce claimed Mangan was the greatest romantic Irish poet, perhaps even more important than Thomas Moore.[30] In discovering Mangan to be an accomplished Orientalist, moreover, Joyce found reinforcement for the Irish fascination with the myth of their supposed Semitic origins.

In his essay brashly titled "The Day of the Rabblement," written within two years of the premier of *The Countess Cathleen*, Joyce attacked the Irish artistic mentality wholesale.[31] Yet the dramatists he was praising – Ibsen, Hauptmann, and others – were not necessarily apolitical; Ibsen himself had challenged the Danish literary movement in the 1880's. But to Joyce, Ibsen's works were more than political; they were "modern": their protagonists were "European" not in their nationalism, but in their radical individualism – their overt sexual explorations, their vernacular speech, their unshakable integrity, their secular humanism, and, even if Joyce liked to avoid such catch-phrases, their social reforms.[32] Moreover, as a "reformed" liberal Catholic, Joyce's scrutinization of the Irish struggle for nationhood was now intensified. His belief in a nationalism springing from the re-Celticized Ireland, to say the least, was uncertain. A "nationalistic aesthetic" that sat under auspices of the Church was of course completely repulsive to him as well. He would thus continue to rebel through a rejection of that to which he was once closest – a liberalism that could not break with Irish Catholicism – and move toward a secular art based on the struggles of the temporal world, be they social, political, gender, or ethnic issues; continental notions about "the Jew" had already found a role in that rebellion.

Summer 1899 was a difficult time for Joyce. Although he matriculated, his performance on his examination could not have pleased him. He felt completely estranged from Catholicism, and his new friends in the L&H had deserted him. Nonetheless, by summer's close, he had become secure in his refusal to acquiesce to what he saw as the Catholic dogmatism of his peers. One of the first products of that new confidence was his essay, "Royal Hibernian Academy 'Ecce Homo.'"

II   A SUDDEN INTEREST IN PAINTINGS

While the events surrounding *The Countess Cathleen* spurred Joyce's rebellion, his break with the Church did not destroy his interest in Christian ideas. It seems that now "Christianity had subtly evolved in his mind from a religion to a system of metaphors."[33] With this new freedom, Joyce undertook to write an essay on a painting he had seen at the Royal Hibernian Academy. The piece that had impressed him was one of three religious works Munkácsy had completed toward the end of his life – works which were receiving a great amount of attention in Britain at the time.[34] The paintings exuded a Pre-Raphaelite vibrancy in their dramatization of three scenes from the life of Christ – Ecce Homo, Christ before Pilate, and Golgotha. Never a real enthusiast of the visual arts, let alone of sacred art, Joyce's visit to the exhibition is an isolated event during his university days.[35] His reaction to the paintings, however, became a ready opportunity to articulate his new aesthetic.

Although by the 1890s Munkácsy's paintings hung in galleries throughout Europe, the artist himself was generally little known outside of his native Hungary. Munkácsy had generally ignored the rising school of Impressionism, yet by the 1870s had gained recognition in Hungary as his country's most prolific artist.[36] But as he was not known as a religious painter, the popularity of his final works is somewhat ironic. Munkácsy's choice of subject matter was usually drawn from his own provincial, peasant background. By 1878, however, his dealer, Charles Sedelmeyer, was encouraging him to paint subjects determined by the tastes of his rich Parisian buyers.

Sedelmeyer had encouraged the artist, who was not a practicing Catholic, to paint biblical and historical scenes from a "Naturalistic standpoint." The dealer offered as an example the success of Ernest Renan's *La Vie de Jesus* (1863), a book Joyce himself would later read and admire in Trieste. Munkácsy, however, wanted to "lift Biblical scenes to the level of literary experience," and create "a really majestic form."[37] After the success of his *Christ before Pilot*, Munkácsy decided to paint the Golgotha and Ecce Homo scenes. The last piece was completed in 1896 when the artist's reputation had begun to decline in Paris, but remained strong in his native Hungary.[38]

In depicting the scene, Munkácsy may have expressed a residual anti-Jewishness from his Catholic upbringing. Indeed, Hungarian admiration of *Ecce Homo* suggests the popularity of the scene among believing Catholics of the era. The scene itself represents the moment in the New Testament in which the Jews as a people are most clearly inculpated. Not appearing in the Eastern Orthodox Church, however, Ecce Homo is a relatively late iconographic subject. By the seventeenth century the scene had been painted in Western Europe by the Van der Weyden brothers, and by the century's close, Rembrandt had treated the scene twice.[39] The nineteenth-century work that influenced Munkácsy was Antonio Ciseri's *Ecce Homo*, completed just before the Italian painter's death in 1891. The importance of the scene as a staple of late nineteenth-century Christian anti-Jewish discourse is suggested in a description of Ciseri's piece by an American iconographer as the depiction of "a nation's fate hanging in the balance [with] the clamor and hatred. . .tipping the beam with direst consequences," sealing the Jews' fate as a "People of Dispersion, kingless and homeless, because they knew not the time of their visitation."[40] The description utilizes a rhetoric about Jewish deicide Joyce himself heard countless times in his youth. Yet when he chose to write about Munkácsy's painting, Joyce disregarded such arguments and instead focused on the painter's Naturalistic technique.

Joyce's essay begins with the thesis that a "drama" can be "frozen in time as in a painting." He justifies the painting as "drama" so as to explain that "modern drama" must portray that which is most common to the human experience rather than that which is most idealistic, religious, or mythic. He finds Munkácsy's Christ effective because "it is Christ as the man of sorrows, his raiment red as of them that tread in the winepress. . .it is literally behold the Man."[41] Focusing on the depiction of Jesus as a human, Joyce remains uninterested in the piece as a representation of the "truth-value" of biblical narrative.

During the course of describing Munkácsy's painting to his reader, Joyce also characterizes the faces and gestures of the figures in the crowd. He believes his premise is reinforced by the grotesque detail which Munkácsy uses to capture the emotions of certain figures. Because of this technique, Joyce praises the artist as a modern "dramatist": "To paint such a crowd one must probe humanity with no scrupulous knife" (p. 35). It is not the representation of "Jewish sin" that impresses Joyce, but how Munkácsy captures the secular "drama of the thrice-told revolt of humanity against a great teacher" (p. 36). Joyce's substitution of the terms "humanity" and "teacher" for the more common "the Jews" and "our Lord" further evinces his new heterodoxy.

Yet, in his descriptions of Munkácsy's figures, Joyce inadvertently reveals certain prejudices that he may have not yet analyzed:

In the heart of the crowd is a figure of a man furious at being jostled by a well clad Jew. The eyes are squinting rage, and an execration foams on his lips. The object of his rage is a rich man, with the horrible cast of countenance, so common among the sweaters of modern Israel. I mean, the face whose line runs out over the full forehead to the crest of the nose then recedes in a similar curve back to the chin, which, in this instance, is covered with a wispish tapering beard. The upper lip is raised out of position, disclosing two long, white teeth, while the whole lower lip is trapped. (p. 34)

One might regard Joyce's descriptions as stereotypical, or perhaps as the reinterpretation of an image that was already based on stereotype. But Joyce's descriptions are, as usual, painstakingly precise. Munkácsy's painting portrays nearly all of its Jewish figures – with the exception of Jesus – in the protofeatures so often found in biblical scenes of masters of the grotesque, such as Bosch. Certainly Munkácsy's choice of two of the three Bible scenes he wanted to paint, *Ecce Homo* and *Christ Before Pilate*, indicates his preference for moments from the Gospels that most incriminate the Jews. But in his rhetorical leap from a description of a face to the phrase "that horrible cast of countenance so common among the sweaters of modern Israel," Joyce may be complicit in Munkácsy's stereotyping. Perhaps both former Catholics were more unconscious than conscious in their prejudice. But Joyce's phrase here suggests that, on a reactive level at least, he still retained the notion that there is an essential physiognomy, perhaps even a psychology, to the Jews as a people.

Telling as well is Joyce's use of the noun "sweaters." The *Oxford English Dictionary* gives a popular nineteenth-century definition of the term "sweat" as "To lighten (a gold coin) by wearing away its substance by friction or attrition." The meaning, originating in eighteenth-century England, thus applies to the noun "sweaters": "One who 'sweats' gold coins," and again to the verb sweating: "the practice of lightening gold coins by friction . . . 1785: Grose Dict . . . Vulgar . . . *Sweating*, a mode of diminishing the gold coin, practised chiefly by the Jews, who corrode it with *aqua regia*."[42] While Joyce may have had this definition in mind, we can't know whether he was using an Irish cliché or revealing his own tendency to stereotype. And although his purpose was to promote his new aesthetic, his "Jewish miser" must have come easily to his pen. Yet the failure to deconstruct a convention so prevalent in Joyce's world does not seem a completely negligent act. Indeed, despite the figure of speech, Joyce's overall discussion of Munkácsy's work flies in the face of an orthodox Catholic view of the tableau, and his defiance of Church doctrine indicates that the concept of Jewish deicide was either offensive or at least unimportant to him by now.

Joyce's first year at University College can thus be charted by his involvement with the L&H, his reaction to Yeats' play, and his writing of the "Ecce Homo" essay. But 1898 through 1900 was also the period during which Joyce established a close friendship with J. F. Byrne. As the character of Cranly in *A Portrait*, Byrne appears as a sounding-board for the troubled Stephen, and his influence on Joyce during their first year at University College was similar to the fictional depiction. Through Byrne, Joyce was also afforded the opportunity to revise his notions about living Jews, as well as their representation in Irish culture.

III   FRIENDS, HEROES, AND SPEECHES

J. F. Byrne played a dual role in Joyce's adolescence as both an older companion and a challenging interlocutor. Through both roles, Byrne indirectly influenced Joyce to complete his break with Catholicism and to begin to consider the Continent as the focus of his artistic future. Joyce first became acquainted with Byrne at Belvedere and soon grew to admire his friend's "common sense." When Joyce enrolled at University College, his relationship with Byrne entered a new, more dependent phase. Aside from Stanislaus, Byrne became one of Joyce's true intimates during the course of his academic career at the college. Byrne believed that Joyce at first "cleaved" to him because the latter found the university intimidating; realizing Joyce's anxiety, as well as his potential as an intellectual companion, Byrne amiably assumed a role he himself termed as "protector."[43] Byrne had a habit of thinking aloud, and enjoyed engaging in arguments with Joyce concerning the Church and both political and aesthetic matters. Joyce's respect for his friend early in their relationship included making Byrne one of the first readers of his poetry.[44] Dublin born but of peasant stock, Byrne represented to Joyce a rugged, conservative mind that wasn't afraid to accept the controversies or paradoxes of any idea, heretical or not.[45] And after he had become acquainted with several of Dublin's Jews through his interest in chess, Byrne's open-mindedness provoked in him a curiosity about the city's Jewish community.

Respected as one of the best young players in Dublin, Byrne met a number of Dublin Jews when he joined the Sackville Chess Club in 1902.[46] One of these members who eventually became a close friend, an immigrant named Moses Zaks, was perhaps one of Joyce's first Jewish acquaintances. A well-educated, short, and swarthy individual, Zaks was of Russian descent and had been trained in his youth to be a rabbi. Like many immigrants, however, he was unable to continue in his calling and eventually became the proprietor of a shop on Redmond's Hill. Byrne's association with Zaks was a close one; the two often dined together at Zaks' home and engaged in evening-long discussions. Some of the ideas the two exchanged certainly became elements of the debates between Byrne and Joyce.[47] Moreover, through his relationship with Zaks, Byrne became interested in several aspects of secular Jewish culture, not the least of which was the life and writings of Baruch Spinoza. After they had known each other for some time, in fact, Zaks requested that Byrne give a lecture on the philosopher to the Dublin Jewish literary club in 1908.[48]

The aspect of Spinoza's personal history that Byrne found most fascinating was the philosopher's excommunication from Judaism and subsequent view of his own Jewish identity. The interest is not very surprising considering Byrne's own struggle with Catholic identity. Indeed, in Trieste, as Joyce was discovering his curiosity about certain key ambiguities of Jewish identity, Byrne was explaining to a group of attentive Dublin Jews that Spinoza, even while excommunicated, might have always considered himself a Jew:

I explained that in discussing the excommunication of Spinoza I had two points in view, both of which I intended to be implicit rather than explicit. [The first of these] was whether Spinoza, as a result of his excommunication and in view of the fact that he never recanted, did or did not, ipso facto, cease to be a Jew. In this connection, I suggested, it would be highly desirable for the Jews themselves to formulate an authoritative definition of the word "Jew." I concluded by saying that the second of my two points was to advert to man's inhumanity to man; an inhumanity that often reveals itself in its most virulent form in man's relationship with his own people – "The near in blood the nearer Bloody." And the deplorable circumstance about this condition is that it appears to exist universally in all human societies.[49]

In the passage Byrne was responding to Zaks' claim that his fellow Jewish members were unaware of the writ of excommunication served on Spinoza by the Dutch Sephardic Rabbinate in 1656. Byrne viewed that ignorance as a failure, present so critically in his own Irish culture, to achieve a unified sense of personal identity and community. His cliché, "the near in blood the nearer bloody" represents his own connection between the struggle for an ethnic Irish identity and those of Jewish identity crises. The confrontation of such grey areas of religious identity sat at the center of many of Joyce's arguments with Byrne, and Byrne's assertions are analogous to the conflicts that would someday underlie Leopold Bloom's life as a "non-Jewish, Jewish Dubliner." Bloom's entire narrative of course would focus on the controversy of what makes a Jew a Jew, and Joyce's displacement on to Bloom of the ambiguities of his own Catholicism and "Irishness" finds one beginning in the connections he and Byrne made between marginal Jewish and marginal Catholic identity. In *Ulysses*, Joyce indeed makes Spinoza Bloom's favorite philosopher.

Byrne's interest in ethnic/religious questions became the raw material for Cranly's discussions with Stephen in both *Stephen Hero* and *A Portrait* about how one could leave the Church and continue to consider oneself an Irish Catholic. The controversy not only had a history in the Joyce–Byrne relationship, but may have been the disagreement over which they first severed their ties in 1904. During an interview years after his completion of *Ulysses*, when asked the question, "[w]hen did you leave the Catholic Church," Joyce laconically replied "[t]hat's for the Church to say."[50]

With Byrne in attendance, Joyce read his essay "Drama and Life" to the L&H in January, 1900, and publicly proclaimed his rebellion against present Irish drama. Joyce's accusations were now precise:

"Shall we put life – real life – on the Stage. No, says the Philistine chorus, for it will not draw."[51] Ibsen, the playwright who inspired Joyce's essay, is only mentioned briefly – once in an allusion to *The Wild Duck*, and, at the end of the paper, with a line from *Pillars of Society*. After Joyce had read his essay he was slapped on the back by a fellow Society member and called "magnificent, but quite mad."[52] He subsequently was given a new nickname among the L&H members: "The Mad Hatter." But Joyce was quite proud of his paper, and soon wrote to the editor of the *Fortnightly Review*, W. L. Courtney, asking him if he would publish such an article. The surprising answer was a qualified no; Courtney was looking for a more specific review of Ibsen's latest work, *When We Dead Awaken*.

"Ibsen's New Drama" (1900), was Joyce's response. The piece was not only a tribute to an artist Joyce would always hold in high esteem, but became the initial source of Joyce's first public recognition in Dublin. For Joyce not only had the piece published in the prestigious *Fortnightly Review* on April 1, 1900, but he was thanked for his praise of the play by Ibsen himself through the editor of the magazine.[53] In the introduction of his essay, Joyce refers to the playwright as having already been "upheld as a religious reformer, a social reformer, a Semitic lover of righteousness, and as a great dramatist."[54] His use of the phrase "a Semitic lover of righteousness," however, is somewhat incongruous. Whether he had previously heard Ibsen called this is unknown; he may have very well created the phrase himself. Ibsen was certainly not Jewish; nor is there any particular reason to believe that Joyce might have thought him to be so. Perhaps in claiming for Ibsen a courageous commitment to his vision, however, Joyce was reminded of the passages of the Old Testament he had learned in his youth. He was, as well, echoing the concept of the Hebraic strictness of mind he had encountered in his reading of Arnold's "Hebraism and Hellenism." Yet Joyce was not using the phrase to suggest antiquated heroism, but a contemporary allegiance to "the true and the good." The label thus implies Joyce's revision during his last year at University College of his concept of "Jewish nature." Once a "sweater of horrible countenance," "the Jew" for Joyce had now also become the embodiment of an agitating righteousness. Later on in 1912, while discussing the English temperament, Joyce used a similar epithet to further describe his view of Semitic characteristics. In his lecture on Defoe's *Robinson Crusoe* to a Triestine audience, Joyce described the Englishman as "not endowed with the intellect of the

Latin, nor with the patience of the Semite, nor with Teutonic Zeal, nor with the sensitiveness of the Slav."[55] Yet even by his graduation from University College, Joyce was ascribing various new qualities of mind to his expanding notions about "Jewish nature," many of which also implied an admirable "continental" mentality. Ellmann indeed states that "before Ibsen's letter Joyce was an Irishman; after it he was a European."[56]

Joyce himself had begun to look to Europe for inspiration. He now began to write more poetry, and even tried his hand at an Ibsen-influenced play, titled *A Brilliant Career*.[57] He taught himself Dano-Norwegian so he could reply to Ibsen. He began jotting down comments in overheard conversations, which would later be dubbed "epiphanies" and would of course become sketches for many of the stories of *Dubliners*. Joyce's reputation as an eccentric grew among his classmates during this period as well. One outcome of reputation is always comparison; through such gossip Joyce's oratory style was compared in 1901 to that of a visitor to the university, a Dublin barrister and nationalist writer named John F. Taylor.

Taylor delivered a speech before the Law Student's Debating Society on October 24, 1901. Joyce attended the presentation and later on in Trieste obtained the pamphlet entitled "The Language of the Outlaw," which Taylor had printed from his notes. Joyce also read excerpts of Taylor's piece that had been printed the next day in the *Freeman's Journal* in a section entitled "The Irish Revival." A dedicated Home Ruler, Taylor was also committed to the widely disseminated program of Douglas Hyde's Gaelic League. In his speech, Taylor used the now conventional Irish–Hebrew simile to portray the inability of the English to comprehend the commitment of the Irish cause.[58] Joyce was pleased with the analogy between the condescension of the Egyptians and that of the English, and Taylor's entire presentation appears to have risen above mere rhetoric for him – the speech, slightly altered to emphasize the metaphor, is of course recited by Professor MacHugh in the "Aeolus" episode of *Ulysses*. Taylor gave Joyce a sense of continuity – the analogy reminded him of the Home Rule discourse of his youth. He indeed retained a delight in his own version of Taylor's words throughout the composition of *Ulysses*; when asked in 1924 to record some of the book for Sylvia Beach, Joyce made MacHugh's passage his first choice.[59]

While at University College Joyce also encountered the Classical studies of Father Henry Browne, SJ, Professor of Greek and Latin and

Dean of Residence during this period.[60] Browne is predominately remembered for rejecting, in the capacity of adviser to the journal *St. Stephen's*, Joyce's essay "The Day of the Rabblement" (1901).[61] Before this, however, Browne's theories on Homer – which drew heavily on Victor Bérard's ideas of the Semitic and Phoenician's origins of the *Odyssey* – may have influenced Joyce's attitude toward ancient Judaism. As Joyce's Latin professor, Browne spoke often about his work in progress, *Handbook of Homeric Study*, which he published in 1905. Browne's ideas, such as "the Phoenicians [being] the Semites of the West, [to discuss them] is to enter upon the question of debt that we Aryans owe to a people we are naturally inclined to hate," may have initiated Joyce's own fascination with Bérard, whom he later read extensively in Zurich.[62]

During his last year at University College, however, Joyce was still enthralled with the French Symbolist poetry and Naturalist drama that had so impressed him in 1898. Joyce's enthusiasm for the Continent had become a means to a new awareness, and France was continually the focus of his attention. The French had always welcomed Irish expatriates, and Joyce may have felt his desire to cross the Channel was somehow within Irish tradition of "the wild geese." He certainly looked to Paris as the city of avant-garde art. Joyce's knowledge of the Dreyfus Affair may also have attracted him to Paris, as a place where rebellion and conflict were open and alive, not buried by what he viewed as the ubiquitous fear of a medieval institution, as in the Church and Dublin.

James Joyce graduated from University College on October 31, 1902. His family had been encouraging him to enroll in the University's Medical School. Although he was initially admitted, his father's financial circumstances kept him from ever attending.[63] Instead, Joyce sailed for France not less than two months after the university rejected him for lack of funds. He petitioned money and services for this trip from several of the more influential figures in Ireland who he had come to know through George Russell. Although Russell had read Joyce's poems, he found them unpromising and declared that one of his other disciples, Padriac Colum, would be the next great voice of Ireland.[64] Yet both Yeats and Lady Gregory corresponded with Joyce that year and undertook to aid him during his stay in Paris. But Joyce knew he was not going to Paris to become a physician; he had already decided he would someday be a writer of international repute.

That trip to Paris was a turning point in Joyce's experiences with "the Jew" as well as with European Jewry. After meeting Yeats in London, Joyce felt he had come full circle in his break with the Irish Renaissance. He was ready for a new outlook on life – ready to become a "European." But in Paris, Joyce would discover a new world of prejudices. Stanislaus once said of his older brother that as a young man, Joyce "preferred people whom the world rated as failures."[65] After reading about Dreyfus, failing to convince his peers of his genius, and rebelling against his own culture, Joyce escaped to Paris to become a bohemian. Viewing himself both an apostate and outcast, Joyce appears to have been sensitive to the anti-Semitism he encountered in his new home. Several years later he would come to believe that as an expatriate, avant-garde writer, he shared a distinct consciousness with the assimilated Jewish intellectual of Europe.

CHAPTER 4

Exile: excursion to the Continent, bitter return

Joyce's time in Paris, from December 1902 until April 1903, represents his first experiences on the Continent. While the trip initially seemed promising, Joyce discovered his own potential for failure in Paris when his plans to become both a physician and a poet collapsed. In the role of dejected foreigner, Joyce felt a kinship with the disenfranchised groups he observed in the culturally mixed Latin Quarter near his lodgings at the Hôtel Corneille. One such group that certainly suggested Stanislaus' "rating of failure" were Parisian Jews, who in 1902 were still the target of Dreyfus-related anti-Semitism. Rather than a religious prejudice, however, Parisian Jew-baiting incorporated stereotypes drawing on a century of theories about racial hierarchy. Such images provoked Joyce's curiosity about the secularized Jew of Europe and became the foundation of parallels he later drew between his own Otherness in British culture and Jewish Otherness on the Continent.[1]

After returning to Dublin for the Christmas holidays, Joyce once again sailed for France on January 23, 1903. On the morning after his arrival, he registered for an admission card to both the Bibliothèque Nationale and the Bibliothèque Saint-Geneviève.[2] He soon discovered that he would have to pay fees immediately to attend classes at the École de Médecine. Not possessing the necessary funds, he began spending his days and nights reading Aristotle, Ben Johnson, and the Symbolist poets. His French at the time was not adequate enough to comprehend the technical terminology of his courses, and his impecuniosity kept him from any immersion in the life of the city.

The ensuing winter months were quite hard on him. He met with some fellow Irishmen – the "wild goose" Joseph Casey and John Synge – but for the most part he was on his own. Nevertheless, Joyce was taken by the ambiance of his new home: a photo postcard of December 15 to J. F. Byrne portrays Joyce looking like a rebellious,

bourgeois adolescent wearing the latest bohemian head wear.[3]
Parisian heterogeneity was a new experience for a young man from
the homogenous world of Catholic Dublin. But although he felt
foreign to those surrounding him, Joyce found something comfortable
about the role of isolated alien viewing his environment from the
perspective of detached observer. One year after his return, he would
leave Dublin to become a lifelong expatriate, ensuring his marginality
to the cultures in which he was to make temporary homes. In that
position as an avant-garde Irish artist living on the Continent, Joyce
became fascinated with the several discourses concerning "the Jew";
but his initial awareness of the impact of theories of Jewish racial
degeneracy began in Paris.

In the atmosphere of rationalistic positivism, anti-Semitism in
France had been fostered early in the century through philological
and anthropological arguments. The noun "Semitism" itself represents
the era's mania for thinking in terms of racial hierarchy, the whole of
which had already affected Joyce as an Irishman who rejected both
Sinn Féin nationalism as well as racial Celticism. As a pseudo-science,
anti-Semitism co-opted religiously based hatred and made it viable
for a secular world.[4] This commingling of ideologies is alluded to in
the very beginning of *Ulysses*, when Buck Mulligan calls Stephen
"Japhet in search of a father" (*U*1.561). Even Catholicism in Ireland
was affected by such theories: "scientific" research about Noah's sons
as progenitors of the Caucasian, Semitic, and Negroid races appears
in the 1893 edition of *The Irish Ecclesiastical Record*.[5]

The conceptual origins of an inferior Semitic race, as opposed to
the superior races of "Indo-European" or "Aryan" descent, reached
back to eighteenth-century philology. Herder's 1767 nationalistic
writings included the notion that language not only united peoples,
but could define a nation's "soul." The racial theories of J. F.
Blumenbach at the University of Göttingen in the 1770s, and
linguistic research on the origin of Greek from Sanskrit by William
Jones in the 1780s laid the foundation for the theory of a Brahman
ancestry of Greek civilization – the beginnings of the ideology of
Indo-European preeminence.[6] Much of German Romanticism later
incorporated Orientalism as a key to understanding the psychology of
European strength and heterogeneity.[7] These differing ideas eventually
coalesced into a single, racialist animus: in 1847, the Indologist
Christian Lassen's publication, *Indische Alterthumskunde*, postulated
that both the Semitic languages and Semitic people lacked the

"balance of all the powers of the soul" which made the Aryan "race" superior.[8]

By the 1880s, theories of Semitic inferiority had served to form political platforms in France and Germany, and to a lesser extent, later on in England. The term "anti-Semitism" had been coined in 1879 by the German socio-economic writer Wilhelm Marr to denote a separate set of prejudices from those of Christian anti-Jewishness.[9] Later in the century, French theorists such as Joseph Gobineau, Ernest Renan, Silvestre de Sacy, and Gustave Le Bon developed arguments about racial inferiority as well, which often emphasized "the Jew" as racial alien and economic parasite. This discourse again indicted "the Jew" as a cultural pariah, whose secret desire was to destroy Christian power by way of an international financial conspiracy.

During the *fin-de-siècle*, the British empire had its own version of a Jewish conspiracy myth, and Joyce was certainly aware of it before arriving in Paris. The London stereotype of the Eastern Jew – dirty, scheming, and even blood-thirsty – bolstered fear of waves of Jewish immigration to that city throughout the last two decades of the century. As a negative reifier of imperial ideology, "the Jew" was seen as "Asiatic" and economically subversive, intent on destroying British power from within; unscrupulous "Jewish business practices" were supposedly backed by an international network of Jewish bankers.[10] Joseph Banister's *England Under the Jews* encapsulated many of these claims; although somewhat of an obscure text, it nonetheless went through three editions from 1901 to 1907.[11] Moreover, to Boer War imperialists, the conspiracy theory also displaced a more realistic fear of German military dominance. In this manner, Jews were cast as German "spies" gaining a foothold on London soil through false claims of religious persecution. Ironically enough, Joyce initially encountered this type of rhetoric at University College and later through Sinn Féin propaganda.

As one born into a struggle of race and culture within an empire, Joyce took special notice of the racially-based French anti-Semitism he readily observed in Paris. He had just left a world where his own people had for years been characterized as "racially inferior" by the English. During his stay in the city, Joyce's youthful awareness of "the Jew" was brought to the forefront of his consciousness, and generated in him a curiosity about French Jews he encountered. Absorbing Dreyfus-related propaganda, Joyce's perception of these "Others" was undergoing an acute change.

When he returned to his hometown in 1903, Joyce met with some Jewish Dubliners. And on an eventful evening in 1904 he may have been aided in a time of distress by one Alfred H. Hunter, who was rumored in Dublin to be both a Jew and cuckold. These experiences played on Joyce's new thoughts about "the Jew" from Paris, further undermining those stereotypes he had encountered to that point. When Joyce began to construct his "Jew" in 1914, he indeed drew on his memories of Paris as well as on his experiences directly after his return.

I   FRANCE AND THE FIGURE OF "*LE JUIF*"

Throughout the nineteenth century, Paris was often referred to as the "first city" of Jewish emancipation. Napoleon's plan for the assimilation of some 40,000 Jews into the new Republic had given him the distinction of "the Liberator of the Jews." Quite positive to French Jewry, the title was often derogatory in the mouths of French nationalists. Napoleon himself had recriminations against the Jews because they "set themselves apart" from the nations where they made their homes. During the Sanhedrin he assembled in 1807, he had declared to leaders of the Parisian Jewish community that the Jews were to swear allegiance to the Republic and no other peoples, including the "Jews of other lands."[12] While discrimination against the Jews lessened under Napoleon, full legal equality was not obtained until the abolition of the *more judaico* in 1846.[13] The impending years of revolution during the 1840s brought a new rise in popular anti-Jewish sentiment, though these forces remained less than a national movement throughout the Second Empire. During the Third Republic, however, the idea that Jews had to be French before they were Jewish became fuel for ardent Parisian anti-Semites. Turning Napoleonic-era rhetoric on its head, anti-Semitic platforms of the 1880s claimed the Jews could relinquish their religion, but never their "Jewishness" – as both a racial and cultural distinction, "the Jew" could never be a true Frenchman.

Yet most urban Jews by this era – 60,000 of them in Paris – sought a single identity as loyal French citizens.[14] The majority of mid-to-late-century Parisian Jews spoke only French and substituted Parisian diet, dress, and social activity for *Kashrut* and *Yiddishkeit*. Even as early as the year of Joyce's birth, this older community of Francophone Jews was embarrassed by the arrival in the city of waves of Yiddish speaking "*Ostjuden*," (Eastern European Jews, religiously orthodox and often impoverished). Such prejudice between Jews was analogous to the ethnic self-hatred Joyce experienced in his own Irish culture, and he made allowance for the phenomenon in constructing Bloom: the "Jewish" protagonist expresses a milder version of prejudice toward "the Jew" throughout his day.

Jewish self-hatred in *fin-de-siècle* Paris is clearly manifested in the work of the journalist Bernard Lazare. At the outset of the decade, Lazare attempted to cope with anti-Semitism by promoting French nationalism among Parisian Jews. His early writings distinguished two types of French Jews. "*Le juif*," the socially evil Jew, was of German or Eastern European extraction and embodied those qualities from which the stereotype of the avaricious Jew was enabled: "*le juif*" was "dominated by the unique preoccupation with making a quick fortune and [made] money the goal of all life."[15] Conversely, "*l'israelite*," the socially progressive Jew, was more refined, of poor to moderate circumstances, assimilated into mainstream French society, and, according to Lazare, should reject all association with the other "moneychangers from Frankfort, Polish bartenders, Galician pawn-brokers, with whom they have nothing in common."[16] Although by the Dreyfus years Lazare had completed a serious study of anti-Semitism and become a spokesman for "Jewish nationalism" in France, his older distinction between the assimilated "*israelite*" and the clannish "*juif*" maintained its currency in French culture well after the turn of the century.

An important aspect of late-century assimilation in France was the effort on the part of Jewish families to place their sons socially above the mercantile world by establishing them as *fonctionaires*. In spite of the Catholic dominance of institutions such as the army, one Alsatian–Jewish family who had successfully landed their son in the military was that of Raphael Dreyfus, father of Alfred. Years later, when Alfred – then a decorated captain in the prestigious General Staff – was arrested on charges of treason, the family was on some level as shocked as other Republicans, Jewish or not.[17]

By Joyce's arrival in 1902, the most tumultuous years of the Dreyfus scandal were over. But a residue of the anti-Semitism surrounding the second trial remained unavoidable in Paris. In addition, French politics had yet to be reconciled after the Affair had deepened the rift between what is often referred to as "the two Frances": the post-1840 division between right-wing Royalist and liberal Republicans. After the Franco-Prussian War, France witnessed a rise in tensions between incumbent Republicans and a growing contingent of disgruntled Royalists. The latter felt the corruption of the Second Republic – especially the loss of the war – was due to the destructive bureaucratic nature of democratic rule. Their stance was violently nationalistic and called for a new France – monarchist, authoritarian, and cleansed of all foreign influence. Their constituency was entrenched in the two most powerful aristocratic institutions, the army and the Church. The discovery in 1894 of a supposed traitor – who was both Jewish and Republican – became the catalyst for Royalists and anti-Semites to build a coalition against permissiveness toward Jews. Studies of the era often postulate that Dreyfus pushed the division of the "two Frances" to the breaking point.

To say the least, the anti-Semitism Joyce encountered in Paris was much more complex than that of his native Dublin. In 1902, anti-Semitic propaganda still issued from both Royalist and leftist elements of the city. United by the pressures of the Reactionaries, however, the Socialist party set a precedent in European history by eventually backing the bourgeois Republicans – by 1898 both parties viewed anti-Dreyfusard actions as the first signs of a threatening tidal wave of archaic monarchism. As noted in the earlier articles in *The Times*, however, the left always maintained its own brand of anti-Semitism disguised as "anti-capitalism." Jules Guerin, founder of the Ligue Antisémitique Française of 1889 positioned himself as radically left-wing, and claimed that "Antisemitism is essentially socialist."[18]

Finer distinctions between these contradictory types of anti-Semitism, however, probably escaped Joyce. But seeking to support himself as a journalist, Joyce became aware of anti-Semitism in general as a volatile aspect of Parisian political discourse. His reviews and articles for both the Dublin *Daily Express* and *The Speaker* during this period represented his only source of income other than the funds shipped to him by his mother.[19] While these writings contain no references to anti-Semitism, they do relay Joyce's growing concern with religion as the enemy of modern art and with violence as the downfall of man.

Joyce's first published review was titled "An Irish Poet," and appeared in the *Daily Express* on December 11, 1902. In his comments on William Rooney's book of patriotic verse, *Poems and Ballads*, Joyce again explained how religious and political enthusiasts provide an audience for incompetent authors, reaffirming his belief that religious didacticism undermines powerful art. In this instance, however, Joyce's rhetoric critiques not only aesthetics, but action: "Religion and all that is allied thereto can manifestly persuade men to great evil, and by writing these verses, even though they should. . .enkindle the young men of Ireland to hope and activity, Mr. Rooney has been persuaded to great evil."[20] Religion and politics as the sources of violence in the West was also the focus of his next review, "A Suave Philosophy," published in the *Daily Express* on February 6, 1903. In reviewing H. Fielding-Hall's book on Buddhism, titled *The Soul of a People*, Joyce registered his contempt for physical force:

Our civilization, bequeathed to us by fierce adventurers, eaters of meat and hunters, is so full of hurry and combat, so busy about many things which perhaps are of no importance, that it cannot but see something feeble in a civilization which smiles as it refuses to make the battlefield the test of excellence.[21]

Later in life, Joyce constructed the same attitude into Bloom's pacifism throughout *Ulysses*. And in the spring of 1903, Joyce's own repugnance to violence was tested. During the preceding January, he had entered into an argument in a Paris bar with the Austrian poet Teodor Daubler. When Daubler became angry with Joyce, he challenged the young "Irish upstart" to a duel. After Joyce had recounted the incident to his brother, Stanislaus asked him what he would have done if the threat seemed more than mere drunken histrionics. Joyce replied promptly " – Started for Dublin by the first train leaving Paris."[22] As a frail, cerebral young man, Joyce's reaction was probably one of simple fear. Later on in life, however, he would declare a commitment to non-violence, as in his often repeated statement to Frank Budgen that he was "not a bloodyminded man."[23] Having already attacked the Church as the ruinous element in Modern Irish art, Joyce now discovered a relationship between religion, politics, and a violence he saw as indigenous to the West; that predilection for brutality was most conspicuous in its French form in the Dreyfus propaganda he was presently observing.

Walking about the city, Joyce encountered a host of articles and placards that called for violence against Dreyfus and the Jews. In that discourse – as in British rhetoric about the Irish – a Jewish racial distinction was inseparable from a supposedly subversive "Jewish politics." As an aspiring journalist, Joyce was reading several Parisian papers, a number of which were Anti-Dreyfusard.[24] Although mainstream papers such as *Le Temps* had by 1903 ceased daily coverage of the events of the Affair, the efforts of popular anti-Semitic cartoonists and writers pushed on throughout the years proceeding the trial at Rennes. Journals such as *Le Libre Parole*, *La Fueille*, and *La Patrie* often ran front-page stories and cartoons about Dreyfus as well as French Jewry in general.[25]

One of the more severely anti-Semitic papers that had a life beyond 1901 was Henri Rochefort's *L'Intransigeant*. The journal's anti-Dreyfus posters, which made use of venomous caricatures of Jewish figures, had been banned by police during the trial at Rennes. The popularity of the paper itself, however, even in 1902, made it available to Joyce at the corner newsstand. The lead article of the December 2 issue (the day after Joyce arrived in Paris), entitled "Les Dessous Du Procès," began with this admonishment:

Il est une chose indéniable, c'est que l'affaire Dreyfus est au fond de tout: au fond de la note de votre tailleur, s'il est juif, qui la diminuera s'il vous sait judaisant et l'enflera s'il vous a deviné nationaliste; au fond de procès qu'on vous intente ou que vous intentez; au fond de vos chaussures au fond de votre potage.

[It is undeniable that the Dreyfus Affair is behind everything. . .it is behind everything down to the bill your tailor gives you: if he's a Jew, he'll lower it if you're Jewish, and raise it if he suspects you're a nationalist. It is beneath all proceedings – all that is intended for you and all that you intend to do – it is beneath your shoes and at the bottom of your bowl.][26]

But even as Joyce read such papers, his own designs for a future in Paris were crumbling.

Joyce's vision of becoming a journalist and poet, of entering the exotic subculture of Symbolist artistes, soon collapsed into a mere struggle to eat. For the first time in his life he knew the isolation of being poor, friendless, and hungry. On his arrival to the city, he felt exploited as an immigrant: "My funds are low because among other things the little Parisian shopkeepers passed old louis off to me and once or twice [even] Italian lire."[27] During his desultory perambulations about the city, he also noticed Frenchmen whose features suggested to him that they were Parisian Jews, and may have felt a connection with them through his now reinforced feelings of isolation and marginality. The faces and conduct of Jews had begun to earn their place in his imagination, and by 1915 Joyce would reach back into his memories of Paris to create Stephen's vision of Jews on the steps of the

Bourse in the "Nestor" episode (*U*2.364–73). Joyce passed the Bourse *en route* to the Bibliothèque Nationale, and the building's structure afforded his imagination a setting in which modern Jews could be linked to the ancient Hebrew money-lenders Jesus had driven from another temple.

Exactly which Parisian pedestrians were in fact Jewish, however, was much more difficult to determine than it would readily appear. Many city-dwellers had similar "oriental" features and complexions to those of the stereotype of "the Jew." This kind of misreading would be especially egregious in the area of the Marais, behind the Hôtel de Ville. Both Alsatian and Russian Jews had been settling there for some time among other Mediterranean peoples, including Italians, Arabs, and Spaniards. During the immigration waves of the 1880s, these areas grew in population; for Eastern Jews, Paris then seemed a safe place to escape the pogrom.[28] On the other hand, to assume that some of the stock traders he observed at the Bourse were Jewish would not have been such an error for Joyce. Given the occupational realities of Paris, many Jews were active there on a daily basis. But while the Parisian Jewish community had produced some of the banking dynasties of the century – the Rothschilds, Pereires, Lazards, and Finlays – most Jews in the city were not wealthy. They were, however, involved in daily business in a very visible way, especially to an outsider curious about European Jewry. Paula Hyman tells us that "[Jews often] worked as agents and stockbrokers...[and] in commerce they were concentrated in several lines of supply, most notably in the garment industry, leather goods, jewelry and furniture."[29]

As intricate as Jewish assimilation had been in France, however, any prejudice Joyce retained from his youth was reinforced by Parisian anti-Semitism. Jew-baiting in the city remained popular in visual and written material in 1903 and did not issue from strictly Catholic anti-Jewish sources. But Joyce was familiar with these stereotypes in a tangential manner: anti-Semitism in Paris was set in the context of racial hierarchy, a discourse that had shaped Irish stereotypes in British culture as well.

II INFERIOR RACES, LESSER HUMANS

The "truth of race" had been of course an important aspect of rationalistic positivism throughout Western Europe. By the middle of the nineteenth century, nationalistic fervor played on the "racial" differences of minority cultures subject to imperial hegemony throughout the Continent. Joyce would later recognize that modern Zionism itself was in a crucial manner a reaction to these new ideas. In Trieste, he would become aware that Theodor Herzl's *Der Judenstaat* was written only after Herzl had covered the Dreyfus Affair for his Viennese paper, the *Neue Freie Presse*.[30] During the Dreyfus era, "the Jew" was transformed for the French from the "betrayer of Christ" to the inferior pariah. Even the converted Jew felt the impact of such theories attempting to crush his identity as a Frenchman by claiming he could not escape his "racial nature" as a Jew. As these theories matured during the decade of Joyce's birth, they often became less "scientific" and more nakedly political. French anti-Semitic writers' reputations grew throughout the later century and their theories were eventually absorbed by Parisian popular culture. Indictments of the inferior natures of the Jewish and Arabic peoples, "the inferior Orient," such as those of Earnest Renan, became the foundation of the caricatured posters Joyce encountered in Paris.

Renan, a major figure of the 1860s who Joyce later read, began his research about race once again through linguistics. In his history of Semitic languages published in 1855, as well as in his most influential work, *La Vie de Jesus* (1863), Renan concluded that he was perhaps "the first to recognize that the Semitic race, compared to the Indo-European one, represents essentially an inferior level of human nature."[31] By the 1870s Renan had established in French intellectual circles a kind of Occidental authoritarianism. Disseminated to the masses, these ideas formed the French image of *"le juif"* as

rabid monotheists who produced no mythology, no art, no commerce, no civilization; their consciousness [was] a narrow and rigid one; all in all they represent *'une combinaison inférieure de la nature humaine.'*[32]

With Renan's theories for support, Gustave Le Bon reshaped the concept of racial inferiority in 1890s Paris with an emphasis on the idea that the Jews alone were a distinct "race." Le Bon believed "each people possess[ed] a mental constitution as fixed as its anatomical characteristics."[33] His rhetoric asserted Jewish identity was comprised of a distinct physical and psychological type, a "nature" that was directly contradictory to the Gallic mind.

Like their German predecessors, French theorists considered themselves "scientists" whose ideas were on the leading edge of anthropological thought. But in 1902, Joyce, as well as most

Parisians, did not often read such works. It took a middle ground of informed journalists to popularize these notions. According to Michael Marrus, "anti-Semites invariably armed themselves with weapons forged in the 'scientific' studies of philology and biology. Edouard Drumont [editor and publisher of the Paris daily *La Libre Parole*] began his massive *France juive* with a discussion of the traditional battle between the Semitic and Aryan races."[34]

Drumont was, in fact, the central voice of the most volatile period of anti-Semitic activity in France – an era coinciding with the first two decades of Joyce's life. After success as a journalist, novelist, and playwright, Drumont set his sights on what he saw as the epicenter of the corruption of the Third Republic: its erosion of standards through the "pernicious Jewish influence." Amalgamating both racial and Catholic anti-Jewish arguments, Drumont produced his muddled yet influential work, *La France juive*, in 1886. With the book's success, the ensuing years found Drumont as the publicly proclaimed leader of French anti-Semitism. In 1889, he helped to establish La Ligue Nationale Antisèmitique de France, the predecessor of the Ligue Antisèmitique Français. In 1892 he founded *La Libre Parole*, one of the leading anti-Dreyfusard journals.

Drumont is mentioned in Stephen's thoughts in the "Proteus" episode of *Ulysses* (*U*3.230–37). Renan's name, as well, comes up in the argument about Shakespeare in "Scylla and Charybdis," when Stephen alludes to Renan's adaptation of *The Tempest*, entitled *Caliban, Suite de la Tempête* (1878).[35] But Stephen's thoughts of both Drumont and Renan do not include either writer's anti-Semitic programs. In Stephen's musings, however, Drumont's name may appear as a result of the anti-Semitism Stephen encountered earlier from both Haines and Deasy. During his wandering on the strand, Stephen's stream-of-consciousness includes Drumont's slander of Queen Victoria: "Drumont, famous journalist, Drumont, know what he called Queen Victoria? Old hag with yellow teeth. *Vieille ogresse with the dents jaunes*" (*U*3.231). The allusion portrays the metonymic nature of stream-of-consciousness while implying Stephen's heightened reaction against authority. Stephen's labeling of the subject as a "famous journalist," however, again ignores Drumont's reputation as an anti-Semite. In these omissions, Joyce suggests Stephen's own lack of sensitivity to the Jewish plight as part of the callowness his character displays throughout the book.

Stephen's reference to Drumont is juxtaposed, as well, to his

thoughts of another Parisian writer, Leo Taxil. Moments before his
memory of Drumont, Stephen mentions Taxil's *La Vie de Jesus*
(*U*3.167). Toward the middle of his career, Taxil brought charges
against Drumont on the grounds that the latter was the leader of an
underground plot to kill all the Jews of France, and was not only
anti-Semitic but anti-Catholic as well.[36] While Taxil had re-entered
the Church by this point and was lashing out with all the vehemence
of the convert, his early reputation was similar to Renan's in so far as
both attempted to demythologize Christ's life and Christianity.
Stephen's reminder to himself in "Proteus" that Kevin Egan should
send him a copy of Taxil's book becomes an aspect of his continuing
non serviam toward the Church. Moreover, the references to Drumont,
Renan, and Taxil all represent the secularization of Christian
narrative, and Taxil's theory of the "cuckolding" of Joseph from *La
Vie* is embedded throughout *Ulysses*.[37] But Joyce must have known
that the educated reader would connect these writers as well through
their involvement with anti-Semitism.

Moveover, the allusions to Taxil and Drumont come in the midst of
Stephen's reminiscence of Paris. In the same breath as the reference to
Drumont, Stephen recalls the Parisian publication *La Patrie*, yet
again fails to make reference to the paper's anti-Dreyfusard politics.
Still, it seems no surprise that when he had confronted Garrett
Deasy's prejudice, Stephen conjured a vision of the Jews he had seen
at the Paris Bourse. Like Joyce, Stephen had absorbed anti-Semitism
in Paris. But at the outset of *Ulysses*, he seems not to have realized that
the experience may be relevant to his own struggle as an iconoclastic
Irishman.

Joyce too returned to Dublin in April 1903 with only a minimal
grasp of the different types of anti-Semitism he had observed. But
while his recognition of those arguments was minimal, their impact
on his conception of "the Jew" was not. Though he avoids overt
reference to Drumont's anti-Semitic reputation in *Ulysses*, in 1903
Joyce was unable to avoid Parisian anti-Semitism in a host of visual
propaganda.

Beside that found in popular cartoons, an element of French racial
anti-Semitism was observable in the fine arts. In impressionist and
post-impressionist works, one finds figures and scenes based on
stereotypes of "the Jew." Even Pissaro, born Jewish himself, did such
work. In his series of sketches entitled *Les Turpitudes Sociales* (1889),

Pissaro drew stereotypical portraits of Jews (well dressed, hooked noses, heavy-set, smirking) in actions such as carrying the "new Golden calf" or symbolizing the "new God Capital."[38] Pissaro's Jews, however, were to him a trope for the "evil of capitalism," and not necessarily a racial truism. He was, moreover, a committed Dreyfusard throughout the Affair.

Pissaro's contemporary, Degas, however, not only painted stereotypical Jewish figures, but was a staunch anti-Dreyfusard and supported the views of both *La Libre Parole* and *L'Intransigeant*.[39] In 1882, the year of Joyce's birth, Degas debuted his piece entitled *Portraits à la Bourse*. Along with his other works based on a vision of the city, this piece enjoyed a great popularity, and Joyce may have viewed it during his stay in Paris. By late 1903, however, the painting had been purchased by Degas' friend and subject of the piece, Ernest May. May himself was a wealthy Parisian Jew who had funded the journal *Jour et Nuit*, to which Degas had been deeply committed.[40]

Portraits à la Bourse portrays May whispering to another stock player while several background figures, all with large, hooked noses, mill about the exchange. It appears that the information being whispered must pertain to that day's activity on the Bourse. In its entirety, the picture invokes the stereotype of "the stock-exchange Jew." Linda Nochlin indeed reads the painting as "a whole mythology of Jewish financial conspiracy."[41] But whether we accept this interpretation or not, the tableau is nonetheless uncannily similar to Stephen's vision of Jews in the "Nestor" episode; the second figure's head tilting to the right recalls Stephen's "maladroit silk hats" (*U*2.366). Yet even if Joyce, who had written of "the horrible cast of countenance . . . among the sweaters of modern Israel," never viewed the Degas, he certainly noticed similar depictions of Jews on posters and in journals throughout Paris.

Inflammatory cartoons of Jews were common in Paris during the Dreyfus Affair and the years beyond. The ambitious poster series of V. Lenepveu entitled "Musée des Horreurs," although banned in 1900, was still to be found about the city in 1902. The artist frequently attached portraits of the heads of Dreyfusard personalities to the bodies of animals such as pigs, dogs, and cows. Created for the opening of the Paris World's Fair on April 15, 1900, the poster entitled *"Bal à L'Elysée"* portrays several animals with the faces of persons who supposedly represent "the Jewish syndicate" of Paris. The Grand Rabbi of France, Zadoc Kahn, is depicted as a dancing monkey, while Émile Zola reclines as a smug pig. Peeping through the entourage is Dreyfus, who possesses the body of a coiled serpent.[42]

The postcard, a new and popular phenomenon in Paris, was also used for this type of propaganda. The Parisian caricaturist Orens designed several pieces from 1899 to 1905 whose sketches depict Dreyfus and others in insultingly awkward positions. One such card is entitled "*Allez en Paix*" and portrays Dreyfus, after his pardon, flinching, while La France and others throw pieces of furniture and a mattress at him.[43] Another, entitled "*Le Cake-Walk Juarès-Dreyfus*," portrays Dreyfus and Jean Jaurès, the Socialist deputy who led his party to support a review of the Dreyfus case, dancing in victory together.

All of these cartoons – many of which also appeared in newspapers – portray Jewish figures with dark, sunken eyes, exaggerated noses, and fat, sloppy, or even bestial bodies. "The Jew's" expression in these pieces is often perversely joyful, as if in some secret triumph. "The Jew" as evil conspirator against the Christian nation, in fact, had deep roots in French culture. The medieval Jew as a cancerous element in league with the devil had its rebirth in modern France with the Abbe Chabauty's influential *Les Juifs nos Maîtres* (1882). Chabauty's religiously based anti-Jewishness was paralleled by the secular anti-Semitism of Maurice Joly. Joly's most popular work, *Dialogue aux Enfer entre Montesquieu et Machiavel* (1864), became one of the sources upon which the French version of *The Protocols of the Elders of Zion* was built.[44]

Whether Joyce himself ever possessed a copy of *The Protocols*, which from 1903 to 1930 saw versions in French, English, Russian, and German, remains unclear. In the "Circe" episode of *Ulysses*, however, Rudolph Bloom "appears garbed in the long caftan of an elder of Zion" (*U*15.248–49). Moreover, the cartoons that accompanied the 1934 French version of *The Protocols*, entitled *Le Péril Juif*, based their representations of "the Jew" – unshaven, heavy eyelids, hooked nose, groping fingers reaching over and digging into the globe – on the Dreyfus-era caricatures Joyce viewed in Paris in 1902–03. Joyce was particularly sensitive to these cartoons because of their similarity to derogatory caricatures of the Irish he had viewed in both English and Unionist journals in Dublin.

Cartoon stereotypes of the Irish had a long history in the British press. By the 1840s, W. H. Maxwell's *History of the Rebellion in Ireland in 1798* made popular its accompanying illustrations by the then famous

George Cruikshank. Cruikshank's drawing portrayed the rebels as heartless barbarians, gleefully slaughtering not only the landowners, but their wives and children as well. While the figures in these drawings were still anatomically human, the ensuing years of British caricatures brought with them a new kind of slander, the "simian Celt," which drew directly from mid-century racialist assumptions.

Responding to the growing popularity of Darwin and Huxley, these new representations intended to suggest the racial inferiority of the Irish. British cartoonists now found a new legitimacy for the portrayal of the "characteristics [of] violence, poverty, improvidence, political volatility, and drunkenness [as] inherently Irish and only Irish."[45] John Tenniel's cartoons in *Punch*, published throughout the 1860s, made popular this portrait of the Irishman as a subhuman being, wanton in his appetites and most resembling an orang-utan in both facial features and posture.[46] This caricature of the "Irish brute" continued to amuse *Punch* readers throughout the 1880s and 1890s in the cartoons of Harry Furniss. Furniss was not only a racial propagandist, but a political cartoonist of wide repute. In August, 1893, in fact, *Punch* carried Furniss' noticeably simian portrait of the Irish member of Parliament, J. G. Swift MacNeill.[47]

During Joyce's adolescence, several Dublin publications made popular the facetious cartoons of the "Irish Paddy" and the "Irish Bull." Designed to amuse the Dublin professional class, these images appeared in magazines such as *The Jarvey* (1889–90) and *The Irish Figaro* (1899–1901), and portrayed Irishmen as more human and heroic than their English counterparts. Yet, while the cartoons of these later serials attempted to lighten political turmoil through images of "good natured Paddy," they often used the simian Celt to display the distortion of "the Irishman" by the British. Two prime examples of this subversion of the simian Celt were produced by John O'Hea for the 1880s publication *Pat* and by Richard Orpen for *The Jarvey*. O'Hea's cartoon, published in *Pat* on January 22, 1880 and entitled "Setting Down in Malice," was a pictorial sequence representing the transformation of a people into stereotype.[48] O'Hea's grasp of stereotyping made the piece a lasting image in the Irish imagination. The cartoon achieved a widespread popularity in Dublin; born the year after its initial publication, Joyce himself probably viewed it more than once. In this triptych of facial sketches, O'Hea demonstrates the simianizing process. The first portrait is of an English cartoonist who has been sent to Dublin by his publication to "furnish truthful sketches of Irish character."[49] The two other faces portray how that same cartoonist converts the human reality to the bestial caricature. The largest portrait, the cartoonist's model, is of a refined Dubliner, well dressed and with a serious countenance. The third and final portrait is the sketch made from this above model by the English cartoonist. Here the gentleman Dubliner has been transformed into a simian Celt: his teeth have become pointed, his complexion darkened, and his expression made one of wanton abandon. He snarls and holds a pistol in his hand.

The darkened complexion in O'Hea's cartoon evinces another nomenclature for the simianized Celt, "the white Negro," indeed a counterpart to "the Jewish Nigger," which was itself a standard reference in both German and French anti-Semitic discourse.[50] The similarity further yokes the "simian Celt" to the era's racialist preconceptions: within the taxonomy of humankind, all non-Caucasians – Blacks, Asians, Indians, Arabs, Jews (whose identity as Caucasians was continuously challenged) – represent lesser types of homosapiens.

In both the caricatures of Jews that Joyce encountered in Paris and cartoons of the Irish he had seen in Dublin, a people were maligned as subhuman by the dominant groups of their respective cultures. Both "the Irishman" as simian and "the Jew" as serpent-conspirator played on theories with which Joyce would later become fascinated. The citizen of the "Cyclops" episode indeed bestializes Bloom while judging his supposed parsimony: "there's a Jew for you. All for number one. cute as a shithouse rat" (*U*12.1761). In 1903 Joyce was not only a politically aware young man, but one who had a growing interest in popular culture – billboards, postcards, and advertisements did not fail to draw his attention.

When he returned to Dublin that year, however, Joyce's friendship with – and soon antipathy for – Oliver St. John Gogarty served as a narcotic to his memories of Paris. Yet by 1905, Gogarty's anti-Semitic nationalism would only add fuel to Joyce's repugnance toward his former drinking companion. Joyce's letters from Rome that year incorporate many derogatory references to both Gogarty's writing and politics. His plans in 1905 to write a story for *Dubliners* based on his encounter with Alfred Hunter, as well as his new interest in texts about the Jews, however, find their inchoate connections in 1903, when he arrived home from Paris after receiving the austere message: "Mother Dying Come Home Father."

III   A BITTER RETURN

April 1903 to June 1904 saw Joyce's troubles grow. After watching May Joyce die a slow death from cancer, he became bitter and lost. Often inebriated and irascible, he spent less time with Stanislaus and became the drinking companion of Gogarty. Then a promising medical student, Gogarty was known among his circle of friends as both a witty vulgarian and an incontinent drinker. Stanislaus believed that Joyce's "riotous" drinking was mostly a product of Gogarty's influence.[51] When Stanislaus castigated his brother for having deserted writing, Joyce responded in language highly influenced by Gogarty: "the matter with you is that you're afraid to live. You and people like you. This city is suffering from a hemiplegia of the will . . ."[52] The expression "will to live" as well as Joyce's use of the medical term "hemiplegia" represent Gogarty's dominance – the medically-minded Gogarty was just then studying Nietzsche. But Gogarty's friendship was from the beginning one that engendered a fearsome competition between him and Joyce as well. Gogarty resented Joyce's "intransigence and air of superiority" and told an acquaintance that he was making Joyce drink "in order to break his spirit."[53] Joyce saw in Gogarty an aloof smugness he cultivated to repress his newly conflicted emotions. Moreover, Joyce felt an envy toward the well-to-do Gogarty who was on his way to achieving a position in society Joyce once devised for himself; Gogarty had already gained a small reputation in Dublin as a clever verse-maker. But these differences were balanced in the beginning of their acquaintance by a mutual desire to see themselves as Bohemian: "they were rebellious; they had the same capacity for ribald laughter, the same sardonic humor, and an identical talent for blasphemy; they both leaned toward low company and had a partiality for taverns."[54] Yet Joyce's drinking and whoring diminished and soon came to an abrupt halt in June, 1904 when he met Nora Barnacle.

When Gogarty returned to Dublin that summer, Joyce ignored him. This new hostility would more or less continue for the rest of their lives. Joyce may have now felt embarrassed at what he had earlier let himself become under Gogarty's sway. Gogarty, as well, was annoyed by Joyce's poem "The Holy Office," in which he was presented as a snob: "Or him whose conduct 'seems to own' / His preference for a 'man of tone.'"[55] Nevertheless, by September Joyce and Gogarty were sharing the Martello tower at Sandy Cove. And it

was of course the alleged "panther incident," fictionalized in the
opening episode of *Ulysses*, that finally caused the complete rupture in
their relationship. When he and Nora were living in Rome, Joyce had
nothing but disdain for his former friend. By this time, Gogarty had
become an outspoken proponent of Arthur Griffith's Sinn Féin
movement, and had written editorials for both *United Irishman* and the
eponymous journal of the organization. Although Joyce remained
ambivalent to much of Griffith's agenda, he could not help but
register his overt repugnance toward Gogarty's propaganda.

In 1906 – not coincidentally the year he also informed his brother
of plans to write a story titled "Ulysses" – Joyce expressed this
ambivalence about Sinn Féin on several occasions. In September he
disagreed with Stanislaus' distaste for *United Irishman*, claiming it as
the "only newspaper of any pretensions in Ireland," and insisting that
"its policy would benefit Ireland very much."[56] Later that month he
praised a speech Griffith had given to the National Council in Dublin,
and highlighted Griffith's plans of a boycott of British goods and the
implementation of national banking, civil service, and educational
systems.[57] In the same breath, however, Joyce noted an objection to a
centerpiece of Sinn Féin rhetoric:

What I object to most in his paper is that it is educating the people of Ireland
on the old pap of racial hatred, whereas anyone can see that if the Irish
question exists, it exists for the Irish proletariat chiefly.[58]

Joyce's direct reference was to the spate of anti-British propaganda
Griffith had used since 1898 to provoke his Irish audience.[59] But
Joyce's "pap of racial hatred" was much more multivalent than this.
Indeed, the socialist tenor Joyce displays here would soon fade in light
of his growing disgust for both Griffith's and Gogarty's anti-Semitism.
In reviewing Gogarty's series of articles entitled "Ugly England,"
Joyce called the writer's ideas "rich," and Gogarty a "scribbler."[60]

The second installment of Gogarty's "Ugly England" series
appeared in Sinn Féin on November 24. The piece accused Jews of
London and Dublin of conspiring economically to control both cities
and eventually the Empire. Gogarty postulated that the "Jew
mastery of England" was a sign of the Empire's decay, and that these
pernicious people were continuing their abuse of the poor in Dublin.
He ended the piece with the admonition "I can smell a Jew. . .and in
Ireland there's something rotten."[61] Joyce sent a copy of this article to

Stanislaus, stating "I send you S.F. with a column of O. G.'s stupid drivel."[62] By the time of the composition of *Ulysses*, Joyce would portray a parallel between imperialist and nationalist anti-Semitism by placing Gogarty's rhetoric in the mouth of Garret Deasy in the "Nestor" episode. As for Gogarty's reputation as a writer, Joyce later wrote to Stanislaus that he would "call such people as Gogarty and Yeats and Colum the blacklegs of literature. . .because they have tried to substitute us, to serve the old idols at a lower rate when we refused to do so for a higher."[63]

Gogarty never imagined that his anti-Semitism would help provoke Joyce's own interest in the Jewish question in Europe. Yet it was only eleven days before his criticism of Gogarty that Joyce had written to Stanislaus about reading Guglielmo Ferrero's *L'Europa giovane* and its chapter on anti-Semitism:

He [Ferrero] has a fine chapter on Antisemitism. By the way, Brandes is a Jew. He says that Karl Marx has the apocalyptic imagination and makes Armageddon a war between capital and labor. The most arrogant statement made by Israel so far, he says, not excluding the gospel of Jesus is Marx's proclamation that socialism is the fulfillment of a natural law. In considering Jews he slips in Jesus between Lassalle and Lombroso: the latter too (Ferrero's father-in-law) is a Jew.[64]

Joyce's enthusiasm here represents his deeper curiosities about "the Jew" now bubbling to the surface. After this, Ferrero's book would join those that provided a textual foundation for Joyce's construction of Jewish identity throughout *Ulysses*. But Joyce's interest in anti-Semitism in 1906 also had a strong link to his negative reaction to Gogarty's articles. The envy and competition he had felt toward Gogarty for some years had now found a single focus. The urbane attitudes Joyce was encountering in Trieste – especially in the company of Jewish journalists – represented to him an antithesis to Gogarty's prejudice, and Gogarty's anti-Semitism appeared now to Joyce as further proof of the provincialism of his former Dublin circle. On one level, simply because of his hostility to his former friend, that hatred worked to subvert any residual anti-Semitism Joyce may have retained. Joyce would later scandalize Gogarty's attitudes – including his anti-Semitism – through the prejudices of Buck Mulligan in *Ulysses*.

During his drinking sprees with Gogarty in 1903, however, Joyce may have on occasion acknowledged some of his friend's anti-Semitic remarks. Not yet having the confidence to confront his new mentor, Joyce responded more to a sense of male comradeship than to his own thoughts on the matter. Indeed, an event during this period involving another of Joyce's friends, Padraic Colum, suggests Joyce still placed a certain amount of credence in some Jewish stereotypes.

Entertaining the idea of starting his own Dublin daily journal, Joyce contacted Colum who later related the following:

He asked me especially did I know any Jewish people he could go to with the project. (It is odd that the creator of the most outstanding Jew in modern literature did not at that time know any of the Jewish community in Dublin.) Jews would be receptive to such a proposition, Joyce thought. I had two Jewish friends, intellectuals, Willy and Harry Sinclair, who had an antique shop in Nassau Street. I brought Joyce into the shop and introduced him to one or the other of the brothers. Of course nothing came out of it in the way of promoting *The Goblin* [Joyce's proposed name for his paper], and I don't know whether my introduction resulted in any friendliness between the two parties. However, one of the Sinclairs gets a line in *Ulysses*: Bloom at one stage along his itinerary remarks "Have a chat with young Sinclair? Well mannered fellow."[65]

Joyce's assumptions here about a Jewish financial backer suggests his belief in the stereotype of "the Jew" as not only moneyed, but inclined to propaganda, or in a less pejorative vein, to journalism in general.[66] Joyce had mentioned to Colum that he wanted to model his project on a sophisticated "continental paper, published in the afternoon."[67] After his experiences in Paris, Joyce's perception of "the Jew" now apparently included the notion that Jews were "cosmopolitan" and "literary." From Colum's statement, it appears as well that Joyce did not know many, if any, Jews in Dublin even by 1903. Other than Byrne's friend Zaks, Joyce had little opportunity to meet Dublin Jews. In either case, Joyce's introduction to the Sinclairs represents his most intimate involvement with Jews before his years in Trieste. Colum's allusion to Bloom's comment in the "Lestrygonians" episode (*U*8.553) may indeed represent the surprise Joyce registered upon meeting the Sinclairs after he had perceived Jews for years through negative stereotypes. Instead of manipulative usurers or conspirators against Christian power, the Sinclair brothers appeared to Joyce as rational, educated Dubliners.

It was ironically during the same year Joyce met the Sinclair brothers that the Jews of Limerick suffered the stoning of their shops and persons.[68] As noted earlier, Griffith defended the instigator of the anti-Jewish actions, Father Creagh, in the April 23 issue of the *United Irishman*. From his observations in Paris, Joyce recognized the erroneousness of Griffith's indictment that "all Jewry [was] seeking to ruin France." Moreover, Joyce may have also begun to re-evaluate both Griffith's bigotry and the Limerick boycott through a much more personal event that occurred this year during his usual nighttime carousing.

IV   THE JEWISH SAMARITAN

During the period in 1906 when Joyce first thought of his "Ulysses story" for the yet unfinished *Dubliners*, he also appears to have already intended to focus on some Irish uses of anti-Jewish myths. In a letter to Stanislaus that directly follows his praise of Griffith's speech, Joyce mentioned that he had a "new story for *Dubliners* in [his] head [dealing] with Mr. Hunter."[69] Although controversy over the actual Alfred Hunter as a model for Bloom continues, it remains a fact that this project became a novel with a protagonist whose identity engages a spectrum of European discourse about "the Jew." The notion that one night in 1904, Joyce, after being severely beaten, was aided and "bucked . . . up generally in orthodox Samaritan fashion . . ." (*U*16.3) by Hunter – whom Joyce and the rest of Dublin believed to be a Jew and a cuckold – was of course first explored in Richard Ellmann's biography.[70] Although Ellmann hinted at the possible inaccuracy of his "Dublin sources," and referred to Hunter's Jewish identity as "putative," he was taken to task by Hugh Kenner for offering as biographical reality what Kenner calls "the Irish Fact" of Hunter as the rescuer of Joyce and Jewish model for Bloom.[71] But whether Joyce ever thought Hunter to be a Jew or not (or whether Hunter actually "rescued" Joyce in St. Stephen's Green), we should not downplay the idea that the story of "Mr. Hunter's Day" – once slated as the crowning story of *Dubliners* – may well have focused on an alienated Dublin Jew. Indeed, it was just two months after Joyce's reference to this "Hunter story," that he expressed his disgust for Gogarty's anti-Semitic articles. Moreover, wedged between those letters was Joyce's correspondence containing his thoughts about Ferrero's *L'Europa giovane*.

The supposed event involving Hunter – which has been argued as the prototype for the decisive action of *Ulysses* – was said to have occurred on the night of June 22. We can fix this date because Joyce's letter to C. P. Curran the following morning opens with an apology for a missed appointment on account of his physical infirmity: "black eye, sprained wrist, sprained ankle, cut chin, cut hand," [and in the next line]: "For one role at least I seem unfit – that of the man of honor."[72] Joyce could have met Hunter before this, and may indeed have heard of him as an object of ridicule in Dublin drinking circles because he was a "less-than-manly," cuckolded Jew. Hunter's name appears as a mourner on July 24, 1904, along with James and John Joyce, at the funeral of the latter's good friend, Matthew Kane, the model for Martin Cunningham in both "Grace" and *Ulysses*.[73] The most famous irony of this "Hunter myth," of course, was Ellmann's discovery during his 1982 revision that he had been previously misled by Stanislaus, and that Hunter was in fact not Jewish.[74] And while it has no impact on reading the representations of "the Jew" in *Ulysses*, the question of whether Joyce thought Hunter to be a Dublin Jew or not still haunts Joycean biography.

As mentioned above, Joyce had also been rewriting the *Dubliners'* story "Grace" in 1906, in which the character Mr. Harford is recalled as being slandered by his "fellow Catholics" as an "Irish Jew" who "never embraced more than the "Jewish ethical code.""[75] In the story, Harford, and his Jewish associate Mr. Goldberg, are indeed moneylenders. But Cunningham's sneer at the mention of Harford's name has more to do with Irish prejudice than with Jewish identity *per se*. Given these elements of "Grace," however, Rodney Wilson Owen speculates that Joyce's proposed "Hunter-story" appears to have been a blueprint for the action of the "Cyclops" episode of *Ulysses*.[76] Joyce's reference to his "Ulysses" story as a "Dublin Peer Gynt," and the fact that the actual Hunter attended Kane's funeral, led Owen to theorize that Joyce intended his Hunter to retire with his fellow mourners to a pub, and then to have been castigated as a "Jew," a pariah in Irish society whose "Irishness" could never partake of Celtic blood-purity or an allegiance to the Church.[77] Thus, after creating Harford, Joyce seems to have recognized the many possibilities of a character who was an "Irish Jew" in more ways than merely the brunt of a Dublin insult.

It may well be that when Joyce coupled his impression of a kindly Dublin Jew with the themes of marginality and paralysis in *Dubliners*, the short story of "Ulysses" was born. But the project as a story died, getting no further than its title.[78] Joyce would instead conclude

Dubliners with the narrative of a character based on his own marginality as an "apolitical" intellectual in nationalist Ireland – "The Dead's" Gabriel Conroy. What happened in the interim between the death of the first story and the birth of the novel, however, is another matter, a matter that was to be played out among the Jewish intelligentsia of both Trieste and Zurich.

But what of the incident the night of June 22, 1904? While references to it have become obligatory in investigations of Joyce's representations of "the Jew," very few thoughts beyond the argument over its mere occurrence have been offered. Perhaps added now to Joyce's youthful preconceptions about Jews, his break with the Church, and his trip to Paris was the memory of the compassionate "Jewish" Hunter. Curiously, Joyce never spoke to anyone about the incident or the impression it left on him. But despite this silence, nagging questions remain. Did Hunter's act of compassion become an element of Joyce's conception of "Jewish nature"? Did Joyce see Hunter as a "good father-figure," one which for him embodied the paternal relationship of Judaism to Christianity? Did Joyce eventually perceive the incident as a foreshadowing of his warm reception into a circle of Jews in Trieste and Zurich – especially of his friendship with Ettore Schmitz (Italo Svevo)? Attempts to answer these questions must first consider Joyce's reading and writing during those relationships, as well as the backgrounds of the individuals he came to know between 1904 and 1914.

Before examining those crucial years on the Continent, however, a step backwards in Joyce's own reading is essential. From 1902 until he "exiled" himself in 1904, Joyce's perception of the role of "the Jew" in Europe was influenced by the broader concept of "Hebraism and Hellenism," which he first read about in Matthew Arnold's *Culture and Anarchy* at University College. When he encountered the writings of Friedrich Nietzsche around 1903, however, Joyce's understanding of Jewish influence in the West was critically altered. Both of these theories may have played a role in Joyce's perception of "the Jewish Samaritan" who came to his aid in 1904, and certainly influenced his later construction of "the Jew" in *Ulysses*.

CHAPTER 5

Cunning and Exile – Greeks and Jews

The concept of "Hebraism and Hellenism" as a centerpiece of efforts to historicize the ideology of "Western civilization" both predates Matthew Arnold's theory as well as finds its more radical avatar in Nietzsche. Bryan Cheyette concedes that Arnold becomes an "admittedly arbitrary starting point" in investigating "the Jew" in British literature.[1] But Arnold's use of "Hebraism and Hellenism" as a means of cultural re-evaluation represents neither an arbitrary moment in the concept's evolution, nor its most profound connection to the political realities of European Jewry. As a mature novelist, Joyce knew both Arnold's and Nietzsche's versions of Hebraic–Hellenistic discourse; Theoharis Constantine Theoharis has aptly demonstrated Joyce's free play with Arnold's Greek–Jewish "balances" in *Ulysses* on both the text's cultural representations as well as on the individual psychologies of both Stephen and Bloom.[2] The use of Arnold to reread "Joyce's Jew" as an attack on, or support of, Victorian liberalism, however, is somewhat limited. As a writer who from late-adolescence onward fashioned himself as "continental" rather than "British," Joyce (as well as the intellectual milieu of *fin-de-siècle* Dublin) recognized Nietzsche's ideas about Hellenic freedom and Hebraic law as the more useful key in the discernment of Western (de)evolution. Dublin enthusiasm for Nietzsche was fostered by his radical position in the German Romantic philosophical tradition, which interested Yeats' circle both for its transcendental elements as well as for its political opposition to Victorian liberalism.

Precisely when Joyce first encountered the representation of "the Jew" within the context of "Hebraism and Hellenism" is unclear; by the time he was composing *Ulysses*, however, he owned both a copy of Arnold's *Culture and Anarchy* as well as several translations of Nietzsche's work.[3] Joyce's initial reading of Arnold – quite possibly in the University College class of brother Thomas Arnold – gave him his first taste of what he later called "JewGreek-GreekJew."[4] In a matriculation-year essay, "The Study of Languages," Joyce seized an opportunity to disparage Arnold: ". . .for the building of intellectual man, his most important study is that of Mathematics. . .in this we are supported by the great lights of the age, though Matthew Arnold has his own little opinion about the matter, as he had about other matters."[5] But Arnold's "sweetness and light" – the goal of a balanced culture – was only the beginning of both Joyce's interest in and subversion of the concept of "Hebraism and Hellenism'; during the depression that followed his return from Paris, Joyce discovered Nietzsche's writings.

Arnold had of course theorized that the re-evaluation of the Hebraic and Hellenistic impulses in British culture would produce a new equilibrium in the temperament of the nation.[6] In chapter four of *Culture and Anarchy*, he examined these two "points of influence [that move] our world," and concluded that recognizing their inseparability "[enlarges] our whole view and rule of life."[7] But on a broader level, Arnold's Hebraism was once again dependent upon the pseudoscientific racialism of Orientalism:

Science has now made visible to everyone the great and pregnant elements which lie in race, and in how signal a manner they make the genius and history of an Indo-European people vary from those of a Semitic people. Hellenism is of Indo-European growth, Hebraism is of Semitic growth. And we English, a nation of Indo-European stock, seem to belong naturally to the movement of Hellenism. But nothing more strongly marks the essential unity of man than the affinities we can perceive, in this point or that, between members of one family of peoples and members of another.[8]

Conversely – although remaining within a racialist framework – Nietzsche's philosophy was strewn with his historical concept of how the zenith of early European culture (Hellenism) had been choked by the Judaic law (Hebraism) and then by its manifestation in Christianity; in declaring God's death, Nietzsche hoped to begin a neo-Hellenism, albeit one with much more revolutionary goals. Thus, rather than asserting the balance of the twin impulses, Nietzsche pitted Hebraism against Hellenism. The two were irreconcilable to him because ancient Judaism, in subverting the Greek "will to power" and supplanting it with a self-hating "slave-morality," had led Western culture down a self-destructive path. Hebraism for Nietzsche had evolved into spiritually paralyzed Christian Europe, and was thus at the center of the *mal du siècle*.

This version of the Greek–Jewish argument was new and provocative to Joyce in 1903. Still in the midst of his own apostasy, Joyce discovered in Nietzsche an ally to his anti-Christian and anti-Catholic attitudes. Like many *fin-de-siècle* intellectuals, Joyce also identified with Nietzsche's aristocratic radicalism, especially his central concept of the *Übermensch*; by 1904 Joyce had toyed with the term to impress his future nemesis at Maunsel & Company, George Roberts, by signing a letter to the editor "James Overman".[9] Most significant to "the Jew" in *Ulysses*, however, Joyce also discovered in Nietzsche a completely new discourse about contemporary Jews as a European people. Indeed, Nietzsche's perceptions of modern Jewry were nearly opposite from his theory of the ancient "Jewish crime" committed against Greek culture, and his assertions about the Jews as a positive social force in modern Europe caught Joyce's attention. The argument provided Joyce with a new language through which to think about Jews as a contemporary community and not merely as an abstract, sentimentalized force called "Hebraism." Arnold introduced Joyce to the binary opposites of Greek and Jew, but Nietzsche lifted the entire discussion for him out of a liberal Christian humanism and into the discourse of political antagonism.

I "THIS FUNDAMENTAL GROUND"

Arnold's interest in the Hebraic aspect of his theory was in part a product of the late-Victorian obsession with religious historiography and the Higher Criticism. While his father had adamantly opposed the enfranchisement of English Jews, Arnold himself had an ongoing interest in Jewish thought and became intrigued with the dichotomy between Hebraism and Hellenism he initially found in the writings of Heinrich Heine.[10] Heine declared that all men were either "Jews or Greeks – either men who ascetically question life and nourish their apocalyptic visions, or men who love life with a realism generated by their personal integration."[11] Arnold's idea for a modern British culture also placed him in the camp of Victorian Higher Critics newly fascinated with Judaism and the Hebrew language.[12] While studying Hebraic scholarship, as well as Spinoza, Lessing, Herder, Heine, and even Moses Mendelssohn, Arnold had also been welcomed into a circle of wealthy, influential London Jews.[13] Here he eventually met the most celebrated Hebraist in England, Emanuel Deutsch. Later on in the century, Deutsch would teach George Eliot Hebrew while she was writing *Daniel Deronda*, and may have been a model for the character of Mordecai in that novel.[14] Upon meeting Deutsch in 1868, Arnold wrote to Lady Constance de Rothschild – his main contact with London Jewry – that he and the linguist had had "a long talk about Hebraism and Hellenism."[15] In addition, Arnold was also a reader of Disraeli's novels, and admired the statesman's "Hebraism" to such an extent that he sent him a copy of *Culture and Anarchy*.[16]

Yet despite Arnold's interaction with Jews and Jewish thought, *Culture and Anarchy* never refers to the Jews' position in contemporary England. Cheyette asserts that "Hebraism and Hellenism nonetheless invoked the 'semitic discourse' of the racialized 'Jew,'" and in doing so, "positioned 'the Jew' as the spiritual and cultural embodiment of the 'essential unity of man' precisely because their [the Jews'] transformation was proof positive of the civilizing power of a necessarily superior 'culture.'"[17] But Arnold's rhetoric presents a "force" called "Hebraism," not a discussion of a struggling ethnic group within English culture. Indeed, beginning with the older Scholastic assumption that Christianity superseded Judaism, Arnold assumes his audience recognizes the term "Hebraism" as a Christian binary opposite to Hellenism, unconnected to the social position of the modern Jew:

Christianity changed nothing in this essential bent of Hebraism to set doing above knowing. Self-conquest, self-devotion, the following not our own individual will, but the will of God, *obedience*, is the fundamental idea of this form, also of the discipline to which we have attached the general name of Hebraism.[18]

The most volatile end of "Hebraism" to Arnold are the spates of puritanical Christian fervor within British history that impede artistic (Hellenistic) expression. Joyce, however, recognized this "Hebraism" as the impulse he himself was excoriating in the "puritanical" attitudes of Irish Catholicism.

Conversely, Arnold's definition of Hellenism was both new and delightful to the artist as a young man, especially if this version of "Greekness" entered Joyce's consciousness before that of Walter Pater. Arnold's Hellenism was indeed a delight for a budding esthete:

To get rid of one's ignorance, to see things as they are and by seeing them as they are to see them in their beauty is the simple and attractive ideal which Hellenism holds out before human nature; and from the simplicity and charm of this ideal, Hellenism, and the human life in the hands of Hellenism,

is invested with a kind of aerial ease, clearness, and radiancy; they are full of
what we call sweetness and light.[19]

In its Pateresque tone, the passage was certainly inspirational to the
author of "The Day of the Rabblement."

But Arnold himself had very different ulterior motives. He asserts
that England is in dire need of a revitalized concept of culture built on
Hellenic principles so as to balance radical Nonconformist and
Establishment Christian arguments – the two streams of "Hebraism"
in contemporary England. Moreover, he re-emphasizes that an
inclination toward Hebraizing (in the form of Christian zealotry) had
a specialized history in English culture, and that in avoiding the
Continent's delight in Hellenism as represented by "the Enlightenment
and the Revolution. . .England has endangered herself in the modern
world."[20] In reverting to their Hebraic potential, moreover, Victorian
culture was losing the harmonizing force of Greek consciousness:

the main impulse of a great part, and that the strongest part, of our nation
has been toward strictness of conscience. They have made the secondary the
principal at the wrong moment, and the principal they have at the wrong
moment treated as secondary. This contravention of the natural order has
produced, as such contravention must always produce, a certain confusion
and false movement, of which we are now beginning to feel. . .[21]

If Arnold hoped to reinvigorate a Hellenism as a means of spiritually
re-empowering the British empire, as an Irishman, Joyce could only
be ambivalent toward such an idea. On a more general level,
however, Joyce was enticed by the balance of opposites upon which
Arnold insists; Joyce's introduction during his university years to the
philosophy of Giordano Bruno had seduced him into celebrating
polar opposites wherever he found them.[22] Arnold himself emphasized
the mental equilibrium that must be achieved through the two
impulses, and reminded his audience that "the governing idea of
Hellenism is *spontaneity of consciousness*; that of Hebraism, *strictness of
conscience*."[23] This dichotomy also fed into Joyce's rebellion against the
Church: to be a Christian was to be paralyzed; to be a Greek was to
think and create freely.

Arnold's overall theory of the binary relationship between Hebraism
and Hellenism was certainly important to Joyce during his University
College years and beyond. By 1902, Joyce was arguing against Oliver
Gogarty's plan to "Hellenize" Ireland by asserting the Irish needed
"Europeanizing" instead.[24] Exactly what he meant by "Europeanize,"

however, was not fully in Joyce's power to define just then. We can speculate, however, that it included the missing element of "the Jew." Yet, by the composition of *Ulysses*, Joyce viewed many aspects of Arnold's argument as specious. The more Joyce had learned about modern Jews on the Continent, the more their secular history necessitated an understanding through a direct focus on their political plight; Hellenizing or Hebraizing his own culture thus became for Joyce another attempt – like the Celtic Twilight – at the reshaping of national consciousness through a politically naive, inviable notion. It is of course the "usurper" Buck Mulligan, modeled on Gogarty, who introduces Hellenism in "Telemachus." And by the "Circe" episode, Lynch's cap makes a mockery of the idea in its flippant response to Stephen: "Ba! It is because it is. Woman's reason. Jewgreek is greekjew. Extremes meet. Death is the highest form of life. Ba!" (*U*15.2098–99).

During his stay in Paris, Joyce witnessed the realities of public anti-Semitism; he returned to Dublin in 1903 with a grasp of the predicament of modern Jewry that undermined Arnold's more ephemeral concept of Hebraism and Hellenism. That theory now lost much of its original lustre. It was at this moment in his life that Joyce first encountered Nietzsche's writings.

II   JOYCE AND NIETZSCHE

In *The Origins of Totalitarianism*, Hannah Arendt asserts that Nietzsche was one of a handful of modern thinkers who recognized the pivotal role played by the Jews in the progress of Europe. Explaining that emancipated Jewry was an "inter-European, non-national element in a world of growing or existing nations," Arendt claims that along with Diderot and von Humboldt, Nietzsche understood "the grandeur of this consistently 'European' existence." She concludes that "Nietzsche, who out of disgust with Bismarck's German Reich coined the word 'good European'. . .[made] his correct estimate of the significant role of the Jews in European history, and saved him[self] from falling into the pitfalls of cheap philosemitism or patronizing 'progressive' attitudes."[25] Writing in the post-Holocaust era, Arendt had the advantage of looking back in time at the foreboding movements of nineteenth-century anti-Semitism. Reconsidering his own assumptions about Jews during the Dreyfus era, Joyce had no such advantage. Yet long before Arendt made her claim, Joyce was affected by Nietzsche's insights into the role of European Jewry.

Joyce had read a fair amount of Nietzsche before he ever left for the Continent. Ellmann tells us that he "came to know the writings of Nietzsche" in 1903.[26] Joyce's "hyperborean" behavior after his return from Paris also indicates a Nietzschean influence, which was aided by way of his relationship with Gogarty, who was also an avid reader of the philosopher. In either case, while living in Trieste, Joyce purchased translations of *The Birth of Tragedy*, *The Joyful Wisdom*, and *The Case of Wagner/Nietzsche Contra Wagner*, each of which was published between 1909 and 1911. Given this fact, Joyce scholars have traditionally proposed that he only came to know Nietzsche after 1909. But by 1902, Nietzsche's ideas had become ubiquitous in the intellectual world of Dublin, especially through the influence of W. B. Yeats. And by 1905, Joyce had included *Thus Spoke Zarathustra* and *The Gay Science* as favorite reading of Mr. James Duffy in the story "A Painful Case." The Nietzsche translations that Yeats was passing around his Dublin circle were, of course, readily available to Joyce.

In *My Brother's Keeper*, Stanislaus comments that in shaping the character of Duffy, Joyce had stolen much of the protagonist's personal reflections from his brother's diary. He goes on to say that "Jim had also lent Mr. Duffy some traits of his own, the interest in Nietzsche and the translation of *Michael Kramer*, in order to raise his intellectual standard."[27] "A Painful Case" was rewritten into its final form in May, 1905 in Trieste. From implications of the short story, it is apparent that Joyce had already grasped the concept of the *Übermensch* from reading Nietzsche's work and not merely as a popular catch phrase. By making Mr. Duffy an admirer of Nietzsche and yet a paralyzed, unfulfilled man, Joyce suggests that Duffy is merely a self-deluded, "straw" *Übermensch*. Even if Duffy reappears as "the man in the mackintosh" in *Ulysses*, he has hardly become a moral superman. In any event, Joyce's ironic use of Zarathustra's message demonstrates the depth of his pre-1909 understanding of a central Nietzschean concept.

Moreover, given the fact that Joyce's Trieste editions were translations, it is unlikely that he ever read Nietzsche in the original; in Dublin, he certainly had to depend upon available English translations.[28] Thus Joyce's Nietzsche – like so many of his Dublin contemporaries – was a product of the translator's art and not of the author's German.[29] Translations of Nietzsche had indeed gained followings in London, New York, and Dublin by 1899, and the Irish

capital was at the forefront of this enthusiasm.[30] Describing this
Dublin reception, David Thatcher states that "Irish writers were, on
the whole, quicker to recognize Nietzsche's importance than their
English counterparts: the names of T. W. Rolleston and Stephen
Gwynn, Stephen McKenna and James Cousins, Shaw and Yeats
immediately come to mind."[31] Topping the list was the Dubliner
most enthusiastic about Nietzsche's ideas, Arthur Symons. In reviewing
the translation of *The Dawn of Day*, Symons criticized the English-
speaking world for not paying closer attention to Nietzsche.[32] Symons
and Yeats together also decided that Nietzsche was the direct
intellectual heir of William Blake; in his 1906 book on Blake, Symons
included a lengthy comparison of the similarities of the two writers'
ideas and paradoxes. Considering the admiration Joyce expressed
early on for Blake, the parallel alone was stimulus enough to pique his
curiosity.

Through his Dublin reading of Nietzsche, Joyce also began to learn
about Nietzsche's refiguration of "the Jew." And by 1907 – the year
Joyce met Ettore Schmitz – translations of *The Dawn of Day*, *Thus
Spoke Zarathustra*, *Human, All Too Human*, *Beyond Good and Evil*, *The
Antichrist*, *Nietzsche Contra Wagner*, and *On the Genealogy of Morals* were
available. The bulk of what Nietzsche postulates about both Judaism
as an historical force and the Jews as a modern people is contained in
these selected texts. Nietzsche's version of the Greek–Hebrew opposition
plays a central role in his discussion of Western culture, as well as in
his theories of the *Übermensch* and the "Will to Power." In his view of
the West's cultural development, Judaism's "triumph" over Hellenism
was fundamental. While that "victory" was problematic, it nonetheless
places Judaism and "Jewishness" at the center of Nietzsche's discussion
of modern Europe.

Indeed, as this chapter will demonstrate, Nietzsche's view of
contemporary Jews became quite influential to Joyce's construction
of Bloom's "Jewishness." Nietzsche's references to the strength of
European Jewry was very new to Joyce – he certainly hadn't read
anything similar in Arnold. Nietzsche had followed Arnold in his
view that Christianity was an outgrowth of Judaism; in the Nietzschean
interpretation, however, Jews had a political existence separate from
their historical identity as the original people of "Hebraism" or as the
forefathers of Christianity. More crucially, Nietzsche's discussion of
contemporary Jewry laid the groundwork for Joyce's later belief that
the Jews had developed an acute "shrewdness of character" (often

pejoratively described by others as "cunning") to combat and endure their marginality.

It should be emphasized, however, that as an early twentieth-century "continental literatus," Joyce's debt to Nietzsche involves more than the latter's discourse on "the Jew." The use of Nietzsche's most popular theories amongst Joyce's generation – who often swallowed the writings whole – was of course widespread. Even random selections from a book as popular as *Thus Spoke Zarathustra* (translated 1896), reveal that Joyce found in Nietzsche a leader in his own rebellion against liberal, bourgeois culture. One common ground for Joyce in particular was Nietzsche's unflinching disdain for "the masses." The prophet's "On Reading and Writing" relays a prime example of this repugnance: "Of all that is written I love only what a man has written with his blood. Write with blood, and you will experience that blood is spirit," and then: "Every one being allowed to learn to read, ruineth in the long run not only writing but also thinking. Once the spirit was God, then he became man, and now it even becometh populace [*pöbel*]."[33] The German *pöbel* here also translates to "rabble." While Joyce never read the original, in his Thomas Common translation he would find Zarathustra's speech no. 28 – originally titled *Vom Gesindel* – indeed translated "The Rabble."[34]

Yet despite Nietzsche's influence on Joyce's generation, one should in the end not consider Joyce himself "a Nietzschean" in the sense that the title implies taking the principal theories – Eternal Recurrence, The Death of God, and the *Übermensch* – as a center of one's philosophical belief. But Joyce's rejection of Christian morality, his commitment to sexual freedom, righteous individualism, and the amorality of art nonetheless place him squarely in the Nietzschean camp. Joyce understood Nietzsche's "transvaluation of Western values" to have penetrated to the core of his own struggle; the philosopher's "sickness of the spirit" is the precise malaise of will that Stephen wars against in both *A Portrait* and *Ulysses*. And when we turn to the influence of "Nietzsche's Jew" on *Ulysses*, there is an unmistakable link between Bloom's "Jewishness" and those representations of "the Jew" found throughout the philosopher's works.

III   "THE GOOD (JEWISH) EUROPEAN"

Like many post-Enlightenment German philosophers before him, Nietzsche had a conflicted relationship with the Jews: first as a subject of study and second as a minority group within German culture.[35] As a philosopher, he was interested in exploring the role of Judaism in the construction of Western consciousness. A central argument of his version of this theory was that Judaic law, a system created out of a "slave-mentality," had "transvaluated" the superior aristocratic Greek culture. In this vein, Christianity is to Nietzsche the final, degenerate flowering of the original Hebraic mentality. As a citizen of Bismarck's Germany, however, Nietzsche was personally engaged with Jewish individuals as both admired contemporaries and as victims of anti-Semitic movements – movements that attracted members of his own circle, including his sister and mentor Richard Wagner.

Nietzsche's conception of the critical role played by Jews in the evolution of Western morality begins in his very first book, *The Birth of Tragedy* (1872) and continues on into his last, *The Antichrist* (1895). His encounter with Jewish individuals and "anti-Semitic Teutonism – or proto-Nazism – was one of the major issues of [his] life."[36] Nietzsche had a high regard for what he deemed the "Jewish intellect," a term that suggests his simultaneous admiration for and stereotyping of Jews. He thought Spinoza's intellect "Jewish" in its sensibility, and Spinoza to be one of the fathers of modern thought (Joyce himself shared this last opinion). His respect for Jewish contemporaries is demonstrated in a letter to his sister describing the Jewish translator of *Beyond Good and Evil*, Helen Zimmern: "I had the privilege of introducing this 'champion of women's rights' (Frl. van Salis) to another 'champion' who is my neighbor at meals, Miss Helen Zimmern, who is extremely clever, incidentally not an Englishwoman – but Jewish. May heaven have mercy on the European intellect if one wanted to extract the Jewish intellect from it."[37] Nietzsche's compliment to Zimmern's "Jewishness" ironically denies her an identity as an Englishwoman – the dichotomy represents a crux of the era's Jewish question. Both of the "Jewish characteristics" Nietzsche intends as complimentary here – an ineluctable political identity and a superlative cleverness – would indeed become part of Joyce's composite of Jewish nature.

Nietzsche's admiration for Jews also effected his personal relationships with fellow German gentiles. Both Wagner's new aesthetic after *Parsifal*, as well as his more general hatred of Jews, finally caused Nietzsche's break with the man he had once idolized as the premier artist of the age. The 1885 marriage of Nietzsche's sister to Bernhard

Forster, a prominent leader of the German Anti-Semitic Movement, further enraged Nietzsche. By 1887, unable to restrain himself, Nietzsche lashed out against her:

One of the greatest stupidities you have committed – for yourself and for me! Your association with an anti-Semitic chief expresses a foreignness to my whole way of life which fills me ever again with ire and melancholy...It is a matter of honor to me to be absolutely clean and unequivocal regarding anti-Semitism, namely *opposed*, as I am in my writings...[38]

Nietzsche would not be party to German anti-Semitism for he held opposite opinions from those such as Wagner about the role emancipated Jewry played in modern Europe. Sander Gilman asserts that this anti-anti-Semitism was a key ingredient in Nietzsche's forming of his anti-establishment self-image.[39] But a by-product of self-interest or not, Nietzsche's characterization of the Jews as "survivors" *par excellence* greatly influenced Joyce's perception of "the Jew." Joyce's belief in "Jewish perseverance" is found in many of his conversational remarks, as well as being woven deeply into Bloom's character.[40]

Throughout his work, Nietzsche addresses the Jews as a subject of study through a paradox of past and present. On one hand they are the ancients who established the "destructive" moral code of the West; on the other they are a contemporary people who have been made by history into a group categorically different from all other peoples occupying Europe. Because their estrangement had transformed the Jews into such a willful people, Nietzsche believed they must assimilate with other Europeans so as to create a superior "new ruling caste for Europe."[41] In this manner Nietzsche is sometimes perceived in relation to the Jews as merely a liberal gentile who views their assimilation as socially progressive.[42] But Nietzsche's blending of European cultures, the basis of his "good European," designates a much more specific role for the Jews.

Above nationalism and religious sectarianism, Nietzsche's "multi-cultural" aristocracy represents the foundation through which superior individuals can strive toward a will to power.[43] By de-emphasizing "the nation" and distilling the strongest qualities of differing cultures, each individual is afforded the opportunity to begin true self-meditation, "the hour of great contempt," and to awake to "perfect self-knowledge and perfect self-transcendence."[44] Joyce's view of the artist *qua* artist, as well as the art he prescribed for his Irish culture, both play on a similar awareness. Always a critic of the notion of a "pure Celtic Irishness," Joyce believed, as emphatically as Nietzsche did, that "[w]here races are mixed, there is the source of great cultures."[45] Because the Jews to Nietzsche were "beyond all doubt the strongest, toughest, and purest race at present living in Europe," their inclusion in this "race-mixture" was essential.[46] As a young man, Joyce did not of course question Nietzsche's use of the murky concept of race. But given the Judeophobia and anti-Semitism he had encountered by 1907, Joyce initially may have had some difficulty believing in Nietzsche's "tough Jews." Nietzsche himself, indeed, only portrays contemporary Jewry as admirable; his "Hebraism" as an historical force is paradoxically opposite.

Although Nietzsche separates Jewish identity into ancient and modern significance, his division differs from the Christian dichotomy between Old and New Testament Jews. To Nietzsche, Christianity was not the antithesis of Judaism, but merely a refined form of the Jewish slave-morality; Jesus had merely inverted the tribal vengeance of Judaism to conceive universal forgiveness. In turn, Paul ruined Jesus' teachings by structuring the Church on a wrathful patriarchy similar to that of the original Pharisaical class. Judaism and Christianity to Nietzsche thus are a continuum; they are not to be opposed. Taken together, they form one of the roots of Western civilization.

This negative yet decisively ancient role becomes the initial framework through which Nietzsche discusses the Jews. He asserts that in its infancy the Greek culture was so entirely Promethean that it threatened to destroy itself through an uncontrollable Dionysian spirit. Through the later influences of Euripides' Apollonian drama and Socratic philosophy, the Hellenic world began an amelioration of this earlier willfulness. The movement led to the predominance of reason as the most culturally admired mental achievement and individuation as the most culturally admired goal. The repression of will that the Hebraic law demanded, however, soon eclipsed even this more sober generation, and the rise of Judaism represents the final blow to the beauty, strength, and equilibrium of Aeschylean Greece.

This disparity between Hebraism and Hellenism arises in Nietzsche's very first work. Distinguishing between the nature of the tragic in the Greek and Semitic, he concludes that in the Greek mentality "the highest that men can acquire they obtain by a crime [the Prometheus myth] and must...take upon themselves its consequences, namely the whole flood of suffering and sorrows with which the offended celestials must visit on the nobly aspiring race of man."[47] This "dignified" crime, however, "contrasts strangely with the Semitic myth of the fall of man in which curiosity, beguilement, seducibility, wantonness – in short, a series of pre-eminently feminine passions – were regarded as the origin of evil."[48] He thus believes "crime is understood by the Aryans to be a man, sin by the Semites a woman." By internalizing the desire to act freely, the Jews to Nietzsche had "feminized" the idea of sin; to the Hebrew mind, acting out of will was Eve's crime rather than her triumph. Unlike the Greek, the Jew was commanded to control his passion, limit his power, and thus internalize his strongest desires.

In creating Bloom's most guilt-ridden anxieties, Joyce drew heavily on this "Jewish impulse" toward internalization. He later noticed a similar tendency to internalize in both the personality and fictional characters of his friend Italo Svevo; ultimately, the tendency became a key component of Joyce's construction of Bloom's "Jewish nature," and Nietzsche's historical explanation appears to have always shadowed and justified Joyce's belief in such a phenomenon.

Yet Nietzsche was not attempting to define the Jews as a "feminine race." Rather, he was noting that the Old Testament set the foundation of the concept of sin as more tempting to the female, defining maleness as that which must resist sinful action to become the beloved of God. (Such passages, however, influenced Otto Weininger to formulate his later theories about the Jews as a "feminized race.")[49] The subsequent arguments about this radical inversion of Greek values are found throughout *The Gay Science*, *Beyond Good and Evil*, and *The Genealogy of Morals*. Nietzsche's concept of the "Jewish slave-morality revolution" thus begins early in his canon, although it is only fleshed-out in his subsequent works.

In his next major work, however, *Human, All Too Human* (1878), Nietzsche reverses his arguments surrounding the Jews; rather than expanding on Judaism's role in the ancient world, he considers how the Jews are to be understood as a modern people.[50] He may have been motivated to turn aside from his initial historical argument by his sister's marriage to Forster. In any event, Nietzsche was impelled in *Human* to assert the value of the community of modern, European Jews to Europe as a whole. These passages introduce Nietzsche's ideas about "mixed race superiority" and the "good European":

By the way, the great problem of the *Jews* only exists within the national States, inasmuch as their energy and higher intelligence, their intellectual and volitional capital, accumulated from generation to generation in tedious schools of suffering, must necessarily attain to universal supremacy here to an extent provocative of envy and hatred. . .So soon as it is no longer a question of the preservation or establishment of nations, but of the production and training of a European mixed race of the greatest possible strength, the Jew is just as useful and desirable an ingredient as any other national remnant. Every nation, every individual has unpleasant and even dangerous qualities, – it is cruel to require that the Jew be an exception. Those qualities may even be dangerous and frightful in a special degree in his case; and perhaps the young Stock-Exchange Jew is in general the most repulsive invention of the human species. Nevertheless, in a general summing up, I should like to know how much must be excused in a nation, which, not without blame on the part of all of us, has had the most mournful history of all nations, and to which we owe the most loving of men (Christ), the most upright of sages (Spinoza), the mightiest book, and the most effective moral law in the world?[51]

Despite his racialism, Nietzsche here subverts the notion of a "Jewish nature" that is "racially" corrupt. Instead he offers a stereotype built from the results of historical pressure, which, in the modern world, finds its most damaging manifestation in the prejudices of the nation-state. This idea of behavior as in part due to cultural influence rather than "racial nature" informed Joyce's attitude toward "the Jew" as well. But as an expatriate who found the exclusions of his culture's Celtic and Sinn Féin movements offensive, Joyce was also affected by this passage as an Irishman. In learning how Jews were viewed as incapable of becoming nationalists because of their supposed allegiance to the "Jewish nation," Joyce recognized that both he and the Jews were victims of the era's rigid nationalistic fervor.

Nationalism was clearly the enemy to Nietzsche as well. One answer for him, however, lay in the social evolution or pan-Europeanism of his "European mixed race." This synthesis of European peoples sat well with Joyce; he himself hoped to remake the Irish into a secular culture that he continually characterized as "European," as if continental struggles for nationalism were inconsequential. On the Continent, Joyce felt drawn to Jewish individuals who seemed to him the embodiments of this multi-cultural "new man"; one such friend of course would be Svevo. The benefits and paradoxes of assimilation were chief preoccupations in Joyce's life; it was indeed the ambiguities of assimilation that became one of the hobby-horses of *Ulysses*.

In *The Dawn of Day* (translated 1903) Nietzsche linked his consideration of the Jews as both an ancient and a modern people. In his reading of this text, Joyce was sensitive to Nietzsche's preference for the Old Testament over the new, and must have found Nietzsche's discrediting of Christian Bible typology fascinating:

But, after all, what can we expect from the after effects of a religion which, during the centuries of its foundation, enacted that stupendous philological farce about the Old Testament. I am speaking of the attempt which was made to snatch the Old Testament from the Jews, under the pretext that it contained nothing but Christian doctrine, and belonged to the Christians as the true people of Israel, whereas the Jews had only usurped it.[52]

If Joyce had never wondered about the flaws in Christian typology before, Nietzsche's discourse planted the seeds for his mature view of the ancient Hebrews, which of course penetrated those Catholic views he absorbed as a child.

The aphorism from *The Dawn* that endured in Joyce's memory more than the others, however, was "The People of Israel." This passage begins by claiming that "[o]ne of the spectacles which the coming century holds in store for us, is the decision regarding the fate of the European Jews." After proposing that the Jews could become the "masters of Europe," Nietzsche relates how centuries of persecution have created an extraordinary "resourcefulness in [the] soul and intellect of our modern Jews." He further explains that:

Each Jew finds in the history of his fathers and grandfathers a voluminous record of instances of the greatest coolness and perseverance in terrible positions, of most *artful cunning and clever fencing* with misfortune and chance; their bravery under the cloak of *wretched submissiveness*, their heroism . . . surpasses the virtue of all the saints. People wanted to make them contemptible by treating them scornfully for twenty centuries, by refusing to them the approach to all dignities and honourable positions, and by pushing them all the deeper down into the mean trades – and indeed they have not become cleaner under this process. But contemptible? They have never ceased believing themselves qualified for the highest functions; neither have the virtues of all suffering people ever failed to adorn them. Their manner of honouring parents and children, the reasonableness of their marriages and marriage customs make them conspicuous among Europeans. [italics mine].[53]

This positive stereotype of "the Jew" obviously became instrumental to Bloom's character. The idea that contending with persecution had made the Jews into a "clever" group, however, is certainly not original to Nietzsche. But Nietzsche's *positive* use of the stereotype, especially the passage's allusion to the strength of the "Jewish family," became a fixture of Joyce's conception of "Jewish nature."

Further on in *Dawn*, Nietzsche also describes Odysseus in much the same language ("shrewd" and "equal to circumstance"). Joyce indeed acknowledged the similarity: in *Ulysses* the shrewdest of Greek warriors is refigured as a highly assimilated Jew.[54] Nietzsche's influence here, as well, predicts Joyce's delight in Zurich in 1917 with Victor Berard's *Les Phéniciens et L'Odyssée* (1902). The "cunning Jew" as parallel to "the shrewdness" of Ulysses implies a common resourcefulness of mind and strength of will. By combining the Jewish stereotype and the classic hero, the negative representation of "the Jew" as perniciously "cunning" is de-emphasized; cunning to Nietzsche is a positive attribute, indeed is tantamount to "Jewish genius." This "shrewdness" opposes the anti-Semitic stereotype of "the Jew" as intrinsically inclined to cheat, lie, steal, and even murder in hopes of usurping Christian and state power.

Surprisingly, however, it is a similar talent for survival that Nietzsche claims for the *ancient* Hebrews in their overturning of the values of Greek civilization. In this later discussion of Hebraism, "Nietzsche's Jew" now comes full circle. The ancient Hebrews' establishment of a morality that destroyed Greek willfulness and created a nation out of slaves represents to Nietzsche one of the great examples in Western history of a mass will to power. The explanation of the Hebraic subversion of the Greek culture, and thus the creation of a new *Weltanschauung*, is spread over several of Nietzsche's books. Walter Kaufmann asserts that although Nietzsche views Judaic law as the beginning of the inhibition of the individual will,

[he] is hoping to initiate a 'revaluation' comparable to that [which he] ascribed to the Jews. . .they are his model. Of course, he does not agree with the values he ascribes to them; but the whole book [*Beyond Good and Evil*] represents a model to rise beyond simpleminded agreement and disagreement.[55]

What the ancient Hebrews did was damaging, but the fact of their accomplishment clearly represents to Nietzsche his ideas of "sublimation" and "will to power." Nietzsche's "shrewd and willful Jew" – now both ancient and modern – thus forms the framework through which Joyce created Bloom's perseverance and cleverness. Such attributes are indicative of a "Jewishness" Joyce desired for Bloom, as well as Joyce's own version of "good Europeanism."

In *The Gay Science*, Nietzsche returns to his initial discussion about ancient Jews, and explains two of the most influential "Jewish inventions," sin and Christianity:

Origin of Sin – Sin, as it is presently felt wherever Christianity prevails or has prevailed, is a Jewish feeling and a Jewish invention. And in respect to this background of all Christian morality, Christianity has in fact aimed at "Judaising" the world. . ."Only when thou *repentest* is God gracious to thee" – that would arouse the laughter or wrath of a Greek: he would say, "Slaves may have such sentiments."[56]

Judaism issues from a "slave mentality", and Christianity is an outgrowth of the original Jewish hatred of their masters: "from the trunk of that tree of revenge and hatred, Jewish hatred – the deepest and sublimest hatred, i.e. a hatred which creates ideals and transforms values, and which never had its like upon this earth – something equally incomparable grew up, a *new love*, the deepest and sublimest kind of love – and, indeed, from what other trunk could it have grown?"[57] This paternal relationship of Judaism to Christianity had a slight but critical difference from the version that Joyce was taught as a Catholic, or even from the one he received in Arnold. Instead of Christianity being the fulfillment of the Law through the miracle of the incarnation, Christianity for Nietzsche was merely the result of a cultural Oedipal drama – the son rebelling against the father, yet ultimately appropriating the father's exact philosophy.

The focus on the similarities rather than the differences of the two religions supported Joyce's rebellion against Catholicism; now he could perceive the entire Judeo-Christian tradition as flawed. Indeed, after reading Nietzsche, Joyce accepted this assault against the Judaic law as fuel for his own disdain of Christian morality. Joyce was soon to discover, however, that complete apostasy like his own was perhaps not as viable for the Jewish apostate. As he would learn on the Continent, the converted or atheist Jew often remained a Jew in his own eyes and the eyes of others. Joyce eventually encountered a living example of this "non-Jewish Jew" in the person of Svevo. But his initial awareness of the ambiguities of Jewish assimilation was certainly effected by his reading of Nietzsche's notions about the schism between Judaism the religion and the Jews as a people.

Nietzsche's premise that Greek culture was overshadowed by an Hebraic slave-mentality is treated in full in *Beyond Good and Evil* and

The Genealogy of Morals. He asserts that the "Jewish victory" becomes the West's downfall, and yet, ironically, its most pertinent lesson:

What Europe owes to the Jews? Many things, good and bad, and above all one thing of the nature both of the best and of the worst: the grand style in morality, the fearfulness and majesty of the infinite demands, of infinite significations, the whole Romanticism and sublimity of moral questionabilities – and consequently just the most attractive, ensnaring, and exquisite element in those iridescences and allurements to life, in the aftersheen of which the sky of European culture, its evening sky, now glows – perhaps glows out. For this, we artists among the spectators and philosophers, are grateful to the Jews.[58]

It is a "grand style of morality" for which Nietzsche believes the Jews are owed a debt. Their "style" was a product of the strength of will; but the morality itself was self-abnegating to the core; by the nineteenth century it had not only become ineffectual, but was a parasite on the body of a new age. In order to understand this "devolution," Nietzsche again re-examines ancient history.

This primary aspect of the Judeo-Christian ideology begins for Nietzsche in the rebellion of a unified group of Egyptian slaves. Here was a view of "the ancient Jew" that was completely new to Joyce:

– The Jews performed the miracle of the inversion of valuations, by means of which life on earth obtained a new and dangerous charm for a couple of millenniums. Their prophets fused into one the expressions "rich, "godless," "evil," "violent," and "sensual," and for the first time coined the word "world" as a term of reproach. In this inversion of valuations (in which is also included the use of the word "poor" as synonymous with "saint" and "friend") the significance of the Jewish people is to be found; it is with *them* that the *slave insurrection in morality* commences.[59]

The psychology of the "Hebrew slave" is the heart of Nietzsche's argument. At the center of the "Jewish revolt" lies an ignoble morality of utility. As a disempowered people, the Hebrews *imagined* revenge rather than *acted* on those desires – thus the creation of an omnipotent, wrathful God. That shift from a physical expression of the will to mental stealth began for the Jews in what Nietzsche terms *ressentiment*. Although Nietzsche intended the French to stand untranslated here, it was mistranslated in the Haussmann version that Joyce read:

The slave revolt in morality begins by *resentment* itself becoming creative and giving birth to values: the resentment of such beings, as real action, the reaction of deeds, is impossible to, and as nothing but an imaginary vengeance will serve to indemnify. Where as on the one hand, all noble morality takes its rise from a triumphant Yea-saying to oneself, slave morality will, on the other hand, from the very beginning, say no to something "exterior," "different," "not itself"; *this* no being its creative deed. This reversion of the value-positing eye – this necessary glance outward instead of backwards upon itself – is part of *resentment*: Slave-morality in order to arise, needs, in the first place, an opposite and outer world; it needs, physiologically speaking, external irritants, in order to act at all – its action is, throughout, reaction.[60]

Ressentiment for Nietzsche encompasses both a resentment of those who rule and a self-resentment of allowing oneself to be ruled. It is an internalization of all violent emotions, and suppresses the impulse toward action such as anger and revenge. Reading only the English term "resentment," Joyce may not have understood such nuances. But the passage nonetheless became influential: in *Ulysses*, Bloom accepts his most unequivocal sense of Jewish identity in "Circe" precisely through internalization and reaction rather than as a product of his own initiative.

By way of this self-hate formed from the internalizing of outward desires, "[t]he greatest and most dismal morbidity was instituted from which humanity has not yet recovered, the suffering of man *from man, from himself*: the consequence of a violent breaking with his past animal history. . .a declaration of war against the old instincts on which so far his strength, his pleasure, and his terribleness had depended."[61] Thus, through generations of adherence to the Law, the manifestation of *ressentiment* became institutionalized:

All that has ever been accomplished on earth against "the noble". . .is not worth speaking of when compared with that which *the Jews* have done against them; the Jews, that priestly people, which finally succeeded in procuring satisfaction from its enemies and conquerors only by a transvaluation of their values – i.e., an act of the keenest, the *most spiritual vengeance*. Thus only it befitted a priestly people, the people of the most powerfully suppressed, priestly vindictiveness. It was the Jews who, with most frightful consistent logic, dared to subvert the aristocratic equation of values (good = noble = powerful = beautiful = happy = beloved of God) and who, with the teeth of the profoundest hatred (the hatred of impotency) clung to their own valuation: "the wretched alone are good; the poor, the impotent, the lowly alone are the good; only the sufferers, the needy, the sick, the ugly are pious; only they are godly, them alone blessedness awaits, – but ye, ye, the proud and the potent, ye are for aye and evermore the wicked, the cruel, the lustful, the insatiable, the godless, ye will also be, to all eternity, the unblessed, the cursed, and the damned!"[62]

Nietzsche's love of personal power is illuminated in such passages, many of which became a basis for Nazi misreadings to support their racial anti-Semitism. But the self-critical Jewish morality was also the ground upon which Christianity was built, and from which modern European angst has grown; the failures of Christian culture are thus impenetrable without positioning the Jews as the perpetrators of the slave-morality. Jewish influence in the West thus lies beyond the grasp of either the anti-Semite or the philosemite; the heart of the matter was the elimination of "the influence of Judaism on European culture in the forms of Christianity and post-Christian humanitarianism."[63]

It is indeed unlikely that Joyce perceived Nietzsche as a racial anti-Semite (although Baumler's and Spengler's later readings of such passages would characterize them as incontrovertibly anti-Semitic).[64] Nietzsche's "Jewish slave revolt," in fact, represents a de-racialized, historical component of his theory of Western development. Although "Hebraism" to him is an absolutely repressive morality, he nonetheless believed it had once fostered a sublimation of the sexual and violent instincts; overcoming such animal impulses was a necessary step in the "will to power."[65] Thus "the Jewish revolt" was simultaneously philosophically abhorrent and admiringly efficient. Since Nietzsche praises modern Jewry and continually registers his disgust with anti-Semitism, Joyce understood those passages that rail against Jewish morality as attempts to dissect the historical causes of the modern European malaise, and not as an expression of hatred toward contemporary Jews.

Sander Gilman has recently argued for a different interpretation of "Nietzsche's Jew." He claims it is indeed tripartite: "the ancient Hebrew, the "archetypical wandering Christian. . .weak and destructive. . .and the Jew as contemporary, the antithesis of all decadence, self-sufficient and incorruptible."[66] But aside from the positive or negative qualities Nietzsche ascribes to each, Gilman believes "all of these moments are, in the last analysis, negative, in that they reduce the perception of a group of single individuals to the generalities of a class.[67] Nietzsche certainly stereotyped Jews in both his ancient and modern arguments. But Joyce wouldn't have perceived Nietzsche's "modern Jew" as a product of such stereotyping. When Nietzsche refers to the Jews as a race, he invokes an entire discourse about racial identity that Joyce's generation took for granted. By imagining a "Jewish nature" for Bloom, to some extent Joyce had to "reduce the perceptions of a group of single individuals to the generalities of a class," or even a "race." Yet in the conflicts discovered at the center of *Ulysses*, Joyce – desipte the *Zeitgiest* of his era – ultimately comes to interrogate many of the era's most pervasive Jewish stereotypes.

Joyce encountered several new representations of "the Jew" in Nietzsche's work. This discourse was very different from either that which his Catholic upbringing had presented or the anti-Semitism he had observed in Dublin and Paris. Nietzsche also presented a Greek–Jewish interpretation of Western culture that revised Matthew Arnold's "Hebraism and Hellenism" – the discordance between the two theories disturbed Joyce and so gained his interest. Moreover, it is important to remind ourselves that Joyce did not "discover" Nietzsche's ideas in Trieste, but brought his knowledge of them with him to the Continent. Nietzsche thus informs Joyce's reading of those texts on the Jewish question that he obtained in Rome, Trieste, and Zurich. Even more, Joyce read through Nietzsche the "Jewishness" of the assimilated Jews who befriended him in these cities. Joyce's later perception of Ettore Schmitz encompasses a "good Europeanism" as well as a self-irony similar to Nietzsche's "hour of great contempt." In both Svevo and his autobiographic protagonists, those traits were coupled with feelings of humility and insignificance; this too may have reminded Joyce of a passage from *The Genealogy of Morals*:

that "tame" man, man hale and hopelessly mediocre and disagreeable has already learned to feel himself as the end and aim, as the sense of history, as "higher man";. . .at a distance from the superabundance of that which is spoiled, sickly, weary and worn out, of which Europe begins to stink today, – hence, at any rate, as something relatively perfect, something still capable of life, something still saying Yea to life.[68]

Bloom's enthusiastic, yet decidedly bourgeois "yea" to life would be shaped by Joyce's perception of his "tame" Jewish friend, Svevo. And by the time Joyce arrived in Trieste, he had also synthesized into his conception of "Jewish nature" Nietzsche's theory about a "Jewish cunning" that sat at the center of "the Jew's" will to survive. His interest now piqued, Joyce began to recognize how the literary culture of his new home incorporated Jewish question(s) into much of its most controversial discourse.

CHAPTER 6

Cunning: Jews and the Continent – texts and subtexts

Joyce's years in Trieste and Zurich have long been suggested as the beginning of his interest in Judaism, Jewish identity, and the Jewish question. As I have demonstrated here, however, this is a narrow view of a broad field of investigation. The oversight may stem in part from the tangential treatment of the subject found in Richard Ellmann's biography. Because Joyce's expatriate years represent his direct involvement with Jews, however, Ellmann was within reason to explore Joyce's interest in "Jewishness" only after his arrival in Trieste. And yet, as I have illustrated through the many discourses about "the Jew" present in Joyce's imagination since childhood, "Ellmann's Joyce" is certainly not the final word on the subject. But life on the Continent did alter Joyce's attitude toward "the Jew" in significant ways. Indeed, his first ten years there represent a desultory and then a very deliberate quest for a well-rounded knowledge about European Jewry, Judaism, and racialist representations of "the Jew."

Joyce's new awareness began with the city of Trieste itself. The life of the town was influenced by a Jewish intelligentsia whose presence was incomparably greater than that of the Jews of Joyce's native Dublin. The relationships he established in his new home offered him an intimacy with several European Jews who had each forged his or her own idiosyncratic assimilated identity. Through these individuals, Joyce came to understand better the nature and spuriousness of stereotypes of "the Jew" he had absorbed to that point. As his awareness of Jewish marginality and assimilation grew, he perceived parallels between the devalued roles played by both the Jews and the Irish in the development of Europe. His new friends in turn became convenient sources of such information. Ettore Schmitz, in particular, appears to have answered Joyce's questions about Judaism and Judaic lore, as well as suggested texts that would eventually play key roles in the construction of Bloom. When Joyce moved to Zurich he

127

befriended or was befriended by still more Jews. Ira Nadel includes Ottocaro Weiss, Stefan Zweig, Paul Leon, Paul Ruggerio, and many others in roles as supportive friends through whom Joyce learned many of the details of Jewish culture and thought.[1]

When Joyce arrived in Trieste, the Jewish question remained a preoccupation of the European intellectual climate. Dreyfus had never been settled to those who viewed the Jews as a threat to French nationality, or transitively, to all nationalisms. The Austro-Hungarian empire, although offering civic freedoms, still harbored a pervasive yet unofficial discrimination against Jews. Kaiser Wilhelm II's Pan-Germanism had earlier given voice to the anti-Semitism of those such as Ernst Hasse and Houston Stewart Chamberlain. Given the frequency with which such arguments entered intellectual discourse, Joyce would eventually recognize his strong desire to articulate his own views on Jewish identity and anti-Semitism, and *Ulysses* would of course become his most poignant statement on those subjects.

In his new home Joyce also gained a greater awareness of continental politics in general. His reading in the city encompassed issues of socialism, anarchism, and Triestine Irredentism, and ultimately served to help him re-evaluate his own identity as an Irishman. But perhaps above all of these areas of investigation was Joyce's growing fascination with "the Jew." The concerns Joyce discovered to be inherent in the Jewish question not only rose above these other subjects, but eventually became the foundation for his most unified position. Joyce was now recognizing that as an ideological tool, "The Jew" was often figured as the root of problems ranging from economic disaster to the failures of nationalistic unity. Thus the knowledge that eventually went into Bloom's "Jewishness" was inseparable from Joyce's experience of what it meant to be European. Bloom indeed constitutes Joyce's attempt to embody the most humane attributes of a European identity in a world still in the thrall of religious, nationalist, and imperial aggression – ideologies Joyce would later dub "the wisdom of the old world."[2]

The texts about Jews Joyce read in Trieste and Zurich played key roles in his composition of *Ulysses* as well. Several of these works represent the type of studies that were popular among the intelligentsia of Trieste, Paris, Berlin, Prague, Vienna, London, and many other important cities during this period. Through these texts, Joyce learned the details of theories asserting a Jewish racial inferiority. Such arguments in turn included several that grew to fascinate him:

Jewish pariahism, international conspiracy myths, the degenerate and "feminized" Jew, a Zionistic or assimilative Jewish destiny. The three works regularly offered as most influential in this respect – all first cited in Ellmann – are Guglielmo Ferrero's *L'Europa giovanie* (1897), Otto Weininger's *Geschlecht und Charakter* (1903), and Maurice Fishberg's *The Jews: a Study of Race and Environment* (1911). The fact that these books issue from three distinct cultures displays the international scope of Jewish question controversies. While Joyce owned and expressed admiration for the Ferrero text, his reaction to both the Weininger and Fishberg books was less vocal. These two texts, however, were quite popular in Joyce's circle during the time he was composing *Ulysses*. And by the time he left Trieste for Paris, Joyce's store of texts concerning Jews included such titles as Heijermans' *Ahaservus*, Turgenev's *The Jew*, Herzl's *Der Judenstaat*, Sacher's *Zionism and the Jewish Future*, Wagner's *Judaism in Music*, Funk's *The Origins of the Talmud*, and still more.[3]

While Joyce also read Freud during this period, he appears not to have perceived in those works a special relevance to Jewish identity. In a lecture on Joyce in 1927, Italo Svevo argued that his friend had written *Ulysses* before ever reading Freud.[4] But Svevo was incorrect. Since 1911 Joyce had been discussing Freud with his pupil Paolo Cuzzi, who, after reading *Five Lectures on Psychoanalysis*, shared Joyce's fascination with parapraxis. Joyce had by that time purchased three psychoanalytic works in pamphlet form.[5] While Joyce may well have known Freud was a Jew, the idea that psychoanalysis was in any manner a "Jewish science" was not a prevalent argument in the era in which Joyce was composing *Ulysses*. Havelock Ellis, whom Joyce had been reading, was of course Freud's immediate predecessor in the field and was certainly not a Jew. Although Freud himself eventually believed his theories to have benefited from the "Jewish position," he only began to make such assertions publicly in his 1925 *Autobiographical Study*.[6]

I have followed an order here that reproduces Joyce's successive encounter with these texts. It must be recalled, however, that Joyce read such works between 1915 and 1920, when he had already known Ettore Schmitz for a decade.[7] Joyce may have sought out books such as Weininger and Fishberg on the advice of his respected friend. But because Schmitz, who was both a Jew and an avant-garde novelist, looms so large in Joyce's biography, I have reserved my discussion of him for the proceeding chapter.

I   TRIESTE, 1905: JEWISH PLACES, JEWISH FRIENDS

Having returned from their brief stay in Pola, Joyce and Nora resettled in Trieste in March 1905. Except for a six month excursion to Rome, they remained in Trieste for the next ten years. Added now to what were to become Joyce's many associations with European Jewry was both his new sense of "exile" and the atmosphere of Trieste – a city that for two centuries had been a center of Jewish assimilation. In his last letter from Pola to Stanislaus, Joyce once again attempted to justify his flight from Dublin:

> I have come to accept my present situation as a voluntary exile – is it not so? This seems to me important both because I am likely to generate out of it a sufficiently personal future to satisfy Curran's heart and also because it supplies me with the note on which I propose to bring my novel to a close.[8]

Joyce had already realized his choice to live apart from his native country as crucial. While it would be a few years before he would make a conscious metaphor of his own "exodus," he nonetheless recognized that his new marginality seemed for him a means toward self-discovery.[9] In his new home, Joyce was befriended by intellectuals and journalists who had each had his or her own struggle with marginality – many of whom were Italian Jews of Eastern European heritage. In Trieste these Jews were both prominent in, and yet Other to, the dominant Catholic culture. An element of that precarious position resulted from the unique character of the city, an Italian free port within the Austro-Hungarian Empire.

Polyglot and predominately mercantile, by the eighteenth century Trieste's commerical reputation was renowned, and social freedom and inclusion in the life of the city was left open to persons who would become successful entrepreneurs, regardless of ethnic background. Thus Jewish merchants immigrated to the city in increasing numbers throughout its life as a thriving port. The ghetto gates were removed in 1785; by the end of the eighteenth century, the Jewish community had risen to some 1,500 inhabitants. Cecil Roth observes that this new influx of Jews made the city "the most important [Jewish community] in the north of Italy."[10]

When Joyce arrived in the city in 1904, many Triestines had devoted the last fifty-five years to an attempt to establish the port as officially Italian. By 1866, young nationalists in the city were keeping a keen eye on Garibaldi's revolution, half-expecting his troops eventually to sail across the sea and claim Trieste as part of a unified Italy. The Irredentist movement (*Italia irredenta*: unredeemed Italy) was born during this period; many of its first leaders were veterans who had fought with Garibaldi. The Irredentists claimed two enemies: the Austrian government and the increasing influence of Slavs and Slavic culture in their "Italian" city.

Indeed, by Joyce's era, most Triestine Jews, if they had any political inclinations, were Irredentist to the person.[11] The Slovene nationalists could not match the organization and popularity of the Irredentists, who were in part directed by some of the city's most prominent Jewish intellectuals.[12] The Irredentists, whose early goal was to become visible in the eyes of the *Risorgimento*, began their movement in clubs and organizations to promote Italianism through education of the youth. One such club, the *Societa Trestina de Ginnastica*, organized in 1863, had had as a member the family of Francesco Schmitz, whose eldest son, Ettore, would later write under the name Svevo.[13] Schmitz became a committed Irredentist, and at twenty had already published articles in the official Irredentist newspaper, *Indipendente*, founded in 1877. Schmitz's brother, Adolfo, who had a more urgent, lifelong commitment to the cause, died on the eve of reunification.[14] *Indipendente*'s more widely read competitor was *Il Piccolo della Serra*, the successful brain-child of another Irredentist Triestine Jew of Hungarian descent, Teodoro Mayer. Mayer too was a central voice of Irredentism in the city. Within five years of Joyce's arrival, he established employment with Mayer and became both tutor and friend to Schmitz. Joyce's growing knowledge of Irredentism, learned mostly through these Jewish Triestines, rekindled his own political biases.

But Jewish influence in the city went beyond nationalist politics. By the end of the nineteenth century, many Jewish families had made their fortunes in Trieste. Parallel with that success often came assimilation through intermarriage and conversion. By 1890, 14 percent of all Jews in the city had married out of their faith; by 1927 the rate of intermarriage was over 56 percent.[15] As was so often the case during nineteenth-century Jewish emancipation, the Jews of Trieste abandoned much of their Ashkenazi culture. In the *fin-de-siècle* city, assimilation included interest in the art and music of Vienna, the learning of German and Tuscan Italian, and a general consumption of the literature and styles of the West. P. N. Furbank characterizes the influence of Jewish Trieste, stating that "[w]hen Richard Burton the explorer was there as British Consul (1872–90) he and his wife regarded 'the enlightened and hospitable Hebrews as their best friends. . .[i]t is the Jews who lead society here, the charities and the fashion; they are the life of the town,' wrote Lady Burton."[16] Joyce had indeed come to a city whose Jewish population was in public prominence. This was quite unlike his native Dublin, whose Jews were small in number, not terribly well placed, and often invisible as a community. But having already read Nietzsche's theory about the Jewish role in European development, Joyce now became more interested in his Jewish acquaintances, as well as those texts that invited the curious into the world of emancipated Jewry.

Joyce's tutoring of other well-to-do Triestines, including Schmitz, was his introduction to the Jewish community at large. Before he established these contacts, however, Joyce had become interested in the general politics of Trieste. His continuing frustrations with Sinn Féin may have motivated him to find in Trieste similarities to his own occupied city. Dominic Manganiello suggests that "for Joyce there were striking political resemblances between the two places. . .Trieste had been ruled by the Austrians for almost as long as the British ruled Dublin, and both cities claimed a language different from that of their conquerors."[17] From memories about his friend of twenty years, Svevo himself said of Joyce that "Trieste was for him a little Ireland which he was able to contemplate with more detachment than he could his own country."[18] By 1915, Joyce had become quite knowledgeable about the Irredentist movement, purchasing Guilio Caprin's *Trieste e l'Italia*, and, at the request of then editor Robert Prezioso, eventually writing articles about Ireland's struggle for independence for *Il Piccolo del Sera*. And through Mayer, *Il Piccolo's* publisher, Joyce became acquainted with several other Jewish writers in the city.

Thus by 1907, Jewish students, friends, and employers had accepted Joyce into their home town – a place from which he and Nora had initially felt estranged. Indeed, Joyce's arrival in the city in 1904 did not bode a promising future. During his first year, Joyce was troubled by an "unfriendly" populace, struggles for a steady income, and the birth of a first child. Describing to Stanislaus his new home, Joyce wrote, "I must, first of all, tell you that Trieste is the rudest place I have ever been in. It is hardly possible to exaggerate the incivility of these people. The girls and women are so rude to Nora that she is afraid to go out in the street."[19] In that same month, however, during the birth of his first child, Joyce found his Jewish landlady an exception to the coldness of the Triestines:

At three o'clock I found Nora in pain. I had no notion it was for birth but when it continued for a long time I went to the landlady and told her. She sent for a midwife and then there was proper confusion if you like. . .Nora had hardly anything made not expecting the event till the end of August. However, our landlady is a Jewess and gave us everything we wanted. . .at about nine in came the old aunt Jewess smiling and nodding '*Xe un bel machiso, Signore.*' So then I knew an heir was born.[20]

Why Joyce felt it necessary to make reference to his landlady's Jewish identity is curious – the allusion is one of the first significations of "Jewishness" he made on the Continent. Indeed, his phrase "old aunt Jewess" appears to indicate that "Jewishness," at this point in his life, had benevolent – here maternal – implications for him. Yet the remark coincides with his comment that very September that he "must get rid of some of [his] Jewish bowels" in order to make his statement to the world.[21] The second allusion is more ambiguous than the first – did Joyce mean to imply "Jewish bowels" as those of cowardice or of compassion; perhaps there was still an association between the two emotions he had yet to reconcile. In either case, both references portray the manner in which the nineteenth-century language of racial-type entered English idioms. Both, as well, reveal that Joyce had not yet sought to deconstruct the preconceptions about "the Jew" that form the foundations of such expressions.

As the allusions represent both a "Jewish kindness" and "Jewish pusilanimousness," however, Joyce was appropriating a discourse with a widespread popularity. "The Jew" as cowardly reached back to the Christian stereotypes Joyce absorbed in Dublin, as well as his reading of Shakespeare, Scott, and others. The suggestion of a "Jewish kindness" may relate to his year-old memory of Alfred Hunter.[22] But apparently even in 1905, Joyce's perception of Jews still relied somewhat on stereotype. Both the "cowardly Jew" and "the kind old Jewish mama" are parallel to nineteenth-century Afro-American stereotypes, and suggests the way in which Otherness plays on similar projections within very different cultures. In any event, Joyce's offhand allusions coincided with his new readings in Trieste, which included many texts about "the Jew."

II PLAYS AND POLITICS

Joyce's perception of Jewish domesticity was influenced by Hermann Heijermans' drama, *Ahasverus* (1893), which he read just five months before Giorgio's birth. Whether Joyce was fascinated at this time with the myth of the Wandering Jew is unclear – in a letter to Stanislaus he had characterized the play as "nothing."[23] Within the next ten years, though, Joyce would envision this myth as one of the more symbolic foundations of Bloom's character. In the interim, in fact, Joyce purchased Eugene Sue's work, *Le Juif Errant* (1831). Regardless of his initial reaction to Heijermans, however, Joyce was introduced through the play to a world he knew little about in 1905: the *shtetl* of Russian Jewry during the era of the widespread pogroms from 1881 onward.

Hermann Heijermans was an assimilated Jew of Amsterdam who, having failed in business on several attempts, became obsessed with Ibsen's Naturalistic drama and began writing his own plays in the early 1890s. *Ahasverus* was his second attempt and first success. It not only portrayed the suffering of Eastern European Jewry under legal persecution from the Czars, but brought to the secular Dutch stage a marginal, rural world little known in the urban West. The play itself, however, was merely one act, less than an hour in playing time. Later on in his career, Heijermans painted a more complete picture of the *shtetl* in his longer works on religious intolerance, *Ghetto* and *Allerziellen*. But while the brevity of *Ahasverus* did not excite Joyce, the play's stark images made a lasting impression on him.

The drama is set in the cottage of a Jewish family living in a *shtetl* near Nizhni Norgorod around 1890. On the morning after a particularly severe pogrom by the Cossacks, the son of the family, Petruska, is missing. He later turns up unharmed, having converted to Christianity to save his life. The unnamed "mother" of the play, while despising her son's cowardly act, nonetheless wants to keep the conversion a secret from the father and reluctantly accepts Petruska back into the household. When the conversion is revealed, the father, Karalyk, becomes enraged, curses and disowns his son. After being cursed by his father, Petruska watches as the Cossacks evict his entire family, including the senile grandmother, but leave him the hovel and its belongings; as a convert he needs no "papers" to stay there. This ironic ending may have impressed Joyce. Petruska is filled with self-hatred because of his actions, suggesting that this final attitude is a product of the Jewish dilemma: either convert and suffer self-loathing, or continue to be "the wandering Jew."[24] Such choices would some day play a role in the conflicts of both Rudolph and Leopold Bloom.

The characters of the committed Jewish father and the forgiving Jewish mother also made an impact on Joyce, especially considering the two comments he made in the letters that surround his reading of the play. Joyce either read the play in Pola, or in Trieste just upon his return. Becoming aware of how visible and influential the urban Jews of Trieste were, Joyce began to draw conclusions about Jewish assimilation in a place that allowed Jews both freedom and respect. Certainly Nietzsche's broad portrait of "modern Jews" was made more complex for him by both the atmosphere of Trieste and new texts such as Heijermans' play. Through reading the play, Joyce also may have perceived parallels in the plight of *shtetl* Jews to that of the Irish peasantry; the drama presented Jewish *shtetl* dwellers as attached to religion with an allegiance undeterred by the threat of death – a martyrdom at the center of the Irish Catholic struggle as well.

But Joyce's main concern for the moment did not lie in exploring such notions. Rather, his uncertain income and steady work on *Dubliners* held most of his attention during this period. Because the Scoula Berlitz could not offer him the amount of hours he desired, Joyce chose to move again within a year of Giorgio's birth. In July, 1906 he took his new family to Rome because he had landed a clerkship in the Nast, Kolb and Schumacher Bank. In that city, as well, Joyce continued his reading about European Jewry.

Joyce disliked Rome because he found it "decrepit," and because it symbolized to him the tyranny of the Catholic church. While living in the city, however, he became more interested in political science, and through that curiosity encountered another theory about the Jews in Europe. In Rome, Joyce began his first in-depth reading about socialism; in Ireland, he had ignored the ideas of Connolly and Larkin. But after studying Nietzsche, Joyce wanted to believe in an internationalist vision, perhaps to wean himself from the nationalism that was such a part of his own legacy. Yet Nietzsche's aristocratic radicalism could hardly have provoked Joyce's turn to the left; the reality of Joyce's economic situation offered a more tangible stimulus toward his socialist thinking. Having been tossed from Zurich to Trieste to Pola because of sporadic employment, Joyce's need to feed his family pushed him to find the type of position he dreaded; taking a post he hated and having to move yet again stirred his resentment of a capitalism that would not support its literary geniuses. One of the most critical outcomes of this interest in socialism, however, was Joyce's newly discovered enthusiasm for the writings of Guglielmo Ferrero.

Although Ferrero had begun his life as a socialist, by the time Joyce read him he had turned to the right. Ferrero's five-volume history of Republican and early Imperial Rome, entitled *Grandezza e decadenza di Roma* (1902–07), established his international reputation.[25] By 1907, Ferrero's works were widely read and viewed as controversial. In Trieste, Joyce had been reading Ferrero's essays in *Il Piccolo della Sera* as well as his books. Ferrero's discussion of the military mentality in *Il Militarismo* (1898) appears to have aided Joyce in constructing Corley in "Two Gallants."[26] Ferrero had married into the Jewish family of Caesar Lombroso – the father and son-in-law had collaborated on the 1893 work, *La Donna delinquente, la prostituta e la donna normale*. Lombroso had written a study in 1894 concerning the Jews, entitled *L'antisemitismo e le scienze moderne*, which not only influenced his son-in-law, but became a source for Maurice Fishberg's 1911 study.[27] On the heels of his successful joint project, and after publishing articles in support of the Dreyfusards, Ferrero published *L'Europa giovane* in 1897.[28]

Joyce may have been attracted to *L'Europa giovane* at the outset because of Ferrero's reputation as an adamant Dreyfusard. Upon reading the book, Joyce felt a pride in Ferrero's inclusion of the Irish as a part of the evolution of Europe, especially because the discussion proposed Parnell as a paradigm of nationalist leadership. The thesis of Ferrero's book, however, was anti-socialist and thus outside Joyce's present political inclinations. But both Ferrero in his early career and Joyce in Rome were more soi-disant than truly committed socialists. While Ferrero was once an avowed Marxist, by the composition of *L'Europa giovane*, he viewed British parliamentarianism as a more viable system.[29] Joyce, of course, never made a commitment to any socialist party, and admitted to his brother that his brand of socialism was "unsteady and illformed."[30] Socialist thought in Joyce's fiction, moreover, often receives an ironic rather than serious mention – a notable example would be Bloom's muddled ideas in the cabman's shelter in the "Eumaeus" episode (*U*16.526, 538).

Nonetheless, Ferrero's theory was indeed "international" in scope. He believed that "economic growth was the barometer of social progress, and that those nations with developing industries represented superior cultures."[31] Included in this discussion of industrial progress in Europe was the role of the Jews in that development. But Ferrero's conception of anti-Semitism in Europe was paradoxical. He postulated that ancient persecution of the Jews was somewhat rational, because the Jews had represented a dangerous sense of mission which often led to bloodshed. He reverses his argument, however, when addressing contemporary anti-Semitism. Since the Jews had lent so much to the progress of the modern industrialized world, Ferrero saw contemporary anti-Semitism as irrational. Contemporary Jewry offered some particular talents that, to Ferrero, were not only part of a "racial" Jewish nature, but seemed manifest in their most superlative form in the Jews.

Foremost among these "positive, active forces in society," was the Jewish "Messianic conscience" or a belief in themselves as the keepers of the world's ethics.[32] Ferrero speculated that each Jew believes he possesses "the secret to man's redemption." He contends that this tendency on the Jews' part had evolved through the centuries, adapting itself to different ages: "[t]heir solution was first Messianic, then Christian, and either socialism or anarchism for contemporary times."[33] Whether Ferrero was Joyce's first encounter with the theory of Jewish messianism is unclear. But Bloom's prophecies in "Circe" that he will lead Dublin into "the new Bloomusalem in the Nova Hibernia of the future," is certainly a parodic use of the idea (*U* 15.1545).

Ferrero believed "Jewish Messianism" was also related to a Jewish "genius for proselytism," which was manifested in the greatest "Jewish creation," propaganda.[34] Susan Humphreys explains that "In Italian the term *propaganda* also means commercial advertising . . . and Ferrero believes that the Messianic spirit is akin to the journalistic one: 'Every great Jewish talent is always a bit of a journalist,' he says."[35] Humphreys further cites Ferrero's theories as influential to Joyce's construction of Bloom's character, although she adds that the use is often ironic, as in Bloom's position as a canvasser rather than a journalist.[36] Both Humphreys and Dominic Manganiello include in their arguments Joyce's "simultaneous" mention of his reading of Ferrero in a letter to Stanislaus of September, 1906, in which Joyce also talks of his plan for a short story about one "Mr. Hunter." While Joyce had been reading Ferrero since his arrival in Trieste, it does not appear he obtained *L'Europa giovane* until the summer of 1906. As

Humphreys herself points out, Joyce's letter of 13 November states he had "just read" *L'Europa giovane*, but what "just read" means is unclear.

This chronology suggests that Ferrero did not introduce Joyce to these theories, so much as he lent credence to an understanding of "Jewish nature" Joyce had been constructing since his youth. To assert that in 1906, Joyce "learned" of the stereotype of the Jew as self-righteous and propagandistic is to overlook the preconceptions of Jews that he absorbed before he left Ireland. The Christian image of "the Jew" as "stiff-necked" surely was an antecedent to Ferrero's claim of a "Jewish Messianism." In Paris, Joyce had encountered anti-Dreyfusard representations of Jews as manipulative and scheming that foreshadowed Ferrero's "propaganda" theory. Ferrero's mention of Brandes' Jewish background, and his assertion that Marx, Lassalle, and Lombroso were three Jews as influential as Jesus certainly fascinated Joyce.[37] But to credit any single text as the foundation of one of Joyce's most complex characters is limiting, to say the least.

If not entirely original in their representations of "the Jew," however, the texts Joyce went on to read did present to him new theories about Jewish nature, and new methods of support for such. Most prominent of the books that affected Joyce in this manner were Weininger's and Fishberg's studies.

II WEININGER AND FISHBERG: "THE JEW" AS FEMININE RACE OR AS A PEOPLE?

Richard Ellmann offers only the minimal evidence of various interviewees to establish that Joyce had read either *Sex and Character* or *The Jews*.[38] Yet from reading *Ulysses*, it is apparent that Weininger's beliefs about "Jewish nature" are both inverted and discredited in the novel, and that Fishberg's assertions about Jewish cultural diversity lend themselves to Bloom's complexity. Both writers are in the end very likely sources for Joyce. But it is important to realize as well that the arguments Weininger makes and those Fishberg refutes were in the air of Joyce's intellectual climate both in Dublin and on the Continent throughout his lifetime. Joyce need not have read either text to have recognized the prevalence of such controversies about "the Jew" in *fin-de-siècle* Europe.

It seems more than a solid assumption, however, that Joyce read Weininger while writing *Ulysses*. The fact that in "Circe," Dr. Punch

Costello states, "Professor Bloom is a finished example of the new womanly man," represents Joyce's borrowing of the exact language of Weininger's theory about the Jewish male (*U*15.1798–99). Again, the popularity of the theory supports this influence – Weininger was one of the most controversial psychobiologists in Vienna after 1903. Moreover, Svevo was a reader of Weininger, and makes direct reference to him in the novel *The Confessions of Zeno* (1923). In Zurich, Joyce's friendship with Ottocaro Weiss also brought him within a circle of psychoanalysts, including Weiss' brother, Dr. Edoardo Weiss, who certainly mentioned Weininger's ideas. By the composition of *Finnegans Wake*, Joyce definitely knew Weininger; the name appears in some of the margin notes of the typescript.[39]

Quite probable as well is Joyce's actual ownership of the Fishberg book. Ellmann's statement that Joyce delighted in Fishberg's discussion of Chinese Jews (the Jews of K'ai-Fung-Foo) is the result of an interview with Ottocaro Weiss. If Weiss' memory was accurate, in Zurich Joyce had a "little book on the Jews by a man named Fishberg."[40] As Ira Nadel points out, *The Jews* is not a "little" book at all, but a comprehensive study occupying 578 pages in its present edition. Despite these discrepancies, a reading of Fishberg seems to indicate Joyce drew on the book heavily for his shaping of Bloom's supposed "Jewish" traits, as well as Molly's appearance. Fishberg's study was attractive because the statistical proof it offered fed Joyce's hunger for Naturalistic detail. This hard scientific information about Jewish physiognomy, eating habits, suicidal tendencies, occupational inclinations, and intermarriage presented to Joyce a composite from which he could select several of Bloom's "Jewish" traits.

Before Fishberg's study is explored, however, Weininger's theories must first be placed in context of the era's broader gender and racial assumptions, and then examined specifically. Weininger's conclusions parallel much nineteenth-century discourse about both Jews and women with which Joyce was surely familiar. Moreover, the book itself represents the type of study of the era that relied on the discourse of scientized racialism, and so lent credence to Jewish stereotypes by giving them "rationalist authenticity."

Weininger's analogies between Jews and women were present in similar form in misogynistic and anti-Semitic popular culture throughout Europe. While the Jewish population of Joyce's Dublin was minimal, such stereotypes were present there as well. Without ever having read Weininger, quite early on in his life Joyce encountered the representation of "the Jew" as "womanly man" – unaggressive "sissies" who shy from drinking, whoring, and fighting. In *Ulysses*, Joyce has a character allude to this view of Jewish masculinity in the most common locus of Dublin conversation, the pub. Nosey Flynn's opinion of Bloom that "God Almighty couldn't make him drink . . . Slips off when the fun gets too hot. . .If you ask him to have a drink first thing he does he outs with the watch to see what he ought to imbibe . . . declare to God he does," suggests the commonality of such a view of "the Jew" (*U*8.979–81). Uninspired by the Irish activities of drinking and gambling, Bloom is indeed perceived as an "unmanly man." While such pub-gossip was in no way "scientific," it nonetheless partook of the gender and racial myths that fed the theories of academic writers such as Weininger. Moreover, this "influence from the streets" was an element of Joyce's notions about "the Jew" that were ingrained in his psyche early on, and so quite durable.

Stanislaus' *Dublin Diary* contains a telling example of this conflation of female and Jewish stereotypes. As part of a tirade against the ignorance of what he saw as the mainstream of Catholic Dublin, Stanislaus includes an image of the working-class female mentality as likened to that of "the Jew":

As for women, they are cowards, probably as great cowards as men but more obviously so, and far more sensual. They want comfort and children, and the more of the former and the less of the latter the better. They really care not a snap of their fingers about anything else. They have the minds of Jews. It is quite beyond their understanding that people should be grievously troubled by the thoughts of their minds. They were the original egoists and from them men have learnt the first principles of a religion which their masculine energy has pushed to such admirable excess . . . They have not a high kind of intellect and their judgments of men and matters are generally valueless . . . But they are careful and for all their sensuality they want marriage. The Jew in them wants the bond.[41]

Stanislaus' thoughts represent "the Jew" in a manner that Joyce absorbed without ever having read his brother's writing – he heard similar ideas in Dublin pubs. In several instances in the diary, however, Stanislaus expresses resentment toward his brother for reading and even "stealing" the thoughts he found there.[42] The above passage was written in 1904, before Stanislaus or Joyce left Dublin or ever heard of Otto Weininger. Not surprisingly, though, Weininger makes a similar connection:

The Jew [like the woman] is always more absorbed by sexual matters than the Aryan. . .The Jews are habitual match-makers, and in no race does it so often happen that marriages are arranged by men.[43]

But the coincidence here is less than novel when placed in the context of the prevalent stereotypes of "the Jew" as less masculine than his European (Aryan) counterpart.

A perception of "the Jew" and "the woman" as cowardly, lying, mercenary, egotistical, and incapable of sublime thought was established in the intellectual discourse of the era as well. Hegel's early characterization of Judaism as a religion without a theology but only a theocracy, one which necessitated the advent of the sublime faith of Christianity, provided a basis through which anti-Semites could castigate Jews as a people without a true "spirituality."[44] Schopenhauer continued this view of Judaism by emphasizing its worldly optimism as faulty, and the Jews' sense of alienation as a characteristic originating in the biblically based view of themselves as "chosen."[45] Schopenhauer also portrayed women as a similarly problematic group due to their lack of logical powers and their habit of resorting to "cunning tricks and lying."[46] Such parallels, in addition to a supposed superiority–inferiority complex in each group, created a popular image of both Jews and women as soulless, devious, illogical beings, several notches below the European male on both an evolutionary and spiritual scale.

Sander Gilman explains this amalgamation of Jewish and female stereotypes as not random, but in part a reaction to the new social freedoms both groups were seeking.[47] As this climate grew more threatening to anti-Semites, including self-effacing Jews such as Weininger, attempts to prove both misogynistic and anti-Jewish arguments became more "scientific." Gilman, in fact, relates several more charges leveled against both women and Jews, such as both groups lacking an innate ability to use language well, and often misusing it for an unabashed self-gain. For Weininger, however, such indictments against the female and Jewish "natures" become symptoms of a "disease" rather than the disease itself. As a scientist, he perceived his mission as the identification of the causes of this malady in hopes of discovering the root of the *mal du siècle*.

As a student in Vienna, Weininger based *Geschlecht und Charakter* on his doctoral dissertation. The study is constructed from his personal theories, biological research, and what he failed to realize were the

most common gender myths of his time. As a Jew who converted to
Protestantism on the eve of his graduation, Weininger has long been
regarded as a prime example of Jewish self-hatred. This type of
self-abnegation was later explored as a specifically "Jewish phenomenon" by Theodor Lessing in his *Der Jüdische Selbtsthass* (1930).
Weininger, however, did not recognize his work as a projection of
self-hate, and believed it to be a seminal study of psychobiology. His
essentialist assumptions about gender, while supported intermittently
by data from experiments on invertebrates, lack any attention to
environmental factors. Gender and Jewish identity, far from being
socio-historic constructs, are for him "Platonic" conditions. And his
suicide in 1903, immediately after his book's publication, has been
viewed by some as the result of a disgust at his own inability to
exorcise those aspects of his psyche he detested as "womanly" and
"Jewish."

Weininger's text appears to be a discussion of gender for the
majority of the work. His initial premise is that "amongst human
beings the state of the case is as follows: There exists all sorts of
intermediate conditions between male and female – sexual transitional
forms."[48] His opening introduces gender intermediacy as the basis for
homosexuality, bisexuality, and the nature of "cellular gender
individuality." In the second half of the study, however, Weininger
becomes interested in defining male and female as "Platonic types,"
and distinguishes the elements indigenous to each. The discussion,
however, becomes progressively one-sided, eventually becoming
clearly misogynistic. Thus the quintessential female aspects – found in
all women and to a lesser degree in some men – are identified as
superficiality, illogical thought, a tendency toward blinding vanity
and self-pity, and the singular sense of purpose in sexual activity so as
to continue but not necessarily improve the human species. Conversely,
that which is intrinsically male – found less often in women – is
characterized as logical thought, self-sacrifice, sublime faith, strength
of will stemming from an intelligible ego, and a desire for the
intellectual advancement of the race.[49] Women who think and
behave in these "masculine" ways have a preponderance of maleness
in their genetic makeup; to Weininger they are aberrations of "the
female." Conversely, Weininger's conclusion about the "womanly
woman" – the essence of femaleness – is that she represents the
negative element in humankind: "Women have no existence and no
essence; they are not, they are nothing. Mankind occurs as male or

female, something or nothing. Woman has no share in ontological reality, no relation to the thing-in-itself, which, in the deepest interpretation is the absolute, is God."[50]

As a young man, Joyce himself was fond of repeating the canard of a Dublin comic that "woman is an animal that micturates once a day, defecates once a week, menstruates once a month, and paturates once a year."[51] Coming of age in the patriarchal worlds of both social Dublin and Jesuit institutions, Joyce had obviously encountered a similar conception of "female nature" before Weininger wrote about it. More importantly, however, Joyce would find a familiarity with Weininger's definition of Jews as *weiblich*, or manifesting those aspects of behavior that are essentially – and negatively – female.

Weininger's penultimate chapter alters the course of his entire study from gender concerns to ethnic ones. Entitled "Judaism," the chapter emphasizes the common assumption of a racially Jewish cowardice in its portrait of "the Jew." The language in this chapter becomes less controlled and is, of course, without experimental or biological support. Weininger's disdain for his Jewish identity is revealed through this change in rhetorical style, a progression from argument and support to mere diatribe. Coming as it does at the end of a book about gender identity, the chapter seems oddly misplaced. Yet Weininger views it as somehow a summation of his definition of gender "types." This is because, as "womanly men," Jews to him are prime evidence of how negative female traits can corrupt the male. The idea once again begins in his definition of "Platonic" Judaism:

I do not refer to a nation or a race, to a creed or to a scripture. When I speak of the Jew I mean neither an individual nor the whole body, but mankind in general, insofar as it has a share in the platonic idea of Judaism...I think of it as a tendency of the mind, as a psychological constitution which is a possibility for all mankind, but which has become actual in the most conspicuous fashion only amongst Jews.[52]

Weininger's theory here is twofold: first, the Jews manifest a negative kind of masculinity, and second, this "Jewish" lack of masculine traits can be found in those who are not Jewish but who display such "feminized" attitudes and behaviors. This dual nature of Weininger's Jew – both as an inferior group and as an inferior "Platonic state" – suggests a central aspect of all stereotype: a negative trait portrayed as superlative in the stereotyped group so as to lessen the onus toward the trait in the dominant group. As a young man, or even in his adult conversations, Joyce appears to have tended toward such stereotyping on occasion. If he had once perceived himself as cowardly, Joyce's use of the term "Jewish bowels" implies that Jews are not only cowardly, but more revealing, that cowardice in a Gentile is best described as "Jewish." By the composition of *Ulysses*, however, Joyce recognized much more fully the tendency to define and purge undesirable aspects of self through projection.

Weininger, however, moves from the idea of a Platonic "Jewishness" and "femaleness" to his castigation of women and Jews as living entities; the process itself is basic to the establishment of Otherness. Moreover, Weininger believed that his Platonic states were manifested not only in individuals, but in races as well: "It would not be difficult to make a case for the view that the Jew is more saturated with femininity than the Aryan, to such an extent that the most manly Jew is more feminine than the least manly Aryan."[53] Given such assertions, a comparison here of Weininger's, Joyce's, and Bloom's attitudes toward Zionism illustrates how Joyce incorporates a fine line of distinction between Weininger's "Jewishness" and Bloom's perception of his Jewish identity in *Ulysses*.

Because to him Jews are undignified, womanly males, Weininger believes that "before Zionism is possible, the Jew must first conquer Judaism. To defeat [his] Judaism, the Jew must first understand himself and war against himself."[54] Joyce's most often repeated statement on Zionism seems to imply a similar belief: "That's [a Jewish state] all very well, but believe me, a warship with a captain named Kanalgitter and his aide named Captain Afterduft would be the funniest thing the old Mediterranean has ever seen."[55] Does this offhand comment suggest Joyce believed that Jews, because they are Jews, are laughable as military men and thus hopeless as aggressive Zionists? As in many of Joyce's casual comments about Jews, there is as much caprice intended in the statement as there is serious belief. As one who both harbored nationalistic feelings for his own persecuted people and often made analogies between the Irish and the Jews, Joyce may well have had a certain amount of respect for Zionism, even if he believed its time had not yet come. As a physically weak, self-proclaimed pacifist from a culture that placed great value on aggressive nationalism, Joyce's ridicule of Zionism was in part a projection of his own insecurities. But his purchasing in Zurich of both Theodor Herzl's *Der Judenstaat* and H. Sacher's *Zionism and the Jewish Future* (1916) implies that Joyce had some interest in the idea.

Moreover, Joyce's friendships in Trieste with two ardent Zionists, Ciro Glass and Moses Dlugacz (the latter the model for the Dlugacz of *Ulysses*), brought him much information about the plausibility of establishing a new Jewish homeland.[56]

Bloom, however, has serious doubts about Zionism: "Nothing doing, still an idea behind it" (*U*4.200). He won't acknowledge the Zionist pork-butcher, Dlugacz, as a fellow Jew, and ultimately concludes that Zionism is the quixotic dream of a "dying" people:

A dead sea in a dead land, grey and old. Old now. It bore the oldest, the first race. . .the oldest people. Wandered far away all over the earth, captivity to captivity, multiplying, dying, being born everywhere. It lay there now. Now it could bear no more. Dead: an old woman's: the grey sunken cunt of the world (*U*4.222–28).

The son of a depressive, radical convert, Bloom's attitude toward Zionism here embodies not only a self-abnegating sense of Jewishness, but suggests a Weiningerian negativity both Jewish and female. Bloom's anatomical metaphor represents Joyce's metonymic manipulation of one of Weininger's central conclusions:

We have now reached the fundamental difference between the Jew and the woman. Neither believe in themselves; but the woman believes in others, in her husband, her lover or in her children, or in love itself; she has a center of gravity, although it is outside her own being. The Jew believes in nothing, within him or without him. His want of desire for permanent landed property and his attachment to movable goods are more than symbolic.[57]

Bloom's "old woman" metaphor represents the womanliness of the Jews through an allusion not only female, but of female decrepitude – "grey sunken cunt of the world." It would thus appear that Joyce perceived Weininger's own self-hatred as a Jew, and built a similar attitude into Bloom's own "Jewishness." But this is not the case. Rather, the implication throughout *Ulysses* is that Bloom's self-deprecation comes not from a "Jewish nature," but from a lack of a strong, unified identity, which pivots on his denial of his own Jewish identity. But while the experience of June 16 invests him with a new strength of conviction about his "Jewishness," which in turn provokes in him an entirely new – and newly assertive – self-acceptance, his exilic, pacifistic position disallows him to ever rediscover Zionism as a viable alternative.

Weininger's anti-Jewish arguments further impressed upon Joyce that the text's "science" was a smoke-screen for a type of internalized self-hatred of which he as an Irishman was well aware. Conversely, the exhaustive data of Fishberg's *The Jews* seems to have earned Joyce's immediate respect.

Based on research of international scope, Fishberg's *The Jews* examines patterns of assimilation – occupational inclinations, physiognomy, endemic diseases, demographics, tendencies to inter-marry – so as to explore the idea of a Jewish "race" and Jewish "racial traits." The final goal of the study is to raise the debate between assimilation and Zionism by arguing that the Jews are not a race or even a people separate from many dominate cultures. As an assimilated American Jew and fellow of the New York Academy of Sciences, Fishberg was interested in Jewish assimilation as a sociological phenomenon. But while he spent decades compiling the research that went into *The Jews*, the preface and conclusion of his book reveal an agenda hidden behind his empirical data. His central assertion is that Zionism stems from the failure of world Jewry to recognize and benefit from its varied cultural identities, which stem in turn from years of assimilation throughout the globe.

Fishberg's argument, written more than a decade after the publication of *Der Judenstaat*, rebuts one of Herzl's initial assertions: "we [the Jews] have honestly endeavored everywhere to merge ourselves in the social life of surrounding communities and to preserve the faith of our fathers. We are not permitted to do so."[58] Reading both Fishberg and Herzl around 1915, Joyce would have been more inclined to agree with the former's conclusions. In a general manner, Fishberg's attitude supports what Joyce had begun to consider after Nietzsche as the homogenizing role of Jewish influence in European culture. At the outset of the twentieth century, a "good" type of assimilation – one in which Jewish identity was retained yet ameliorated so as to synthesize into host cultures – seemed a plausible solution to the Jewish question. While Joyce may be included among these hopeful assimilationists, his attitude is tinctured with the reluctant but firm suspicion that hatred is more enduring in humans than acceptance.

Fishberg's prefatory comments are meant to color the reader's reception of the ensuing mass of factual data. Relying on his research, he asserts that Jews believe themselves to have been "committ[ing] race suicide" through intermarriage and the subsequent relinquishing of that which makes them distinguishable as a group – dietary laws, daily rituals, and differences in dress.[59] He is confident, however, that his book establishes two aspects of "Jewishness" that combat both the notion of "race" and its "suicide." He argues that the Jews are in no way a "race," because their ethnicity varies the world over – Jewish communities manifest different "racial" features, from Indian, Chinese, Sephardic, Ashkanazi, and more. Through its investigation of these communities and their differences, Fishberg believes his study proves the notion of a single Jewish race to be a myth. He also asserts that intermarriage and assimilation do not eradicate Jewish identity, and that a sense of "Jewishness" can be retained without destroying one's sense of nationality. If Jews could recognize such possibilities, he believes, anti-Semitism would be rendered ineffectual.

Fishberg's argument against a Jewish race is supported admirably through his research. That support also parallels Joyce's own view of racial traits as more myth than truth, not only for Jews, but for his own Irish people as well. Fishberg's second premise, however, seems to stem from the bias of a secular, scientific view, which may have blinded him to the endurance of religious hatred as a continuting factor in the persecution of Jews.

Indeed, in his support of assimilation, Fishberg views not only race but religion to be irrelevant as well; the Jews are not a race, and religion, he asserts, should not be the basis for any nationalism. He also believes the modern, "secular" Jewish and Christian worlds to be nearing a point of complete synthesis:

The fact that differences between Jews and Christians are not everywhere racial, due to anatomical or physiological peculiarities, but are solely the result of social and political environment, explains our optimism as regards the ultimate obliteration of all distinctions between Jews and Christians in Europe and America. . .Both Jews and Christians have been contributing to this end, the former by discarding their separative ritualism, and thus displaying willingness to bridge the gulf which separated them from others, and the latter by legalizing civil marriage.[60]

Although he may have found Fishberg's brand of optimism attractive, Joyce could not accept it in his fiction; while he drew on the book's statistics to inform Bloom's character, Joyce shaped the events of June 16 to contradict Fishberg's hopeful preface here. Bloom has intermarried, converted, and possesses little precise knowledge about his Jewish background or religion. Yet he still must endure anti-Semitism and an identity crisis that cuts to the heart of his well-being as either Jew or Irishman. Moreover, while the citizen of the "Cyclops" episode obviously finds Bloom repulsive as a man, he becomes enraged only after Bloom makes a sacrilegious comment about the incarnation – "By Jesus, says he, I'll brain that bloody jewman for using the holy name" (*U*12.1811). What begins as an argument about Sinn Féin nationalism thus degenerates into a hatred based on the oldest tensions between Jew and Christian. The peace-making abilities of Fishberg's "hard statistics" apparently did not convince the author of *Ulysses*.

And yet, on another level, that hard science caught Joyce's eye; Fishberg's data seems a likely basis for Bloom's and even some of Molly's personal traits. For example, aspects of Bloom's physiognomy may well issue from Joyce's reading of Fishberg. While Fishberg asserts that shortness of stature as a Jewish trait is merely another racial myth, he does report that, on average, Jews of Lithuania and Poland are the shortest, while those in England and the United States have an average height much taller than that of other Jewish communities.[61] Again, this trait stems from the type of populations into which the Jews assimilate. In this manner, Bloom's height, 5'9', becomes less of a clue to Joyce's belief or disbelief in the stereotype of Jewish shortness (*U*17.546). Aside from this, Bloom's "Mediterranean" features also may have been inspired by Fishberg. The book lists such Sephardic features as: "long black hair and beard, large almond-shaped eyes, a melancholy cast of countenance, an oval face and a prominent nose – in short the type of Jews represented in the paintings of Rembrandt."[62] Bloom is reported in "Ithaca" to have a "full build, olive complexion, [and] may have since grown a beard" (*U*17.2003). As another model for Bloom, of course, Svevo had similar Sephardic features, but was not of a "full build."

Fishberg also appears influential in Joyce's construction of Bloom's attitudes toward the Jews as a "nation." In "Cyclops," Bloom is confused about a proper definition of nationhood (*U*12.1423, 1428). Fishberg, on the other hand, believes that the Jews could only be considered a "nation" before emancipation, because then their dress, religious practices, eating habits, and creeds were all for the most part identical. Conversely, he believes emancipation and assimilation to have unequivocally nullified this status. He argues that the idea of Jewish "nationhood" is now only a tool of anti-Semites creating a myth of the Jews as "a separate nation living among other nations."[63] The exact argument was of course a rhetorical centerpiece of nationalistic anti-Semitism throughout *fin-de-siècle* Europe. Fishberg's ideas thus aided Joyce in his rendering of the anti-Semitic taunting of Bloom by the citizen and elsewhere in *Ulysses*. Bloom's putative "Jewishness" is more suspect than it might have been in another place or time because of the aggressive nationalism he encounters in Dublin, in 1904.

Although Molly's Jewish identity remains a contested aspect of *Ulysses*, some features of her character seem borrowed from Fishberg as well.[64] This borrowing may stem from Joyce's desire to have Molly appear Jewish in her darkish features, so as to entice Bloom (as she did Joyce). These include Fishberg's account of Sephardic Jews of Spanish descent returning to Gibraltar after it came under British rule; the popular notion that Sephardic women often have "radiant eyes" and "bewitching elegance and charm"; and that "Spanish and Andalusian women are said by some to owe their charms to these beautiful eyes, which are alleged to have their origin in the small quantities of Semitic blood which flows in their veins."[65] Compare this to Molly's "southern charms," her humming of "two glancing eyes a lattice hid," and her reference to "the rose in my hair like the Andalusian girls used" (*U*18.1338, 1595, 1603). Even more influential, Fishberg includes a page-size print of a "Jewess, Tangier, Morocco."[66] The tableau is a profile portrait of a seated, buxom, dark-haired woman in her mid-thirties. She is dressed in the traditional garb of the Sephardim, and stares pensively – in several ways a portrait of Molly.

The Jews thus offered Joyce a wealth of statistics about Jews the world over, as well as theories of Jewish assimilation and the demythologizing of the concept of a "Jewish Race." The book may have so fascinated Joyce that he sought out more texts offering other arguments about Jewish assimilation and Jewish "racial" traits.

III   RESEARCH PROJECTS – MORE BOOKS ABOUT JEWS

Joyce's reading of Fishberg was undertaken around the same period as his reading of Turgenev's short story "The Jew," as well as Herzl's *Der Judenstaat*, Wagner's *Judaism in Music*, Carlos Cattaneo's *Ricerche economiche sulle interdizioni imposte della legge civileagli israeliti*, and Sacher's *Zionism and the Jewish Future*. Each of these texts played a role in shaping Bloom and representations of "the Jew" in *Ulysses*.

Turgenev's story plays on stereotypes of the Jew as cowardly, unprincipled, and willing to huckster anything – including a daughter. The Russian soldiers in the story who encounter the Jewish antagonist find him repugnant in appearance, language, and behavior. Joyce's admiration of Turgenev as a novelist may well have lent a certain amount of credence to his reading of the short work's portrayal of this itinerant Jewish merchant. But the Jewish character in the story is a "*shtetl Jew*," one who has little direct connection to the urbanized, assimilated Jew Joyce was constructing in Bloom.

Herzl, on the other hand, had answered for himself, and perhaps for Joyce as well, the Jewish question of race and assimilation more relevant to urban Jews:

We are a people – one people.
We have honestly endeavored everywhere to merge ourselves in the social life of the surrounding communities and to preserve the faith of our fathers. We are not permitted to do so. In vain we are loyal patriots, our loyalty in some places running to extremes; in vain do we make the same sacrifices of life and property as our fellow citizens; in vain do we strive to increase the fame of our native land in science and art, or her wealth by trade and commerce. In countries where we have lived for centuries we are still cried down as strangers, and often by those whose ancestors were not yet domiciled in the land where the Jews had already had experience of suffering.[67]

Whether Joyce found Herzl's Zionism a convincing solution for the Jewish question is debatable. But the passage's theory of Jews as united the world over by the ubiquitous prejudice leveled against them earned Joyce's empathy. As one of Herzl's arguments against the viability of complete assimilation, the Jews are "a people" not because of common racial bonds, but because of their universal victimization.[68] This definition of "Jewishness" is of course one of the most solid platforms upon which Leopold Bloom can claim his own Jewish identity; no matter what he feels himself to be – Irishman, Irish-Hungarian, Jewish-Irishman or Irish Jew – his community perceives him to be solely and unequivocally a Jew, and thus as the Other.

Wagner's text, *Das Judenthum in der Musik*, is based on this perception of Jews as a distinct race of "strangers." Wagner asserts that because these "wanderers" have no culture of their own, they have made a "science" of aping the language and art of the most influential cultures of Europe. Postulating that art and music are extensions of speech, Wagner claims the Jews, as a people who must adopt the speech of the dominant culture, can never create their own art-language. Lacking any racial genius, the Jews can only mock the work of their host culture: ". . .in the position of a foreign tongue to the

Jew has our entire European civilization remained. . .the Jew can naturally but echo and imitate, and is perforce debarred from fluent expression and pure creative work."[69]

This argument offered Joyce another parallel between the Irish and what Wagner calls *Judenthum* or "Jewdom." Joyce was born into a generation of Irishmen who made it their mission to create an Irish art which could not be accused of a similar mimicry of English culture. While Joyce did not think himself part of the Renaissance, he nonetheless shared the movement's belief that an "Irish literature" could be written in the English tongue. Leaders such as O'Leary, Yeats, and AE all wrote the majority of their works in a language not "racially" Irish, and at times Yeats had indeed opposed Hyde's vision of a Gaelic speaking Ireland. To Joyce, of course, the very notion of an Irish nationalism built on racial Gaelicism was preposterous. In *Ulysses*, Irish art is symbolized for Stephen in the cracked looking-glass of a servant, implying that self-reflexivity for the Irishman can only be fragmented (U1.146). But even if Stephen recognizes that his "soul frets in the shadow of [the English] language" (P, v), Joyce – as well as most Renaissance writers – demonstrated that a people can "adopt" a language and over generations make it their own. Joyce even believed that such "borrowing" went beyond mere competence; he insisted that in the case of the Irish, having a language forced on them created the necessity of forging a unique literature out of the imposed tongue: "The Irish, doomed to express themselves in a language not their own, have stamped it with their genius and compete for glory with other civilized countries. . .this is called 'English literature.'"[70] Finally, beside this linguistic controversy, Joyce realized by this moment in his career, that Wagner was merely stretching for new arguments to express his incontinent hatred of Jews; Joyce had already come to believe that the Jewish contribution to modern European culture was essential.

Carlo Cattaneo, an economist for the *Risorgimento*, wrote his essay in 1836 in response to an argument between France and Switzerland surrounding the right of Jewish citizens to own land in areas where they were traditionally forbidden to do so. Cattaneo offers a clear defense of the "treachery" of Jewish usury: since the Jews had been forbidden for centuries to become part of mainstream European economy, they were forced to become moneylenders. By continuing this situation for so long, and barring Jews from higher education and liberal occupations, European cultures failed to take advantage of such a resourceful people. Cattaneo presents examples of emancipated Jews, who by their achievements demonstrate what occurs when a Jew is "set free":

Mendelssohn, who wrote excellently on the immortality of the soul, was a Jew; Spinoza, who made his name in the boldest flights of idealism, was a Jew; the engraver Jesi is a Jew, the composer Meyerbeer is a Jew; Basvi, the lawyer who defended Andrea Hofer in Mantua, is a Jew; Rubino Ventura, a Jew from Modena, leads the army, which he trained in European tactics, of the powerful sovereign of Lahore. The art of usury is not a matter of blood, but one of education and rank; and the Jews are capable of other kinds of goods and other kinds of evil.[71]

This listing of notable Jews as a means of defending the Jewish people is a prototype of Bloom's litanies of famous Jews in the "Cyclops" and "Ithaca," and Dominic Manganiello as well as several other critics of *Ulysses*, have previously observed the parallel.

In Zurich, Joyce purchased Harry Sacher's *Zionism and the Jewish Future*, a collection of essays concerning the development of Zionism as both an idea and a reality. Sacher, a Zionist writer and associate of Chaim Weizmann, would be instrumental in helping to draft what was ultimately to become the Balfour Declaration. The introduction to *Zionism*, written by Weizmann himself, attempts to justify a Jewish homeland in Palestine through a discussion of historical anti-Semitism. By the close of his essay, Weizmann presents a simile that must have pleased Joyce:

When the aim of Zionism is accomplished, Palestine will be the home of the Jewish people, not because it will contain all the Jews in the world, but because it will be the only place in the world where the Jews are the masters of their own destiny. . .Palestine will be the country in which Jews are to be found, just as Ireland is the country in which Irishman are to be found, though there are more Irishmen outside of Ireland than in it.[72]

Sacher's text also offered hard statistics about the growing number of farm cooperatives and plantation companies in Palestine. It was indeed from articles such as S. Tolkowsky's "The Jews and the Economic Development of Palestine," that Joyce shaped the parodic "Agendath Netaim" advertisement that Bloom discovers in the "Calypso" episode.[73]

Perhaps most fascinating of Joyce's borrowing from Sacher's text, however, are the possibilities presented in the last essay, "The New

Jew: a Sketch" by Nachum Sokolow, another close colleague of
Weizmann.[74] The narrative telescopes Sokolow's meetings over the
years with an acquaintance who he first met as "a much sought after
young *bocher* in the *Bet-Hamidrash* of [his] birthplace."[75] Encountering
the young man years later, the narrator is disappointed that the
erstwhile Talmudist has become disenchanted with the Judaism of
emancipated Jewry. Joyce appears to have been fascinated with the
protests of the unnamed and self-proclaimed "outsider," who asserts
that Jews have lost their ancient sense of a centered, organic
Jewish-self. Most influential to Joyce, however, was "the outsider's"
answer to the narrator's question, "[a]re you, then, a Jewish
Nationalist?":

If nationalism means hostility, the persecution of other nations, narrow-
mindedness and racial fanaticism, I reject it. It is opposed to all my
convictions, impulses, longings and interests as a Jew. But if nationalism
means being at one with one's own people, then I am a Jewish nationalist.[76]

The passage is a blueprint for Bloom's rebuttal to the citizen's
jingoism in "Cyclops": "Persecution [says Bloom] all the history of
the world is full of it. Perpetuating national hatred among nations"
(*U*12.1417–18). It is this episode in which Bloom declares himself a
Jew for the first time; Joyce found a ready guide in the "outsider's"
struggle for a "new Jewish identity." Sokolow's acquaintance,
however, eventually heals himself by moving to Palestine: he becomes
a farmer and thus reestablishes his "Jewish center" by living close to
the land of his forefathers. Joyce, of course, had other plans for Bloom,
who as a marginal Jew and urbanized Irishman doubts the very
plausibility of Zionism.

From reading these above texts and still others, Joyce became acutely
aware of the prevalence and contradictions of European anti-Semitism.
Fishberg in particular offered a cogent argument that the concept of a
"Jewish race" was a fallacy. Instead, the text provided support for the
variety of Jewish peoples, aiding Joyce in the construction of Bloom's
complexity, which embodies many different cultural influences, yet
retains the longing for his father's legacy of an acknowledged Jewish
identity.

Joyce's own notions about "Jewishness" were expanded greatly
through his encounter with the above texts. But his friendships with
Jews, especially Ettore Schmitz, were irreplaceable as vehicles

through which he learned of the paradoxes of Jewish assimilation. Joyce and Schmitz eventually shared a mutual respect that lent itself to the broadening of both individuals – a commitment that played a key role in the shaping of Bloom and of the central ideas in *Ulysses*.

CHAPTER 7

Cunning: The miracle of Lazarus times two –
Joyce and Italo Svevo[1]

The basic facts of Joyce's friendship with Schmitz were first presented
in the original Ellmann biography (1959). But while references to
Schmitz as a model for Bloom have since become standard fare in
Joyce studies, Svevo's status as a literary artist whose work influenced
Joyce's constructions of "the Jew" has largely been ignored. Joyce's
pre-*Ulysses* reading of Svevo's first two novels indeed begs investigation
as a central moment of the former's awareness of how a character can
embody a certain "Jewishness" without the necessary attributes of
Halachic Jewish identity. To understand this intertextual influence,
however, Svevo's own sense of "Jewishness," as one who was raised in
a Catholic culture, eventually converted to that religion, and yet
professed atheism throughout his life, must be grasped. This chapter
thus reviews Svevo's Jewish background and adult perception of his
Jewish identity, the fortuitous meeting of Joyce and Schmitz, and
finally the influence of the older Triestine's work on the younger
Irishman.

As an outcome of the reputation he earned through his Berlitz
tutorials, Joyce began in 1907 to tutor Schmitz, at the time an unread
Triestine novelist who had written under the pseudonym "Italo
Svevo."[2] Within two years of that meeting, however, Schmitz would
play a critical role in the completion of *A Portrait*. But Schmitz's
advice about the composition of *A Portrait* was only one of many
positive outcomes of the relationship between himself and Joyce.
From the beginning, the younger tutor and older student discovered
they had an unexpected rapport. Schmitz's wife, Livia, explained
that Joyce was delighted to find in Schmitz "a mentality similar to his
own, an analytic method he found congenial."[3]

Compared to Joyce's other Triestine acquaintances, Schmitz was
curiously complex: a novelist, a Jew, an Irredentist, a convert, a
devoted husband, and an apathetic businessman who often hid

155

behind the facade of being a mundane bourgeois. Fascinated with Schmitz's Hungarian–Triestine–Jewish background, Joyce became intrigued with him immediately. As their friendship grew, the two soon discovered that they shared a similar cynical enthusiasm, a temperament that was at once wry yet often piously compassionate. When they exchanged writings, each also gained a profound respect for the other as an artist. But for Joyce, Schmitz's work was of interest not only because of its avant-garde nature, but because both the man and his characters represented a secular "Jewishness" with which Joyce was growing more and more fascinated.

Joyce came to regard Schmitz as a friend, a father-figure mentor, and a symbol of Jewish marginality; Schmitz's presence caused Joyce to once again revise "the Jew" he had been refiguring since he left the insular world of Dublin. The relationship he built with Schmitz also contributed to his psychological awareness as an author; indeed, Joyce's growth as a writer and his knowledge of the complexity of Schmitz's "Jewishness" were inseparable. Schmitz's devotion to Naturalistic literature, his self-ironic humor, and his eventual disclosure that he was a novelist all seem to have formed the initial bonds between him and Joyce. And although by 1907 Joyce had in fact met many of Trieste's prominent Irredentists and intellectuals, Schmitz became the object of Joyce's interest and affections in a manner quite different from those other acquaintances.[4]

From all biographical accounts, Schmitz appears to have been a kindly, introspective, highly creative man. While he believed himself to be a competent writer, and had been publishing since his adolescence, he seems always to have been riddled with self-doubt. Although he converted to Catholicism in later life, he was raised in a family that practiced the Jewish religion and associated exclusively with other Jews. His continual witticisms were almost always directed against himself, suggesting a type of humor Freud labeled as indicative of a particularly "Jewish" self-irony.[5] The protagonists of Schmitz's novels are overtly autobiographical, and Joyce recognized this fact immediately.

Considering Schmitz's own Jewish background and his warm, self-deprecatory temperament, scholars have of course long suggested him as a model for Bloom.[6] It was indeed after developing an intimacy with his new friend for seven years that Joyce finally began his "Hunter story" as a novel.[7] Stanislaus stated that after the war Svevo had "asked him to tell him something about Ireland and the

Irish – My brother had been talking to him so much about Jews that Svevo wished to get even with him by holding forth on the Irish.''[8] But despite these established influences, many aspects of the two writers' relationship remain unclear. Did Joyce perceive Schmitz from the outset of their relationship as Jewish? Did he perceive Schmitz as a manifestation of "the Jew" he had been constructing since the Hunter incident? Did the protagonists of Svevo's novels serve to reinforce this view of "Jewishness" for Joyce? Did the author and his novels affirm Joyce's assumptions about "Jewish doubt" and "Jewish cunning?" We can begin to answer such questions by first exploring Schmitz's background and his own sense of "Jewishness."

I   ''IS HE A JEW OR A GENTILE OR A HOLY ROMAN OR A
         SWADDLER OR WHAT THE HELL IS HE?''

Schmitz was born of Jewish parents and ritually circumcised, and the atmosphere of his boyhood home indicates his Jewish identity was deeply ingrained from the start. In adulthood this self-image would indeed always take precedence over his Catholic identity. While the Schmitzes did not keep the laws of *Kashrut*, they did observe the Sabbath and all the Jewish holidays. P. N. Furbank suggests that the Schmitzes were in high regard as "good Jews" in their Jewish community, and cites the fact that in 1880 Svevo's father, Francesco Schmitz, was elected *Hatan Bereshit* of his congregation.[9] In addition to any Yiddish used in his home, Schmitz read Hebrew as a young man and may have retained the ability throughout his life.

Schmitz's conversion to Catholicism after the birth of his first child, as well as his lifelong atheism, have often been suggested as the basis for both Bloom's religiously diverse background as well as his agnosticism. But while Schmitz, just as Bloom, was never certain if religion had much validity whatsoever, neither could escape his own ethnic Jewish identity. As an adult, Svevo's religious orientation became irrelevant to his perception of his own "Jewishness." And by 1907, Joyce also understood religion – that is, its practice and belief – not to be the only criterion through which to judge Schmitz a "Jew."

Francesco Schmitz early on wanted to instill in his children a pride in their heritage as German-speaking subjects of the Austro-Hungarian Empire. While his sons were young he made arrangements for both to attend the Brussel Trade and Education Institute in the village of Segnitz-am-Main near Würzburg, a school for the sons of Jewish businessmen. The headmaster at the time of Ettore's attendance was a Jew from Hesse named Samuel Spier, whose dominance at the school included attempts to maintain a cultural awareness for his Jewish students. During his years there, Schmitz visited Vienna and other cities in Austria, and his latter years at Segnitz coincided with Georg von Schoenerer's Austrian campaign of the Pan-German anti-Semitic movement. Returning from a visit to Vienna in 1885, Elio, Schmitz's youngest brother, had told his family "I saw no one but anti-Semites."[10] But in Trieste, the Schmitz family did not encounter such overt anti-Semitism. Furbank relates that because of the age, acceptance, and assimilation of its Jewish community, anti-Semitism in Trieste was minimal.[11] This assertion about the city may well be true, especially during Ettore's formative years. When he returned to Trieste in 1878, however, Schmitz encountered anti-Semitic rebuffs.

By 1880 Schmitz had made several desultory attempts at the beginning of a writing career, and his foundering encouraged his father to help him find a business career. Francesco soon obtained an interview for Ettore at the enterprise of Mettle Brothers, a German business in Trieste. After waiting for hours in their anteroom, however, Schmitz was never called for the interview. Elio Schmitz later said that "nothing came of [the interview] because the applicant [was] an Israelite."[12] Suffering this insult, Schmitz for the first time in his life felt the sting of personally directed anti-Semitism. And it was no coincidence that his next writing venture was a brief article on Shakespeare's *The Merchant of Venice*. Accepted by *L'Indipendente* on December 2, 1880, the article was in fact his first publication.

The premise of his essay, "Shylock," states that its author, "like that renegade Heine," is concerned with "reconcil[ing] his enthusiasm for Shakespeare with the veneration he still felt for the beliefs of his ancestors."[13] The piece absolves Shakespeare of any anti-Jewishness, and proclaims that Shylock embodies the victimization of ghetto Jews and their "inmost suffering essence." Although Schmitz wrote the essay in anticipation of the opening of the play at the city's theater, its theme nonetheless portrays his early recognition of the legacy of prejudice against the Jews. The essay also foreshadows Schmitz's growing sense of secular Jewish identity – as in his later statement "It isn't race that makes a Jew, it's life."[14]

Although the anti-Semitic movement never gained a foothold in Trieste, there were several attempts to stir anti-Semitic sentiment there during Schmitz's lifetime. In 1898, a Jesuit named Pavissich began a series of political lectures that attacked the city's powerful National Liberals and Socialists and slandered the Jews. During that same year, Karl Lueger, the president of the anti-Semitic Viennese Christian Socialist Party, came to campaign in the city but was generally unwelcome. In 1899, however, the Triestine Christian Socialist periodical *L'Avvenire*, published a feature titled "the Jew and his Portrait," which portrayed Triestine Jews with "monstrously" stereotypical features.[15] While Schmitz never commented publicly on these incidents, he was certainly aware of them.

Schmitz married Livia Veneziani in 1896, and entered the segment of the Triestine business community that had welcomed intermarriage between Catholic and Jew for nearly a century. Livia was the daughter of Gioachino Veneziani, the wealthy manufacturer of a patended anti-corrosive paint.[16] After the birth of their first daughter, Livia Schmitz fell seriously ill and began to claim that her sickness was a consequence of the sin of having married a Jew; Schmitz in return suggested he make a present to her of his baptism. Characteristically, he said of Livia's reaction to his offer that "[m]y poor wife, still suffering from fever, received the news with such joy that I have never troubled to decide whether it was the Jewish God or the Christian who performed the miracle."[17]

Living in liberal Trieste, however, Schmitz came to believe "Jewishness" was as much a state of mind as it was a religious or racial affiliation. Because he was an atheist, his view of "Jewishness" did not include a belief in the "Jewish destiny" of having to reconcile oneself to God or religion. But Schmitz's comments on the subject suggest his sense of "Jewishness" included a melancholy pessimism based on an acute awareness of historical injustice. Livia Schmitz described her husband's disposition as "melancholy [from] accepting that suffering was an inevitable part of life."[18] Schmitz's remark about Kafka attests to his sense of Jewish identity as characterized by this melancholy: "Yes, he was a Jew. Certainly, the Jew's position is not a comfortable one.'[19] Schmitz implies that melancholy is not an innate, "racial" quality, but a product of the Jew's subject position. Joyce's view of the Irish as a melancholy people found a parallel here. By 1907, Joyce had not only denied the idea of the "pure race" of his Celtic background, but had called James Clarence Mangan's melancholy "a type of his race," only in so far as "history encloses him so straitly that even his fiery moments do not set him free from it."[20]

During his now famous lecture on Joyce in 1927, Svevo revealed some other aspects of his perception of "Jewishness." After describing Bloom as "the little Jew who delights us and arouses our compassion," he explained that Bloom is the true "dreamer" – one who dreams with a foot in reality. He named this temperament *"Il fantastico practico,"* the practical dreamer. Svevo was recognizing his own double in Bloom. The unspoken connection – which Joyce perceived as well – is that this practical dreaming is an ingredient of Svevo's sense of his own "Jewishness"; Joyce, of course, perceived parallels in the "Jewish dreamer" and the typical "Irish nature."[21] Curious as well is Svevo's description of Bloom as a "little" Jew. In the "Ithaca" episode we discover that Bloom is 5'9½", hardly a "little" stature (*U*17.86–87). Despite this fact, it appears Svevo's perception of Bloom may have included the aspect of Jewish stereotype that depicts male Jews as smallish compared to their "European" counterparts. Included in the image of Jewish diminutiveness was an implied sense of both physical weakness and disease. And indeed, Svevo's own self-image as a Jew was affected by such stereotypes of "Jewish disease," especially as a mental pathology; his autobiographic protagonists are all highly nervous, timid, psychologically troubled, and obsessively introspective.

Several years after Schmitz's marriage, an English admiral suggested that the family open a branch of their business in Britain. Because Schmitz knew a smattering of English, he was chosen to make the trip to discuss the matter further. In a few months his wife joined him, and they later managed a trip to Ireland. Although the Irish countryside "delighted" Schmitz in all its "beauty and peace," once again "the difficulties his slight knowledge of English caused at every step depressed him."[22] Because he had to return to England several times in the subsequent years, in 1907 he decided to begin again the English lessons he had dropped in 1903. He inquired about such lessons at the Scuola Berlitz, and during his inquiry was delighted to be informed about a witty young Irishman who had gained a reputation as a private tutor among the wealthy of the city.[23] He soon contracted Joyce for thrice weekly lessons for both him and his wife.

II "JEWGREEK IS GREEKJEW: EXTREMES MEET"

From its beginning, the interaction between Schmitz and Joyce was anything but simple language instruction. Student and teacher very soon left grammar behind and embarked on conversations about literature and other varied topics. From all appearances, theirs was the type of enthusiastic dialogue that occurs when two people unpredictably discover themselves to be of like mind. As Schmitz helped Joyce with idiomatic Triestine expressions and Joyce shaped the phrasing of Schmitz's English, each became fascinated with the other's opinions. Schmitz was twice the age of his young teacher, and their friendship, although warm and gracious, had a kind of respectful formality.[24]

Joyce may have reminded Schmitz of his once close companion, the painter Umberto Veruda. After years of brotherly relations with Schmitz, Veruda had died suddenly in 1904 at the young age of thirty-seven. Veruda lived a Bohemian life of flamboyant dress, drinking, and frequent travel. To Schmitz, he appeared to be a living antithesis of the mercantile-bourgeois atmosphere of his father's and the Veneziani households. Livia Schmitz reveals that when Veruda died, she saw her husband "for the first time lying on his bed, weeping like a child."[25] Much later in life, after Joyce immortalized Livia through using her long hair and name as models for the character of Anna Livia Plurabell, Schmitz sent Joyce a portrait of his wife painted by Veruda.[26] Livia observed that after Veruda's death something died in her husband. When Joyce surfaced in Schmitz's world, however, the young man appeared to be an "Irish Veruda."

Reciprocally, Joyce felt that his new student would make a good sounding-board for his writing. Before the close of their first year of lessons, Joyce had brought the manuscripts of both *Chamber Music* and *Dubliners* to the Schmitz household. Joyce did not make a habit of offering his works to new acquaintances. But he must have believed that Schmitz would be an intelligent and trustworthy audience. Stanislaus indeed states that Schmitz and Joyce

rarely met except as middle-aged pupil and boyish teacher, yet such meetings were as useful to my brother as to Svevo. Any literary artist who plays the part of Robinson Crusoe for a long time does so at his own peril; and from the time when my brother left Dublin until the Great War sent him to Zurich, Svevo was the only man of letters with whom he was on terms of some intimacy.[27]

That intimacy not only motivated Joyce to offer his books to Schmitz, but on one occasion, having been encouraged by Livia, Joyce actually read to the couple the entire manuscript of "The Dead."[28] When

Joyce finished, Schmitz congratulated him while Livia quietly left the room; she returned with a bouquet of flowers she had picked from her garden and presented them to Joyce. The moment of recognition was, according to Stanislaus, "the first genuine and spontaneous sign of pleasure in the literary work of that outcast artist."[29] And while Joyce felt proud over the display of appreciation for his talents, the reading also precipitated a personal disclosure from Schmitz.

Soon after Joyce's reading, Schmitz revealed that he was a novelist himself who had given up writing shortly after his marriage and the publication of his second novel. He presented Joyce with "two little blue-bound volumes with yellowing pages, *Una Vita* [*A Life*] and *Senilità* [*As a Man Grows Older*]."[30] After recognizing the quality of Schmitz's work, Joyce soon committed himself to helping the world rediscover Ettore Schmitz as Italo Svevo. Furbank tells us that Joyce had returned to his flat on the evening that Schmitz had offered the novels and told Stanislaus, "Schmitz has given me two novels of his to read; I wonder what kind of thing it is."[31]

When he arrived at the Schmitz household for the next lesson, Joyce had finished reading both works. He subsequently learned that the novels had been published years before, were badly reviewed, and had fallen into obscurity – thus ending "Svevo's" career as a novelist. Joyce informed Schmitz that he was a neglected great writer, and that there were passages in *Senilità* that rivaled the best prose of Anatole France. If Stanislaus' memory serves, Joyce had already memorized a few of the passages he admired, and quoted them to Svevo with "huge satisfaction."[32] According to Livia, this was one of the most exhilarating moments of her husband's life:

These unexpected words [from Joyce] were a balm to Ettore's heart. He gazed wide-eyed at Joyce, delighted and amazed. Never had he thought to hear such praise of his forgotten novels. That day he could not leave Joyce; he accompanied him all the way back to his home Piazza Vico, telling him about his literary disappointments. It was the first time he had opened his heart to anyone and showed his profound bitterness.[33]

Stanislaus described Joyce's reaction by stating that "[m]y brother has never praised nor disparaged half-heartedly."[34] And this assessment was demonstrated over the ensuing twenty years; after congratulating Schmitz, Joyce began to spread his high opinion of the books around Trieste's literary and journalistic circles. Most of his pupils and associates, however, "laughed in his face," claiming Svevo's Italian was "impure" – the Triestine dialect rather than the "literary" Tuscan – and that his novels could not be taken seriously. Joyce called the detractors "semi-illiterates," and continued to claim Svevo was the only modern Italian writer in which he had any interest. Some fifteen years later, Joyce's hopes of bringing Svevo to the world were fulfilled. In 1926, after Joyce gave copies of *The Confessions of Zeno* to Valéry Larbaud and Benjamin Cremieux, Schmitz's writing became a Parisian *cause célèbre*; by 1930, Svevo's reputation was secured.[35]

After Joyce's initial affirmation of Svevo's talent, the latter's commitment as a friend and admirer became unshakable. While Joyce continued to give "lessons" to his friend, the face of their relations changed irrevocably. Schmitz would now often visit Joyce's flat at 32 via Baerriera Vecchia and remain there until late into the night, discussing literature and laughing with his friend.[36] After about a year of this new level of intimacy, Joyce felt Svevo would make a good critic of his own work. And by February, 1909 Joyce had given Schmitz the novel he had been salvaging from the former *Stephen Hero* and was then struggling to finish – a struggle that by April of that year had come to a complete impasse.

To disguise his frustration, Joyce offered the unfinished piece as a new type of English lesson: he asked Schmitz to read chapters I through III and write a criticism of them as an English exercise.[37] The request, however, was obviously one born of desperation rather than of inventive pedagogy; Joyce had not only found himself lost for nearly a year as to where to move in the novel after chapter III, he had also spent the entire year discouraged at not finding a publisher for the completed *Dubliners*. For one of the first times in his life, Joyce had severe writer's block. But miraculously, Svevo's written response woke Joyce from his nightmare of unproductivity and gave him the impetus to finish the novel.

In the letter, Schmitz supports Joyce's decision to include the full texts of the sermons Stephen hears in chapter III, and praises Joyce's Naturalistic detail. He also admonishes Joyce against giving "the appearance of strength to things which are in themselves feeble, not important. . .if you had to write a whole novel with the only aim of description of everyday life without a problem which could affect strongly your own mind. . .you would be obliged to leave your method and find artificial colours to lend to the things the life they wanted in themselves."[38] Schmitz's imagined "whole novel of everyday life" made an impression on Joyce; he seems to have reserved the criticism as a challenge toward the shape of his next project. But the more tangible reaction to the letter was Joyce's announcement to Stanislaus a few days later that he was ready to get back to work.[39] He did, indeed, revise parts of chapter 1, which, along with the other chapters, now contained Svevo's handwritten editing, as Joyce had requested. Joyce went on from that point steadily to finish *A Portrait*. He seems also to have been infused with new courage about the publication of *Dubliners* – he sent the manuscript off to Maunsel & Co. in Dublin very shortly thereafter.

Schmitz's comments about retaining the sermons may have been accepted not so much because of their content, but because of their source. Nineteen years older than Joyce, Schmitz always appeared to the young writer as avuncular, if not as a compassionate father-figure. Moreover, Schmitz at some point also seems to have represented to Joyce an antithesis to his own biological father. Although of the same generation as John Joyce, Schmitz did not drink, gamble, nor boast about his money or his past; he was a devoted father and husband; he was soft-spoken and by some accounts even shy. In Zurich, it was Schmitz's portrait, and not that of his own father, that hung above Joyce's desk.[40] Perhaps most significant to Joyce was the creative energy and healthy curiosity at the center of Schmitz's temperament; Joyce saw in those qualities a reflection of his own.

Schmitz, of course, was also a Jew. Joyce had retained the belief from his Catholic background that Jews were the spiritual fathers of Christianity, even though they had betrayed Christ and thus fallen from their chosen status. Through his ongoing reading of Nietzsche, however, he had been able to discard completely the representation of the Jews as deicidal. Now his perception of the Jews was influenced by their secular image as marginalized Europeans, yet as one of the "strongest" contemporary peoples in Europe. Schmitz was a type of Jew who Joyce had never met before; he was not reminiscent of the immigrant shopkeepers Joyce knew of in Dublin, nor was he like the "*shtetl* Jews" Joyce had encountered in Heijermans' *Ahasverus*. Schmitz was precisely the type of Jew Joyce had begun mentally constructing: continental, multi-cultural, and polyglot; alienated, introspective, kind, creative, and self-ironic; an artist yet a family man; cynical yet humble; pragmatic yet a daydreamer – "*Il fantastico practico.*" Joyce thus transformed Schmitz into a kind of benevolent "Jewish European father" even by the time he received the latter's advice about *A Portrait*.

Schmitz also exemplified to Joyce how one could be non-practicing or perhaps even non-matrilineally Jewish (as in Bloom's case) and nevertheless perceive oneself as a Jew. This sense of Jewish identity laid the groundwork for Bloom's final recognition of his own "Jewishness." Schmitz's warmth and hospitality, moreover, may have reinforced Joyce's memory of his possible brief but influential encounter with Alfred Hunter. The middle-aged Jew helping the young Irishman in this manner became a repeating pattern in Joyce's life, and would soon become both plot-device and motif in *Ulysses*.

Similarities in the above comparisons to Leopold Bloom are obvious. Not so obvious, however, was the direction Joyce's imagination took, from focusing on a young, narcissistic character such as Dedalus to creating a mature, compassionate character such as Bloom. Even as early as 1906 – the year Joyce mentioned his story "dealing with Mr. Hunter" – there seems to have been brewing in his imagination a new character that would represent "everyman" in a manner opposite to that of Stephen's portrayal of "the artist." This everyman to Joyce would be polytypic – Jewish, Christian, atheistic; occidental and oriental; artist, businessman, Samaritan; father, lover, son. Schmitz, and subsequently Bloom, was all of the above, Stephen barely one. During his composition of *Ulysses*, Joyce in fact told Frank Budgen that "Stephen no longer interests me to the same extent [as Bloom]. . .he has a shape that can't be changed."[41]

Indeed, Schmitz's comments were as integral to Joyce's self-worth as they were to his accomplishment as an artist. Joyce's need to create paternal role-models in this manner goes beyond any "anxiety of influence'; it represents his attempt to locate mentor father-figures who became pivotal to his own masculine self-image. The construction of new "good-fathers" embodies Joyce's need to psychologically replace a father whose attention and guidance were erratic, and who seemed to personify the most devastating ends of Irish culture's male gendering; John Joyce's spend-thrift, overly morose, dipsomaniacal, and generally self-delusory nature was of course often an embarrassment to Joyce. All of this hesitancy toward his father made Joyce even more attracted to Schmitz; still more, Joyce found in Schmitz's ambivalence to Judaism and yet strong sense of Jewish identity a correlative for his own "anti-Catholic Catholic Irishness."

In many ways, Joyce's relationship with Schmitz completed his own search for a "good father" – a compassionate older man, indeed perhaps like Alfred Hunter. Joyce's perception of Schmitz as a

"European" writer and attentive older friend may have fused with the image of Hunter as a kind, "good European." Because he perceived both of these men to be unequivocally Jewish, Joyce filtered his perceptions of them through those representions of "the Jew" he had been encountering in so many texts. The combination of living and textual source reinforced his intrigue with European Jewish controversies, and with that growing fascination, "Joyce's Jew" took a decisive step toward becoming the hero of *Ulysses*. But as mentioned above, during his apprenticeship under Schmitz, Joyce also discovered Svevo's art as inspiration for his own. After reading Svevo's first two novels, Joyce ruminated over their autobiographical protagonists for the next seven years. What he ultimately perceived as those characters' "Jewishness" indeed became pivotal to his construction of Bloom.

III   SCHMITZ AS ITALO SVEVO: BACKGROUNDS OF HIS NOVELS

In 1927, after basking in two of the three years of notoriety that came to him just before his death, the sixty-five-year-old Svevo was asked to give a lecture at the literary club of the Milanese publication *Il Convegno*.[42] The director of the salon, Enzo Ferrieri, invited Svevo to give a talk about his old friend James Joyce. Ferrieri also mentioned that he would appreciate it if Svevo would focus specifically on *Ulysses*, a work about which the Milan community had heard much praise but was generally uninformed. In that speech, Svevo stated that: "Joyce, as he would say himself, drew Dedalus forth from his pocket, while he had to go seek Bloom in the wide world."[43] Humility or diplomacy aside, Svevo may not have recognized that the "wide world" in which Joyce sought Bloom was ultimately the Schmitz villa. When once asked why Bloom was of Jewish-Hungarian descent, Joyce responded: "Because he was" – almost certainly a reference to Schmitz.[44] But Joyce also perceived Schmitz's "Jewishness" in the protagonists of his first two novels, *Una Vita* (1889) and *Senilità* (1898).

Schmitz's dream of becoming a novelist had withered in the bud. After placing reviews and short stories in *L'Indipendente*, he published his two novels, both of which immediately fell into obscurity. Schmitz believed his second effort to have been a masterpiece, and the lukewarm reception brought a premature, self-imposed end to his career. In commenting on the reaction to his novels, he stated: "there is no unanimity so perfect as the unanimity of silence."[45] But Schmitz's depression over the rejection of his novels was not the whining of an untalented, self-deluded bourgeois. On the contrary, having survived with little support from his loved ones, his work had grown through the study of some central figures of nineteenth century letters: Schopenhauer, Stendhal, Flaubert, Zola, Freud, and even Weininger, to name only a few. Written in his own dialect, psychologically insightful, and overtly Naturalistic, Schmitz's work was indeed avant-garde. Aside from admiring their narratives, Joyce himself appears to have been curious about the novels' sources. An aspect of that curiosity may have been connections he perceived between those influences and the "Jewishness" he had been constructing from his impressions of Schmitz.

Early on in his career Schmitz had come under the spell of Zola's writing, and Joyce easily identified the Naturalism of the two novels. The moral purpose Zola claims for his work in the preface of the 1877 *L'Assommoir* was enticing to Svevo's non-religious, yet "Jewish" sense of ethics. In Svevo's first two novels, his protagonists, Alfonso Nitti and Emilio Brentani, are traced conspicuously as products of environment and heredity. While coming to understand their actions to some extent, they can in the end only respond to their determined "natures." Joyce recognized an element of Svevo's fictional environment as the atmosphere of the European *mal du siècle*. But what heritage did he perceive as the basis of Svevo's characters' tendencies and actions? As we shall see here, the answer appears to be a Jewish one.

After discovering Schopenhauer, Svevo created his own blend of Zolaesque Naturalism and Schopenhauerian pessimism. At first the two thinkers might seem irreconcilable. But Schmitz's comment that Schopenhauer was "the first to become aware of us – [those] sick people, the sort who think [as] healthy fighters, [similar] to men who act, [related, but] like two different animals," implies a connection to Zola.[46] In creating Nitti and Brentani as this type of "fighter," Svevo demonstrates that "the will" is best depicted through the natural forces that play on a character's destiny – à la Zola. Zola's Naturalism impressed upon Svevo the "truth" of the Darwinian evolution of human character. Just as central to Svevo's beliefs, however, is Schopenhauer's comment that the "observer [was] as much a finished product of nature as the fighter."[47]

Svevo's creation of Alfonso Nitti was, in his own words, to be "precisely the Schopenhauerian affirmation of life which is so close to its negation [so that] the ending of the novel [would be] as abrupt and crude as the member of a syllogism."[48] Nitti was to be an egoist who fails to perceive how threatening his delusions actually are. Refusing to realize both his timidity and superiority complex as products of his immaturity, he ultimately commits what Schopenhauer labels the "useless and foolish act" of suicide.[49] Rather than a crime against God, the individual, or society, suicide was to Schopenhauer an error stemming from faulty reasoning: "suicide thwarts the attainment of the highest moral aim by the fact that, for a release from this world of misery, it substitutes one that is merely apparent. But a *mistake* to a *crime* is a far cry; and it is as a crime that the clergy of Christendom wish us to regard suicide."[50] Recalling religious arguments against suicide, Nitti asserts that they are not so much logical conclusions against the act, as much as expressions of the wish to live.[51] Suicide for Schopenhauer, however, was a useless act because, as an assertion of the will against the will, it could never achieve its goal; the will as the thing-in-itself can never be annihilated. As an emphatic affirmation of will, suicide is an act against moral freedom, the most exemplary form of which is asceticism. Far from being such a renunciation, the suicide "wills life, and is dissatisfied merely with the conditions under which it has come about for him."[52]

Joyce recognized Schopenhauer's ideas about suicide in *Una Vita*, and that influence became another element of the novel that Joyce found relevant to his own construction of "Jewish nature." By the year Joyce left Trieste he had purchased translations of both Zola's and Schopenhauer's work.[53] Thus while Joyce never privileged any German philosopher's rationale over the "sharp sword reason" of Aquinas, he nonetheless was drawn to Schopenhauer's work after reading Svevo's novels. Reading later in Weininger that "the Jew" was inherently self-destructive, Joyce's curiosity about the act of self-annihilation was piqued; his fascination with "Jewish suicide" ultimately found its expression in the pivotal role played by Rudolph Bloom's suicide in *Ulysses*. That suicide, which continually haunts Bloom, can be viewed as a Schopenhauerian assertion of the will against the power of circumstance; for the elder Bloom, "circumstance" was inextricable from his identity as a Jew in Catholic Ireland.

Directly after Svevo's death, Joyce in fact alluded to his belief in the Jewish predilection for suicide. In a letter in 1928 to Harriet Shaw Weaver, Joyce suspected Svevo of the act:

I have also bad news. Poor Italo Svevo was killed on Thursday last in a motor accident, I have no details yet but only a line from my brother and so I am waiting before I write to his widow. Somehow in the case of Jews I always suspect suicide though there was no reason in his case especially since he came into fame, unless his health had taken a very bad turn. I was very sorry to hear of it but I think his last five or six years were fairly happy.[54]

The passage is often suggested as proof of Joyce's acceptance of the stereotype of Jews as cowardly and thus prone to taking their own lives. But Joyce's reading of *Una Vita* and Schopenhauer implies a slightly different version of "Jewish suicide." Rather than an indication of "Jewish weakness," the propensity for Joyce was refigured as an outcome of the willfulness of "the Jew." What first appeared as surrender now expressed, oddly enough, a will to power. In the case of Svevo's "suicide," however, Joyce was unaware when writing his letter that his old friend had not been driving the automobile in question.

Around 1908 Schmitz was introduced to the theories of Sigmund Freud. But like Joyce himself, Schmitz never wanted to admit his art owed any significant debt to Freud. Schmitz also appears not to have considered the science of psychoanalysis as a product of "Jewish thinking" either.[55] Psychoanalysis to him added to one's self-awareness, but was ultimately a process without a goal. Although he had apparently read a good deal of Freud, in 1926 Schmitz would only remark that "I had read some books by Freud in 1908 if I'm not mistaken." Asked about the validity of those theories, however, Schmitz answered with the rhetorical question: "What writer could forgo at least thinking in terms of psychoanalysis?"[56] Notwithstanding these disclaimers, Schmitz's reading of Freud would indeed solidify for some years, and ultimately lay the groundwork for his return to novel writing in *La coscienza di Zeno* (*The Confessions of Zeno*) in 1923.

Perhaps most significantly, Schmitz was also influenced by Otto Weininger's theories. Edoardo Weiss, who Schmitz met through his brother-in-law, introduced the writer to Weininger around 1903. Edoardo, the brother of Joyce's friend in Zurich, Ottocaro Weiss, eventually studied with Freud in Vienna and became one of the first Italian psychoanalysts. (Joyce may have been introduced to both Weininger and Freud through Weiss as well.) In any event, Weininger's conception of "the Jew" as weak, anxiety ridden, and tortuously self-analytic certainly influenced Svevo's construction of his central characters.

One of Svevo's earliest critics, Giacomo Debenedetti, concluded that the author's protagonists were a product of his own self-hatred

as a Jew. After reviewing all three novels, Debenedetti met the
author in 1928. It was on that occasion that Svevo, while discussing
a project on Kafka he had been contemplating, mentioned in his
understated style that the "Jewish position" was "certainly not a
comfortable one."[57] One year later Debenedetti contributed an
article to a special edition of *Il Covegno* devoted entirely to pieces
about the recently deceased Svevo. Debenedetti's essay, entitled
"Svevo e Schmitz," explored Svevo's identity crisis as a bourgeois, a
Naturalistic author, and a self-effacing Jew.[58] This last aspect of
Svevo's personality was demonstrated, according to Debenedetti
(who was a Jew himself), in the creation of self-abasing characters
who are hounded by their author. Debenedetti further suggested
that the protagonists were embodiments of Weininger's depiction of
"the Jew" as decentered, self-loathing, and rampant projector of his
own sense of inadequacy. He asserted that Svevo apparently felt a
kinship with his characters as Jews, yet simultaneously punished
them "with an implacability, a taste for vengeance, recalling the
passionate ferocity of the semitic anti-semite. . .[Svevo] mercilessly
harries his hero and leads him to defeat, yet at the same time he
accompanies him with an intense fellow-feeling, a defensive sympathy
like that of racial solidarity."[59]

While acknowledging Debenedetti's insight, most critics consistently
reject his theory about Svevo's identity crisis with his own "Jewishness."
Furbank believes Debenedetti "got it wrong" when he accused Svevo
of being a self-hating Jew, and Naomi Lebowitz claims that
Debenedetti's "assumptions about Svevo's evasion of his Jewish
heritage remain tenuous and highly questionable."[60] These writers
may be accurate in their aversion to Debenedetti's theory of a direct
influence of Weininger on Svevo. But as a Jew who converted to
Catholicism, an incompetent businessman, and an avant-garde,
alienated artist, Schmitz often felt himself to be outcast from Trieste's
bourgeoisie, and in this position, he did not escape the tincture of a
self-loathing he associated with his Jewish identity. Despite the city's
liberal atmosphere and Svevo's lack of references to Judaism in his
writing, it is absurd to imagine that in the era in which he lived Svevo
lacked a decisive sense of himself as a Jew. An analysis of Svevo's
protagonists is indeed made fruitful when bringing to bear the idea
that they are products of a mind quite affected by *fin-de-siècle* discourse
about "the Jew."

IV　JOYCE READS SVEVO'S ''JEW''

Through studying Svevo's protagonists, Joyce discovered how stereotypical traits can be investigated within complex characterization. He may have read Svevo's protagonists initially as romantic-egoists, unassociated in any direct manner with "Jewishness." But after learning of Weininger's theories, Joyce recognized the "feminized Jew" in the behavior of Svevo's central characters. And Joyce's perception of Schmitz's own "Jewishness" served only to reinforce such a reading. To reconsider Svevo's characters in this manner, however, Joyce had to perceive them as Jewish despite the fact that neither is directly mentioned as such. But one must recall that Joyce's readings of both Nitti and Brentani were entirely informed by the intimacy he had with their creator. Unlike most readers of Svevo, Joyce knew early on just how autobiographical his protagonists actually were. Unlike most readers, Joyce also perceived Schmitz as the embodiment of a type of "Jewishness" he now found fascinating – secular, introspective, humane, and idiosyncratically clever. In this manner, Joyce was preconditioned to read Svevo's autobiographic anti-heroes as "Jewish." That sense of Svevian "Jewishness" resides at the core of Joyce's analysis of both protagonists – linking their traits with Bloom's "Jewishness" affirms this assumption.[61]

The religious ambiguity of Svevo's protagonists may have been a first clue for Joyce. In *Una Vita*, Nitti's religion is cloudy. When visiting his mother's grave it appears he is in a Christian cemetery; later on, he refers to his "Christian" name in his signature on a letter (*A Life*, pp. 311, 391). Both references imply he may be Christian. But given the predominantly Catholic world in which the story is set (obviously an unnamed Trieste), these allusions are easily dismissed as products of a Christian-influenced vernacular. In *Senilità*, Brentani's religion is never revealed, while the characters who surround him speak of confession and are again obviously Catholic. In their random thoughts on God, Nitti and Brentani have a tendency toward agnosticism, if not atheism, and neither character ever speaks of a secular Jewish identity. These same aspects initially seem true of Zeno Cosini, the main character of Svevo's third novel, *Zeno*. This illusion remains until a final memory of his childhood seems to reveal Zeno actually to be a Jew.[62] The progression from Nitti's ambiguous Christianity to Brentani's lack of any religion to Zeno's Jewish identity seems a product of Svevo's coming to terms with his own sense of "Jewishness." Svevo may finally have recognized that those qualities he had been projecting on to his main characters were to him "Jewish." First published in 1923, however, *Confessions* did not affect Joyce's creation of Bloom.

In the second novel, the name Brentani was also a sign from Svevo to his Italian audience. In the north of the country especially, a name derived from a place-name often signals to the Catholic Italian that the bearer may be a Jew. Svevo took the name from the area around the Brenta river, a vacation spot of wealthy northerners, and he may have done so to clue his readers as to the ethnicity of his protagonist. He wouldn't need to belabor the point beyond this; in turn-of-the-century Trieste, Catholic and Jew had mixed so completely that one could readily believe in a character who lived his life as a Catholic but was in fact ethnically a Jew. But whether Joyce would have been sensitive to the name's implication is difficult to know.

Nonetheless, after making his own connections through Svevo's protagonists, Joyce transformed the stereotype of the "weak feminized Jewish male" into the admirably compassionate and engagingly complex Bloom. But inverting stereotype is not the same as denying it. In Joyce's world, stereotype was not often, if ever, questioned as an empowering tool of a dominant culture. The social science of the era is of course replete with premises based on the concept of "racial nature," and indeed, throughout the nineteenth century, stereotype was not a subject of sociological study, but a "truth" about racial "essence." Joyce did not rise completely above those assumptions. In reading these novels after he had established an intimacy with Schmitz, however, Joyce was offered a sounding board to test both stereotype and his changing conception of "the Jew."

Yet Svevo's protagonists are far from mere stereotype or caricature. Rather, they are three dimensional creations whose stories and psychological portraits are quite intricate. But they do portray basic characteristics that embody some of the era's most pervasive stereotypes of Jewish males. Svevo invested each protagonist with an equivocating, timid masculinity he believed was a projection of his own self-image as a Jew, but avoided declaring either of the characters as such. Svevo's joke thus could well have been on himself: the absence of any mention of "Jewishness" in his first two novels seems to have been a product of his own self-abnegation as a Jew; he represented the stereotype, but refused to either acknowledge or explore it.

But Joyce saw through Svevo's smoke screen. He read Nitti and

Brentani as embodiments of the "weak effeminate Jewish nature" he had heard about throughout adulthood. Moreover, Joyce may have been pre-emptively armed with his memory of Hunter as "the compassionate Jewish cuckold'; and, indeed, by his Zurich years, the "Europeanized" Joyce was discovering depictions of "Jewish nature" everywhere. Because they were the literary products of his Jewish friend, Nitti and Brentani became for Joyce part of this composite of "Jewishness."

While Nitti and Brentani never declare themselves Jews, they continually express feelings of alienation from their *petit-bourgeois*, intellectual milieu: they perceive themselves to be more sensitive than other men; they have convinced themselves that they alone among their associates have a true "artist's nature"; they feel their relations with women are much more equivocal than the exploits they hear from others, and they continually berate themselves for "thinking too much." Inveterate daydreamers, they are compelled by their loneliness to imagine an idealized love outside of the bounds of their economic class. Acting on these dreams, however, each discovers himself weak, contradictory, and obsessed with being cuckolded. If an overt struggle for Jewish identity is added to these characteristics, one easily discovers Joyce's Bloom.

Svevo's protagonists are also clerks: Nitti an entry level correspondent for the prestigious Maller bank; Brentani a "subordinate. . .in the Insurance Society" (p. 2). By making them clerks, Svevo gave the characters a position that allows sustenance while promoting a deadly monotony – a situation ripe for the daydreams of the bourgeois romantic. Bloom's daydreams are aided by the nature of his occupation as well; wandering around Dublin, his imagination reels. Before he was a canvasser, Bloom was an actuary for small-time cattleman Joe Cuffe, and a subordinate employee of the Drimmie Insurance Company of Dublin.[63] Working to maintain their *petit-bourgeois* status, Bloom, Nitti, and Brentani become confused about the role of their imaginative, compassionate natures. Unlike Svevo's protagonists, however, Bloom eventually recognizes that his struggle with "Jewishness" includes coming to terms with that compassion.

Moreover, Nitti's and Brentani's occupations are uninspiring because each has unrealized dreams of being a writer. Neither one, however, makes any concerted effort to write; the role is merely another of each man's romantic delusions. Nitti has yet to publish, but decides early on in his narrative to write a study of German idealism and Italian philosophy he tentatively titles *The Moral Idea in the Modern World*. He never writes the first word. Brentani, like Svevo, has published a novel which was initially praised and then forgotten; he has yet to write anything since. Like Bloom, both characters possess a "touch of the artist" about them (*U*10.582). Yet like Bloom as well, neither have a vital commitment to art – they are all paralyzed by obsessive introspection and self-doubt.

Nitti–Bloom

Alfonso Nitti is a twenty-two-year-old man who has come to the city to work in the Maller bank. Immature and egotistical, he continually projects his idealized perception of women on to his elderly mother, whom he characterizes as "so simple, so good" (*A Life*, p. 3). Lonely and homesick, he develops a condescending superiority. An element of that self-image is his desire to live the moral asceticism of the contemplative life – Svevo's version of Schopenhauer's renunciation of the will. Nitti's preoccupation with proving himself a potent male, however, subverts his vision of righteous abstinence.

Nitti rejects as beneath him the attention of Lucia Lanucci, the daughter of the family with whom he is living. Lucia is, indeed, similar to Nitti's mother – working class, uneducated, frail, compassionate. After refusing her, he consoles himself by musing, "Man should be able to live twice, once for himself and once for others. . .If he'd had two lives, he thought, he would dedicate one to the Lanuccis' happiness" (p. 205). That "second life" ironically represents the bourgeois mediocrity Nitti refuses to recognize in himself. His ego is much too fragile to admit how similar his own situation is to that of the Lanuccis.

In reaction to these pressures, Nitti becomes infatuated with the bank owner Maller's daughter, Annetta. A snobbish dilettante, Annetta is aloof and often cruel. While vying for her attention among several other suitors, Alfonso recognizes he is falling in love with her. The narrator, however, suggests the attraction as unrequited and regressive: "He did not go so far as to dream of being loved. . .His was the dream of a vicious boy, in which she abandoned herself to him coldly, for pleasure, to revenge herself on a third person, or even out of ambition" (p. 124). In spite of a haunting guilt about his fantasy, Nitti seduces her.

Nitti indeed delights in punishing himself. He no sooner consummates his love with Annetta than he takes her calculated advice for their "future" and flees the city. Back in his village he tends to his sick mother until she dies. In the "womb" of his hometown he recognizes the destructiveness of his love for Annetta, and renounces her for a life of asceticism. He believes he is "doing right according to a definite moral code" (p. 307). He begins to refigure himself as someone who has always been persecuted because his superiority inspires feelings of jealousy and repugnance (pp. 380–81). He soon returns to the idea that his "nature" will only be satisfied when he has sequestered himself from the world. In the end, his visions of Annetta, his mother, and the "contemplative life" all deflated, he decides that the ultimate asceticism is suicide. He deludes himself into believing he has renounced the will to live, when his suicide is an act of pure will.

Most influential to Bloom, Nitti's defense mechanisms are products of his tendency to internalize. Like Bloom, Nitti is more introspective than those who surround him because, as he himself notes in the beginning of his narrative, he is "timid" – he has the tendency to turn his aggressive will inward (pp. 11, 16). This timidity represents one of the key avenues through which Joyce perceived both Nitti and Brentani as Jews. Joyce was hearing echoes of Nietzsche's theory of the *ressentiment* of the original Hebraic philosophy – the internalization of vengeance. In *Una Vita*, Nitti's timidity is portrayed as solely a product of his Oedipal struggle; his perception of "the female" is caught between the sexual and virginal mother. Confused, he turns his frustration inward. While this tendency is found in Joyce's protagonist as well, Bloom has the added support for his isolation by recognizing, in a very undeluded manner, that he appears as Other to the gentiles who surround him because he is perceived as a Jew. By the end of his narrative Bloom thus believes he has found a locus for his problematic internalizing – his struggle to identify himself as a Jew. And rather than further fragmenting the self, Bloom's "Jewishness" ultimately empowers him. In this manner, Bloom's victory begins in Joyce's recognition of Nitti as a product of Svevo's negative perception of his own "Jewishness." Rather than yielding to the assumption that such "Jewishness" was racial, however, Joyce eventually realized self-abnegation to be a product of the internalization of societal and cultural blame.

As noted earlier, the concept of "the timid feminized Jew" was prevalent in much nineteenth-century social discourse; Weininger merely represents the particular use of the stereotype with which Svevo and Joyce appear to have been most familiar. Nitti is, indeed, "feminized" in the Weiningerian sense. Nitti's self-conceptions are always multiplying and becoming contradictory; he can find no "center." While he recognizes his own willfulness, he also finds he is paralyzed. Repressed to a point of self-loathing, he finds satisfaction in masochistic relationships, not the least of which is his love affair with Annetta.

Earlier on in the narrative, Macario, the aggressive male to whom Annetta ultimately becomes engaged, implies his dominance through a metaphor. Nitti himself acknowledges that Macario's friendliness may be a product of the former's "docility and smaller size" – Nitti's presence buoys Macario's delusion of masculine prowess. In spite of being used in this manner, Nitti reveals that the role "pleases him" (p. 104). Later on, while the two are sailing, Macario points out the predatory nature of some gulls:

"made just for fishing and eating," philosophized Macario. "How little brain it takes to catch a fish! . . . What has brain to do with catching fish? You study, you spend hours at a desk nourishing your brain uselessly. Anyone who isn't born with the necessary wings will never grow them afterwards. Anyone who can't drop like lead on prey at the right second by instinct will never learn . . . One dies in the precise state in which one is born, our hands mere organs for snatching or incapable of holding." (p. 107)

When Nitti subsequently asks, "And have I got wings?" Macario sarcastically replies, "yes, to make poetic flights."

Perceiving himself be of this same ilk, Joyce displaced his own timidity through making his "Jew" embody a "feminized masculinity." Joyce's "Jew" thus eventually disarmed his own anxieties about being a Shem instead of a Shaun.[64] But while Joyce's Shem cannot act, he can dream and he can write. And after perceiving Nitti as the "feminized Jewish male," Joyce must have already begun to recognize that that sense of "Jewishness" was also tantamount to the artistic temperament – the shaper of selves and creator of realities, yet the man who cannot aggress, cannot act. In Svevo's second novel, however, it is precisely the imagination's healing capacity to project, condense, and recreate that the new protagonist discovers as curative.

Brentani–Bloom

If Nitti had survived his suicide attempt, perhaps he would have matured into Emilio Brentani – or Leopold Bloom. Brentani is older and more self-aware than Svevo's first protagonist; he has not only recognized his own tendency to daydream, but has even written and published a novel. Although he is not destroyed by his unconscious conflicts, he still manifests some disturbingly self-destructive behavior. Brentani and Nitti in fact share a melancholy that is nearly identical; Svevo himself claimed that "Alfonso [Nitti] is obviously a blood brother to the protagonists of the other two novels."[65] Yet, Brentani has known the power of being a creator, although he believes his works to be "insignificant" and himself to be "still in the preparatory stage" of life (*Senilità*, p. 2).

Brentani, though, is thirty-five-years-old when the novel opens. Having abandoned his writing, he has spent years in the creative vacuum of nursing his invalid sister, Amalia, and feeling impotent and alone. Once again an egoist with the tendency to internalize, Brentani also idealizes "the female" – or the type of female who can act as the antithesis to the sterile maternalism of Amalia. The opening of the book introduces the dichotomy between the siblings: "he who was an egoist . . . she who was like a mother in her unselfish devotion" (p. 1). As a sickly, maternally compassionate woman who accepts Brentani's timidity, Amalia may have influenced Joyce's creation of Gerty MacDowell in "Nausicaä."[66] When Brentani, out on a stroll, spies the seductive Angiolina Zarri, however, problems begin.

Brentani's love for Angiolina grows strong yet remains duplicitous. He vacillates between acknowledging his (re)creation of her as a virginal vision, and fearing that she is a promiscuous seductress, betraying him with a host of other men. Conscious of his capacity for delusion, Brentani, like Nitti, feels the need to punish himself. But Brentani fulfills this need through subtly encouraging Angiolina to cuckold him. Perceiving himself as disempowered, introspective, and timid, he also believes he deserves to be punished.

Brentani's troubling attitude toward his lover is indeed a prototype for the same in Bloom. Brentani's preoccupation with being cuckolded reminded Joyce of another of his mental pictures of "the Jew," perhaps again based on the actual Alfred Hunter. (One cannot help but also recall Joyce's masochistic and cuckold fantasies throughout his life). From the beginning of his affair, Brentani is aware of transforming Angiolina into an innocent creature of sheer physical beauty. He imagines himself her savior, who through education can rescue her from her prison of poverty and ignorance: "Poor Child . . . In return for the love he hoped to receive from her he could only give her one thing, a knowledge of life and the art of making the most of it" (p. 16). Later in the narrative he expands his fantasy about her "rescue" into an idealized socialism. Angiolina, however, can't understand him, and argues that "the working classes are jealous good-for-nothings, and will never succeed no matter how much you do for them." Brentani soon abandons her education, astonished that his "child of the people" is on the "side of the rich" (p. 165–66). His fantasy about becoming the mentor of a wild, beautiful, "child of the people" plays on his perception of Angiolina as a working-class woman; she is the completely sensuous female who will help him escape his neurotic bourgeois internalizing. Naomi Lebowitz sees in this desire an embodiment of Freud's idea that the subject believes he is "short-circuiting [his] Oedipal conflicts through dalliance with the lower classes."[67]

Joyce himself was of course fascinated with the idea of pygmalionism. He once explained Blake's aversion to cultured and refined women as "his unlimited egoism want[ing] the soul of his beloved to be entirely a slow and painful creation of his own."[68] Joyce would indeed interrupt his composition of *Ulysses* to recreate this type of relationship between Richard Rowan and his wife, Bertha, in *Exiles*. Moreover, Joyce's own relationship with Nora encompassed elements of the same scenario. But Bloom does not seek or even "create" Molly out of a class below his own; he finds her in his own neighborhood.

Like Bloom, however, Brentani knows himself to be a chronic daydreamer. Brentani knows further that he is struggling to create an imaginary woman out of Angiolina, one which he goes as far as renaming *Ange* (p. 43). At times he recognizes Angiolina/Ange as his poem, his novel, his artwork (see p. 147). The actual Angiolina Zarri, however, is little more than an opportunist, and the character whom Brentani ultimately discovers her to be might result from Svevo's partial acceptance of Weininger's theories about women. At the outset of her relationship with Brentani, Angiolina suggests that she become his mistress, and that they both seek out a third party "on whom to put the burden of any complication that might arise from their relationship, and whom it would be great fun to deceive" (p. 32). Already agitated at the photographs of former admirers that decorate her bedroom, Brentani at first rejects this idea, but soon acquiesces. He recognizes the deceit in both her and their relationship, but would rather punish himself as a cuckold than extinguish his romantic delusions.

Thus again like Bloom, Brentani willingly participates in his own betrayal. And just as Bloom enacts a self-punishment by constantly comparing himself to Blazes Boylan, so Brentani negotiates his own masculinity by comparing himself to his friend, the sculptor Stefano Balli. The narrator of the story, in fact, introduces Balli as "a man in the true sense of the word, [who] submitted to no outside influence, and in Brentani's company had almost the sense of being with one of many women who were entirely dominated by him" (p. 11). Brentani is a "woman" in the presence of Balli who is "a true man"; Bloom becomes a woman through his guilt-induced hallucinations in "Circe." Once again Svevo's protagonist is the feminized male, the Weiningerian "Jew." Brentani indeed laments "why could he not be like Stefano and just amuse himself with women" (p. 44).

After Balli meets Angiolina, the suspicion that they are attracted to each other continually haunts Brentani. Balli, on the other hand, reprimands Brentani for his softening delusions about Angiolina. When Brentani invites Balli and one of his girlfriends to dinner with him and Angiolina, Balli indeed succeeds in tempting Angiolina by insulting and teasing her. Brentani dubs the meeting "the veal dinner," suggesting himself as a sacrifice of innocence. The dinner is repeated several times, with "Emilio condemned to silence, Margherita and Angiolina prostrate at the feet of Balli" (p. 78). Brentani's fantasies soon include an image of himself "on his knees before [Angiolina], exactly in the position in which it would have been most easy to humble him, if [she] should have thought fit one day to give him a kick" (p. 80).

The entire scenario is reminiscent of Sacher-Masoch's *Venus in Furs*, a book that was as fascinating to Svevo as it was to Joyce. Joyce not only makes Bloom a reader of Sacher-Masoch, but *Venus and Furs* appears to have suggested to Joyce the "feminized Jew's" masochism as partially homoerotic. Joyce indeed suggested to Frank Budgen that a reader should ultimately recognize "an undercurrent of homosexuality in Bloom as well as his loneliness as a Jew."[69] But after reading Weininger, such aspects of Bloom must have been connected in Joyce's mind through the idea of a "feminized Jewish nature."

Balli, however, soon demonstrates his own egoism to be as fragile as that of his "feminized" friend. Svevo unmasks Balli through the subplot of Amalia's infatuation with the sculptor. When Balli notices the attention that the lonely invalid is paying to him, he is repulsed by her need. Yet, satisfied with the captive audience, he delights in telling his life story to her over several dinners at the Brentani home. When Emilio realizes the infatuation, he finds an excuse to stop the dinners. It is then that he recognizes the depth of his own egoism in his plans for Angiolina. He decides to "devote himself wholly to his sister [and] live for duty alone" (p. 94). But he vacillates between this commitment and the pleasure he receives from Angiolina, which he now fully recognizes as masochistic. Not coincidentally, Balli soon informs Brentani that Angiolina has in fact several other lovers. Concurrently, feeling rejected by Balli, Amalia begins to deteriorate, lapses into delirium, and dies; upon her death she is discovered to have been a secretive alcoholic. The "aggressive and confident" Balli, however, denies any role in Amalia's tragedy. He can only express an ironic admiration for the neighbor who aids Emilio in nursing Amalia in her death throes. When Balli observes, "simple goodness like that moves me more than the loftiest genius," his words ring with hypocrisy (p. 210).

In disclosing Balli's aggressiveness as a flimsy egoism, Svevo introduces the opportunity for Brentani to revise his view of his own sense of masculinity. Initially, Brentani experiences an epiphany about what he imagines as the core of his problems with women: "'Yes,' . . . he felt he was saying something which ought to strike shame . . . into the hearts of all the elect among the human race – 'it is the wealth of images in my brain which makes me inferior'" (p. 111). "The elect among the human race": too much thought, too many visions make of potentially superior men, inferior men. After reading the passage, Joyce must have recalled Weininger's accusation that "internal multiplicity is the essence of Judaism." And it is the stereotypical decentering aspects of "the feminine" that Svevo next makes Brentani perceive in himself. He first recognizes such qualities while observing his sister and Balli: "How like Amalia was to himself . . . the desire to please produced in her a state of embarrassment which made it impossible for her to behave naturally" (p. 120). Thus acknowledging his own submissiveness, Brentani decides to break with Angiolina for "the last time." As he progresses with this plan, he suddenly recalls his past commitment to art, when the death of his father had provoked him to write:

It was then that he had written his novel, the story of a young artist whose intellect and health are ruined by a woman. He had portrayed himself in the hero, his own innocence and gentleness of nature. His heroine he had pictured after the fashion of the time as a mixture of woman and tiger [and] . . . with what confidence he had described her! He had suffered and enjoyed with her and sometimes even felt that he harbored in himself that monstrous hybrid of tiger and woman.(p. 145)

Brentani now realizes how he has been transforming Angiolina, and soon recognizes the process as a means of projecting his own feminine self. Despite the analysis, however, by the end of the narrative Brentani has lost the maternal Amalia and subsequently banished the promiscuous Angiolina. Yet rather than choosing the self-defeat of Nitti's "rationalized" suicide, Brentani is buoyed by a new vision. Memory and desire mix to form a mental image that ultimately synthesizes his dichotomous notions of "the feminine." Key aspects of his perception of both Angiolina and Amalia now become a basis for his own renewed selfhood.

With Brentani's unexpected dynamism, we arrive at the closing climatic moment of *Senilità* that once made a memorable impact on Joyce.[70] Among other qualities, Joyce admired the lyricism of Svevo's Triestine Italian. In translation the passage retains both its lyrical beauty and substantive irony:

Angiolina underwent a strange metamorphosis in the writer's idle imagination. She preserved all her own beauty, but acquired as well all the qualities of Amalia, who died a second time in her. She grew sad and dispirited, her eye acquired an intellectual clarity. He saw her before him as on an altar, the personification of thought and suffering, and he never ceased loving her, if admiration and desire are love. She stood for all that was noble in his thought and vision during that period of his life.

Her figure even became a symbol. It was always looking in the same direction, toward the horizon, the future from which came those glowing rays, reflected in rose and amber and white upon her glowing face. She was waiting! The image embodied the dream he had once dreamed at Angiolina's side, which that child of the people could not understand . . .

Yes, Angiolina thinks and sometimes cries, thinks as though the secret of the universe had been explained to her or the secret of her own existence, and is sad as though in all the whole wide world she could not find one single solitary *deo gratis*.(pp. 244–45)[71]

Brentani infuses his new construction of Angiolina with his sister's compassion and his own idiosyncratic melancholy. And even if the "new Angiolina" can find no "*deo gratis*" in the world, Brentani himself has discovered another grace: the imagination's capacity to transform what was once neurotic projection into revitalized versions of self. In this, Brentani may represent the notion that "cruelty, subterfuge and self-delusion are imperishable," but he nonetheless achieves a kind of balance his blood-brother Nitti could not, and that his heir, Leopold Bloom, would struggle toward and achieve on June 16.[72]

Brentani's ability to form an adjusted self-image from his fragmenting Otherness thus became for Joyce a key aspect of his own revised version of "Jewish cunning." Cunning for Joyce now pivoted on a heightened capacity for strategies that defend against self-destructive behaviors. Bloom's eventual "Jewishness" may be inseparable in this manner from a prominent stereotype of "the Jew"; but, like Nietzsche before him, Joyce's "cunning Jew" represents a positive rather than negative social force. Jews to Joyce were now not "shrewd" because of their financial dealings or conspiratory schemes, but were clever in how they managed their own minds. Disempowered socially, "the Jew" for Joyce re-establishes power through recognizing difference as an *enabling* Otherness – a lesson Joyce himself had learned about his own sense of "Irishness." In Bloom, traits that must be purged from traditional interpretations of masculinity – melancholy, introspection, self-doubt, daydreaming, emotionalism, physical weakness, compassion – become fused into a supremely adaptive self. Thus out of sheer psychological survival, the marginal Jew – like the alienated writer – recreates himself, and in the process exposes his own culturally-based false-consciousness.

Moreover, whether Svevo perceived his protagonists as Jews or not, as their stories unfold it becomes clear that *all* the male characters in his novels delude themselves as to the power and value of their own masculinity. This is true of the confident and aggressive types who seem examples of Weininger's "internally solid Aryan," such as Macario or Balli, or the doubting and unstable protagonists who can be likened to "Weininger's Jew." Considering, then, how fragile each of these male characters become, in the final analysis Svevo's supposed displacement of his own "inferior Jewish masculinity" on to his protagonists must be read as ironic. All of his males are "weak" in that they are prone in some manner or another to immense self-delusion. Yet his "Jewish" characters, despite this, reach surprising levels of self-recognition – an ability he unequivocally denies to the other characters.

Svevo's portrayal of these different types of male delusions captivated Joyce as well. And in reading Brentani as a Jew, Joyce added to his conception of "Jewish nature" the ability to recognize the most devastating delusions of an overly aggressive masculinity; in this, "Joyce's Jew" evinces the pose of unabashed machismo. Apparently, Joyce surmised that because Jews had for so long occupied the role of the disempowered Other, the Jewish male possessed a special insight into male chauvinism. Through such a consciousness, the marginal Jew becomes acutely sensitive to the failures of patriarchy – especially those of nationalistic and religious intolerance. Joyce would indeed construct in Bloom's psychological make-up just such a sensitivity. Yet a belief in a "Jewish insight" into the folly of masculine aggression may seem at first to suggest Joyce's complicity with Weininger: the subversion of male chauvinism would appear to be more the privilege of the disempowered female. But perhaps Joyce once again turns the idea on its head by making Bloom's sensitivity into a positive rather than negative trait.[73] Yet while Bloom would soon be fending off bullies through passive resistance, the end of *Ulysses* offers no social victory for the lonely, marginal Jew. The social question, however, was less pliable to Joyce than the psychological one (as it was to many living Jews of the era). Indeed, Bloom's acceptance of his Jewish identity ultimately reconnects him to memories that had severely haunted him before. Unfortunately, however, his negative social status as "the Jew" among Christian, nationalist Irishmen remains unaltered by that change.

Yet despite Bloom's problematic social marginality, Joyce discovered through reading Svevo that there was no dishonor in being a chameleon. The nineteenth century had made marginal Jews such as Schmitz pragmatic about the construction of selfhood; reserving a sense of oneself as a Jew while taking on new identities was one of the most poignant lessons of cautious assimilation. Moreover, even the attempt to totally annihilate one's Jewish identity through radical assimilation often met with obstacles that somehow kept at least a remnant of the Jewish-self alive. Motivated by an overwhelming self-loathing, Otto Weininger had formed his notion that such "internal multiplicity" was the curse of "the Jew"; perhaps only a self-hating Jew could have invented such a theory. As a much less tortured thinker, however, Joyce had celebrated complexity of character even in his youth – Ulysses became his childhood hero in part because of such a dynamism. In Joyce's own *Ulysses*, when Bloom recognizes key aspects of his temperament as "Jewish" in a definitively positive manner, he accepts his difference and converts what he once perceived as weakness into his most humane and admirable strengths. Both Svevo and the protagonists of his novels had been central models for Joyce's construction of this protean "Jewish-self."

CHAPTER 8

Ulysses

E l'epopea di due razze (Israele-Irlanda) e nel melemimo tempo il ciclo del corpo umano ed anche una storiella di una giornata (vita).[1]

Ulysses is Leopold Bloom's book.[2] While the narratological complexity of the novel has fostered much debate over its status as a work of realism, it remains unquestionable that the central focus of the narrative becomes Bloom.[3] Joyce's experiments with novel form, which indeed often deny the reader the sustained illusion of fictive reality, came to fruition in *Ulysses*; by the composition of *Finnegans Wake*, the rudimentary structures of story-telling no longer held much interest for him. Karen Lawrence explains that in depending on "third-person narration, dialogue, and dramatization of scene," the first six episodes of *Ulysses* lull the reader into false narrative expectations, which are of course later subverted to expose Joyce's boredom with the "staples of the novel."[4] But despite the eccentricities of episodes such as "Oxen of the Sun" or "Ithaca," there exists *throughout Ulysses* the framework of a very traditional realist novel: consciously contrived plot, intricate characterization, representation of extrinsic social relationships, implied ethical meaning(s) – a constant and coherent cause and effect from character to action. Readers may continue to view Joyce as the hidden "hero" of the text, but Bloom is without a doubt the hero of the narrative's most fundamental interests. It is Bloom's struggle for a viable Jewish identity in Christian/nationalist Dublin that forms the core of "the story" – the essential suspense of plot that enables the dynamism of central characters. As a new type of protagonist, Bloom was Joyce's act of departure: by imagining his Irish Ulysses as a marginal Jew, Joyce exposed the Otherness of two of the most disenfranchised peoples in Europe, and simultaneously discovered a neutral paternal figure to which he could lead the embittered ex-Catholic Stephen.

Both of these fictional strategies of course embody some of Joyce's most self-defining experiences. Describing the project to his translator, Carlo Linati, Joyce did not hesitate to begin a description of his work with the above epigraph.

Bloom's coming to terms with his "Jewishness" through the memories of his deceased father and son indeed parallels Stephen's crisis with Catholicism embodied in the memories of his mother. But Stephen's desultory efforts are overshadowed by Bloom's piqued struggle. Ultimately, Stephen merely deflects his memories and what they portend; he remains a static character who wanders out of the book without achieving any substantial victory over his anger and confusion. Bloom, on the other hand, confronts his own "Jewishness" as well as his anti-Semitic attackers, and so achieves a sense of equilibrium and perhaps even a renewed masculine power. Because like so many Modernists, Joyce was on some level a Romantic, he allows Bloom this transcendent sense of self – one which for the character becomes inseparable from his Jewish self. Bloom thus holds the most profound moral weight of the narrative on both the level of form and content; he is simultaneously the text's central dynamic character as well as Joyce's very austere representation of marginal Jewry in pre-Holocaust Europe.

To reread the principal narrative of the novel, then, it is imperative that we perceive Bloom through both of these designations. It is imperative because, ironically, Bloom's conflicts also reveal how European discourse about "the Jew" subverted the mythic, ahistorical humanism at the center of Modernist aesthetics. So many of those Jewish intellectuals who sought through aesthetics to escape their "Jewishness" ultimately recognized that society – even their new "Modernist" milieux – would not let them do so. While Bloom is in no way an avant-garde artist, his "non-Jewish Jewishness" nonetheless resides in this manner at the heart of his character. Theories of Jewish psychology, paradoxes of marginal Jewry, and the history of Jewish emancipation all intersect in Bloom. This dynamism issues from Joyce's recognition of the complexity of Jewish identity as well as his criticism of "the cult of the nation" in modern Europe.

As demonstrated in this study, nineteenth-century discourse about "the Jew" in *Ulysses* forms a unifying element of the text's representational qualities. Indeed, the heteroglossia of the novel often centers on voices embodying the many discourses of "the Jew" in Europe. Bloom's struggle as a Jew evinces Joyce's mature recognition of the role of Jewry in both the past and future of Europe. Bloom also represents Joyce's concern with marginal groups and the transformation of complex individuals into self-hating, alienated Others. While Bloom is absent from the first three episodes, his crisis with his own "Jewishness" is prefigured in the anti-Semitism of Mulligan, Haines, and Deasy. Their arguments in turn provoke Stephen's thoughts about "the Jew" well before he meets Bloom in nighttown. At the opposite end of the book, Bloom *as a Jew* fails in his attempts to befriend one of the more promising gentiles he apparently has ever met. After Bloom falls asleep in "Ithaca," the novel's representation of *fin-de-siècle*, marginal Jewish identity comes to an incomplete close. From our post-Holocaust perspective, that social indeterminacy may even appear prophetic.

Bloom's conflicts over his own "Jewishness," as well as representations of "the Jew" that have left their mark on him, are thus an entrance into an entirely new reading of the book; ultimately, Joyce's inconclusive ending becomes the denouement of such a reading. Moreover, the social realism of *Ulysses* cannot be grasped unless the narrative is read within the context of the era's Jewish question – Joyce's knowledge of those arguments as well as our own late twentieth-century understanding of them. Reading Bloom's struggle with "Jewishness" allows us to fully recognize the value of the novel as social commentary, despite Joyce's ambivalent posturing or his formalistic experimentation. As mentioned in my opening, however, a refusal to look uncompromisingly at Bloom's struggle to define himself as a Jew has resulted in a kind of lipservice within the Joyce establishment. When Joyce is praised for representing in Bloom the alienation of "the modern everyman," Bloom's Jewish identity is acknowledged yet made irrelevant to detailed political and cultural concerns in one stroke. Standing in the face of such failures to read Bloom, this chapter explores the text precisely from the point of view that Bloom's struggle as a Jew is the axis on which the realist novel of *Ulysses* revolves.

It indeed appears that a discussion of "the Jew" was present in Joyce's earliest plans for *Ulysses*. Sometime around the completion of *A Portrait*, Joyce began to take notes toward his next project. The first mention of a work with the title *Ulysses*, other than Joyce's letters to Stanislaus in 1906, can be found in the 1914 version of *Giacomo Joyce*. Near the end of that poem, Joyce makes an allusion to a dream he had about Oliver Gogarty:

I kissed her stockings and the hem of her rust-black dusty skirt. It is the other. She. Gogarty came yesterday to be introduced. *Ulysses* is the reason. Symbol of the intellectual conscience . . . Ireland then?[5]

By this period, Joyce had already verbalized his aversion to Gogarty's anti-Semitism, and the terms "other," "*Ulysses*," and "intellectual conscience" here can be taken as a germ of the book; the excerpt presents the feminine Other (Popper), the book's title, and an implication of Gogarty's anti-Semitism as vehicles to explore the European intellectual conscience, Irish or otherwise. Ellmann surmised that *Giacomo Joyce* was composed between 1911 and 1914.[6] These dates, Joyce's relations with Svevo, and the Jewish subject of the poem itself suggest that from the beginning Joyce was aware that his new work would incorporate arguments about Jewish identity.[7] When he moved to Zurich, Joyce's friendships with other Jews of course helped him to construct and focus Bloom. And as I will illustrate here, there is sufficient proof in the manuscripts of *Ulysses* to suggest that as Joyce revised his book in that city, he became more aware of the need to emphasize Bloom's "Jewishness." Throughout the available gatherings of typescripts, notesheets, and printer's placards, one finds Joyce repeatedly penciling in lines that become crucial to portraying Bloom's progressive awareness of his Jewish consciousness.

As much as any other locus of meaning, *Ulysses* is "about" questions surrounding European Jewry: assimilation, Zionism, xenophobia, the psychology of scapegoating and stereotype, nationalistic pariahism. Both the cultural position of "the Jew," as well as normative Jewish identity, have changed irrevocably since Bloomsday because of events Joyce did not live to see: the historicizing of Auschwitz, the maturation of American Jewry, the establishment of the state of Israel. The questions *Ulysses* raises through Bloom's struggle as a Jew, however, remain pertinent in a world where neither damaging stereotype nor aggressive nationalism have disappeared.

I   BLOOM'S ABSENCE: THE *TELEMACHIA*

Because no Jewish characters appear in the *Telemachia*, questions about "Jewishness" in those episodes initially seem irrelevant. Stereotypes of "the Jew" issuing from religious and political ideologies, however, unify all three episodes. The absence of Jewish characters is Joyce's point: the specter of "the Jew" in this first section shadows the narrative and represents the essence of prejudice. By the close of the

Telemachia, many stereotypes of "the Jew" have insinuated themselves into Stephen's more ethereal thoughts. Stephen, who desires to be both ahistorical and apolitical, cannot escape either of these realities; from the beginning of his day to its close, a persistent foil to his Romantic posture is the anti-Semitism he encounters from one end of Dublin to the other.

At the midway point of the *Telemachia*, Stephen begins to fantasize about "dark men." As representations of the Oriental Other, these dream-Semites appear to him as allies in his apostasy, mysterious comrades-in-arms to his anti-Christian, metaphysical struggle. But impinging on these satisfying images are salvos of bigotry from external forces. Throughout the course of the narrative, Stephen will be challenged to discard his generalized "Orientalism" for the specific realities of one particular Irish Jew's identity struggle. That challenge arises from both the book's barrage of anti-Semitic arguments, and, of course, from Stephen's meeting with Bloom.

In "Telemachus" the characters of Buck Mulligan and Haines introduce several types of discourse that become central to the entire text. Mulligan, the mocking usurper, and Haines the empowered, ignorant hater, immediately interrupt and exacerbate Stephen's struggle with paternalism. Both of these interlocutors, not coincidentally, begin to articulate their positions through anti-Semitic rhetoric. In the Linati schema, Joyce named the art of the opening episode "theology"; in the Gorman-Gilbert schema he renamed the episode's symbol "the heir."[8] As Catholics, Stephen and Buck know that Christianity is the heir of Judaism, Jesus is the heir of the Judaic God, and that they themselves are the rebellious heirs of a Church-dominated culture. Buck is the "untonsured" leader of their Black Mass; his first words mock the entire Judeo-Christian tradition by drawing on a piece of Catholic liturgy taken from the Hebrew: "Introibo ad altare Dei" is St. Jerome's Vulgate version of the Hebrew in the first line of Psalm 43: 4: "*Va-a-vo-ah el mizbaj elohim*," "Then I will go unto the altar of God" (*U*1.6).[9] A mocking of theology, and of God "the collector of prepuces," is apparently underway (394).

But theology in Ireland cannot escape politics. Mulligan describes Haines as a "bloody English[man]" who is "bursting with money and indigestion" (52-53). The insult prefigures the economic slander Haines himself will level at English Jews. The theological introduction gives way to political friction, and thus begins the text's intricate foreshadowing of Bloom. In the midst of "theology," Joyce presents stereotype, hate, and economic envy as age-old religious weapons in the hands of modern political rivals. In this struggle, the disempowered internalize their marginality and often project their self-hatred on to other disempowered groups. Thus Buck, the wild Catholic heretic, is also an Irish anti-Semite. This is Joyce's reading of Dublin, 1904; the "cracked looking glass of a servant" reflects an image so striated that its beholder finds solace by projecting on to "masters" and "servants" alike (159).

As a Brit sympathetic to Celticism, Haines appears to have conquered a relevant prejudice to these Irishmen – he even speaks Gaelic to the peasant milkwoman. In broader terms, however, Haines has conquered nothing; he has merely transferred his impulse for bigotry to the most common type of economic anti-Semitism: "I don't want to see my country fall into the hands of German Jews. That's our national problem, I'm afraid, just now" (666–68). It seems Haines was in error when he explained that "history" was to blame for problems with the commonwealth; history isn't the culprit, "the Jew" is – "when in doubt persecute Bloom" (U15.976–77).

Haines indeed becomes the voice of some central elements of turn-of-the-century British anti-Semitic discourse. Based predominantly in economic rather than religious arguments, this rhetoric continues throughout the book in both nationalistic and imperialistic forms. Such discourse allows Joyce to undermine stereotype as a tool of political agendas; but, even more significantly, he also implies through it that imperial and nationalist ideologies rely on similar types of subjugation of the Other. In this respect, the episode's allusion to South Africa aids the reader in understanding the underlying nature of Haines' "liberal" politics.[10]

Implying Haines' background, Buck states "his old fellow made his tin by selling jalap to Zulus or some bloody swindle or another" (156–57). Buck's slander parodies the exploitation inherent in colonialism. But a subtle irony arises, however, when Haines himself later makes his comment about the Jews. The Irishman perceives the Englishman as an economic exploiter; in turn the Englishman figures "the Jew" as the economic parasite. Joyce was well aware of such antagonism in both English and Irish political discourse during the years of the Anglo-Boer confrontation.

From the war's earliest beginnings, liberal British voices disseminated the idea that a network of Jewish financiers had encouraged the war. Since Irish nationalists were opposed to the confrontation, anti-war-anti-Semitism played right into their hands. As one condescendingly sympathetic to the Irish, Haines represents the imperialist who found an unexpected common hate with Irish nationalists. A character such as Haines may well have been a reader of Arnold White's *The Modern Jew*, published in London, in 1899. Among other charges of international conspiracy, White accuses the Jews of possessing a monopoly on Johannesburg's press and financial worlds. In a pamphlet in 1902, White claims there was only one firm of first rank in Johannesburg that was non-Jewish, and that the Jews were behind the prolonging of the war for their own financial gain.[11] Haines' reference to "German Jews" does not represent some amorphous "scapegoating," but is Joyce's allusion to a specific anti-Semitism native to Dublin at the turn of the century.

When Buck himself turns against Haines in an attempt to reingratiate himself to Stephen, Joyce uses the ensuing reference to Oxford to initially lambaste Matthew Arnold's brand of liberalism. Thus "the Jew" remains in shadow here by way of the implied insult to Arnold's Hebraism and Hellenism. After asserting the need for an Irish neo-Hellenism – "together we might do something for the Island . . . Hellenise it" (158) – Mulligan suggests that they get rid of Haines by "ragging" him in the manner of Oxfordian hazing rituals. The allusion provokes in Stephen a vision of one of the more famous of these stunts involving an underclassman named Clive Kempthorpe. But as Bernard Benstock has previously observed, Stephen has never been to Oxford, and his "memory" must be a second-hand invention based on Mulligan's version of the event.[12] In either case, the entire vision leads to, and indeed ends in, the allusion to Arnold:

Shouts from the open window startling evening in the quadrangle. A deaf gardener, aproned, masked with Matthew Arnold's face, pushes his mower on the sombre lawn watching narrowly the dancing motes of grass-halms.
    To ourselves . . . new paganism . . . *omphalos.*(172–76)

As both Seamus Deane and Bryan Cheyette point out, the deaf gardener tending to his small plot and ignoring the adjacent violence stands as an obvious metaphor for Joyce's view that Arnold's *Culture and Anarchy*, as rehabilitating "social theory," was the product of an overly poetic, liberal British blindness to the injustices of imperialism.[13] Stephen, as well, will have no truck with such a romantic "new paganism," even in the guise of Mulligan's vulgar aestheticizing of Arnoldian theory. Later on in nighttown, however, Stephen's uncertainty about his own "Hellenic" and "Hebraic" impulses will again conjure "the Siamese twins, Philip Drunk and Philip Sober, two Oxford dons with lawnmowers . . . both masked with Matthew Arnold's face" (*U*15.2512–14).

Resisting both Haines' and Mulligan's "politics," Stephen again returns to theology. The drowned man, the missing one, lies out in the bay "full fathom five," as in Ariel's song. Stephen imagines "the man that was drowned" lying face-up in the sun; looking toward heaven, the man speaks the words, "Here I am" (673–37). The phrase is a translation of the Hebrew from Genesis: "*ha-esh v'ha-e-zim ah-nee*" – "Here am I," the words spoken by Abraham to his son on Mount Peniel, the phrase spoken by God to Abraham moments later. As an Hebraic allusion, the words foreshadow Bloom, in that both he and Stephen are "drowned men," searching in the depths of patriarchy for meaning. The drowned man – now Stephen's image of himself – is calling to the father. In the proceeding lines, Buck in fact brings up Bannon's "photo-girl" in Westmeath, who must be Milly Bloom (686). Bloom the father is calling back. Stephen is lost – "I will not sleep here tonight. Home also I cannot go" (739–40). His frustration finds its most readily accessible target in Mulligan, the "usurper." But Haines' bigotry represents a key role in Stephen's dilemma as well: enter Garrett Deasy's history lesson.

Because "Nestor" concerns historiography, the episode amplifies the previously introduced anti-Semitic discourse by suggesting it as a singular manner of rereading Western history. Stephen's reference here to Vico Road encouraged A. M. Klein long ago to read the episode as an embodiment of the Viconian cycles of history.[14] Notwithstanding Vico's theory that the Jews live outside of historical cycles, the episode asks how "the Jew" becomes an element of Western culture in its present appropriation by both liberal Christian and nationalist ideologies. When the episode opens, Stephen is in fact giving a history lesson; in his subsequent discussion with Deasy, history remains the focus through allusions to economics, nationalism, eschatology, and memory. All of these subjects are avenues for a radical historiography; but in Deasy's perception, it is just as important to read each one for its undercurrent of the destructive "Jewish influence." Deasy in this vein is once again the evil twin of Bloom; both read history through "the Jew," but toward diametrically opposed ends.

As his students reiterate the "facts" of history, "Asculum . . .
Pyrrhus . . . 279 B.C . . . *Another victory like that and we are done for,*"
Stephen recognizes these as merely selected parts of an ever-changing
narrative (*U*2.11, 12, 13). He is reminded that memory "fables" facts
into a collection of stories that "time brand[s] and fetter[s] [and]
lodg[es] in a room of the infinite possibilities they have ousted"
(49–51). To Stephen, history is a consciously constructed limit of
possibilities. As narrative, history may be at its best as metaphor;
Stephen has just won his own Pyrrhic victory against both Mulligan
and Haines. But Stephen's disbelief in "history as truth" is rebutted
by Deasy's sense of history as the transcendent work of God. As
muddled as Deasy's arguments are, that sense of the past makes
Stephen squirm.[15]

Stephen is soon confronted with an impromptu math tutorial.
While sympathizing with the unkempt, confused boy, Sargent,
Stephen recalls the "algebra" he has used to prove his *Hamlet* theory.
In turn he begins to perceive the numbers on the page as some sort of
elaborate "morrice" of figures or "imps of fancy of the Moors"
(155–57). He summons two historical names that evince the Eastern
flavor of mathematics: "Averroes and Moses Maimonides, dark men
in mien and movement, flashing in the mocking movements the
obscure soul of the world, a darkness shining in the brightness which
the brightness couldn't comprehend" (158–60). Averroes completes
the tone of the vision as the Oriental melding with the Occidental, but
was of course of the Islamic culture, and not a Jew. Maimonides,
however, not only foreshadows Bloom as a "dark man in mien and
movement," but will be echoed in Deasy's reference to the Jews:
"they sinned against the light" (361). Stephen's words are a parody of
John 1:5. As an apostate "dark-horse," Stephen searches for spiritual
allies, and it has been noted previously that he is "clearly attracted to
those dark, semitic powers which are said to be undermining
Britain."[16] But for now he perceives these as simply "dark men" – the
Oriental Other – as they represent to him infidels or subversives to
Church and state; they are to this extent merely literary specters and
have no tangible social corelatives.

Stephen repeats this vague longing for "the Oriental Other"
throughout his day. As in the Orientalism of his predecessor James
Mangan, Stephen's dreams of those such as "Haroun al Raschid"
also represent the Irish fantasy about the mysterious Semitic origins of
the Milesian Celts (*U*3.366). But this vision of the dark Other is

ultimately another aspect of Stephen's heady Romanticism. The fantasy, however, will soon buckle under pressure applied by Deasy and others. Stephen's most viable opportunity to subvert those Liberal or religious forces he views as destructive only arises when he begins to focus not on some specious "Orientalism," but on a specific, living Jew. Moreover, Deasy's anti-Semitic outbursts here in "Nestor" begin not in eschatology or exotic cultural myth, but again, like that of Haines, in conspiratory economics.

Deasy's fatherly advice, "Money is power," and his boast, "*I paid my way, I never borrowed a shilling in my life . . . I owe nothing*," indicates a pettiness of mind to Stephen (253–54). Deasy next asserts that, as one who knows the value of a pound, he knows the cost of freedom – even nationalist freedom. All of this Unionist propaganda bores Stephen. But Deasy has been stirred: the problem with foot-and-mouth disease is just a symptom. Ireland is ignoring commercial common sense; something is amiss Deasy can't quite name: "I am surrounded by difficulties, by . . . intrigues by . . . backstairs influence by . . ." (343–44). Deasy implies that Stephen and his generation don't comprehend the true nature of the times; they must ask themselves who is behind Ireland's economic turbulence, who is chipping away at the empire from within? Deasy's rejoinder indeed echoes Haines' discourse:

He raised his forefinger and beat the air oldly before his voice spoke.
– Mark my words, Mr. Dedalus, he said. England is in the hands of the jews. In all the highest places: her finance, her press. And they are the signs of a nation's decay. Wherever they gather they eat up the nation's vital strength. I have seen it coming these years. As sure as we are standing here the jew merchants are already at their work of destruction. Old England is dying. (345–51)

Jews secretly control the banks and the media – brainwashing innocent Christians while they ruin them financially. Deasy's allegations soon somersault, however, through several different types of anti-Semitic myths. Joyce here begins an expansion of the range of anti-Jewish voices in the text, emphasizing the protean nature of Jewish hatred during the era. It is not only the press and the bankers behind this conspiracy, but the Jewish merchant as well. Jewish conspiracy transcends class and institution; all Jews, no matter what their livelihoods, resources, or politics, are working toward the domination of the Christian empires – Joyce thus incorporates into the attitude his memories of Arthur Griffith's journalistic attacks on "the Jew." Indeed, Deasy's ground-rules for success now include the breaking of what he imagines are "the great Jewish coffers," the definitive obstacle to European culture, imperial or nationalistic; once again, "the Jew" is the common enemy.

But the false accusation piques Stephen's attention: " – A merchant, Stephen said, is one who buys cheap and sells dear, jew or gentile, is he not?" (359–60). Stephen's rhetorical question exposes Deasy's paranoia, and the bigot now falls back on religion in a typical nineteenth-century admixture of religious and social arguments against "the Jew." To Deasy, Jewish usury as an historical necessity is merely a disguise – the devil works in mysterious ways: "They sinned against the light . . . And you can see the darkness in their eyes. And that is why they are wanderers on the earth to this day" (361–63).

Deasy's new argument is biblically based, and thus rouses the Catholic component of Stephen's imagination. In his Jesuit-trained memory, Stephen hears Deasy's words echoing his earlier reference to St. John: "And the light shineth in darkness, and the darkness comprehended it not." But for Stephen to entertain the Christian belief in Jewish blood-guilt is tantamount to "serving a master" he flatly rejects. To combat these remnants of Catholic doctrine, Stephen recalls his trip to the Paris Bourse, the single moment in his life when he was presented with the opportunity to observe a large group of Jews:

On the steps of the Paris stock exchange the goldskinned men quoting prices on their gemmed fingers. Gabble of geese. They swarmed loud, uncouth, about the temple, their heads thick-plotting under maladroit silk hats. Not theirs: these clothes, this speech, these gestures. Their full slow eyes belied the words, the gestures eager and unoffending, but knew the rancours massed about them and knew their zeal was vain. Vain patience to heap and hoard. Time surely would scatter all. A hoard heaped by the roadside: plundered and passing on. Their eyes knew their years of wandering and, patient, knew the dishonors of their flesh. (364–72)

In the passage, Joyce echoes his "Ecce Homo" essay, as well as draws on his own experiences of Paris in 1902. But to Stephen, the vision is a sincere rebuttal to Deasy's scriptural argument. Sympathetic as the vision may be, however, it does not escape stereotype. The Jews, "a hoard heaped by the roadside," may appear to Stephen to be brothers to the Irish. But Jews in Stephen's mind remain nervous, plotting victims, whose place in the world appears to be as mythical pariahs. While Deasy's grotesquery offends his sensibility, Stephen's vision does not attempt to destroy prejudice, but merely exchanges it for the pleasures of an aestheticized, mythologized "Jew." The reaction is typical of Stephen, whose "conduct is marked chiefly by refusals: . . . surrounded by deniers, he must deny them."[17]

Stephen also alludes to Christ chasing the moneychangers from the Temple, and makes a less than complimentary analogy of Jewish brokers as "geese" as they go about their business. One could surmise that the architecture of the Bourse aids Stephen in transforming contemporary stock-traders into the Jews who Christ condemned. But this perception of ancient (and thus mythical) Jews subtly corroborates Deasy's scriptural argument for Jewish accursedness; in his "vain patience to heap and hoard," Stephen in a manner unintentionally supports Deasy's Jewish financial conspiracy theory. Stephen at this point is unwilling, or unable, to imagine Jews as differentiated individuals, and his vision of Jews at the Bourse is little more than a projection of his sense of himself as an outcast.

As a result of the vision, however, Stephen does recognize at least one crucial element of his own paradigm. In answer to Deasy's accusation of Jews "sinning against the light," Stephen asks "Who has not" (73). Apparently Stephen understands the sin constructed into the Christian stereotype of "the Jew" as simply a human possibility, projected and idealized into an identifying mark of a people. Through ideological reinforcement, such identities of course become disseminated, and through generations, become unquestioned. This process indeed resides at the center of "the nightmare of history" from which Stephen is "trying to wake" (377).

In a typescript of this episode, Joyce penciled in a preceding line: "What if that nightmare gave you a back kick?" (379).[18] Directly after his comment about history, Stephen had glanced out of the window at the scoring of a rugby goal. A back-kick might wake Stephen from his nightmare of solipsism, and he will soon be kicked by history – the history of Jewish emancipation – incarnate in the form of Bloom.

But Deasy continues to fulminate his "old world" beliefs, veering from a pedestrian eschatology to a biblically based misogyny: "all human history moves toward . . . the manifestation of God . . . a woman first brought sin into the world" (380–81, 390). In the Linati schema, Joyce labeled the "sense" of this episode "the wisdom of the old world."[19] Even without a substantial rebuttal from Stephen, Deasy becomes laughable. Chasing after Stephen at the end of the

episode, he shouts "Ireland, they say, has the honor of being the only
country which never persecuted the Jews" (437). Again he demonstrates
his ignorance – Dublin had a three-century-old Jewish community,
and that very April, 1904, the Limerick anti-Jewish riots had
occurred. In Deasy's punch line, "because she never let them in,"
Stephen hears a "coughball of laughter . . . dragging after it a rattling
chain of phlegm" (443–44). Deasy's words echo with the death-rattle.
To Stephen, Deasy's economic "Bible lesson" is nothing more than a
rationalization of his prejudice. In Stephen's last sight of Deasy he
sees "on his wise shoulders through the checkerwork of leaves the sun
[flinging] spangles, dancing coins" (448); the perception reveals
again the materialist hatred behind Deasy's flimsy religiosity. Stephen
thus flees Deasy's earth-bound rhetoric and strolls off to Sandymount
strand in hopes of gaining eternity.

In "Proteus," Stephen's thoughts about the "ineluctable modality of
the visible" indeed suggest his obsession with penetrating the material
world and achieving transcendence. When he had attempted to grasp
the essence of "the Jew" in his vision of the Bourse, however, Deasy's
arguments had pulled him back. Politics in "Proteus," however,
again intrude on Stephen's metaphysical musings, although he still
refuses to recognize the relevance of anti-Semitism to these allusions.
This process adds to the episode's dominant motif of change as the
only constant. Yet, Stephen's thoughts on anti-Semites and dark
Others begin to undergo a transformation here as well, which will
enter a dormancy until he meets up with Bloom in nighttown.

Committed, of course, to his self-image as an apolitical artist,
Stephen has allowed the anti-Semitism he encountered earlier to
merely drift from his mind. Alone on the strand his mind reels in the
metaphysics that preoccupy him in his search for a deep, abiding
truth. After testing his *Nacheinander* and *Nebeneinander*, Stephen again
returns to a Judeo-Christian allusion in his joke about telephoning
Eden. But having parodied Genesis, Stephen thinks of his own birth.
In copulation, his parents enacted the will of God: Stephen imagines
his consubstantiation with his mother as a metaphor for the "divine
substance wherein Father and Son are consubstantial" (*U*3.49–50).
Once again, Stephen misses the mark; he attempts to align the
corporeal consubstantiation of parent and child with the mystery of
the Trinity.

He now repeats the name of Arius, one of the four heresiarchs he had remembered earlier in "Telemachus." After the experience with Deasy, however, Arius' theory of Jesus' unconsubstantiality with and inferiority to God cannot escape an association in Stephen's thoughts with "Jewish fathers" and "Christian sons."[20] Stephen's problems throughout the episode have surrounded "schisms": Arius' ideas of course played a key role in the triple schism of Constantine's Nicaean council, as well as in the schism of the Orthodox Church from the Roman. But the West's first great schism was that of the Christian with the Jew; like Stephen's own personal struggle, that rift too was provoked when a son usurped the position of a father.

In this manner, Joyce introduces a key portmanteau word of the episode. Stephen thinks: "Where is poor dear Arius to try conclusions? Warring his life long upon the contransmagnificandjewbangtantiality" (51). Joyce's term incorporates "consubstantiality," "transubstantiality," "magnificat," "Jew," and "bang" for Stephen's "noise in the street." The construction incorporates Stephen's dilemma over Christology and his own future: his meeting with a Jew becomes his bond to a non-biological father, and thus opens the possibility of his own transformation into a spiritual, ecumenical son.

Stephen's sighting of the pigeonhouse recalls another Catholic mystery. The symbol of the Holy Ghost as *pigeon* in French reminds him of the Virgin Birth and the writings of M. Leo Taxil. Taxil asserted in *La Vie de Jesus* (1884) that the archangel Gabriel, in the form of a dove, "cuckolded" Joseph; Bloom the cuckold hovers around Stephen's thoughts. Recalling his acquaintance with the Irish expatriate and reader of Taxil, Kevin Egan, Stephen's mind soon drifts back to Paris.[21] After Stephen's vision of Parisian Jews at the Bourse, Joyce cannot resist interjecting some anti-Semitic rhetoric into Stephen's stream-of-consciousness. Stephen soon thinks of Taxil, Edouard Drumont, and Ernst Renan, all three of whom played their part in the development of French anti-Semitism.[22] These associations may be a by-product of the anti-Semitism Stephen had previously encountered, but their presence in his imagination appears solely based on their identity as heretics and historical theorists – and one whose anti-British vehemence rendered for Stephen a memorable insult to Victoria (232, 494). Even his reference to the journal *La Patrie*, whose anti-Dreyfusard attacks Joyce read in Paris, fails to remind Stephen of the arguments he encountered earlier in the tower and in Dalkey.

As his thoughts of Paris wane, Stephen sympathizes with the aging

Kevin Egan (267–70). His final sentiment about Egan, "they have forgotten Kevin Egan, not he them. Remembering thee, O Sion," is a sarcastic remark referencing old metaphors of the plight of the ancient Hebrews and the Irish nationalist cause (263–64). The allusion is to Psalm 137:1 – "By the rivers of Babylon, there we sat down, yea, we wept, when we remembered Zion." But to embittered ex-nationalists, such similes are shrill, and have little relevance to Jews living in Dublin or elsewhere.

Stephen soon recalls the dream from which Haines appears to have awakened him the night before. In sleep Stephen found himself on a "street of harlots" confronting first the apparition of "Haroun al-Raschid," and then "That man" who held a "melon" against his face. The reference to the renowned Caliph of eighth-century Baghdad is linked to the book's leitmotif of the popular Dublin pantomime, *Turko the Terrible*. In "Telemachus," Stephen recalled his mother's delight over a performance of this show (U1.259–63).[23] As a fictionalized Haroun al-Raschid appears in this pantomime, Stephen's dream of the Caliph also embodies his lingering remorse over his refusal to his mother.

Stephen's dream and the actual pantomime also represent the hold Oriental tales had over the Irish imagination during this period. As alluded to earlier in this study, one of Joyce's initial recognitions of how Orientalism stimulated his imagination occurred during his University College years when he became interested in James Mangan. His *Dubliners'* story "Araby," of course, makes ironic use of Mangan's name, doubling the mystery of the Orient by coupling it with the boy's obsession with a female; for Joyce, the Oriental often possessed a female flavor. Stephen too dreams of the mystery of the Orient: his "street of harlots" can be viewed as a harem image – its mention of al-Raschid recalls the high-point of medieval Islamic culture.[24]

Unfortunately, however, "that man" invades Stephen's Oriental vision and shoves a melon in his face. The street of harlots will become nighttown, and "the man," of course, foreshadows Bloom. Bloom's taste for melons, his bowler translated to the French *melon*, and the "mellow yellow smellow melons" of Molly's buttocks all will later demystify the offending fruit of Stephen's dream. Melons and bowlers, however, have little to do with historical questions of Jewish identity. Yet as a depoliticized trope, this eccentric symbolism surrounding Bloom as "the mythic Jew" typifies readings of "the

Jewish aspect" of the book as far back as Stuart Gilbert's study.[25] But it is not so much Stephen's dream as a prefiguration of Bloom "the Oriental man" that is relevant to Jewish identity. It is rather the intrusion of an unwanted association within the dream that becomes a key to Bloom's "Jewishness." Perceived as a Jew, Bloom will appear as an "intrusion" into Irish culture and social discourse throughout the book – the threatening presence of the Other that literally haunts the dominant culture. In his dream, Stephen was made to smell the fruit because "that man" said it "was the rule" (68). Later on in the day, Bloom's annoying presence will suggest on several occasions repressed "rules" of social harmony to both Stephen and his fellow Irishmen.

II   BLOOM THE JEW

With the introduction of Bloom in "Calypso," Joyce abandons "the Jew" as solely a racialized element of cultural production, or even as a defense-mechanism projection of non-Jews. All the characters presented in the the *Telemachia* perceived Jews through stereotype. But in Bloom the projections come home to roost: the stereotypes are now captured from the inside out. Recognizing his own Jewish background, Bloom has throughout his life refigured his identity by juggling – and often internalizing – a host of learned representations of "the Jew."[26] Occasionally, Bloom joins other Dubliners in their projections on to "the evil Jew," attempting to purge those unwanted aspects of himself. But as the day of June 16 progresses, Bloom begins to re-evaluate and negotiate his "Jewishness" in new and crucial ways; by the closing episodes, his Jewish identity has become astoundingly multivalent, and his selfhood has been redefined into a much less self-defeating shape.

Bloom's morning: Calypso

It is pure Joyce to introduce a "Jewish" character through his taste for offal, which in the very next scene becomes an un-kosher pig kidney. Organ meats were not a very common dietary staple of lower-middle-class and working-class Dubliners in 1904.[27] The nearest approximation of such delicacies in the diet of Bloom's north end of the city might be the English-influenced steak-and-kidneys, or the popular pig's-cheeks mentioned in "Araby."[28] Because he is of Hungarian-Jewish extraction, however, Bloom's "relish for the inner organs of beasts" is a cultural marker of Jewish identity – one which becomes completely secularized with the pork kidney. Eastern European Yiddish diet, from Polish *shtetls* to Budapest, included organ dishes as staples, such as *Gefilte Mintz* (stuffed spleen), *Lungen* (sauteed lung) and *Kishke* (stuffed intestines). In this serio-comic manner, Bloom is different than his fellow Irishmen even in his taste for breakfast. Thus his "non-Jewish Jewishness" here informs something as basic as his eating habits.

In his desire for a kidney on June 16, however, Bloom chooses a pig's organ solely for its freshness: "Thursday: not a good day either for a mutton kidney at Buckley's . . . Better a pork kidney at Dlugacz's" (*U*4. 44–45). Bloom's satisfying pork kidney suggests the rationalization of Levitical law that was, and still is, an element of Jewish assimilation throughout the West. By the "Circe" episode, the kidney indeed becomes transmuted in Bloom's imagination into the shape of the "new Bloomusalem" – a symbol of the potential harmony of assimilation (*U*15.1549). Bloom's breaking of *Kashrut* is necessary to define the type of Jew Joyce wants to represent – one who is marginal to Judaism yet has been formed in part through Jewish culture. In this vein, Joyce is unrelenting in his portrayal of Dublin Jewry; he redoubles the irony not only by introducing Dlugacz as a Jewish pork-butcher, but a Zionist one at that. Dublin Jewry in this first glance appears as a cruel joke – the one about "an Irish Jew."

Bloom and Dlugacz are nonetheless finely-tuned representations of a Jewish identity crisis that was fresh from the tensions of the Dreyfus Affair. Although an apostate from Judaism, Bloom's ethnicity parallels Joyce's view of his own anti-Catholic Irishness. To be born a Catholic Irishman, reject the Church, and then to call oneself the great Irish writer of his era appears to have been parallel in Joyce's mind to being uncircumcised, unkosher, agnostic, and still thinking of oneself as a Jew.

As Bloom passes O'Rourke's pub, he wonders at the drinking habits of Dubliners. He thinks "where do they get the money . . . Save it they can't. What is that, a bob here and there, dribs and drabs" (126–33). Later in the day, Bloom's frugality and abstinence are both suggested as "Jewish traits" by intoxicated Catholic Irishmen. Nosey Flynn in "Lestrygonians" and the citizen in "Cyclops" both perceive Bloom through stereotypes of the "cheap, unsociable, devious Jew." In constructing Bloom as a private, frugal man, Joyce may be complicit in the stereotype; yet his version lessens the negativity and thereby disarms it. Perhaps the stereotype had become for Joyce a kind of historical analogue – Bloom's Hungarian-Jewish background does not include the inherited Irish propensity for social drinking and gambling. On the other hand, Bloom is not welcomed into pub discourse because he is perceived as an "un-Irish" Jew. Joyce begs the reader to recognize the vicious circle. Yet, when Bloom enters Dlugacz's shop – a "Jewish" establishment – he encounters only silence.

Dlugacz's name and looks are based on the actual Moses Dlugacz of Trieste, who was Joyce's student and friend from 1912 to 1918. An ordained rabbi from a family of Ukrainian rabbis, Dlugacz's ardent, vocal Zionism appears to have been Joyce's first encounter with such. Living in Trieste, Dlugacz had little chance of gaining a congregation, and after establishing Hebrew classes for Triestine youth, he became a food merchant and eventually emigrated to Palestine.[29] As a "wholesale supplier of cheese and meat products to the Austrian army," Dlugacz trafficked in non-Kosher products, just like his fictional counterpart.[30] Yet here again Joyce is shrewdly accurate: it was not uncommon for the assimilated Jew to work in "un-Jewish" environments – even as a pork-butcher – and still maintain an identity as a Jew, or even a Zionist. The fictional Dlugacz seems a likely representation of this kind of Jew; immigration and economics make strange bed-fellows, and kosher butchers didn't do too well in Dublin.

Joyce intends the "ferreteyed porkbutcher" in "Cyclops" to be Bloom's *landsman*. Before they part, the two Hungarian Jews stare into each other's eyes, and Bloom withdraws "his gaze after an instant . . . No: better not: another time" (186–87). Estranged as they are from both Judaism and a sense of Jewish community, what other sign can the two exchange? Upon entering the shop, Bloom had picked up one of the sheets of paper Dlugacz has cut for wrapping his meats. Bloom's canvasser's eye reads over the advertisement for "the model farm at Kinnereth on the lakeshore of Tiberias," and catches the name of the renowned Jewish philanthropist Moses Montifore (154–56). Curiously, though, the space-salesman Bloom does not evaluate the advertisement for effectiveness as in his usual response; instead, he appears interested in its content. The address seems to make Dlugacz a recipient of mail from The Palestine Land Development Company, whose actual offices were indeed located at Bliebtreustrasse 34–35, Berlin.[31] Bloom gloats as his suspicions about Dlugacz are confirmed: "I thought he was" (156).

Recognizing Dlugacz as a secretive Zionist, Bloom now calls the butcher's "ferreteyes" "foxeyes" (186). Dlugacz, the "Jewish por-kbutcher," now appears wily to Bloom; later in the episode Bloom recalls the deep, rich tone of Dlugacz's voice, and calls him an "enthusiast" (492–93). Bloom perceives the butcher as virile and possessing a strength of conviction as a Jew – the opposite from the type of "Jewishness" Bloom imagines he embodies.[32] Later in the Ormond Bar, Bloom associates "Dlugacz' porkshop bright tubes of Agendeth [and] a gallantbuttocked mare" with another aggressive male, Blazes Boylan (*U*11.884–85).

After reserving for "another time" a mutual affirmation of their Jewish identities, Bloom scrutinizes "gravely" the advertisement for Agendath Netaim. He imagines a Palestine alive with growth, a Jewish world blossoming in oranges, olives, and the pride of territoriality. The dream embodies the sentiment expressed in the lyric of *Hatikvah*, a song Bloom exits the novel singing. As "unJewish" as Bloom appears, his vision initially depicts Zionism as an Edenic rebirth. But while he ultimately decides that Zionism has "nothing doing," he does acknowledge that "still [there is] an idea behind it" (200). And indeed, the vision also reminds him of his former ties to the Dublin Jewish community and his old Jewish friends: "poor Citron in Saint Kevin's Parade . . . and Mastiansky with the old cither . . . [and] Moisel" (205–09).[33] Each figure, however, is also tied to an intrinsic sympathy surrounding "the Jew" as sufferer, and the concept of Zionism becomes another unviable and thereby pathetic attempt at redemption.

Thus Bloom's warm Oriental memories of citrons and Jewish comradeship are easily altered. A cloud covering the sun radically changes his vision: Palestine becomes a wasteland, and then, "Dead: an old woman's: the grey sunken cunt of the world" (228). For a moment, Bloom's sense of Jewish nationalism had been aroused into an idealized dream: a future fellowship with a Jew, a future Eden in Palestine. But Bloom refuses the hope. His sense of alienation is too complete; he is not accepted as an Irishman by others, and he will not accept himself as a Jew. Later we learn that his self-image as a "Jewish male" – effeminate, weak, overly compassionate, and cuckolded – perpetuates that isolation. His negative vision of Palestine and Zionism thus ends in an image of female decrepitude. In this manner, the vision further introduces the shadow of Weininger and "the feminized Jew" into the text, which will continue to haunt Bloom throughout the day. Indeed, "Agendeth Netaim" will resurface in

Bloom's imagination at key moments of his confrontation with his own "Jewishness" – perhaps most revealingly in nighttown. For now, Bloom's regard for "Jewishness" dulls even further when his thoughts turn to Molly and "poor Paddy Dignam"; the final allusion to Judaism in the episode occurs in Bloom's quip about his cat as "kosher," in which he reveals either his ignorance or forgetfulness about the Levitical prohibition on consuming blood; for now, Judaism again regresses to another of Bloom's little private jokes (277).[34]

Bloom's midday: Lotus-Eaters *through* Sirens

Throughout his day, events, objects, and persons remind Bloom of his father. In each instance, these memories of the elder Bloom invoke emotions surrounding Judaism, Yiddish culture, and a lost sense of Jewish identity. Remorse over the plight of his father, who ironically converted to Protestantism, is Bloom's most meaningful tie with a religious Jewish identity. The upshot of each brief memory, however, is more often a lament for "poor papa's" suicide than any tangible desire on Bloom's part to become *Halachically* Jewish. Bloom is, indeed, foggy about the few scraps of Jewish ritual and liturgy his father has passed on to him. Further, Bloom is an agnostic and at times even an atheist: memories of his father praying or observing Jewish law appear pitiable to him. Just as in his jibes at Catholicism, Bloom's paternal "Jewish remnants" seem sadly futile. They represent a sorrowful man's attempt at reconciliation with a religion that is, like all religions to Bloom, unfortunately only a comforting mythology. Bloom indeed demonstrates his view of Judaism as merely another "false religion" in "Lotus-Eaters" by comparing the communion wafer with matzoth (358).

Bloom's memories of his father, however, involve more than a condescending sympathy. While religion is archaic to him, the plight of his father as an alienated, immigrant Jew is not. That legacy indeed represents one of Joyce's beliefs about the essence of his own ethnicity – "jews and Irish remember the past."[35] In his final moments of waking consciousness in "Ithaca," Bloom in fact repeats his doubts about God and religion, but reaffirms his lifelong struggle to remember his father's European journey as a persecuted, exiled Jew (U17.1903–15).

At mid-morning, as Bloom walks toward the chemists, he spies an advertisement for a performance of the play *Leah* (U5.194).[36] He remembers having once seen this drama, and recalls that the female lead, Mrs. Bandmann Palmer, had just last evening performed the role of Hamlet. He jokes to himself about transvestism, Hamlet being a woman, and Ophelia committing suicide because of the discovery. But the subject of suicide rarely holds any humor for Bloom. He recalls his father's high regard for *Leah*, which in the past had been performed under several different titles. The elder Bloom apparently repeated select passages to his son:

Nathan's voice! His son's voice! I hear the voice of Nathan who left his father to die in grief and misery in my arms, who left the house of his father and left the God of his father. Every word is so deep, Leopold.(*U*5.203–06)

Rather than generating guilt over his apostasy from Judaism, however, the memory again reanimates Bloom's pity for "poor papa, poor man" (307). Bloom's "Judaism" may have devolved to only a sense of filial piety, but such memories ultimately represent to him one of the double-binds of assimilation, one which, in his father's case, became poignantly tragic. Leaving "the God of our father" seems to have been suggested to the young Leopold as the "sin" behind the family's problems. But Bloom knows that when his father took his own life, his business venture in Ennis was failing miserably.[37] It was during those last years of his father's depression that Bloom had ridiculed him for returning to his Jewish faith.[38] Although Bloom has always regretted that disrespect, his sorrow mainly surrounds the suicide, not the blasphemy. Like many living, assimilated Jews of his era, however, Bloom's sense of himself as a Jew cannot be extinguished through mere apostasy.

Note the progression of Bloom's thoughts. *Leah*, a play about Jewish matriarchy, becomes a joke about transvestism, which in turn becomes a reference to suicide, and so finally evokes pity for a guilt-ridden Jew. "Jewishness", androgyny, weakness, and suicide mark the pattern of this memory. And Joyce's delight in the associative power of the imagination becomes obvious here. Bloom represses these elements of his own self-image by projecting them on to "poor papa," who as a suicide deserves only sympathy. But Bloom himself often feels he is as much an emasculated – read Weiningerian – pariah as he imagines his father felt about himself.

Bloom's sense of difference issues from several aspects of his personality, not the least of which may be discovered in his linguistic habits. While we assume he speaks English with an Irish brogue, on occasion Bloom underscores his thoughts with Yiddish. As Hebrew was primarily a liturgical language in 1904, these Yiddish terms again represent Bloom's cultural "Jewishness." He uses such expressions throughout the day, as in his estimation of Denis Breen as "Messhugga" (*U*8.314). These snippets of another language now become mostly an intimate inner-voice, a manner of personal emphasis, perhaps parallel to the use of Gaelic of many turn-of-the-century Dubliners (as in the citizen's use of Irish in "Cyclops"). Bloom thus appears to have a different mother tongue from other Irishmen – as will be confirmed in "Ithaca" (*U*17.724-60).

Perhaps more significant than his smattering of Yiddish, however, is Bloom's situation as apprehended by most other Irishmen: he cannot avoid being perceived as a "Jew" by those who surround him, and anti-Jewish rhetoric appears to confront him daily. On the morning of June 16, evidence of that ubiquitous perception occurs as he rides to Paddy Dignam's funeral in the "Hades" episode. When Bloom's fellow mourners suggest that Reuben J. Dodd's usury is a "Jewish act" – "of the tribe of Reuben" – Bloom sits by in careful silence. He endures Cunningham's suggestion that Bloom himself has somehow suspiciously avoided debt, and then suffers Simon Dedalus' curse on Dodd – "Drown Barabas!" (*U*6.261, 274). Bloom attempts to deflect the first insinuation by offering the story about the junior Dodd's swim in the Liffey (251–92). But the reference to Dodd as a "Jew" nonetheless has made a deep impression on Bloom. Later in the day, it appears he tacitly accepts Dodd as a "dirty Jew," when, catching sight of Sir Frederick Falkiner, he is reminded of the magistrate's reprimand of the gombeen man (*U*8.1158–61). Later in nighttown, Bloom's fantasies include Dodd as a Judas figure. When Bloom's "Jewishness" becomes an outlet for his self-hatred, he willingly participates in the stereotype of "the Jew" as unscrupulous in usury – Shylock without a heart. In the carriage, however, Bloom is perhaps the sole passenger who best understands the historical dynamic behind the stereotype. His failure to register this understanding, even in his own thoughts, demonstrates his avoidance of his Jewish consciousness that is ironically most crucial to his claim as an Irishman; without confronting the first, he can never fully accept himself as the second.

Once inside the cemetery, Bloom further reveals the ambiguity of his Jewish identity in his stream-of-consciousness about rites of burial. At one point he recalls the Jewish custom of burial with a clod of earth from Israel: "Bit of clay from the holy land" (*U*6.819). He views the wish as a final expression of the Jew's desire to be "protected" by God, which is to Bloom another delusion of religious belief. When thinking of his own death, Bloom remembers the plot he has apparently purchased in this Christian burial ground: "Mine over there toward Finglas, the plot I bought. Mamma, poor mamma, and little Rudy" (861–62). Critics have pointed to this plot as further proof of Bloom's perception of himself as a Gentile. [39] But Bloom wants to be buried next to his mother, who unlike his father, was interred in Dublin and was of course not Jewish. On the other hand, Bloom has buried his son here – at the time of Rudy's death, Bloom had yet to recognize his son as one of the strongest links to his sense of "Jewishness." Bloom indeed often wants to view himself as a Dubliner but not a Jewish Dubliner. Prospect Cemetery in Glasnevin is where middle-class Dubliners, as well as Irish patriots such as Parnell, are buried.

Bloom recalls his father's Judaism again in "Aeolus," when a typesetter's work reminds him that Hebrew is written from right to left. In this instance, after ridiculing aspects of the Passover ritual, he decides that the lyric of "Chad Gadya" ("One Kid") "sounds a bit silly till you come to look into it well. Justice it means, but its everybody eating everyone else. That's what life is after all" (*U*7.206–14). Now "poor papa's" religiosity strikes a meaningful note. It is this specific meaning, moreover, that becomes a catalyst for Bloom's sudden acceptance of himself as a Jew later on in Barney Kiernan's pub; when Bloom defends passivity and love as above nationalism and violence – "that's not life for men and women, insult and hatred" – he publicly declares himself a Jew for the first time in the novel (*U*12.1481–82). But in "Aeolus," the previous stereotype of Dodd has already impinged on Bloom's view of his father's Jewishness. Judaism remains another "silly" religion to Bloom, but surprisingly, Judaism's "obsolete" ritual now suggests a meaning – a meaning Bloom recognizes as a cornerstone of his personality; as a pacifist, Bloom knows that non-aggression is central to his beliefs. And his compassion, which often pains him as another aspect of his weak, effeminate nature, nonetheless becomes a main vehicle for his sense of himself as a Jew. Judaism certainly can't claim a monopoly on compassion, but Bloom's identity as a Jew will become to him inseparable from his own heightened empathy for living things.[40]

Thus influenced by Weininger and Svevo alike, Joyce establishes here a key element of his "Jew" as the tendency toward internalization and compassion. Taking Weininger as a model rather than an authority, however, Joyce will portray Bloom's fear that his compassion is part of his "effeminate Jewish nature" as a product of the internalization of stereotype. But during the midday hours, that recognition on Bloom's part has yet to be made.

After the twin "monsters" of Platonism and Aristotelianism have been introduced in "Scylla and Charybdis," Stephen launches into his *Hamlet* theory. But Mulligan soon enters and begins mocking both Stephen and the act of scholarly dialectic in general. Stephen has sent Buck a telegram bearing the message "*[t]he sentimentalist is he who would enjoy without incurring the immense debtorship for a thing done,*" implying that Buck's Hellenism is hollow (*U*9.550-51). Mulligan, of course, actually eschews intellectualism, and by the close of the episode has composed the opening of his play which suggests that "library types" are merely weak "masturbators." It is this cynicism about the "unmanly" act of critical discourse that provokes Mulligan to slander Bloom as he makes his way toward his research for the Keyes advertisement (*U*9.586–87):

Voluble, dutiful, he led the way to all the provincial papers, a
  bowing dark figure following his hasty heels.
  The door closed.
– The sheeny! Buck Mulligan cried.
He Jumped up and snatched the card.
– What's his name? Ikey Moses? Bloom.
He rattled on:
– Jehovah, collector of prepuses, is no more. I found him over in the museum where I went to hail the foam born Aphrodite . . .
  Suddenly he turned to Stephen:
– He knows you. He knows your old fellow. O, I fear me, he is Greeker than the Greeks. His pale Galilean eyes were upon her mesial groove . . . (*U*9.602–16)

Buck here refers to Bloom's interest in the question of whether a statue of a goddess would possess an anus (*U*8.930–31). But his warning to Stephen that Bloom is "Greeker than the Greeks," coupled with the previous "sheeny" and "Ikey Moses" are Buck's way of insinuating that, as a Jew, Bloom is "womanly," and thus a kind of "scheming homosexual pervert." The anti-Jewish composite is furthered when Stephen theorizes that Shakespeare must have had experiential insight into the Jewish position to create Shylock.[41] Stephen is merely attempting to point out that the dramatist drew from "real life" to create his most profound characters, but an offended John Eglinton interrupts: "Prove that was he a jew . . . " (763). At the close of the episode, Stephen and Mulligan stand in opposition (the two represent the whirlpool and the rock themselves) as Bloom passes between them. Mulligan again suggests that Bloom, "the wandering Jew," "lusts after" his friend, but Stephen has already associated Bloom with the man in his dream who appeared on the "street of harlots" (1206–12). Although Stephen finds Buck's ranting insulting, he cannot yet grasp the ramifications of Bloom's presence. But he is hopeful: "A creamfruit melon he held to me. In. You will see" (1208).

In "Wandering Rocks," allusions to the Dublin Jewish community and both Bloom's "Jewish effeminate nature" and "Jewish generosity" again suggest the duplicity of "the Jew" in Irish Culture. As Ned Lambert points out the historical value of Saint Mary's Abbey off Capel Street, he is careful not to exclude its association with Dublin Jewry:

This is the most historic spot in all of Dublin. O'Madden Burke is going to write something about it one of these days. The old bank of Ireland was over the way till the time of the union and the original jews' temple was here too before they built their synagogue over in Adelaide Road.(*U*10.409–13)

But while Jews have been an element of Dublin history since the seventeenth century, Bloom "the Jew" to a vulgar roustabout such as the *Dubliners'* recycled Lenehan is only a joke as a "real man."

In relating his private narrative of how he was once able to fondle Molly in Bloom's presence, Lenehan implies that the latter is either so oblivious or so pacifistic that he will not challenge those who would have their way with his wife. But the joke causes its audience, M'Coy, to both smile and grow "grave" (578). M'Coy's rejoinder attempts to defend Bloom: " – he's a cultured, allaround-man, Bloom is, he said seriously. He's not one of your common or garden . . . you know . . . There's a touch of the artist about old Bloom" (581–82). Although the comment recognizes Bloom as a compassionate, creative thinker, such an honor – especially given the implied suspicion of homoeroticism behind it – is dubious to most of the Irishmen Bloom encounters on June 16; indeed, the dubiousness is more often than not suggested as an element of the perverse, "effeminate nature" of "the Jew."

By the close of the episode, two of the more humane Dubliners in the story suggest another irony about Bloom's "Jewishness" as they perceive it. While observing the fund for Dignam's widow, Martin

Cunningham and John Wyse Nolan notice that Bloom has signed on
for a donation of five shillings (974).⁴² Cunningham signs on for the
same amount, and acknowledges the right-mindedness of Bloom's
gesture. Later on in "Cyclops," this act appears inspirational to
Nolan's support of the set-upon Bloom (*U*12.1419). In response to
Cunningham, however, Nolan "quotes elegantly . . . I'll say there is
much kindness in the jew" (980). The statement is an allusion to *The
Merchant of Venice*, Act i, Scene iii, when Antonio considers the
absurdity of Shylock's pound-of-flesh collateral, and readily agrees
to the proposed bond. Nolan's left-handed compliment suggests that
as a Jew, Bloom's acceptance always competes with stereotype –
even in the case of an unadulterated act of kindness. Thus the
Irishman's Christian compassion is suggested as categorically different
than that of Bloom. Nolan is of course being wry; but the fact that
Bloom is one of the most generous of the group makes the joke a
bitter pill. Beneath the humor lies the suggestion that if they prick
Bloom he'll bleed, but it will be a Jew's blood, still somehow distinct
from their own. On some level, perhaps even in his formative years,
Bloom has always been aware of being perceived as different in this
essential manner.

In "Sirens," haunted by Boylan's impending insult, Bloom wanders
into the Ormond bar. The enchanted singing here not only aids him
in forgetting Boylan's "jingle," but inspires in Bloom a surprising
recognition of heritage. Joyce intended "Sirens" to close the middle
episodes of the book; provoked by Ben Dollard's song, Bloom here
finally discovers the courage to affirm his roots. Preoccupied with the
impending adultery, Bloom notes how Dollard was once a young,
brawny man; the memory of Molly's laughter at Dollard's bulge in
Bloom's borrowed knickers explains things to him: "well of course,
that's what gives him the base barreltone. For instance eunuchs"
(559–60). Bloom "measures" his masculinity against Dollard and
Boylan in a manner similar to his earlier assessment of Dlugacz. These
men are to Bloom his mirrored opposites: strong, talented, aggressive,
virile. Dollard's rendition of "The Croppy Boy" recalls for Bloom
another strength of conviction: "All gone, all fallen. At the siege of
Ross his father, at Gorey all his brothers fell. To Wexford, we are the
boys of Wexford, he would. Last of his name and race" (*U*11.
1063–65). Oddly enough, this staple of the Irish folk-imagination
provokes an unexpected recognition from Bloom:

I too. Last of my race. Milly young student. Well, my fault perhaps. No son. Rudy. Too late now. Or if not? if not? if still?

He bore no hate. Hate. Love. Those are names. Rudy. Soon I am old. (1066–69)

Bloom believes himself to be a "mixed middling": he is both an Irishman and a Jew; he is male, yet he has come to perceive many of his traits – compassion most prominently – as negatively "female attributes." When he hears an Irish elegy, however, he thinks not of an Irish identity, but of a Jewish one. Even before his vision outside of the brothel in "Circe," he harbors here the sentiment that, had the child lived, Rudy would have perpetuated a sense of Jewish patriarchy in his world.

Celebration of patriarcal victories is of course a bulwark of Irish culture as well. But Bloom's remorse over the loss of his paternity doesn't parallel the most common Irish response to dead sons and lost causes. Since "Jewishness" to Bloom is diasporic, it does not have a homeland and thus can have no aggressive nationalism. Without a territory to defend, there can be no sanctioned acts of terror. Bloom's growing sense of his own "Jewishness" – precisely because it is unterrritoried, exilic, and assimilated – embodies a heritage of blood that need not spill any to remain intact. The beauty of ethnicity to Bloom can only be one of exile, regeneration, and the continuity of ethical values.[43] "Jewishness" here implies an education of the heart, rather than one of the hands – a similar lesson to the one Mrs. Dedalus had prescribed for her son at the close of *A Portrait*.[44] Bloom's accompanying flatulence to a text of the dock-speech of Robert Emmet – an Irishman who was ready to kill and of course died in the name of nationalism – suggests a new song for this Irish Jew (1275–93); Bloom is "done" with at least one level of his confusion.[45]

Bloom's afternoon: Cyclops *to* Nausicaä

Demonstrations of the deconstructive nature of Joyce's language and narrative structure have often focused on the "Cyclops" episode. The reasons behind this are many: the introduction of a new narrator referred to only as "the collector of bad and doubtful debts" and later as the *Nameless One*; the ironic distance "the arranger" narrator achieves through a parody of mythic heroism and teasing pathos toward Bloom; the capturing of Dublin pub-humor in all its grittiness; and finally, the feeling on the part of many readers that, despite this subterfuge, the episode maintains a deadly seriousness about xenophobic nationalism, anti-Semitism, and the incontrovertible call for compassion toward the Other.[46] The infamous "Love loves to love love" passage (*U*12.1493–501), which directly mocks Bloom's impassioned expression of fraternal piety, has often been viewed as the most stinging attack on the sentimentality of benevolent toleration, which, previous to its intrusion, appears to be a viable polemic to the citizen's bigotry.

Yet despite such ambiguity, many readers of *Ulysses* often recognize "Cyclops" as one climax of the novel. Since most of the "action" in the "Circe" episode occurs only in the mind, "Cyclops" portrays Bloom's most crucial interpersonal conflict. Indeed, the time he spends in Barney Kiernan's pub is critical for Bloom: his dignity is insulted, his reputation impugned, and his person threatened. As the negative highlight of his day, the incident becomes engraved in his memory as "that altercation with a truculent troglodyte" (*U*17.2050). Any sense of seriousness in the "gigantic humor" of this episode appears to arise from Bloom's newly discovered assertiveness. Indeed, pathetic as the drunken citizen and frightened Bloom may be, their muddled confrontation presages Bloom's further recognition of the double-bind created by his Irish–Jewishness. By the end of the episode, Bloom emerges from the cave of Cyclops to reaffirm that he is not "Noman," but a very complex someone.

Bloom's stream-of-consciousness is of course usurped in this episode by the unnamed narrator. Without the lullaby of his own inner-voice, Bloom is coaxed into a territory not his own – the enemy territory of drunken patriots. Although the Gorman-Gilbert plan presents the art of "Cyclops" as "politics," there are few politically informed voices in Barney Kiernan's. Most of the supporters of Sinn Féin here erroneously believe that Bloom, of all people, has suggested to Arthur Griffith how the Irish could make use of the "Hungarian system" (*U*12.1636).[47] Through recycled *Dubliners* figures such as Hynes, Lenehan, and Doran, Joyce once again thumbs his nose at what he believes are some of the lowest common denominators of his home town. He also portrays, just as he did in "Ivy Day in the Committee Room," how politics can become a brutal travesty in the hands of uneducated jingoists. The cast of locals who the narrator recalls as having been in the pub that hour, including himself, are indeed for the most part ignorant opportunists. "The citizen," based on an aging Michael Cusack, is perhaps the blackest comedic figure of them all.[48]

Cusack, a stout, burly man who walked around Dublin with a

blackthorn stick, a large dog by his side, and called himself "citizen Cusack," was of course one of the more outspoken nationalists of his day. It at first appears curious, however, that Joyce chose to place many of Griffith's sentiments in the citizen's mouth rather than in some anonymous supporter of Sinn Féin, and we may never know precisely how much Joyce was thinking of Cusack as he formed the citizen. But given the common nickname, the citizen of "Cyclops" must have had some essential correspondence to the actual Cusack in Joyce's mind. Cusack's nationalism, like that of the young Griffith, was initially based on Davis' Young Ireland movement, and from 1882 onward Cusack had "immersed himself in Davis' writings" from the *Nation*.[49] But by the 1890s, Cusack was a committed supporter of Griffith. While some limited copies of Cusack's journal, the *Celtic Times* (founded in 1887), have recently become available, there appears to be no evidence that he was ever publicly anti-Semitic. Cusack's biographer laconically states, however, that as a young man, the athlete and teacher from county Clare was "full of prejudices of all kinds."[50] Moreover, it is likely Joyce himself only met Cusack briefly, while the former was attending University College.[51] In a 1906 letter to Stanislaus from Trieste, Joyce made only a cursory reference to Cusack's death.[52] But even if Joyce knew few actual details of Cusack's life, the man's public image and sports program seem to have lent themselves neatly to the needs of "Cyclops." Apparently, Joyce believed the connection between an aggressive republican and anti-Semite like Griffith and an organizer and sportsman like Cusack was their dogmatic racist Celticism, as well as their mutually aggressive temperaments.

Cusack, like Griffith, was obsessed with "Irishness" and Ireland for the Irish, and became the first treasurer for the Gaelic Union in 1883. He had launched the Gaelic Athletic Association (GAA) the following year, and was primarily responsible for its most successful venture, the ban against all those who would play in "English" games and accede authority in Ireland to the Amateur Athletic Association of England.[53] But during the height of his influence, Cusack continually made use of Griffith's type of reverse racism against the English. Moreover, Cusack was a man not to be crossed, even by his own compatriots, and his pugnaciousness soon lost him the leadership of his association through several arguments over policy with an editor of the *Freeman's Journal*, and then with the politically active Archbishop Croke.[54]

In his prime Cusack was a bigoted and forceful patriot, and by the

years Joyce chose to portray him, he had not only bullied his way out
of the public eye, but was indeed somewhat of a drunken, broken
man. Nevertheless, the impact of the GAA was immense: "[m]ore
than the Gaelic League, more than Arthur Griffith's Sinn Féin, more
than even the Transport and General Workers Union and of course
far more than the movement which created the Abbey Theater; more
than any of these the Gaelic Athletic movement aroused the interest
of large numbers of ordinary people throughout Ireland."[55] Yet,
ironically, such popularity incensed Joyce because he always had
higher standards for his own people; they hadn't supported a superior
man like Parnell in his time of need, but rallied behind the idea that
ancient games were a kind of linchpin of their patriotism. The very
setting of this episode – a Dublin pub dedicated to glorifying contact
sports, violence, and gore – is indeed based on such sentiments.

The citizen is thus in part Joyce's reconstruction of the stereotype of
"the simian-Celt" or Irish brute who can only think with his fists.
Indeed, Joyce may reveal his own self-deprecation as an Irishman
here; it appears to have been easier for him to investigate and subvert
stereotype in his "Jew" than in this portrait of an aggressive Irish
patriot. But the citizen is not all projection or even parodic
fun-and-games. Had we met him in his athletic prime, perhaps his
republicanism would appear to be more than just blarney.[56] The
citizen doesn't have time for Celtic twilights; his sentiments are more
of the "bloodyminded" Jacobin type: " – Its on the march . . . To hell
with the brutal Sassenachs and their *patois*" (1190). The nation to him
must be forged through violence; Joyce underscores this with the
citizen's paramilitary phrases: "stand and deliver"; or "on point
duty" (128–379). As aged and drunken as he may be, when nations of
citizen-Cusacks-Griffiths become empowered, the Blooms of the
world are threatened by more than a biscuit tin.

As soon as he is spotted in his "gloryhole" in the pub, the citizen
indeed becomes the voice of Griffith's yellow journalism. When
informed that the "markets are on a rise," he immediately invokes
undocumented imperial causes – "Foreign wars is the cause of it . . .
It's the Russians wish to tyrannize" (138, 140). By his composition of
"Cyclops," Joyce knew well that the era's anti-imperialistic propaganda
often preceded Jewish conspiracy theories; he had of course inscribed
the same type of discourse previously in the words of Deasy and
Haines. Moreover, Griffith himself was inspired to begin his political
life after two years in South Africa, where he became incensed about

the Boer War and imperialism.[57] A great part of both Irish and British reaction to the situation in South Africa throughout the 1890s focused on Jewish economic involvement there, and often made the claim that the growing confrontation was inspired by Jews who stood to gain from a victory on either side.[58] In this scenario, imperialism was only the tip of the iceberg – imperialists were suggested as the dupes of the larger "Jewish conspiracy." Joyce underscores such inflated bigotry with the ensuing mock heroic description – "the figure seated on a large boulder . . . " (151–205). This, then, becomes Joyce's one-eyed monster: a looming, xenophobic patriotism that plays on the most convenient hatreds to fuel its cause.

From the opening of the episode, the reader is offered a kind of smorgasbord of religious, economic, and nationalistic anti-Jewishness. The narrator introduces the taunting in his initial story about Moses Herzog, "the little jewy getting his shirt out" (*U*12.30). The first reference to Bloom is "the prudent one" who gave Joe Hynes the tip on *Throwaway*. Bloom's nickname here evinces one of the reasons he feels isolated from other Dubliners – he doesn't drink or gamble or indulge in pub-boasting. Not drinking, and more incriminating, not "standing a round" when supposedly he has just reaped his winnings, are identifying marks of "the Jew" to the citizen and his companions: "Courthouse my eye and your pockets hanging down with gold and silver. Mean bloody scut. Stand us a drink itself. Devil a sweet fear! There's a jew for you! All for number one. Cute as a shithouse rat" (1759–61). The slander, which plays on the bestial nature of Dreyfus-era caricatures, is again simple projection; it's the citizen who is "all for number one" – his own gullet and his own idea of "the pure nation."

Noticing Bloom outside the pub, the citizen asks, "What's the bloody freemason doing" (300). Given that the citizen perceives Bloom as a Jew, the insult obviously references the kind of Jewish-world-conspiracy rhetoric Griffith often invoked, and Joyce thus now evinces the previous allusions to Bloom's freemasonry as merely another form of anti-Semitism. The citizen thinks Bloom is a foreigner, a "cursed" Jew, and a "Mister knowall" – but he'd be willing to accept a drink from him (838). When he confronts the citizen, however, Bloom becomes "a wolf in sheep's clothing," interested only in "swindling the peasants and the poor of Ireland'; the citizen will have "no more strangers in [his] house" (1150–51). Joyce achieves a parallel here to Deasy's earlier Unionist anti-Semitism in "Nestor," and thus again demonstrates how the two political opposites appropriate the same discourse about "the Jew." Yet as the embodiment of bigotry, the citizen slanders everyone but his own – the French, the English, the Germans – any people can become a target of his displaced self-hatred.[59]

But unlike Deasy, the citizen is looking for a fist-fight, and in fact invites Bloom into the bar and makes conversation with him (409). Bloom indeed soon becomes annoying to everyone present. His loquaciousness is unwelcome in a place where speech is used only for cursing or boasting about heroism. The "secrets" of his Hungarian–Jewish past, his money dealings, and his supposed Freemasonry make him suspect. He asserts that physiology, not virility, is responsible for the hanged Joe Brady's erection.[60] He proposes the skills of tennis over the brutality of boxing; he believes that "drink [is] the curse of Ireland"; when the "Canada swindle" is brought up, he suddenly becomes to the others an example of "the Jew," "coming over here to Ireland filling the country with bugs" (464, 945, 684, 1141). When "Garryowen" sniffs Bloom's leg, the narrator reminds us of an essential element of "the Jew'; they even smell different – "I'm told those jewies does have a queer odor coming off them" (452–53).[61]

When Bloom engages him in a discussion about training animals by a method of kindness, however, the citizen finally appears to grasp the implications of his interlocutor's argument. The citizen's "rebuttal" suggests that the true "patriot" can't forget injustice; solidarity and vengeance are sweeter than love: "the memory of the dead . . . *Sinn Fein!* says the citizen, *Sinn Fein Amhain!* the friends we love are by our side and the foe we hate before us" (519, 523–24).[62] Bloom's worst offense by far is thus his Jewish Otherness – he's not included in "Ourselves Alone," and his mere existence in Ireland challenges the cult-of-nation fantasy.

To the other patrons as well, national identity rests on a kind of pseudo-blood-right, and for Bloom that in itself is a murky subject:

– And after all, says John Wyse, why can't a jew love his country like the next fellow?
– Why not? says J. J. when he's quite sure which country it is.
– Is he a jew or a gentile or a holy Roman or a swaddler or what the hell is he? says Ned. Or who is he? No offence, Crofton. (1628–32)

Martin Cunningham offers his own explanation – "He's a perverted jew . . . from a place in Hungary and it was he drew up all the plans according to the Hungarian system. We know that in the castle"

(1635-37). Ironic as it may be, Bloom on occasion apparently supports Sinn Féin, and his co-operative, non-violent programs are supposedly always waiting in the wings. But when his ambiguous Jewish-Irishness is layered over the ambiguity of race, blood, and allegiance, the Fenian mind reels in confusion. Bolstering their own self-definitions, the gang of patriots must revert to an older discourse of difference. Even if he's for the cause, Bloom can't be trusted because he's also a Jew: " – A wolf in sheep's clothing, says the citizen. That what he is. Virag from Hungary! Ahasuerus I call him. Cursed by God" (1666-67). Nations can crumble, blood may be mixed, and Protestants in Dublin have long been welcomed into the cause, but, despite the fact that he may change his surname, a Jew is a Jew – deicidal from the start.

But Bloom, of course, has much broader concerns – he wants to portray himself as *agape* – or *tzedakah* – incarnate. Military aggression, corporal punishment, bravado, "force against force" are all the same to him, and he'll have no part in any might for right:

– Persecution, says he, all the history of the world is full of it. Perpetrating national hatred among nations.(1417–18)

The citizen and his band of drunks are uninterested in such "sissy-talk." The more humane members of this ironically dubbed "sinhedrim" (1125), however, are compelled to address Bloom's assertion – especially because it issues from the mouth of an "alien" Jew: "– But do you know what a nation means? says John Wyse" (1419). Apparently, Bloom doesn't know the answer; he is at first contradictory – "a nation is a people living in the same place – Or also living in different places." Then, he is presumptive – "What is your nation if I may ask? says the citizen. – Ireland, says Bloom, I was born here. Ireland" (1422-31). The art of "Cyclops" in the Linati schema is "surgery," and Bloom has now cut into both the citizen's wrath and his own identity crisis.[63]

When Bloom declares he also "belongs to a hated and persecuted race," he acknowledges himself a Jew and so verbalizes a key aspect of his dilemma. His confused attempts to answer the question of what precisely defines a "nation" – landed or rootless – emphasize the idea that a nation is an ideology; and in his case, the implication in turn presents a central tension of the era's Jewish question. The entire discussion, moreover, introduces a subtext of nationalist arguments: is citizenship the main criterion for membership in a nation? Is one bound to a nation by birth alone? Is "dual allegiance" to both one nation and another people ultimately contradictory? Could a believing, Zionistic Jew (both of which, ironically, Bloom is not) ever have been a true national? Could Joyce be an Irish nationalist as an expatriate writer whose work centered on impugning several mainstays of his own culture?

Bloom's understanding of Rabbinic Judaism is of course incomplete, and he's a confirmed atheist, but again, in many ways, he remains a Jew. His lineage is at least three-fourths Jewish.[64] He was born and raised in Ireland, yet his most strongly held beliefs are based on a sense of "Jewishness" that has been diluted through his father's and his own radical assimilation. He is not a Zionist, but an Irish nationalist who is dogmatically pacifist, a prophet of peaceful coexistence – "the opposite of hatred"; Yet, in vital ways, he regards these attitudes as remnants of his Judaism (1484). But if he won't hate or die for the cause, does he really believe in Ireland for the Irish? He is both a "perverted" Irishman and a "perverted Jew"; one can be neither in the citizen's nation (1635). In every sense, then, Bloom is a threat to the ideology of racial purity. Bloom now recognizes that he is, indeed, "neither fish nor flesh" – a compassionate Jew in an Irish "rogue's gallery" pub, he cannot escape being perceived as emasculated and devious. But if he's "Ahasuerus . . . that white-eyed kaffir," then he now has an identity he can hold on to and examine – the authentic Jew.[65] This may not be the most profound sense of a Jewish identity, but it is nevertheless a revelation for Bloom; recognizing himself to be a Jew whose self-perception as such has been formed greatly through stereotype, Bloom begins his own victory over self-abnegation. (Not by coincidence, he also appears to be one of the most compassionate "Christians" to pass through Barney Kiernan's on June 16.)

Joyce rewards Bloom in the episode with two final gifts, one serious, one parodic. When the citizen shouts his most vitriolic sarcasm, "Three cheers for Israel," Bloom becomes confrontational (1791). Perhaps he had been foolish to confront the citizen altogether – one can't argue with drunken irrationality. But now it is no longer a matter of gentlemanly disagreement. As an apostate Jew – "the non-Jewish Jew" – Bloom is not only empowered, but believes himself to be in good company:

– Mendelssohn was a jew and Karl Marx and Mercadante and Spinoza. And the Savior was a jew and his father was a jew. Your God.

– He had no father, says Martin. That'll do now. Drive ahead.
– Whose God? says the citizen
– Well, his uncle was a jew, says he. Your God was a Jew. Christ was a Jew
like me.(1804–09)

Bloom's list has often been regarded as a prime example of his foggy
thinking, here about "his own people." But this assumption again
suggests "Jewishness" as an either/or question of religion, which it is
not. Joyce's joke is thus on the reader, not on Bloom. With the
exception of Mercadante, each of the names suggest a "Jewishness"
similar to Bloom's.[66] Moses Mendelssohn of course advocated a new
type of emancipated Judaism assimilated to the ideas of Western
rationalism and was condemned for it by orthodox German Jewry.
His grandson, Felix Bartholdy, ultimately considered himself "Jewish"
even after baptism into the Protestant Church. On one level, Marx's
early anti-Semitism can be viewed as a devastating result of the type
of Jewish self-abnegation Bloom embodies. Spinoza was excommunicated – which is not the same as denying one's Jewishness – for
his blasphemous philosophy.[67] But Jesus is the best example: a
political misfit, he transgressed Hebraic law and considered himself
a new, more divinely inspired Jew ('Christ was a Jew like me"
embodies Joyce's predilection for heretics; to the Pharisees, Jesus
was precisely the kind of revolutionary Joyce admired.) In a 1922
revision of his printer's placard, Joyce had in fact penciled in the
final "Your God" of Bloom's speech here to emphasize the theological
as well as the historical division between Jew and Christian.[68]
Bloom's list of "non-Jewish Jews" is more a recognition of his own
type of "Jewishness" than a good defense of the citizen's insult. In
"Ithaca," Bloom will indeed recite to Stephen a similar list of names
in attempting to demonstrate the genius of Jewish assimilation
(*U*17.711–23).[69]

While the citizen remains seated throughout Bloom's list of
"important Jewish figures," the reference to Jesus' Jewish identity
inspires in the former a profound religious hatred. In the text's terms,
he has been "properly riled" by the "bite from a sheep" (*U*16.1639–40).
Despite the ensuing slapstick hilarity, Joyce is having a field-day with
the dialogic between religion and nationalism. The citizen's subsequent
fulminations are riddled with irony: "I'll brain the bloody jewman for
using the holy name. By Jesus, I'll crucify him so I will" (*U*12.1811–12).
Drawing on the attitudes of both Griffith and Cusack, Joyce suggests
that beyond Christian, patriotic, or Celtic allegiances, the citizen

represents the convolutions both bigotry and violent republicanism make to sustain their hatreds.

The second gift Joyce offers is Bloom's new mantle, "ben Bloom Elijah" (1916). The narrator closes his story with Bloom escaping the biscuit tin. The "arranger" voice that has continually undermined that narration with pseudo-mythic language, now parodies Bloom as the prophet who heralds the coming of the Messiah. But while Bloom-Elijah answers God's call in Hebrew – "*Abba, Adonai*" (Father, God) – the glorious trajectory of his flaming chariot is given the prosaic description of "at an angle of fortyfive degrees over Donoghue's in Little Green street like a shot off a shovel" (1917–18). The final simile here subverts the "muscular gigantism" of Bloom's effort, offering instead a local, unadorned cliché. Bloom has been given his moment of glory; he is now off to the strand to engage in one of the most prosaic of all acts.

Undoubtedly, the web of narrative complication and inflated, parodic language in "Cyclops" disallows a reader to sustain either an unmitigated pathos toward oppression or an admiration of chauvinistic aggression. Instead, Joyce evokes the spontaneous doubt that often arises when debating a compassion for "the Other" against deep religious and nationalistic feelings of unity. The love of "my people" and the ideal of unconditional love for humankind both have their untenable elements, and perhaps their own kind of lies as well. But despite his underdeveloped argument or what has been called his "lunatic has-been" opponent, Bloom as a Jew has escaped the cave of the one-eyed giant, the monster of ancient hatreds renewed under the guise of modern patriotism.[70] As this type of newly reaffirmed Jew, however, he has not yet escaped the torture of his own psyche.

As the sun sets on the strand in "Nausicaä," Joyce reveals two essential aspects of Bloom's struggle with a Jewish identity. Bloom's gaze at Gerty MacDowell suggests that much of his sexual satisfaction is completely dependent on the internalizing force of fantasy. Bloom has been dreaming all day about past encounters and his prospective liaison with Martha Clifford; but when he acts on his urges, it is through the voyeurism and masturbation of a lonely person denying or even fearing the need of human contact. Is this Joyce's portrayal of Bloom at his most internalizing moment and so his most "Jewish" in a Weiningerian sense? Joyce is certainly not passing an ethical judgment on Bloom as a "pervert" (although public masturbation certainly crosses the line of social acceptability) but demonstrating the severity of Bloom's isolation and self-doubt. Bloom needs the protection of distance and fantasy to achieve orgasm, and the flirtatious Gerty (who is herself repressed and alienated by her handicap) provides him with this day's opportunity. But does Bloom himself perceive his guarded, timid act as stemming from his "Jewish nature?" If so, he has internalized the stereotype to a devastating degree.

In detumescence, Bloom rearranges himself and mumbles "this wet is very unpleasant. Stuck. Well the foreskin is not back. Better detach. Ow!" (*U*13.979–81). The reader now discovers that Bloom is uncircumcised and so further excluded from a Rabbinic Jewish identity. Within moments, Bloom again verbalizes both his ignorance of Jewish custom, as well as his condescending view of Judaism: "And the tephilim no what's this they call it poor papa's father had on his door to touch. That brought *us* out of the land of Egypt and into the house of bondage. Something in all those *superstitions* because when you go out never know what dangers" (1157–60, italics mine). Bloom is both alienated and confused (his "danger" is manifesting itself in his bedroom as he speaks, and he is the "cuckoo" of the closing lines of the episode).[71] His pronoun "us" here includes himself as a Jew, but he gets the sentiment backwards, and reiterates his view of Judaism as merely another set of archaic superstitions. Rather than being merely another typical Bloomian error (as this line is so often cast), the reversal in his reference to Exodus suggests Bloom's ironic, modern sensitivity to the historical persecution of the Jews. Thus he won't perceive himself as a Jew in his own right, but includes himself in the constructed cultural pariahism of European Jewry. In the final phrases of the episode, even Gerty's purple perception of Bloom ultimately includes his Otherness: "she noticed at once that the *foreign* [italics mine] gentleman that was sitting on the rocks looking was / *Cuckoo/Cuckoo/Cuckoo*" (1301–02). Where does one in such a marginal subject-position and with so tortuous a self-image as Bloom go to discover a center, an identity that fosters self-worth, purpose, and a sense of belonging? . . . Nighttown?

Bloom's night: Circe *through* Penelope

While "Circe" is strewn with Yiddish, Hebrew, and Jewish allusions, the references at first seem pivotal only to Bloom's secular masochism/ Messianism. Having publicly affirmed himself a Jew in Barney

Kiernan's, Bloom has meandered for the rest of the evening. In
"Oxen of the Sun," among a group of Irishmen, he once again
became an outcast as the man who sides with the female and glorifies
the maternal (*U*14.1060–109). Despite this, Bloom's victorious
declaration of "Jewishness" in "Cyclops" has failed to transform him
into a potent father or forgiven son. Molly, Rudy, and Rudolph
Bloom still haunt him; tracking Stephen and Lynch, however, Bloom
enters an environment that unlocks his repression. Again, however,
the catalyst here initially appears not to be his "Jewishness", but
rather his impression of nighttown as the place in which it seems
possible to exhume his sexual skeletons.

Bloom's skeletons, however, have much to do with his timidity.
Even the fantasies for which he feels the most guilt – Gerty, Josie
Breen, Mary Driscoll – hardly deserve the label "sexual aggression."
Bloom's "crimes" are predominantly voyeuristic and masturbatory.
He punishes himself for this by empowering "the female" in his
psyche in the forms of Molly, Bella, and other miscellaneous women,
all as dominatrices. Whipped and degraded, he imagines he has
reached the nadir of timidity.

There can be no doubt that Joyce makes Bloom perceive himself as
timid, in part, because of his "Jewishness"; in his most degraded
position beneath the boot of Bello, he renames himself "Ruby
Cohen" (2966, 3108). Indeed, of all the hoops Bloom jumps through
in "Circe," his struggle with "Jewishness" demands the most masochistic
exercises. Even after "Cyclops," he continues to define his bisexual
guilt by way of his Jewish identity. But although Bloom has not yet
realized it, Joyce has made him "Weininger's Jew" only in so far as he
denigrates or parodies his own "Jewishness." Bloom's timidity, rather
than a "racial trait," stems in part from his internalization of the
social censure of the compassion and passive tolerance Judaism
prescribes. Once he establishes his "willpower" in confessing his
"sins" (3216), Bloom's "timid-compassionate-'Jewishness'" becomes
no less than a complete masculinity – a gendering that moves beyond
his dominant culture's assumptions about maleness and into those
Bloom will accept as both Jewish and redemptive. That new identity
is ultimately expressed through both his rescue of Stephen and his
subsequent vision of Rudy. (4422-54, 4962–67).

Jewish allusions reside at the core of each of Bloom's four fantasies
in "Circe." Bloom's initial vision in nighttown suggests a reprimand
from the spirit of his father. Rudolph Bloom wears "the caftan of elder

of Zion," and he and his son converse in Yiddish. The description of
Rudolph's appearance here draws on and parodies the rhetoric of the
infamous *Protocols of the Elders of Zion*; rather than a conspiratory
mystic in league with Satan to overthrow Christian power, Rudolph
is a figure comically burdened with only the vestments of the
stereotype; his function in Bloom's imagination is rather to once again
fulfill a self-flagellation over forgetting one's "Jewish roots." Ad-
monishing Bloom about running with "the drunken goy," the senior
Bloom embodies the father searching for the prodigal son – the whole
of which reminds Bloom of Mosenthal's *Deborah* (Bloom's *Leah* in
"Lotus Eaters," 252, 264). But again the religious allusion itself has
little impact on Bloom. What does upset him, however, is the memory
of his father's disappointment when, as an adolescent, an inebriated
Bloom had ruined his clothes in a race (268–72).[72] Rudolph's chiding
recalls Bloom's afternoon in "Cyclops" – *"goyim nachez"* ("gentile
satisfaction or pleasure"). In this Bloom recognizes his "Jewishness"
here as the imperative of a secularized self-control, ironically Judaism
as religion distilled to its most potent and pragmatic social message.

Bloom's defender during his first trial is J. J. O'Molloy, one of the
Irishmen who earlier in Barney Kiernan's had at least entertained the
notion of an Irish Jew as something more than a joke (*U*12.1630).[73]
Cast in the position of the accused, Bloom fortifies his own defense
with malapropisms of Judaism – "shitbroleeth" – and traditional
stereotypes – "I am being made a scapegoat of" (770, 786). In his
closing arguments, O'Molloy reinforces Bloom's self-defense by
referring first to Hebraism – "The Mosaic code has superseded the
law of the jungle," and then to scapegoating – "when in doubt,
persecute Bloom" (969, 975). As expressions of Bloom's claim to a
Jewish identity, both arguments appear to him to have some validity.
Bloom thus imagines Dlugacz standing on the shores of the Lake of
Kinnereth, and "holding in each hand an orange citron and a pork
kidney" (988–89); the new vision of the proud Zionist momentarily
includes Bloom as represented by the kidney.

But Bloom has yet to conquer his "Jewish timidity." At the trial's
close, Bloom's guilt produces Sir Frederick Falkiner, with "Mosaic
ramshorns" and "black skullcap" (1165, 1173). As an authoritarian
figure, Falkiner is now both an anti-Semite and an aggrandized
"Jew" (Moses). Thus, Jewish self-abnegation such as Bloom's empowers
the anti-Semite. Falkiner indeed condemns him to the accompaniment
of the jury's cries, "Who'll hang Judas Iscariot" (1176).

Bloom "wakes" from this fantasy to another in which Zoe Higgins speaks Hebrew to him (1332). As a "Higgins" she may be a distant relative of Bloom's Jewish maternal grandfather; in Bloom's vision she becomes a kind of a Jewish confidante, who, in stealing his potato talisman, forces him to confront, in an unprotected manner, his most devastating fears. His ensuing "Messianic dream" is thus nothing more than a wish-fulfillment, imagined in parodic largesse, about the acceptance of his assimilation. "Chief magistrate Bloom's" inauguration banner is, of course, "[a] streamer bearing the legends Cead Mile Failte and Mah Tob Melek Israel" (1399–1400).[74] After commissioning his "new Bloomusalem" to be built in the shape of a "pork kidney," Bloom is blessed by citizen Cusack himself (1618). Bloom's declaration in Hebrew, however, is a mockery of Judaic lore: "Aleph Beth Gimmel Daleth Hagadah Tephillim Kosher Yom Kippur Hanukah . . ." (1623–5). With the exception of the first four letters of the Hebrew alphabet, his proclamation merely repeats, nonsensically, the snippets of Hebrew and Yiddish he recalled during the course of the day.[75] To Bloom-the-Messiah, however, his ability to pray as a Jew is trivial compared to his plans for an egalitarian Ireland: "Union of all, jew, moslem and gentile . . . Free money, free rent, free love and a free lay church in a free lay state" (1685–94). "Joyce's Jew" has now become a parody of Ferrero's secularized "Messianic Jew" – Ferdinand Lassalle as the "tragic comedian."[76]

To his persecutors, such a plan – Hungarian or not – could only issue from the mind of a revolutionary, "perverted Jew." Bloom's Messianism indeed provokes a satirical list of the ways in which he believes he is perceived by others – a shopping-list of alterity and self-hatred. To the Church he is "an episcopalian, an agnostic, an anythinginarian seeking to overthrow our holy faith" (1712). To Dr. Mulligan he is "bisexually abnormal"; to Dr. Costello, he smells like a Jew: "The *fetor judaicus* is most perceptible" (1795).[77] In Bloom's defense, Dr. Dixon asserts that the subject is "a finished example of the new womanly man" (1798-99). Besides which, "he is about to have a baby."

Bloom proves his bisexual-Messianism by indeed giving birth to a litter, then transforming into a host of historical figures, several of whom were Jewish by birth (1821-51). Imagining himself a "finished example," however, Bloom for the first time places a positive twist on his "effeminate Jewish nature." But while he may have partially accepted what he believes to be a type of androgyny, he has not solved the anxiety surrounding it as a "Jewish condition." Thus he is soon dubbed in ancient Hebrew *"Azazel"* (scapegoat) and *"Belial"* (worthless) by the phantoms of his former Jewish friends (1899, 1907); he now conjures Reuben J. Dodd as a "blackbearded Iscariot," and then accepts the "high pointed hat" of the medieval Ghetto Jew (1918, 1928). His Messianic dream concludes in a prayer incanting each of his roles on that day. As absurd as these titles sound – "Kidney of Bloom . . . Wandering Soap . . . Midwife of Most Merciful" – they nonetheless represent in comic summary essential aspects of Bloom's most humane potentials. In this he confirms his status as the half-breed, the mundane, the compassionate, the timid, the alienated, the Other. Now he must confront his most devastating identity – the cuckold.

Bloom's grandfather, Lipoti Virag or Virag Lipoti, occupies a curious role in the next fantasy. Bloom never knew his grandfather, but he does possess a photograph of "Rudolf Virag and his father Leopold Virag" taken in 1852 in Hungary (*U*17.1875). After salivating over the whores, and imploring his grandson to assert himself as a sexually potent male, the specter of Virag howls at the moon. The "old world" phantom then launches into a tirade about the legends surrounding Jesus. His fulminations begin, ironically, with an inversion of a common German slander for the Jews – *"verfluchte goyim"* (accursed gentiles) (2570–76) and move through a histrionic diatribe about sexual "truths" and Christian "lies." Virag's appearance is thus marked by psycho-sexual babble, a bitter defamation of Jesus, the "unscrewing" of his head, and his final "quack!" (2637–38). Bloom imagines his grandfather – a "crazy Jew" spouting Yiddish notions about sexual deliverance and anti-Christianity – as a kind of cartoon nightmare. The once persecuted ancestor offers little direction, except to "make hay while the sun shines." To Bloom, Virag's manic mock-psychosis is a symbol of the exasperating history of Jewish victimization – a history that for the moment appears best represented as a sardonic joke.

Henry Flower, Bloom's "romantic, Savoir's faced" alter ego now enters and draws the latter's attention as the personification of one of his options – the romantic delusion of promiscuity (2483). With Bloom's mind momentarily hypnotized by Flower's piano playing, Joyce switches the focus to Stephen's consciousness so as to reintroduce the unsolved tensions between his impulses of "strictness and spontaneity" – or as he had been reminded that morning, between

"Hebraism and Hellenism." Bloom's struggle with his own masculinity (which for him still resides in the thick of his "Jewishness") remains irrelevant to Stephen, the "no voice … finished artist" (2508). Yet as the embodiments of Arnold's twin impulses of Western culture, "Philip Drunk and Philip Sober" still persist as diametric opposites to Stephen; their contradictory advice falls to absurd chatter, and is soon rendered inaudible by Joyce's return to Bloom's vision and Virag's running sexual harangue.[78] Virag's banter now becomes pseudo "Kama Sutra instruction" to Henry Flower-Bloom (2543–56); after, the grandfather shouts his farewell "Dreck!" and disappears into the wall with a "Quack!" Thus in light of the power of sexual energy and the horror of Christian persecution of the Jews, "Arnoldian balances" appear here to be nothing more than inconsequential "shit."

For Bloom, moreover, there is method in Virag's madness – the grandfather's sex-crazed imperative doesn't completely miss the mark for his grandson. In circuitous fashion, Bloom's final fantasy will indeed ultimately re-establish his masculine potency. When he hears what seems to be Boylan's voice in the outer hall, Bloom suddenly puts on "Svengali's fur overcoat … and gives the sign of past master" (2721–24). The magic spell incorporates two dominant stereotypes of "the Jew" as supernaturally devious: George du Maurier's Svengali was the modern personification of medieval legends about "the Jew's" mesmerizing powers; "Past master" alludes to the mysteries of Bloom's Freemasonry, which of course embodies Jewish world-conspiracy myths.[79] Bloom insulates himself through stereotypes of the "Jewish sorcerer" – stereotype internalized, yet now revised and empowering. And the announcement of this arcane "Jewish power" is soon followed by the appearance of Bella Cohen, the mystical "massive whoremistress" (2722).

As a kind of "magical Jewess" herself, Bella Cohen's witchcraft includes gender metamorphosis; her dominance–submission play with Bloom releases his guilt as a cuckold. Bloom imagines Bella as the feminine element of his own person – Jewish, libidinous, but yet now empowered. Punishing himself for his sexual inactivity, Bloom transforms first into a submissive homosexual, and then into a degraded woman. After the bondage and humiliation of Bello's discipline, Bloom finally admits his "sin" (3216). The fantasy is a prime example of Joyce's encoding of his own residual Catholicism into Bloom's "Jewishness"; when Bloom "confesses" to the "sexual priest" Bello, a chorus of Jewish Dubliners appear to mourn the death of the old Bloom: "Darkshawled figures of the circumcised, in sackcloth and ashes, stand by the wailing wall, M. Shulomowitz, Joseph Goldwater, Moses Herzog . . . " (3220–25).[80] These Rabbinic Jews recite the *Shema* over the "recreant" Bloom. But they do not recite *Kaddish*, the prayer for the dead.

Bloom is not dead; he is transformed. In the ensuing fray with the nymph, Bloom recalls his masturbatory life as originating in a youthful sacrifice "to the god of the forest" (3353). And in a kind of Joycean "romantic transcendence," Bloom now suddenly and insightfully realizes that there is nothing degenerative about him; his lack of aggressiveness as compared to other males is now seen in a transformed and acceptable light. Bloom's sexual "transgressions" are little more than expressions of his own sexual temperament, which is perhaps a bit more passive and consciously polymorphous than most, but hardly criminal. His problems reside neither in masturbation nor in voyeurism, nor in the internalizing impulse behind both acts, but in the lack of sexual contact with another human – most importantly Molly. In his recognition of his sexuality as both permissible and tied to qualities (internalization and non-aggression) he now views as "Jewish" in a *positive* sense, Bloom becomes empowered as both a man and a Jew.

During the remainder of his time in nighttown, Bloom fulfills his potential as both Jew and self-accepting male – he now knows the two were inseparable for him. He becomes active rather than reactive – the "cunning" Jew he always knew he was – and puts his cleverness to good use by aiding the suffering Stephen. He keeps Bella from overcharging Stephen and Lynch (3581). He accepts his punishment resolutely, and allows Boylan's hat to be hung on his "cuckold's antlers" (3762–64). Along with that of his new ward Stephen, he perceives his reflection in a mirror as the face of William Shakespeare; the two wanderers – one Irish, one Jewish – now join ranks with all artists, daydreamers, and cuckolds: the Shems of the world united. He uses his knowledge of both Freemasonry and the Dublin Jewish community to control Bella's threats of calling the police (4298-304). (Bella's subsequent cowering is another of Joyce's use of stereotype – as an assimilated "Jewish mother" she is subdued by Bloom's threats of exposing her son, and so ruining his chances at Oxford, his ticket to legitimacy within the dominant culture.) In response, Bella, "(almost speechless)," mumbles "Who are. Incog!" (4309) Bloom is, indeed, *incognito*, in the disguise of the marginal Jew: he is the Jew other Jews refuse to recognize; he is the Irishman other Irishmen will not accept. But he overcomes this challenge as a Samaritan, and as a Jew who now understands one of the basic tenets of Judaism as neither masculine nor feminine; he thus fulfills himself as a *mensch*, a mixed-middling who cares for individuals more than doctrines or sectarian solidarity; he is Joyce's Jewish Alfred Hunter aiding the wounded stranger.[81]

Hugh Kenner asserts that Bloom never hallucinates in "Circe" – what appears as fantastical to him in nighttown happens entirely in his mind's eye.[82] If this observation is correct, the figure of Rudy at the episode's close is not actually "seen" by Bloom, but is merely a final dream-image. Regardless of the nature of its manifestation, however, Rudy's phantom appears to be reading Hebrew and kisses the page in an imitation of the Jewish ritual of kissing the *siddur* (*U*15.4955–67).[83] Rudy has become a *Jewish* "fairy boy of eleven."

Joyce's revisions of the Rudy scene indeed demonstrate that the boy became "Jewish" as Joyce recognized what was needed to suggest the nature of Bloom's revelation. In the 1918 printer's placard, Rudy is simply "a boy of eleven in a Eton suit, holding a book in his hand. He reads inaudibly, smiling."[84] In revising for page proofs, Joyce subsequently penciled in the line "He reads *from right to left* inaudibly, smiling" (italics mine).[85] In a later proof, at some point Joyce added "kissing the page" to the end of this line.[86] As he revised, Joyce thus realized that Rudy's "Jewishness" had to be emphasized to clarify the nature of Bloom's nighttown experience.

As masochistic as Bloom's fantasies have become in nighttown, he was, as well, constantly undeterred in his avuncular mission toward Stephen. Just before seeing Rudy, Bloom watches over Stephen in "orthodox Samaritan fashion." Although he "stands irresolute," Bloom has acted on his impulse to nurture in a directed, confident manner (4922). Bloom has now become a Jew in his own eyes, but not one that manifests the stereotype of "Jewish degeneracy." Bloom is thus a new kind of Jew to himself: admirably compassionate, masculinely nurturing, active, and worthy of being a Jewish father.[87]

In "Eumaeus," safely sequestered in the cabman's shelter, Stephen and Bloom engage in a somewhat desultory conversation. After their respective visions in the brothel, each appears wearied and disturbed. In nighttown, identities and roles have been so thoroughly shaken that both wanderers now appear somewhat confused, and contrived role-playing in the tavern still shadows more solid interpretations of self.[88] Having himself assumed the role of Good "Jewish" Samaritan, Bloom suggests the shelter's proprietor is none other than the notorious Invincible, "skin-the-goat" (*U*16.322). When the "soi-disant sailor" portrays himself as a worldly-wise traveller, Bloom suspects his postcard, and thus his stories, to be fraudulent (489). Most significantly, it is in the shelter that Bloom will test his new role as Jewish Dubliner.

The first discussion in which both Stephen and Bloom participate fully concerns "the existence of a supernatural God" (771). After seeing the ghost of his mother, Stephen has revealed he is still a believer, although everything he says in the shelter is redolent with bitterness and sarcasm. Bloom, however, slipping into the role of paternal authority, is quite literal. Faith to him is "a matter of everyman's opinion," and the existence of God has in no way been "proved conclusively by several of the bestknown passages in the Holy Writ" (779, 773). This assertion of Bloom's agnosticism appears at odds with his new role as the father of a pious, Jewish Rudy. When the citizen's name arises out of a discussion of nationalism, Bloom in fact admits: "He called me a jew and in a heated fashion offensively. So I without deviating from plain facts in the least told him his God, I mean Christ, was a jew too and all his family like me *though in reality I'm not*" (1082–85, italics mine). Bloom's declaration implies that he is and is not a Jew, which, while contradictory, is perhaps quite accurate.

On one level, Bloom believes that "in reality" Rabbinic "Jewishness" is the only valid Jewish identity. Since he cannot qualify as such, he also implies that his previously earned "Jewishness" has now become merely another of the roles that the cabman's shelter offers. "In a non-committal accent," Stephen reminds him that Paul himself recognized Christ's "Jewishness" – "*Ex quibis . . . Christus . . . secundum carnem*" (1091–92).[89] But Stephen is as mocking as he is supportive. Bloom's agnosticism, on the other hand, is balanced by his sense of social outrage as a Jew:

Jews, he softly imparted in an aside in Stephen's ear, are accused of ruining. Not a vestige of truth in it, I can safely say. History, you would be surprised to learn, proves up to the hilt Spain decayed when the inquisition hounded the jews out and England prospered when Cromwell, an uncommonly able ruffian who in other aspects has much to answer for, imported them. Why? Because they are imbued with the proper spirit. They are practical and proved to be so. I don't want to indulge in any because you know the standard works on the subject and then orthodox as you are. But in the economic, not touching religion, domain the priest spells poverty . . . I'm, he resumed with dramatic force, as good an Irishman as that rude person I told you about at the outset and I want to see everyone, concluded he, all creeds and classes *pro rata* having a comfortable, tidy-sized income . . . That's the vital issue at stake and its feasible and would be provocative of friendlier intercourse between man and man. At least that's my idea for what its worth. I call that patriotism. *Ubi patria*, as we learned a smattering of in our classical days in *Alma Mater, vita bene*. Where you can live well, the sense is, where you can work.(1119–40)

The monologue, one of Bloom's most impassioned, is too often read as another of his muddled diatribes. It has even been suggested that Bloom here falls prey to stereotyping Jews. But while Bloom may depict the Jews as victims, he is nonetheless attempting to be historically "objective." His mention of Cromwell, for example, would make the most tolerant Irishman indignant; yet he acknowledges Cromwell's crimes even though they have little association with his argument. Moreover, while Bloom may stereotype Jews as economically shrewd through both the Cromwell and Inquisition allusions, both examples in this instance have factual antecedents.[90] Although his confused Latin is laughable to the Jesuit-trained Stephen, Bloom's insinuation that priests are a bane to sound economics must be enticing to the young anti-cleric. As generalizing as Bloom's points may appear, his speech in a way reaffirms his identity as a Jew because he addresses social injustice specifically *through* the Jewish position. To Bloom, Jewish pariahism seems to lie in economic questions. His egalitarianism is thus his "Jewish compassion" now taken from the personal to the political.[91] Moreover, he is colloquial and elegant here without being pedantic – a quality to which Joyce always aspired. Bloom's argument praises Jewish pragmatism, which in his own life has meant "the proper spirit" toward assimilation and affability. Bloom may generalize Jews as victims who have developed an indefatigable talent for survival. But one may well ask whether such a generalization is solely a product of stereotype or sound historical commentary.

Moreover, Bloom has to make his point quickly and quietly. The cabman's shelter is hardly the place to extemporize on injustices perpetrated on the Jews. But when he later entices Stephen into the safe ground of 7 Eccles Street, Bloom indeed shakes-off his other identities and becomes, for both himself and his lost friend, an Irish Jew.

With the Catholic Irishman and Irish Jew now isolated, "Ithaca" replays the rhetoric of the Celtic–Hebraic heritage and its similes, and confronts the discourse of race and racial type. The trope is revised in this penultimate episode, suggesting that the two "races" are bound in the modern world by their mutual "dispersal, persecution, survival and revival" (*U*17.55–56). Bloom has by this hour acknowledged that his "Irishness" also contains a viable, yet non-religious "Jewishness;" But Stephen, as a future Irish "bard" who has just seen his mother's spirit, has neither escaped his romanticism nor the remnants of his Catholicism. The catechism between reader and narrator of "Ithaca" on this level becomes an attempt to distinguish racial myth from ethnic reality.

Joyce begins by casting Bloom as a "racial Jew," Messianic by "nature," who "bears in his arms the secret of the race, graven in the language of prediction" (*U*17.340–41). The description not only paradoies Professor MacHugh's rendition of Taylor's speech in "Aeolus," but confuses religious mission with racial nature; Bloom's satisfaction in aiding Stephen is now cast as having "brought a positive gain to others . . . Light to the gentiles" (352–53), a parodic variation of the imperative in Deuteronomy that the Hebrews be a "light unto the nations." The dialogic continues with the myth that, as Irishman and Jew, Stephen and Bloom are indeed descendants of the same "race." This mutual heritage initially presents a means through which Bloom and Stephen may relate as long-lost brothers, if not as Jewish father and Christian son. Bloom, indeed, first offers fatherly advice – personal hygiene and good nutrition – in hopes of establishing Stephen's surrogate sonship (229–52). But the narrative voice pushes the connection beyond Bloom's pseudo-paternal schemes:

Did either openly allude to their racial difference?

Neither.

What, reduced to their simplest reciprocal form, were Bloom's thoughts about Stephen's thoughts about Bloom and about Stephen's thoughts about Bloom's thoughts about Stephen?

He thought that he thought that he was a jew whereas he knew that he knew that he knew he was not.(525–31)

In this racial context, Bloom's "Jewishness" is ironically still a matter of perception. Joyce revised the passage to include Stephen's thoughts about Bloom, when the original version of the second question here had originally ended with Bloom's thoughts about Stephen.[92] Now, whether Bloom is a Jew or not is in fact "the simplest reciprocal form" of both of their thoughts. Stephen is as curious about Bloom's "Jewishness" as Bloom is as about Stephen's perception of him as a Jew – the gaze between Jew and non-Jew verbalized.[93] After the day's occurrences, it is little wonder that Bloom now fully believes he is perceived as a Jew by other Irishmen. But Stephen believes Bloom is not a Jew, and further, that Bloom knows this. The syntactical confusion of the answer represents the estrangement Jews and Gentiles – especially the Irishman, who is Gentile yet still Other to Europe – must excise if they are to come to an understanding of the other's position; Joyce thus presents here in serio-comic form the difficulty of members of disempowered groups perceiving each other as individuals beyond stereotypes. Apparently both Stephen and Bloom have discarded prejudice, and so may be able to proceed as "racial blood-brothers." But the constructed mythologies of race are a poor vehicle through which to establish friendship, even more so because the Irish and Jewish "races" have been so thoroughly mythologized and exploited as elements of religious, nationalistic, and imperialistic discourse.

As much as Irish–Israelite rhetoric had nourished Parnell's campaign, the adult Joyce here demonstrates that he did not place much credence in those legends of common origin. Joyce's refusal to capitalize the word "Jew" throughout *Ulysses* further indicates his distrust of the nineteenth-century concept of racial determination in the modern world. Joyce appears to consider "Jewishness," then, as neither religion nor race, but as an accepted self-image and personal commitment. While it was no myth that both the Jews and the Irish had been victimized by imperial and religious intolerance, Bloom and Stephen themselves know there was little scholarly worth to the seventeenth-century Irish histories which fostered the Irish–Hebrew legends.[94] Stephen's *Pisgah Sight of Palestine or the Parable of the Plums* is indeed little more than a bitter parody of a simile that once sustained a nation. But the Irish-as-the-lost-tribe-of-Israel is only that – a simile. It offers no help to the identity struggles of either Stephen or Bloom. Thus the narrator prepares the reader for each man's disparate reactions to the myth: "What two temperaments did they individually represent? \ The scientific. The artistic" (559–60).

As in his attitude toward Catholicism, Stephen does not so much demythologize the simile as he bitterly parodies it. Always the romantic, he leads with his imagination, reading his world either through allegory or parody. Still unable or unwilling to disarm his anger at the Church, Stephen will never reconcile his "Irishness" with his identity as an avant-garde artist.

Bloom, however, deconstructs Stephen's myth by answering his *Pisgah* parable with a list of Jewish "seekers of pure truth" (709–24). This series of names echoes Bloom's list in "Cyclops." While each figure here exemplifies to Bloom the "postexilic eminence" (710) of Jewish achievement, he nonetheless divides his list into two categories. At first his "seekers" are all religious figures (Moses, Maimonides, Mendelssohn, 709–14). His "other anapocryphal illustrious sons," however, represents four assimilationists who each achieved a precedence in his own field, despite such obstacles as conversion, excommunication, or even tragic death (721–22).[95] Like Stephen's "two Dublin vestals," Bloom's Jewish heroes, religious or not, all have been refused entrance into the promised land. In "exile," however, they have succeeded in their own cultures through varied and valuable accomplishments – hardly analogous to spitting plum pits. This is Bloom's "epistle to the Irish romantic": if survival means compromise, it need not mean complete severance from ethnic identity (a lesson Joyce learned in part from observing Svevo and his other Jewish friends). Bloom underscores the point by singing *Hatikvah*, the Hebrew lyric about hope and return:

What anthem did Bloom chant partially in anticipation of the multiple, ethnically irreducible consummation?

> *Kolod balejwaw pnimah*
> *Nefesh, jehudi, homijah.* (761–64)[96]

Forgetting the remainder of the lyric is typical of Bloom, but he nonetheless continues his lesson to Stephen through "a periphrasitc version of the general text" (768). Bloom may not recall the complete Hebrew, but he remembers the meaning: "As long as deep in your heart the soul of a Jew still stirs . . . " Stephen the ascetic-romantic-idealist, however, will have none of this watery ambiguity and pragmatic compromise. Encouraged by Bloom to "chant in a modulated voice a strange legend on an allied theme," Stephen elects not a tune of Irish hope (and he knows many), but the Judeophobic *Ballad of Little Harry Hughes*.[97]

As one of the only musical scores included in *Ulysses*, the "chanted legend" stands as a conspicuous departure from traditional novel format.[98] Joyce meant to catch and focus the reader's attention, and one needn't stretch too far to recognize the ballad as Stephen's final statement on the questions of Bloom's acceptance as a Jew. Bloom first reacts to the song "with unmixed feeling. Smiling, a jew, he heard with pleasure and saw the unbroken kitchen window" (810–11). Considering the long history of Jewish persecution, Bloom is initially reminded that, as a Jew in Dublin, his life has been relatively calm. Hearing the song's allusion to ritual murder, however, he becomes "unsmiling"; he recognizes his own Irish Milly as a potential victim of charges against "a jew's daughter, all dressed in green" (830–31). Bloom also recalls that accusations of Jewish ritual murder are not limited to medieval legend – in all likelihood, Bloom's attitude here may be constructed from Joyce's knowledge of the 1911 Beilis murder trial in Russia.[99] Bloom's ensuing list of "evidences for and against ritual murder," though, is inappropriately named; Bloom in fact recites to himself a rational, sociologically based explanation as to why the myth of ritual murder exists at all (844–49).

But while Stephen may not be an anti-Semite, he is, by the close of the book, quite a nihilist. The narrator invites the reader to recognize this:

Condense Stephen's commentary.

One of all, least of all, is the victim predestined. Once by inadvertence, twice by design he challenges his destiny. It comes when he is abandoned and challenges him reluctant and, as an apparition of hope and youth, holds him unresisting. It leads him to a strange habitation, to a secret infidel apartment, and there, implacable, immolates him, consenting. (832–37)

Who is "the victim" here, Bloom or Stephen? Readers have assumed in the past that the passage refers only to the latter. Despite its inescapable anti-Jewishness, Stephen's "ballad" may have represented to him his own victimization as a son, an outcast, and an Irishman. And his "condensed version" here may also be his final judgment of Bloom's "Jewishness." Stephen insinuates that Bloom's "Jewishness" – as "the victim predestined" – parallels his own perception of himself as an outcast Irishman. He alludes to the psychology of the victim as not only informing Bloom's day, but having governed the older man's choices to remain both alienated and cuckolded. Stephen thus remakes Bloom in his own image; as an Irishman refusing the Church, politics, and even amiable social intercourse, Stephen feels he has escaped his own victimization, and seems to imply that Bloom should follow suit.

But Stephen fails to gain any significant empathy for the Other disenfranchised Irishman. He refuses to accept the specifics of Bloom's life and history as a Jew, and instead reverts to the easier notion of "the scapegoat." He implies that any inheritor of the legacy of victimization cannot break free while maintaining an ethnic identity. The Jew, like the Irishman, "must wake from the nightmare of history" and surrender his ethnicity, which to Stephen must always encompass what he feels is a degrading religious component. He exits the novel as he entered it, emphasizing his "victory" over Catholicism by mocking a prayer for the dying (1230–31). Stephen thus maintains his illusion that in leaving his religion he has left his problems as an Irishman. He walks away, enveloped by the night; but it is the darkness of his self-imposed isolation that truly swallows his departing figure.

The "questioner-voice" is left with a compassionate, lonely character, who, however psychologically healed he may have become, remains caught in the throes of a overwhelming cultural Otherness. Despite Stephen's possible return, the reader cannot help but feel that Bloom has lost another opportunity for friendship with a member of the empowered group through which he must negotiate his identity as a Jew. Joyce subsequently pays careful attention to Bloom's "Jewish artifacts" in the ensuing encyclopedic descriptions. These objects evince Bloom's "Jewishness" as not simply a reaction to that day's anti-Semitism, but an integral part of his lifelong self-making, now fully recognized and accepted.

Caught in his double-bind as an Irish Jew, and now even more apprehensive about nationalistic divisions, Bloom sadly burns the *Agendeth Netaim* prospectus he had saved throughout his day. His lack of enthusiasm for Zionism again characterizes Jewish assimilationists of the era – an attitude Joyce encountered in his Jewish friends in both Trieste and Zurich. Conversely, Bloom's library suggests the reach of his Jewish interests: *Thoughts from Spinoza*, *Philosophy of the Talmud*, Gustave Freytag's *Soll und Haben*, and *The Hidden Life of Christ* (1372–94). The titles are metonyms of Jewish rationalism, Orthodox Judaism, economic anti-Semitism, and Jewish ecumenical tolerance and curiosity. Subsequently, when the possibility of pursing any number of Bloom's fanciful financial schemes are questioned, Jewish philanthropists – Rothschild, Guggenheim, Hirsh, Montefiore . . . etc. – who could offer aid are described as "possessing fortunes in six figures, amassed during a successful life, and joining capital with opportunity the thing required was done" (1748–50). The captioning of such names as merely "honest capitalists" is in stark contrast to the conspiratory accusations Joyce encountered throughout his life pertaining to the wealthiest Jewish families of Europe. Through the episode's catechism, the reader further discovers that Bloom still owns his father's *Haggadah* as well as the suicide note, and that Judaism as religion now appears to him as "not less rational than any other beliefs or practices . . . " (1902). Indeed, immediately previous to the discovery of Bloom's new tolerance toward Orthodox Jewish practice, the questioner uncovers why it is that Bloom continues to harbor a remorse pertaining to his father's suicide (1893-1901):

Why did Bloom experience a sentiment of remorse?

Because in immature impatience he had treated with disrespect certain beliefs and practices.

As?

The prohibition of the use of fleshmeat and milk at one meal: the hebdomadary symposium of incoordinately abstract, perfervidly concrete mercantile coexreligionist excompatriots: the circumcision of male infants: the supernatural character of Judaic scripture: the ineffability of the tetragrammaton: the sanctity of the sabbath. (1893–901)

Again Joyce is not random in his selection of Bloom's regrets: the passage covers some of the most vital pillars of Orthodox Jewish practice: Kashrut, the imperative of community (although ironic in Joyce's term "coexreligionist"), circumcision, belief in the Bible as the word of God, the mystery of the divine presence, the observance of the Sabbath as more significant than that of other holidays. The narrator finally suggests that Bloom's entire day has followed, in the disguise of his "non-Jewish Jewishness," mock-ritualistic acts of ancient and modern Judaism – "The preparation of breakfast (burnt offering): intestinal congestion and premeditative defecation (holy of holies) . . . " and so on (2042–59). Thus with his regrets and his doubts – even with his confusion over and lack of allegiance to *Halacha* – to Joyce at least, Bloom can be viewed as having lived the life of a Jew; in this, he becomes Joyce's literary foil to a host of pernicious representations of "the Jew," as well as confirms some essential commitments of a viable Jewish identity.[100]

While Molly Bloom's status as a Jewish character has divided readers of *Ulysses* for some time, her "Penelope" episode monologue nonetheless ties together the remaining threads about Bloom's "Jewishness." John Henry Raleigh demonstrates that Molly's genealogy is impenetrably murky, and that attempts to read her as Jewish are very tenuous.[101] Conversely, Phillip Herring claims that because Molly's unwed mother's name, "Lunita Laredo" (*U*18.848), was also the name of a prominent Jewish family of Gibraltar during the era, Molly can indeed be considered Jewish in the *Halachically* matrilineal sense.[102] Herring's theory, however, has some problems that once again reveal just how complex Joyce's manipulation of Jewish identity becomes. In the line previous to giving the name, Molly admits that she never knew her mother – "my mother whoever she was" (846–47); given the further implication that she was also a prostitute, Lunita Laredo could well have been an alias for many obvious reasons. More significantly, however, Molly's allusions to places and things Jewish – "jews burial place . . . [her] being jewess looking . . . old longbearded jews in their jellibees and levites . . . [sleeping on the floor] the way the jews used when someone dies . . . Im sick of Cohens old bed . . . " (*U*18.834, 687, 1185, 1247, 1498) – in no way reveal that she has ever considered herself a Jew. And self-perception is a key to Joyce's puzzle here; while one does not become a Jew simply by declaration, the entire text of *Ulysses* has gone to great lengths to demonstrate, through Bloom, that the establishment of a Jewish identity must be based on the psychological affirmation of a "Jewishness," which in turn must be based on at least the central tenets of Judaism, a compassion for Jews and other sufferers, and the ability to rise above pernicious stereotypes of "the Jew." Neither of these are relevant to Molly, who considers herself an Irish Dubliner of Spanish-Moroccan descent by way of Gibraltar. Her own "Jewishness" to her – if she indeed can claim any at all – is merely incidental.

Yet despite her distance from Jewish identity and Judaism, Molly nonetheless perceives Bloom as a superior type of male in part because of a "Jewishness" she believes resides at the heart of who he is "when he's at home." Molly's monologue of course encompasses her history, dissatisfactions, fantasies, infidelities, and pleasures of the sexual life. In this vein, Bloom is perhaps as problematic as any other man she has ever known. She indeed finds several of his habits repulsive: "of course hes mad on the subject of drawers," "trying to make a whore of me," "any man thatd kiss a women's bottom . . . hed kiss anything unnatural," "if he wants to kiss my bottom I'll drag open my drawers and bulge it right out in his face . . . he can stick his tongue seven miles up my hole" (289, 96, 1402, 1520–22). Bloom's fetishes once again reveal both his scatological fascination and his masochism. But the apparent increase of such habits since Rudy's death suggest Bloom's "perversity" as tied in part to his identity crisis as both a father and a Jew. Thus, as noted by Ellmann and many others, Bloom's nighttown experience presages the possibility that he may now once again desire complete vaginal intercourse with his wife.

Although Molly herself has always been flirtatious, and seems to have wanted no more children after Rudy, she states that "its all his [Bloom's] own fault that I am an adulteress" (1449–50, 1516). Indeed, prior to this day, Bloom's self-doubt as a male and a Jew may well have provoked in him the self-destructive idea that he deserves (perhaps now, "deserved") to be cuckolded, deserved to be punished by a more powerful, more "masculine" male. Yet despite Bloom's habits, or Molly's claim that he "pimped" Boylan for her, his presence in her life has always represented something beyond sexual need, perhaps even beyond carnality itself. It was Bloom's Jewish *menschlichkeit* that first attracted Molly:

yes he said I was a flower of the mountain yes so we are flowers all a womans body yes that was one true thing he said in his life and the sun shines for you today yes that was why I liked him because I saw he understood or felt the way a woman is and I knew I could always get round him and I gave him all the pleasure I could . . . (1575–80)

And his empathy and compromising nature have indeed remained at the center of her devotion:

Mad Poldy anyhow whatever he does always wipes his feet on the mat when he comes in wet or shine and always blacks his own boots too and he always takes off his hat when he comes up in the street . . . (225–28)

making fun of him then behind his back I know well when he goes on with his idiotics because he has sense enough not to squander every penny piece he earns down their gullets and looks after his wife and family . . . (1276–79)

I was in mourning that 11 years ago now yes hed be 11 though what was the good of going into morning for what was neither one thing nor the other the first cry was enough for me . . . of course he insisted hed go into mourning for the cat . . . (1307–10)

Bloom's failure as a lover has not squelched his concern as one who loves; he is and has been throughout his turmoil considerate, gentle, family-minded, and socially refined in his own Bloomian manner.

Indeed, the positive sense of "Jewishness" he has finally recognized in himself on June 16, Molly has apparently always held as their saving grace.

United in their eccentric arrangement in bed, the Blooms once more confirm their precarious devotion. Surrounded by the objects that galvanize his Jewish identity and kept by the female presence that reinforces his role as a *mensch*, Bloom the weary Jew sleeps. Forgiving Molly and having asserted his new found confidence, Bloom rests with all disenfranchised Jews of pre-Holocaust Europe, and deservedly so. But Joyce's earlier abandonment of Bloom before the novel's close in "Penelope" becomes the final comment on the social plight of his era's marginal Jewry: unaccepted by his countrymen, unable to completely reattach himself to his people, Bloom remains lost, unhappy, and at home.

Conclusion

James Joyce's refigurations of a range of European cultural assumptions about "Jewishness," as well as his confrontation of anti-Semitic nationalism, are invaluable. Joyce sought to challenge his era's dominant discourse surrounding "the Jew" by presenting a character who was a Jew, but also not a Jew, viewed both from within and from without. By imagining Bloom's conflict as one of Jewish identity, Joyce achieved an empathy for the paradoxes of Jewish marginality perhaps unequaled by any writer since. Moreover, Bloom's triumph embodies Joyce's beliefs in precisely which aspects of a positive "Jewishness" are most empowering: recognizing his own sense of Judaically-based "Jewishness" and thus rising above stereotype, Bloom the uncircumcised-converted-agnostic-cuckold re-establishes his self-respect as a Jew and as a man, and thus reaffirms his responsibility toward humanity. To read the realist novel that is *Ulysses* without recognizing this dynamism at the center of its narrative is, essentially, to misread *Ulysses*.

The idea that culture can only be re-evalutated from the position of the Other has of course become one of the intellectual staples of our age. Realizing how alienated his own sense of "Irishness" had made him to the Irish, British, and European cultures of his day, Joyce confronted his own Otherness by becoming fascinated with another type – perhaps the most entrenched "Other" in all of Europe. Bloom's final acceptance of his own "Irish-Jewishness" represents a victory for difference by demonstrating how essentialist and constructivist theories play on the act of self-making. And if the experiences of June 16 begin for Bloom a reshaping of his identity, then such a breakthrough indeed centers on his "Jewishness."

But like Stephen Dedalus, the character who Joyce abandoned to create Bloom, the apostate author may have never solved his own conflict with Irish Catholicism. Joyce could leave the Church, but could never stop being Irish – whatever that finally meant to him. Bloom as well could be an Irishman, but not at the cost of denying his Jewish identity. Both author and character discovered, however, that one's "individuality" must contend with one's history before it can be whole. Bloom's struggle indeed examines how lost religious values can be synthesized into a predominantly secular consciousness. Joyce himself, however, seems to have displaced his need of the same by the very act of creating Bloom; he disarmed his own apostasy through Bloom's reconciliation with Jewish values. The Catholic Irishman may have thus anonymously returned Alfred Hunter's kindness by insisting, through Bloom, that the idea of an adjusted Irish Jew was no joke; Joyce portrayed such an identity as a viable psychology merely waiting for a reciprocal social consciousness.

Toward the end of his life Joyce indeed experienced at first hand how pervasive the Otherness of "the Jew" actually was. It is now well known that when he applied for a visa to enter Switzerland in 1940, Joyce was initially denied entry by the *Kantonal Fremdenpolizei* of Zurich. Inquiring on Joyce's behalf about the refusal, a Zurich friend was informed that the visa had been rejected on the grounds that Joyce himself was a Jew.[1] Acquaintances of Joyce, including Jaques Mercanton, testified to the proper authorities that Joyce was not Jewish. But it took several more reapplications and newly imposed fees before Joyce was allowed to enter the country.[2] While involved in the debacle, Joyce punned to his friends: "*que je ne suis pas juif de Judée mais aryen d'Erin.*"[3] Coming from the man who created Bloom, the casual remark might at first seem representative of how readily even the most original minds of the era could rely on the language of racial myth. Listening to Joyce's French, however, it appears more likely that he could not resist laying bare the anti-Semitism of Swiss "neutrality" through some linguistic humor.

When Joyce formerly lived in Zurich, many of his associates, of course, had been Jews. But the Swiss authorities' claim was also based on Joyce's reputation as the author of *Ulysses*. Joyce himself had thus experienced the prejudice-by-association-to-stereotype that he had once placed at the center of his novel. Fortunately, however, both he and Bloom could survive in a world that had not yet begun to act-out such hatred through an attempt at genocide.

European Jewry, from the Orthodox to the marginalized, indeed experienced a respite of persecution between the Dreyfus Affair and the Second World War, an era Stefan Zweig called "The Golden Age

of Security."⁴ After a century of attempting to enter nationalist
Christian societies, being burdened with myths that created "the
Jew" for both religious and racial ideologies, and with no territoried
nationalism of their own, the Jews had become the symbol for the
devious, the unprincipled, the cowardly, "the feminine," the subversive.
During the after-shock of Dreyfus, however, several European
societies experienced a temporary hesitation toward anti-Semitic acts
as a result of witnessing the extent of French xenophobia. That period
indeed produced works that offer keen insight into the assimilated or
marginal Jew's double-bind, such as Weininger's *Geschlecht und
Charakter*, Charles Peguy's *Notre Jeunesse*, and Joyce's *Ulysses*. But the
thunder embodied in Joyce's penetrating depiction of Bloom, "the
non-Jewish Jew," would not erupt into a storm for some fifteen years
after the publication of *Ulysses*. Living in the wake of that storm, we
must learn to reread the novel in light of the cultural assumptions
about "the Jew" which Joyce lived through, and in the context of
those ideologies that became the nightmare from which we have yet
to awake.

Notes

INTRODUCTION

1 As quoted in Richard Ellmann, *James Joyce*, revised edition (London: Oxford University Press, 1982), p. 709. In an interview with Ellmann in 1954, Maria Jolas remembered Joyce's remark.
2 The term "Halachically" refers to the third phase of historic Judaism, the Talmudic or Rabbinic tradition. Talmudic commentary on Levitical Law, along with the Law itself, are referred to in Hebrew as *Halachah*, derived from the verb, *lalechet*, meaning "to go" (*Halachah* literally means "the way to go"). Within this context, Bloom would not be considered a Jew because his mother was apparently not born of a Jewish woman and never converted to Judaism, and because he was never allowed to enter "the covenant" through ritual circumcision. Joyce certainly knew that the lack of these two Rabbinic markers of Jewish identity would exclude Bloom from such, and so make his struggle to view himself as a Jew definitively complex.
3 Bryan Cheyette, *Constructions of "the Jew" in English Literature and Society: Racial Representations, 1875–1945* (Cambridge: Cambridge University Press, 1993), p. 3.
4 Valéry Larbaud, "Ulysses'" in *Joyce: the Critical Heritage*, vol. 1, ed. by Robert H. Demming (New York: Barnes & Nobel, 1970), pp. 252–62. The review was originally published as "James Joyce," in *Nouvelle Revue Française* 18 (April, 1922): pp. 385–405.
5 Budgen, *James Joyce and the Making of Ulysses* (Bloomington: Indiana University Press, 1960), pp. 273.
6 *The Critical Heritage*, vol. 1, pp. 292–96. His first article, "An Irish Comment on *Ulysses*," was published in *Claxon* (Winter, 1923–24): pp. 14–20. The second piece, "The Jew Errant," was published in *Dublin Magazine* 2:1 (1963): pp. 11–24.
7 *Ibid.*, pp. 13–14.
8 See Magalaner, "The Anti-Semitic Limerick Incidents and Joyce's 'Bloomsday,'" *PMLA* 68 (1953): pp. 1219–23.
9 For the first piece, see Levitt "The Family in Bloom," in *New Light on Joyce from the Dublin Symposium (Dublin, 1969)*, ed. Fritz Senn (Bloomington:

Indiana University Press, 1972), pp. 141–48. See also Levitt, "A Hero for Our Time: Leopold Bloom and the Myth of *Ulysses*'" in *Fifty Years: Ulysses*, ed. Thomas Staley (Bloomington: Indiana University Press, 1972), pp. 132–46; and "The Humanity of Bloom, the Jewishness of Joyce," *The Seventh of Joyce*, ed. Bernard Benstock (Bloomington: Indiana University Press, 1982), pp. 225–28. Levitt's investigation of Talmudic allusions in the *Wake*, "The New Midrash: *Finnegans Wake*," in *1992 Joyce Studies Annual*, ed. Thomas Staley (Austin: University of Texas Press, 1992), pp 57–70.

10 Sultan, *The Argument of Ulysses* (Columbus: Ohio State University Press, 1965).

11 Other writers who have discovered sources for "Joyce's Jew" and their role in *Ulysses* include Ellmann, Edmund Epstein, Bernard and Shari Benstock, Daniel Fogel, Patrick McCarthy, Marilyn Reizbaum, Robert Byrnes, Cheyette, and still more. Various articles include: Shari Benstock, "Is He a Jew or a Gentile or a Holy Roman?," *JJQ* 16 (1978): pp. 493–97; Fogel, "James Joyce, The Jews, and *Ulysses*," *JJQ* 16 (1979): pp. 498–501; Epstein, "Joyce and Judaism," *The Seventh of Joyce*, ed. Bernard Benstock (Bloomington: Indiana University Press, 1982), pp. 221–37; Stanley Sultan, "'What the hell is he? says Ned': Why Joyce Answers the Question with a Question," *JJQ* 23, 3 (1986): pp. 217–22; Robert Byrnes, "Bloom's Sexual Tropes: Stigmata of the 'Degenerate' Jew," *JJQ* 27:2 (Winter 1990): pp. 303–23. Among the most controversial of such pieces are twin articles by Erwin Steinberg, in which he asserts that from every perspective – religious, cultural, political, ethnic – Bloom cannot be considered a Jew. See "James Joyce and the Critics Notwithstanding, Leopold Bloom is not Jewish," *Journal of Modern Literature* 9:1 (1981): pp. 27–49; and "Reading Leopold Bloom/1904 in 1989," *JJQ* 26:3 (1989): pp. 397–416.

12 See Fiedler, "Bloom on Joyce: Or Jokey for Jacob," and "Joyce and Jewish Consciousness," in *Fiedler on the Roof: Essays on Literature and Jewish Identity* (Boston: David Godine, 1991), pp. 31–46, 47–58.

13 See "The Jewish Connection Con't," in *The Seventh of Joyce*, ed., Bernard Benstock, pp. 229–38. Her most recent piece,'Swiss Customs: Zurich's Sources for Joyce's Judaica," appears in *JJQ* 27:2 (1989): pp. 203–18.

14 *Ibid.*, p. 395. Ellmann learned of the joke through an interview between Dr. Robert Collinson and Robert Mayo. For a discussion of the convention of such ethnic jokes in twentieth-century Britain, see George Orwell, "Anti-Semitism in England," in *England, Your England and Other Essays* (London: Secher & Warburg, 1953). pp. 66–80, 76.

15 See Ira Nadel "The Incomplete Joyce," in *1991 Joyce Studies Annual*, ed. Thomas Staley (Austin: University of Texas Press, 1991), pp. 86–100.

16 The term "Jewish question" had a specific and general use throughout the century. After Jewish emancipation, the term became an abbreviation for questions such as "Can the Jews assimilate into Christian society?

What should be done with a people who are both religiously and 'racially' different from ourselves?" In his essay "On the Jewish Question" (1843) Marx used the topic as one of the first vehicles through which he defined the problems of the bourgeoisie. He was responding to Bruno Bauer's essay entitled "Die Judenfrage" (1842). For a discussion of how "the Jewish question" arises in the writing of many converted, self-hating Jews, see Sander Gilman, *Jewish Self-Hatred: Anti-Semitism and the Hidden Language of the Jews* (Baltimore: Johns Hopkins University Press, 1986), pp. 7, 11, 20, 197.

17 Referring to Hitler's campaign against the Jews in 1938, Joyce appeared unsurprised when he told Maria Jolas that anti-Semitism was "one of the easiest and oldest prejudices to 'prove.'" See Ellmann, *JJII*, p. 709. Interview with Maria Jolas, 1954.

18 *Ibid.*, p. 395. Although Ellmann gives no source for the comment, it is similar to many of the statements Joyce made to Frank Budgen while composing *Ulysses*. Ellmann believed that Joyce made these "Irish-Jewish connections" qualities of Bloom's mind.

19 See Derrida, "Edmond Jabès and the Question of the Book," in *Writing and Difference*, translated by Alan Bass (Chicago: University of Chicago Press, 1978), pp. 64–78. Joyce's choice of the name "Shem" for H. C. Earwicker's bookish dreamer son suggests the qualities ascribed to Shem the son of Noah, the biblical progenitor of the Hebrew people. Shem's disposition is reflected in Jacob's devotion to study and books, especially as he is compared to his brother Esau, whose chief characteristics of physical agility, marksmanship, and aggressiveness Joyce in turn gives to Shem's brother, Shaun.

20 Both groups were portrayed as cultural pariahs and often reduced to a single phrase: the continental "Jewish question," and "the Irish question" that Parnell and Gladstone had filibustered over throughout the Home Rule era.

21 See Isaac Deutscher, *The Non-Jewish Jew and Other Essays*, ed. Tamara Deutscher (London: Oxford University Press, 1968).

22 While many of Joyce's traits have been synthesized into Bloom's character, Bloom is in no way strictly autobiographical. One of the most influential failures to grasp this was Wyndham Lewis' comment in *Time and Western Man* (1927), in which he posited that Bloom was merely a "romantic self-portrait" of the mature author. See *The Critical Heritage*, vol. I, p. 363.

23 Arendt, *The Origins of Totalitarianism* (New York: Harcourt, Brace, Jovanovich, 1973), pp. 3–120.

24 *Jew's Body* (London: Routledge, 1991), p. 5.

25 Herring, *Joyce's Uncertainty Principle* (Princeton: Princeton University Press, 1987), p. xiii. Herring states: "I have tried to avoid the morass of intentionalism," but that "in adding 'principle' to 'uncertainty' in the title, I admit that my aim was to suggest a devious authorial strategy the

Irish have always associated with Joyce." One can only wonder why Herring does not find such a strategy applicable to Joyce's manipulation of Bloom's Jewish identity, which is by far the most complex and interesting construction in the novel.

26 *Ibid.*, p. xiii.

27 Both of these facts can be drawn from *Ulysses*, but Bloom's genealogy is best explained in John Henry Raleigh, *The Chronicle of Leopold and Molly Bloom:* Ulysses *as Narrative* (Berkeley: University of California Press, 1977), pp. 11–21.

28 See Epstein, "Joyce and Judaism," p. 221.

29 Jeremy Hawthorn, *"Ulysses, Modernism, and Marxist Criticism,"* in *James Joyce and Modern Literature*, eds. W. J. McCormack and Alistair Stead (London: Routledge & Kegan Paul, 1982) pp. 112–125, quote p. 114. See Charques, *Contemporary Literature and Social Revolution* (London, 1933), p. 92; Radek, "Contemporary World Literature and the Tasks of Proletarian Art," in *Problems of Soviet Literature*, ed. H. G. Scott (London, 1935), p. 154. For Lukàcs, see below.

30 Lukàcs, *The Historical Novel*, translated by Hannah and Stanley Mitchell (Lincoln: University of Nebraska Press, 1983), p. 286.

31 Theodor Adorno, "The Position of the Narrator in the Contemporary Novel," in *Notes to Literature*, translated by Sherry Weber Nicholsen, (New York: Columbia University Press, 1991), vol. I, pp. 30–36, quote p. 32.

32 Adorno, "Extorted Reconciliation: On George Lukàcs' *Realism in our Time*," in *Notes to Literature*, p. 225.

33 See Cheyette, "'Jewgreek is greekjew',": the Disturbing Ambivalence of Joyce's Semitic Discourse in *Ulysses, 1992 Joyce Studies Annual*, ed. Thomas Staley. (Austin: University of Texas Press, 1992), pp. 32–56, 33. See also *Constructions of "The Jew,"* pp. 206–67.

34 Deane, "'Masked with Matthew Arnold's Face': Joyce and Liberalism," *James Joyce: The Centennial Symposium*, eds. Morris Beja, Phillip Herring, Maurice Harmon, and David Norris, (Chicago: University of Illinois Press, 1986), pp. 9–20.

35 For a conservative view of Arnold's influence on *Ulysses* see Theoharis Constantine Theoharis, *Joyce's Ulysses: an Anatomy of Soul* (Chapel Hill: University of North Carolina Press, 1988). Theoharis demonstrates how Bloom and Stephen have "Greek" and "Jewish" aspects to their temperaments, but that Bloom has synthesized these to the greater degree, see pp. 142–99.

I *SILENCE*: FAMILY VALUES

1 Richard Ellmann, *James Joyce*, p. 373. Joyce's quote came from Frank Budgen's memory of their conversations in his article "James Joyce," in *Horizon* 3 (February, 1941), p. 107.

2 See Joyce's rendition in "Aeolus" of John Taylor's 1901 speech, which incorporated this metaphor, (*U*7.828–70).

3 See Howard Morley Sachar, *The Course of Modern Jewish History* (New York: Dell, 1958), pp. 228–9.

4 Pinchas Lapide, *Three Popes and the Jews* (New York: Hawthorn Books Inc., 1967), pp. 80–81.

5 See Norman Cohen, *Warrant For Genocide: the Myth of the Jewish World Conspiracy and the Protocols of the Elders of Zion* (New York: Harper & Row, 1966) pp. 65, 152.

6 See Cecil Roth, *The History of the Jews: From Earliest Times to the Six Days War* (New York: Schoken Books, 1961), pp. 353–4. For a detailed account of the myth's origins and history see Joshua Trachtenberg, *The Devil and the Jews: The Medieval Conception of the Jew and its Relation to Modern AntiSemitism* (New York: Meridian Books, 1961), pp. 124–39.

7 Ellmann, *JJII*, p. 463.

8 James Joyce, *Ulysses: The Corrected Text*, eds. Hans Walter Gabler, Wolfhard Steppe, and Claus Melchor, (New York: Random House, 1986), 17.801–28. All subsequent citing will appear in text in episode and line numbers.

9 Joyce's "Harry Hughes" draws on one or more of several versions of the ballad, which Frances Child lists as no. 155 from its earliest appearances through eighteen variations. See Child, ed., *The English and Scottish Popular Ballads*, vol. III (New York: Folklore Press, 1956), pp. 240–43.

10 See Roth, *History of the Jews*, p. 208. Child cites the *Annals of Waverly*, the *Chronica Majora* of Matthew of Paris, and the *Annals of Burton* as three of several sources in which renditions of the case first appeared. See Child, *Popular Ballads*, pp. 235–40.

11 See Kevin Sullivan, *Joyce Among the Jesuits* (New York: Columbia University Press, 1958), appendix, p. 239.

12 See Fiedler, "The Roots of Anti-Semitism: a View from Italy," in *Fiedler on the Roof*, pp. 3–29.

13 See Sander Gilman, *The Jew's Body*, pp. 93–103, 119–20.

14 Sachar, *Modern Jewish History*, pp. 242–60.

15 Paula Hyman, *From Dreyfus to Vichy: the Remaking of French Jewry, 1906–1939* (New York: Columbia University Press, 1979), p. 64. Hyman drew this statistic from Lloyd P. Gartner, *The Jewish Immigrant in England*, p. 274.

16 Paul Blanshard, *The Irish and Catholic Power: an American Interpretation* (Boston: The Beacon Press, 1954), p. 191.

17 Clair Huchet Bishop, *How Catholics Look at Jews: an Inquiry into Italian, Spanish, French, and Italian Teaching Materials* (New York: Paulist Press, 1974), p. 31. See also *Twenty Years of Jewish-Catholic Relations*, eds. Eugene J. Fisher, A. James Rudin, and Marc H. Tanenbaum (New York: The Paulist Press, 1986), pp. 126–29. French Catholicism would also become an identifiable influence on the Irish Church by the eighteenth century.

Several of Joyce's Jesuit instructors appear to have spent time in France during their novitiate years.

18 As quoted in Emmet J. Larkin, *The Consolidation of the Roman Catholic Church in Ireland, 1860–1870* (Chapel Hill, NC: The University of North Carolina Press, 1987), p. 286. All excerpts from Archbishop Cullen's letters in this book are taken from The Papers of Paul Cullen, Dublin Diocesan Library.

19 Stephen J. McCormick, *The Pope and Ireland – Containing Newly Discovered Historical Facts Concerning the Forged Bulls Attributed to Popes Adrian IV and Alexander III, etc.* (San Francisco: Waldteful, 1889), p. 164.

20 See Chester Anderson, *James Joyce and his World* (London: Thames & Hudson, 1968), pp. 10–11.

21 See Ellmann, *JJII*, p. 25. See also Anderson, *James Joyce*, p. 13.

22 Anderson, *ibid.*

23 Stanislaus Joyce, *My Brother's Keeper* (New York: The Viking Press, 1958), p. 19.

24 Ellmann, *JJII*, p. 25.

25 Sister Anthony Marie Gallagher. OSF, *Education in Ireland*, dissertation, Catholic University of America (Washington, DC: Catholic University of America Press, 1948), pp. 67–69.

26 *Ibid.*, pp. 72–77.

27 See Ignatius Murphy, *A History of Irish Catholicism, vol. v: Catholic Education* (Dublin: Gill and McMillan, 1971), p. 28–33.

28 Richard Whately, *Lessons on the Truth of Christianity, Being an Appendix to the Fourth Book of Lessons, For the Use of Schools* (Dublin: published by direction of the Commissioners of National Education, and reprinted by express permission at Montreal by Armor and Ramsay, 1846), pp. 28, 72.

29 *My Brother's Keeper*, p. 7.

30 *A Portrait, Text, Criticism, and Notes*, ed. Chester G. Anderson (New York: The Viking Critical Library, 1968), p. 7. All subsequent references cited in text.

31 Ira Nadel, *Joyce and the Jews* (Iowa City: University of Iowa Press, 1989), p. 188.

32 See *Thom's Irish Almanac (Thom's Directory of Ireland)* 37–45th annual publication (Dublin: Alexander Thom & Co.), 1880 edition, 37th publication, pp. 1363–64. Scanning the names on Nassau Street for the same year, several distinctly Jewish names, such as Solomons or Cohen can be found. Given Joyce's own parody of the tendency of Jews to change their names (Virag to Bloom), however, Nadel's assumption does have a foundation.

33 See also Don Gifford, *Joyce Annotated: Notes for* Dubliners *and* A Portrait of the Artist as a Young Man, (Berkeley: University of California Press, 1982), p. 176.

34 *Ibid.*, p. 230.

35 See Peter Costello, *James Joyce: the Years of Growth, 1882–1915* (New York:

Pantheon Books, 1992), p. 67.

36 For Marcus and other Jewish Blooms of Dublin, see Louis Hyman, *The Jews of Ireland: from Earliest Times to the Year 1910* (Shannon: Irish University Press, 1972), pp. 169–76. For Leventhal, see Ellmann, *JJII*, p. 513.

37 Stanislaus Joyce, *Reflections of James Joyce by his Brother Stanislaus Joyce*, translated from Italian by Ellsworth Mason (New York: The James Joyce Society, 1950), p. 10.

38 James Joyce, *Stephen Hero*, edited from the manuscript in the Harvard College Library by Theodore Spencer and incorporating the additional manuscript pages in the Yale University Library and the Cornell University Library. John J. Slocum and Herbert Cahoon, eds., (New York: New Directions, 1963), pp. 131–37. All subsequent citations in text.

39 See Hyman, *Jews of Ireland*, p. 218.

40 *Ibid.*, p. 142. Three students enrolled that year as "other denominations" than Catholic, Protestant, Wesleyan, and Methodist. One of these was William Isaac, who graduated the Medical Course with honors. Four Dublin Jewish families had the name Isaac during the first decades of the century. See *Report of the President of Queen's College, Cork: Year Ending March 31, 1868*, (Dublin: Alexander Thom, 1868), p. 3. See also Louis Hyman, *The Jews of Ireland*, pp. 55, 96.

41 *Ibid.*, p. 52–54.

42 *Ibid.*, pp. 105–13.

43 *Ibid.*, pp. 109–11.

44 *Ibid.*, pp. 105, 155–65.

45 I am indebted to Father Fergus O'Donoghue, SJ for this nomenclature for the area around South Circular Road and Clanbrassil Street, the Jewish community of Dublin during the years John and James Joyce lived there. The present Jewish community has moved further south, toward Rathgar. There is an Irish-Jewish Museum on Walworth Road, Dublin 8. Interview, Father Fergus O'Donoghue, SJ, Milltown Park, Dublin 6.

46 See Hyman, *The Jews of Ireland*, pp. 63, 181.

47 See Ellmann, *JJII*, pp. 15–16.

48 See F. H. O'Donnell, *A History of the Irish Parliamentary Party*, vol. 1 (London: Kennikat Press, 1970), pp. 47–200.

49 *Ibid.*, p. 17.

50 Cecil Roth, *Benjamin Disraeli: Earl of Beaconsfield* (New York: The Philosophical Library, Inc., 1952), p. 84.

51 See Sarah Bradford, *Disraeli* (New York: Stein and Day, 1983), p. 329.

52 Smith's attacks were in part due to Disraeli's publication of *Lothair* (1870), in which an Oxford don who resembled Smith was characterized as a "social parasite." Burton's pamphlet claimed Disraeli's "Jewishness" was the source of his corrupt politics. See Colin Holmes, *Anti-Semitism in British Society 1876–1939* (New York: Holmes & Meier Publications Inc.,

1979), pp. 11–12, 55–58.

53 See Bradford, *Disraeli*, pp. 86–88.

54 Roth, *Disraeli*, p. 86. After O'Connell's remarks at the Dublin Trades Union meeting, Disraeli responded in Parliament by stating, "Yes, I am a Jew, and when the ancestors of the right honourable gentleman were brutal savages in an unknown island, mine were priests in the temple of Solomon."

55 See Louis Hyman, *The Jews of Ireland*, pp. 114, 115, 158.

56 Edward Norman, *A History of Modern Ireland 1800–1969* (Baltimore: Penguin Books, 1973), p. 16. The quote is from Disraeli's speech to the House of Commons on the Home Rule motion, in 1874.

57 *Ibid.*, p. 131.

58 See Bradford, *Disraeli*, pp. 386–87.

59 *Contarini Fleming*, part I, chapter II. I am indebted to Sarah Bradford for calling this passage to my attention.

60 See Edgar Rosenberg, *From Shylock to Svengali: Jewish Stereotypes in English Fiction* (Stanford: Stanford University Press, 1960), p. 178. See also pp. 177–80.

61 See *Letters of James Joyce*, vol. II, ed. Richard Ellmann (New York: Viking, 1966), pp. 81, 86.

62 From "The Shade of Parnell," in *The Critical Writings of James Joyce*, eds. Ellsworth Mason and Richard Ellmann (Ithaca: Cornell University Press, 1989), p. 226.

63 *Ibid.*, p. 164.

64 See Weldon Thornton, *Allusions in Ulysses: an Annotated List* (Chapel Hill: University of North Carolina Press, 1968), p. 391.

65 See Eyal Amiran, "Bloom and Disraeli: on the Side of the Angels," in *English Language Notes* 27:3 (1990): pp. 53–57.

66 See Nadel, *Joyce and the Jews*, p. 164.

67 F. H. O'Donnell, *A History*, p. 102.

68 See Deane, "'Masked with Matthew Arnold's Face,'" p. 11.

69 Eliot, *Daniel Deronda*, (New York: Penguin, 1988), p. 775. For a discussion of Arnold's influence on Eliot, See Cheyette, *Constructions of "the Jew,"* pp. 13–54.

70 While Joyce read Eliot, *Daniel Deronda* does not appear in his Trieste library alongside his copies of *The Mill on the Floss* and *Romola*. See Ellmann, *The Consciousness of James Joyce* (London: Faber & Faber, 1977), appendix, p. 107.

71 See Bernard Shillman, *A Short History of the Jews in Ireland* (Dublin: Cahill, 1945), p. 114. While not a documented fact, the Jewish origins of Delia Parnell are related by Shillman as follows: "The mother of another Irish leader, Charles Stuart Parnell, was of Jewish extraction. Her maiden name was Delia Tudor. She is reported to have told the correspondent of the *Daily Telegraph* that 'my son is descended from the line of a tribe of Judah, from the Jews who took refuge in Spain; and there

the name, which afterward became famous in Wales, was changed to Tudor.'"

72 See R. F. Foster, *Modern Ireland: 1600 to 1972* (New York: Penguin, 1989), pp. 38–43.

73 See Geoffrey Keating, *The History of Ireland*, (Kansas City: Irish Genealogical Foundation, 1983). pp. 2–100. Originally translated by David Comyn and Patrick Dineen (London: Irish Texts Society, 1902–14).

74 Foster, *Modern Ireland*, p. 210, n. 10. Vallancey apparently never learned Gaelic.

75 Nadel, *Joyce and the Jews*, pp. 88, 156, 161.

76 See Louis Hyman, *The Jews of Ireland*, pp. 180, 335, n. 128. Keating's book was translated by Father Patrick S. Dinneen and published in 1908 for the Irish Texts Society.

77 *Critical Writings*, p. 156; Nadel, *Joyce and the Jews*, p. 156.

78 *Critical Writings*, p. 225.

79 See Louis Hyman, *The Jews of Ireland*, pp. 219–21.

80 One such article by Davitt was published in *The Jewish Chronicle* of London, in July 1893. Davitt's discussed here the failure of Parliament throughout the eighteenth century to pass naturalization bills for minorities. As both Catholics and Jews were barred from guilds and other business practices during the period, Davitt asserted the two groups once shared a similar discrimination.

81 Davitt, *Within the Pale: the True Story of Anti-Semitic Persecutions in Russia*, (London: Hurst and Blackett, 1903); republished, (New York: Arno Press, 1975) for The Modern Jewish Experience. Sydney Feshbach first speculated this text was a source for Joyce, see Feshbach, "A Merchant, Stephen Said," *JJQ* 19:3 (1982): pp. 349–50.

82 The Limerick crowd was moved to violence after the anti-Jewish sermons of one Father Creagh. Creagh accused the Jews of attempting to overthrow the Catholic Church, and also voiced the myth of ritual murder, provoking a rampage through the city's Jewish area. Marvin Magalaner suggests Joyce's knowledge of the affair may have been behind his choice of the year of Bloomsday. See "Limerick Incidents" pp. 1219–23. Creagh may have been inspired by the actions of a Dublin public figure, Frederick Falkiner, KC. Falkiner regularly berated Jewish defendants in his court. While he apologized in 1892, in 1902 he had again told a Jewish rioter that he was "a specimen of [his] race and nation that causes [them] to be hunted out of every country." See Louis Hyman, *The Jews of Ireland*, p. 163. Bloom makes reference to Falkiner's "strawcalling" of Reuben J. Dodd in "Lestrygonians" (*U*8.159).

83 See Magalaner, "Limerick Incidents," pp. 1219–20.

84 Louis Hyman, *The Jews of Ireland*, p. 216.

85 *Freeman's Journal*, January 18 1904.

86 See Steinberg, "Persecuted. . .sold. . .in Morocco Like Slaves" in *JJQ* 29:3 (1992): pp. 615–22.

87 See Abbott, *Gladstone and Disraeli*, p. 143.
88 See *The Workshop of Dedalus: James Joyce and the Raw Materials for a Portrait of the Artist as a Young Man*, eds. Robert Scholes and Richard Kain (Evanston, IL: Northwestern University Press, 1965), p. 104.
89 See William Murphy, *The Parnell Myth and Irish Politics, 1891–1965* (New York: Peter Lang, 1986), pp. 51–53.
90 Ellmann, *JJII*, p. 144.
91 Joyce, "The Shade of Parnell," in *Critical Writings*, p. 228. In closing this essay, Joyce stated his now often quoted reference to the Irish choosing not to throw Parnell to "the English wolves howling around him," but to "[tear] him to pieces themselves."
92 *Dictionary of Quotations*, eds. John Daintith and Hazel Egerton, et al. (New York: Macmillan, 1987), p. 291.
93 These three quotes all derive from Joyce's writings from 1907–12. The first line is from "Fenianism" (1907), the second from "The Home Rule Comet" (1910), and the last, of course, from his bitter poem, "Gas from a Burner" (1912). See *Critical Writings*, pp. 190, 213, 243.

2 SILENCE: JESUIT YEARS – CLONGOWES AND BELVEDERE

1 See Ellmann, *JJII*, p. 27. See also Budgen, *Making of Ulysses*, p. 317.
2 Ellmann, *JJII*, p. 118; *Ulysses*, 1.46, 209.
3 See James W. Reites, SJ, *St. Ignatius of Loyola and the Jews*, unpublished dissertation, Gregorian University, Rome. Excerpts published in *Studies in the Spirituality of the Jesuits* 13:4 (September, 1981): pp. 1–47.
4 *Ibid.*, p. 30–1.
5 See William V. Bangert, SJ, *A History of the Society of Jesus* (St. Louis: Institute of Jesuit Sources, 1972), pp. 470–72.
6 See Louis McRedmond, *To The Greater Glory of God: a History of the Irish Jesuits* (Dublin: Gill and Macmillan, 1991), pp. 149, 158–67.
7 Kevin Sullivan, *Jesuits*, p. 41. Ellmann too was disappointed with the dearth of records at Clongowes, see *JJII*, p. 35.
8 From Edward Fitzpatrick, *St. Ignatius and the Ratio Studiorum* (New York: McGraw-Hill, 1933) as quoted in Sullivan, *Jesuits*, p. 73.
9 See McRedmond, *Greater Glory*, p. 177–78.
10 Sullivan, *Jesuits*, p. 47. see note #69: facts taken from a note attached to the Clongowes *Prospectus*, 1886.
11 See Robert Schwickerath, SJ, *Jesuit Education: its History and Principles* (St. Louis: B. Herder, 1904), pp. 585–91.
12 Budgen, *Making of Ulysses*, p. 258.
13 See Sullivan, *Jesuits*, p. 29.
14 *Ibid.*, pp. 77–78.
15 Conmee's memoir about the traditional ways of Catholic Ireland, *Old Times in the Barony*, is mentioned in the "Wandering Rocks" episode of *Ulysses* (10.161–62). Joyce's characterization of Conmee in the first

section of the episode initially appears to be one of an affable, elderly man, naive to the prejudices or hypocrisy that his religious commitment might perpetuate.

16 Sultan, *Argument of Ulysses*, p. 211.
17 Stanislaus Joyce, *Brother's Keeper*, p. 238.
18 Bruce Bradley, SJ, *James Joyce's Schooldays* (New York: St. Martin's Press, 1982), p. 124.
19 Lambert McKenna, Rev., SJ, *The Life and Work of Rev. James Aloysius Cullen* (London: Longmans, Green, and Co., 1924), pp. 100–03.
20 See Chester Anderson, *Joyce and his World*, p. 24.
21 Sullivan, *Jesuits*, p. 134.
22 *Ibid.*, p. 122.
23 Bradley, *Schooldays*, pp. 124–25.
24 *Ibid.*, pp. 131–32.
25 Translated from the French by Rev. Charles Gobinet DD, Father Cullen's edition published (Dublin: James Duffy, 1867). See Bradley, *Schooldays*, p. 125–26.
26 Charles Gobinet, DD, *The Instruction of Youth in Christian Piety* (Boston: Patrick Donahoe, no date given), pp. 34–37.
27 See Ellmann, *JJII*, p. 46; Gorman, Herbert, *James Joyce* (New York: Farrar and Rinehart, 1939), p. 45.
28 Sullivan reports that Joyce was examined on *Ivanhoe* in his Matriculation examination. He concludes the topic would have been an easy task for Joyce, because of his probable reading of the novel during his Belvedere years, pp. 158–59. Unfortunately, Sullivan was in error when he assumed the topics Joyce was tested on were given in the Royal University Calendar, 1900. Joyce had taken the Summer examination in 1899. His topics were given in the 1899 Calendar. Joyce most probably read *Ivanhoe* as a young man, but was never examined on the novel at University College Dublin. For a discussion of the scholarly oversight, as well as implications of the actual topics on which Joyce was examined, see my article, "Joyce's Matriculation Examination," *JJQ* 30:3 (1993): pp. 393–407.
29 Joyce, *Dubliners: Text, Criticism, and Notes*, eds., Robert Scholes and A. Walton Litz (New York: The Viking Critical Library, 1976), pp. 25, 29. Subsequent citing appears in text.
30 See J. F. Byrne, *The Silent Years: an Autobiography with Memoirs of James Joyce and Our Ireland* (New York: Farrar, Strauss, and Young, 1953), pp. 21–25.
31 *Ibid.*, p. 23.
32 *Ibid.*, p. 22.
33 See Thomas Seccombe, "Ivanhoe," *Times Literary Supplement*, December 18, 1919.
34 Sir Walter Scott, *Ivanhoe* (New York: Signet Classic, 1962), pp. 93, 122, etc. All subsequent page references appear in text.

35 See Ellmann, *JJII*, pp. 342–46.

36 See Mahaffey. "*Giacomo Joyce*," in *A Companion to Joyce Studies*, eds., Zack Bowen and James Carens (Westport: Greenwood Press, 1984), pp. 387–420; quoted material, p. 412.

37 Joyce, *Giacomo Joyce* (New York: The Viking Press, 1968), p. 11. Subsequent citing appears in text.

38 *Paradise Lost*, book IV, ll. 304–05.

39 Mahaffey also views Dante's Beatrice as one of the central intertextual sources for the female subject of *Giacomo*, see her "*Giacomo Joyce*," pp. 406–10.

40 See Freud, *Beyond the Pleasure Principle*, translated by James Strachey (New York: W. W. Norton, 1966). Freud of course emphasized that the human attraction toward darkness and mystery stems from the thanatos-impluse.

41 Mahaffey, "*Giacomo Joyce*,"p. 388. Quoted material from *Giacomo Joyce* appears on p. 14.

42 *Selected Letters of James Joyce*, ed. Ellmann (New York: The Viking Press, 1966), pp. 233–34.

43 Scott, introduction to the 1830 edition of *Ivanhoe*, p. xiv.

44 *Ibid.*

45 An 1820 review of *Ivanhoe* places the suffering of the Jewish characters as foremost in the book's use of historical "fact" to explain prejudice. See "Ivanhoe: A Romance," in *New Monthly Magazine and Universal Register*, 1820 (January–June, 1820), pp. 73–82. One hundred and fifty years later, Edgar Johnson characterizes the Jewish presence in the novel in a similar manner: "Isaac and Rebecca are in fact at the moral heart of the novel – the Jews are revealed in historical perspective not as villains but as victims." See Johnson, *Sir Walter Scott: the Great Unknown* (New York: Macmillan, 1970), pp. 743–45. See also Edgar Rosenberg, *From Shylock to Svengali* pp. 73–115.

46 Sullivan, *Jesuits*, p. 160, n. 26.

47 See Georg Lukàcs, *The Historical Novel*, pp. 19–88.

48 Lukàcs, "Realism in the Balance," in *Aesthetics and Politics* ed. Ronald Taylor (London: NLB, 1977), p. 57.

49 See also Leonard Albert, "Ulysses, Cannibals, and Freemasons," in *A.D.* 2 (Autumn, 1951): pp. 265–83.

50 I am indebted to Ira Nadel's work for bringing these allusions together, see *Joyce and The Jews*, p. 211.

51 *Ibid.*, p. 230.

52 W. D. Killen, DD, *The Ecclesiastical History of Ireland* (London: Macmillan, 1875), vol II, p. 510.

53 Fahy, who was not a Jesuit, but a priest of the Holy Ghost Order, founded the Maria Duce organization in the US. His support of fascism and anti-Semitism was similar to the 1930s radio-sermons of the American priest, Father James Coughlin.

54 Letter from Father Fergus O'Donoghue, Milltown Park Jesuit Community, Dublin 6, Ireland, August 26, 1991.

55 See the *Catalogus Provinciae Hiberniea*, Collegium SS, Cordis Mungretense at Convictus, years 1882–87. See also McRedmond, *Greater Glory*, p. 216–20.

56 Edward Cahill, SJ, *The Framework of a Christian State* (Dublin: Gill and Sons, Ltd., 1932), p. 221. Leo XIII's words are again from the *Humanum Genus*.

57 *Ibid.*, pp. 240–41.

58 Although Cahill was a respected member of the Society during the *fin de siècle* and beyond, he is today viewed as quite an embarrassing anomaly. Interview with Father James Hennesy, Director of the Jesuit Community, Buffalo, New York, June 28, 1991; and Father Fergus O'Donoghue, Milltown Park, Dublin, August 4, 1991.

59 See *Portraits: Belvedere College Dublin, 1832–1982*, eds. John Bowman and Ronan O'Donoghue (Dublin: Gill and Macmillan, 1982), pp. 15–16.

60 *Ibid.* p. 15.

61 See Father T. Morrissey, SJ, *A Page of Irish History: the Story of University College, Dublin 1883–1909* (Dublin: McGill and Sons, 1930).

62 See *Our Colloquium: Papers on the Spiritual Exercises*, Thomas Finlay, SJ, Censor Deputatus, and Laurentius Kiernan, SJ, Prep. Provost Hibernia (Dublin: Cahill, 1930), pp. 45–47.

63 See McRedmond, *Greater Glory*, p. 182.

64 See George Mosse, *The Crisis of German Ideology: Intellectual Origins of the Third Reich* (New York: Grosset & Dunlap, 1964), pp. 129–30.

65 Correspondence with Fergus O'Donoghue, SJ, Milltown Park, Dublin, November 1, 1991. I am indebted to Father O'Donoghue for his research on Finlay's background from two sources: Morrisey, *A Page of Irish History*, and George O'Brien, "Fr. Thomas Finlay, S.J.," in *Studies* 29 (March, 1940): p. 27.

66 Bowman and O'Donoghue, *Portraits*, p. 16.

67 See J. F. Burns, *Shop Window to the World: the History of the Masonic Boys' School, Dublin* (Dublin: Published under the authority of the Board of Governors of the Masonic Boys' School, no date), pp. 3–5.

68 See Louis Hyman, *Jews of Ireland*, pp. 52, 59. Hyman believes that the Hebraic influence in Freemason ritual may have attracted Dublin Jews in the eighteenth century for obvious reasons, but that Jewish involvement in the organization was more of a factor because of the bridge it created for the many social gaps between Jews and Christians in the city. Indeed, the Institute for Irish Studies on Merrion Road is now housed in a building that was erected as a school for orphaned daughters of Freemasons, and the front tower of the structure has a large Star of David on its facade.

69 See Louis Hyman, *Jews of Holland*, pp. 197, 202.

70 Finlay may have influenced Joyce's thoughts on Thomism at University College Dublin. See Sullivan, *Jesuits*, pp. 166–69.

71 See Ellmann, *JJII*, pp. 37–39.

72 *Ibid.*, p. 38.

73 *Ibid.*, pp. 38–39.

74 Three months after their trip to Cork, Joyce and his father may have read of an assault in that city on a Lithuanian Jewish immigrant named Jacob Sayers. The incident occasioned letters of protest to Samuel Montagu MP from Justin McCarthy and John Redmond. See Louis Hyman, *Jews of Ireland*, pp. 221–22.

75 See Robert M. Adams, *Surface and Symbol: the Consistency of James Joyce's Ulysses* (New York: Oxford University Press, 1962), pp. 104–06. See also Robert Boyle, SJ "A Note on Reuben J. Dodd as 'a dirty Jew'," in *JJQ* 3 (Fall, 1965), pp. 64–66; and Patrick A. McCarthy, "The Case of Reuben J. Dodd," in *JJQ* 21:2 (Winter, 1984): pp. 169–75. These two articles assert that Dodd is not meant to be Jewish. The argument is based on Joyce's earlier creation of the character of Harford in the story "Grace." Harford, called an "Irish Jew" by fellow Dubliners, is later spotted at the retreat, thus confirming that he is not Jewish. Boyle and McCarthy argue that Harford is a prototype for Dodd – both characters are "Jewish" in their occupations, but not in their religion nor ethnicity.

76 *Ibid.*, p. 38. See also Patrick McCarthy, *Ulysses: Portals of Discovery* (Boston: Twayne Publications, 1990), pp. 78–79.

77 C. P. Curran, *James Joyce Remembered* (New York: Oxford University Press, 1968), pp. 26, 36.

3 SILENCE: UNIVERSITY YEARS – THE CHURCH, DREYFUS, AND AESTHETICS

1 See Ellmann, *JJII*, p. 65.

2 A list of the clergy's positions hostile to Irish freedom was conspicuously long: the abandonment of the Irish Tenant League in the 1850s, Cardinal Cullen's disapproval of the Fenian movement, the 1890s castigation of Connolly's and Larkin's Socialism, and, of course, the desertion of Parnell after some twenty years of support. See Edward Norman, *A History of Modern Ireland*, pp. 151–53, 161–64, 196–232.

3 Curran, *Joyce Remembered*, p. 107–08. See also W. G. Fallon, "Jim Joyce at Belvedere," in *Portraits: Belvedere College, Dublin, 1832–1982*, pp. 45–48.

4 Ellmann, *JJII*, p. 58.

5 See Sullivan, *Jesuits*, p. 195.

6 As quoted in Liam Miller, *The Noble Drama of W. B. Yeats* (Dublin: The Dolman Press, 1977), p. 41. The text of the pamphlet is reprinted in Lady Gregory, *Our Irish Theater* (Gerards Cross: Colin Smyth, 1972).

7 Ellmann, *JJII*, p. 67.

8 See the *Calendar* for 1900, Royal University of Ireland. Joyce enrolled for and underwent the Honors examination, but appears to have done so poorly that he was only awarded a "pass" for his answers. While the National University of Ireland has a record of Joyce's entering and

presenting for the Honors paper, his name does not appear in the *Calendar* for 1900 under the "Honors in English" list. Interview, October, 1991, Ms. N. Moynihan, Archivist, The National University of Ireland.

9 See Davison, "Joyce's Matriculation Examination." See also, Sullivan, *Jesuits*, p. 158–59.

10 Joyce, "The Day of the Rabblement," *Critical Writings*, p. 70.

11 Joyce, indeed, later became friends with Zweig in Zurich. See Zweig, *The World of Yesterday* (Lincoln: University of Nebraska Press, 1964), pp. 43–45.

12 As quoted by Straumann in his essay "Last Meeting With Joyce," in *Contexts of Literature: an Anglo-Swiss Approach* (Bern: A Francha, 1975), pp. 65–68. For information on Straumann, see Reizbaum, "Swiss Customs: Zurich's Sources for Joyce's Judaica," pp. 207–10.

13 See Jean-Denis Bredin, *The Affair: the Case of Alfred Dreyfus*, translated by Jeffrey Mehlmen (New York: George Braziller, Inc., 1986), pp. 152–80, 237–42.

14 The circulation of *The Times* from 1899–1900 was approximately 35,642. One of the largest consumers of that circulation was Dublin City. Interview, Reference Librarian, *The Times*, London offices, January 17, 1991.

15 See Hugh Oram, *The Newspaper Book: a History of Newspapers in Ireland, 1649–1983* (Dublin: MO Books, 1983), p. 70.

16 *Freeman's Journal*, January 17, 1898, p. 5.

17 *The Times*, January 13, 1898, p. 3.

18 *Ibid.*, January 20, 1898, p. 5.

19 *Ibid.*, September 1, 1899, p. 6. The article goes on to diminish the guilt of the Vatican itself in this indictment, but blames Roman Catholic organs such as *Civilita Cattolica*, for "stirring up religious fanaticism." This journal was mentioned previously as a well-known disseminator of anti-Jewish propaganda, see pp. 22–23 of this study.

20 See Terence de Vere White, "Arthur Griffith," in *The Shaping of Modern Ireland*, ed. Conor Cruise O'Brien (Toronto: University of Toronto Press, 1960), pp. 63–73, specifically p. 64.

21 *Ibid.*, p. 72.

22 Griffith, "Foreign Notes: Dreyfus Party Plotting the Disarmament of France," *United Irishman*, July 29, 1899, front page.

23 Foreign Notes: "The Popular Joy of Europe," and "Persecution as a Political Dodge Against Alliance," *United Irishman*, November 11, 1899, front page.

24 *United Irishman*, April 23, 1904, front page.

25 See the paper from February through August, 1906.

26 See Gogarty's series of articles "Ugly England," which ran in Griffith's *Sinn Féin*, from November 24, to December 1, 1906.

27 See Stephen Brown, *The Press in Ireland: a Survey and Guide* (New York: Lemma Pub., 1971), pp. 60–100.

28 *The New Ireland Review* 9 (1898): pp. 153–62. Quoted passage appears on

page 160.

29 For a discussion of this periodical and its role in the Celtic Revival, see Richard Fallis, *The Irish Renaissance* (Syracuse: Syracuse University Press, 1977), p. 117. See also Stephen Brown, *The Press*, pp. 60–100.

30 Curran, *Joyce Remembered*, pp. 31–32.

31 Had he gone back that next night in 1899, however, Joyce might have been impressed with Edward Martyn's Naturalistic play *The Heather Field*; see Fallis, *Irish Renaissance*, pp. 89–90.

32 Curran, *Joyce Remembered*, p. 29. As "the reformer" often spoke from the margins of culture, Joyce found himself drawn to marginal groups more and more. Once he was on the Continent, Jewish intellectuals would become his group of choice.

33 *Ibid.*, p. 66.

34 See Andras Szekely, Introduction, *Mihály Munkácsy*, (St. Paul: Control Data Arts, 1981), p. 5.

35 See *My Brother's Keeper*, pp. 178–79. Stanislaus relates that Joyce never had a vested interest in sacred art, or visual arts in general.

36 Szeleky, *Milhály Munkácsy*, pp. 6–11.

37 *Ibid.*, p. 38.

38 *Ibid.*, p. 39.

39 Jameson and Esterlake, *The History of Our Lord as Exemplified in Works of Art* (London: Longmans Green, 1890), pp. 93–95.

40 Albert E. Bailey, *The Gospel in Art* (Boston: The Pilgrim Press, 1931), p. 345.

41 Joyce, "Royal Hibernian Academy 'Ecce Homo'," *Critical Writings*, p. 37. Subsequent page references appear in text.

42 *Compact Edition of The Oxford English Dictionary*, vol. II (Oxford University Press, 1971), p. 3190.

43 Byrne, *Silent Years*, p. 40–41.

44 Stanislaus Joyce, *Brother's Keeper*, p. 171.

45 *Ibid.*, pp. 171–73.

46 Byrne, *Silent Years*, p. 178.

47 *Ibid.*, p. 184.

48 *Ibid.*, pp. 182–85.

49 *Ibid.*, p. 185.

50 As quoted by Ellmann in *JJII*, p. 65. The original source was Morris L. Ernest's book, *The Best is Yet* (1945), p. 118.

51 *Ibid.*, p. 44.

52 Curran, *Joyce Remembered*, pp. 11–12.

53 Ellmann, *JJII*, p. 74.

54 "Ibsen's New Drama," *The Critical Writings*, p. 48.

55 For a translation of this lecture see the *Buffalo Studies*, edited from Italian manuscripts and translated by Joseph Prescott, (New York: University of New York at Buffalo Press, 1964), pp. 7–25.

56 *Ibid.*, p. 75.

57 Ellmann, *JJII*, p. 80.

58 *Freeman's Journal*, October 25, 1901, p. 7.
59 See Ellmann, *JJII*, p. 775 n. 47. Although the recording was uncirculated for years, it is now available on LP entitled *Lestrygonians: James Joyce reads excerpts from Ulysses and Finnegans Wake*, Cademon label, no. TC1340. Joyce's choice of the passage is related in Sylvia Beach, *Shakespeare and Company* (New York: Harcourt, Brace, 1959), pp. 170–73. I am indebted to Theoharis Constantine Theoharis for pointing out this source, see his *Joyce's Ulysses*, p. 216.
60 See Costello, *Years of Growth*, p. 217.
61 See *Critical Writings*, p. 68–69.
62 I am indebted to Peter Costello for this quotation from Browne's work, see *The Years of Growth*, p. 218. *Handbook of Homeric Study* (Dublin: Browne and Nolan, 1905). Costello does not give a page number. For Joyce's own study of Bérard, see Nadel, *Joyce and the Jews*, p. 27.
63 *Ibid.*, p. 106.
64 See Ellmann, *JJII*, pp. 100, 109, 134; see also Fallis, *Irish Renaissance*, p. 144.
65 Stanislaus Joyce, *Brother's Keeper*, p. 217.

4   *EXILE*: EXCURSION TO THE CONTINENT, BITTER RETURN

1 Ira Nadel agrees with this assumption. He states: "In absorbing the attacks on Jews [Joyce] no doubt felt some identity with his marginality in France in 1903 as a 'foreigner' as the Jews were repeatedly portrayed in the French and Irish press." See *Joyce and the Jews*, p. 68.
2 Ellmann, *JJII*, p. 120.
3 *Ibid.*, photograph section, p. vii.
4 For an account of the racialist ideology behind anti-Semitism, see Leon Poliakov, *The History of Anti-Semitism*, vol. III, translated by Miriam Kochan (New York: The Vanguard Press, Inc., 1975). In his conclusion, Poliakov asserts that anti-Semitism as a "science" was fueled by the need to retain a belief in the Jews as a cursed, alienated people in an age when economics and social theory had usurped the power of religion. See pp. 458–72.
5 See "The Ethnological Table of Moses," in *The Irish Ecclesiastical Record* 14:3 (1893): pp. 213–33.
6 Martin Bernal, *The Black Athena: the Afroasiatic Roots of Classical Civilization* (New Brunswick: Rutgers University Press, 1989), vol. II, pp. 219–23.
7 *Ibid.*, pp. 229–40.
8 Christian Lassen, *Indische Alterthumskunde* (Bonn, 1847) vol. I, p. 414. As quoted in Poliakov's *History of Anti-Semitism*, pp. 317, 535.
9 See Poliakov, "The Racist Reaction," pp. 323–474.
10 See Poliakov, *History of Anti-Semitism*, pp. 458–72.
11 See Colin Holmes, *Anti-Semitism in British Society*, pp. 37–43.
12 See Paula Hyman, *From Dreyfus to Vichy: the Remaking of French Jewry*,

1906–1939 (New York: Columbia University Press, 1979), pp. 3–11. Hyman uses Diogene Tama, *Transactions of the Paris Sanhedrim*, (London, 1807), pp. 181–96, 88–101.

13 See Stephen Wilson, *Ideology and Experience: Antisemitism in France at the Time of the Dreyfus Affair* (London: Associated University Press, 1982), pp. 169–70.

14 See Jacob Katz, *From Prejudice to Destruction: Anti-Semitism, 1700–1933* (Cambridge, MA: Harvard University Press, 1980), pp. 299–300.

15 Bernard Lazare, "Juif et israelites," *Entretiens politiques et littéraires*, vol. I, September, 1890, p. 176, as quoted in Michael Marrus, *The Politics of Assimilation: a Study of the French Jewish Community at the Time of the Dreyfus Affair* (Oxford: Clarendon Press, 1971), p. 169.

16 *Ibid.*, p. 170.

17 *Ibid.*, pp. 180–81.

18 See Stephen Wilson, *Ideology and Experience*, p. 180.

19 See *Letters*, vol. II, p. 26. In this letter to his mother dated February 8, 1903, Joyce speculates that if she can help him obtain work from the *Irish Times* he could make up to 200 pounds a year.

20 Joyce, "An Irish Poet," *Critical Writings*, p. 86.

21 Joyce, "A Suave Philosophy," *Ibid.*, p. 94.

22 Stanislaus Joyce, *Brother's Keeper*, p. 200.

23 Budgen, *Making of Ulysses*, p. 256.

24 See Ellmann, *JJII*, p. 119. Joyce read newspapers to educate himself about the city. He also wanted to become a correspondent for the *Irish Times*, see *Letters*, vol. II, p. 26–27.

25 For an analysis of the role many of these publications played in the Affair, see Stephen Wilson, *Ideology and Experience*, pp. 9–10, 173–75. It may appear that by 1903 the Affair had been brought to a close. In 1901, as a gesture toward reunification, a coalition of the right and left facilitated the pardoning of Dreyfus by French President Emile Loubet. But even up to Dreyfus's reinstatement to rank in 1906, Anti-Dreyfusard journals continued their campaign, claiming the Affair was not a military or political controversy; it had been and still was a product of the subversive Jewish element eroding French culture.

26 *L'Intransigeant*, December 2, 1902, front page.

27 *Letters*, vol. II, pp. 24, 29, 37, 19, respectively.

28 Marrus, *Politics of Assimilation*, p. 16–17.

29 Paula Hyman, *From Dreyfus to Vichy*, p. 47.

30 See Nadel, *Joyce and the Jews*, p. 72–74.

31 Ernst Renan, *Histoire générale et système compré des langues Sémitiques* (Paris, 1855) pp. 4–5. See also Edward Said, *Orientalism* (New York: Vintage Books, 1979) pp. 132–45. See as well Marrus, *Politics of Assimilation*, pp. 10–13. Joyce owned two books written by Renan: *The Life of Jesus*, (London: Watts, 1913); and *Souvenirs d'enfance at de jeunnesse*, (Paris: Calmann-Levy, 1883); see Ellmann, *Consciousness of Joyce*, appendix, p. 125.

32 Said, *Orientalism*, p. 142. The quote is from Renan's *Histoire générale*, pp. 145–46.
33 Gustave Le Bon, *Lois Psychologiques de l'Evolution des Pueples* (Paris, 1894), p. 5, as quoted in Marrus, *Politics of Assimilation*, p. 14.
34 Marrus, *Politics of Assimilation*, p. 14.
35 Thorton, *Allusions in Ulysses*, p. 178.
36 For a discussion of the Taxil–Drumont relationship and how Joyce weaves it into *Ulysses*, see Marvin Magalaner, *Time of Apprenticeship: the Fiction of the Young James Joyce* (New York: Abelard-Schuman, 1959), pp.49–71. Magalaner uses Jean Drault, *Drumont: La France Juive et La Libre Parole* (Paris, 1935) as his source for this discussion.
37 See Magalaner, *Time of Apprenticeship*, pp. 54–8.
38 See Linda Nochlin, "Degas and the Dreyfus Affair: a Portrait of the Artist as an Anti-Semite," in *The Dreyfus Affair: Art, Truth, and Justice*, ed. Norman Kleebatt (Berkeley: University of California Press, 1987), pp. 96–116. The direct quotations are from Pissaro's own words, from Ralph Shikes and Paula Harper, *Pissaro: his Life and Work* (New York: Horizon Press, 1980), p. 231.
39 *Ibid.*, p. 107.
40 *Ibid.*, p. 113. During the Dreyfus Affair, the friendship between Degas and May all but disintegrated.
41 *Ibid.*, p. 101.
42 See Kleebatt, *The Dreyfus Affair: Art, Truth, and Justice*, plates, p. 249.
43 *Ibid.*, p. 203.
44 Cohn, *Warrant for Genocide*, pp. 73–76.
45 For a discussion of the development of this type of caricature, see L. Perry Curtis, *Apes and Angels: the Irishman in Victorian Caricature* (New York: George Braziller, Inc., 1971), pp. 20–22, 29–69.
46 *Ibid.*, pp. 29–46.
47 *Ibid.*, p. 55.
48 *Ibid.*, p. 72.
49 *Ibid.*, p. 71.
50 For simianized Celt as "white negro" see Curtis, *Apes and Angels*, pp. 1–3, 13–15. For a discussion of the concept of "the Jewish nigger," see Gilman, *Jewish Self-Hatred*, pp. 7–12, 206–07, 231.
51 Stanislaus Joyce, *Brother's Keeper*, p. 245.
52 *Ibid.*, p. 247–48.
53 *Ibid.*, p. 245.
54 J. B. Lyons, *Oliver St. John Gogarty: the Man of Many Talents* (Dublin: Blackwater Press, 1980), p. 211.
55 Ellmann. *JJII*, pp. 166–67. For introduction to poem and notes on the text, see *Critical Writings*, pp. 149–52.
56 See *Selected Letters*, p. 102.
57 *Ibid.*, pp. 110–11. Griffith's speech was given at the Rotunda in Dublin on September 1906.

58 *Ibid.*, pp. 110–11.
59 See de Vere White, "Arthur Griffith," *Shaping of Modern Ireland*, pp. 63–73, specifically p. 64.
60 See *Selected Letters*, pp. 108, 110.
61 *Sinn Féin*, November 24, 1906, as quoted in Dominic Manganiello, *Joyce's Politics* (London: Routledge & Kegan Paul, 1980), p. 131, 243, n. 80.
62 *Selected Letters*, p. 138.
63 *Ibid.*, p. 125.
64 *Ibid.*, p. 128.
65 Mary and Padriac Colum, *Our Friend James Joyce* (New York: Doubleday & Co., 1958), p. 56.
66 See Peter Gay, *Freud, Jews and Other Germans: Masters and Victims in Modernist Culture* (New York: Oxford University Press, 1978), p. 20. See also Nadel's discussion of Jews as supposedly predisposed to Journalism and publicity, *Joyce and the Jews*, pp. 150–51. Joyce would find a detailed evolution of exactly why and how "the Jew" was predisposed to propaganda and journalism in his reading, in 1906, of Guglielmo Ferrero's *L'Europa giovane*. For a detailed discussion of Ferrero's book see below, chapter VI.
67 Colum, *Our Friend*, p. 55.
68 See above, pp. 37–38; p. 251, note no. 82.
69 *Selected Letters*, p. 112.
70 See *JJII*, pp. 161–62, 230.
71 Ellmann's source for the event and Hunter's supposed Jewish identity was a letter from a W. P. D'arcy, who claimed to be the son of Bartell D'arcy, model for the character in "The Dead." See Ellmann, *JJII*, p. 762, n. 51. D'arcy claimed to have heard this story from John Joyce. Kenner suggests that through personal experience he knows D'arcy to have been a less than reputable source. See Kenner, "The Impertinence of Being 'Definitive,'" in *Mazes* (San Francisco: North Point Press, 1989), pp. 101–12, (revision of his review of Ellmann's revised biography, *Times Literary Supplement*, December 17, 1982).
72 *Selected Letters*, pp. 21–22.
73 See Louis Hyman, *Jews of Ireland*, p. 169.
74 See Ellmann, *JJII*, p. 230. See also Costello's *Years of Growth*, p. 231:

At the time of the encounter with Joyce, Hunter was living on the Ballybough Road. Later he lived (as Joyce seems to have been aware) in May Street, off Clonliffe Road, up to 1916. In 1921 Joyce asked his aunt Josephine if she knew what had become of Hunter, but it is likely that by then he had passed out of her knowledge. An advertising agent by trade (as was Leopold Bloom) Alfred Henry Hunter died on the 12th of September 1926 in rooms at 23 Great Charles Street (off Mountjoy Square, by then a slum). He was only sixty.

Costello's reference to Joyce's request of his aunt for information on Hunter can be found in his letter of October 14, 1921. See *Selected Letters*, pp. 285–86.

75 "Grace," in *Dubliners*, p. 159. See also above, chapter II, n. 75.
76 See Owen, *James Joyce and the Beginnings of Ulysses* (Ann Arbor: UMI Research Press, 1983. pp. 3–9.
77 In his diary in 1907, Stanislaus had written that "Jim told me he is going to expand his story 'Ulysses' into a short book and make a Dublin 'Peer Gynt' of it." See Ellmann, *JJII*, p. 265.
78 *Selected Letters*, p. 145; letter of February 6, 1907.

5   *CUNNING AND EXILE*: GREEKS AND JEWS

1 Cheyette, *Constructions of "The Jew,"* p. 4.
2 See Theoharis, *Joyce's Ulysses*, chapter 4: "Joyce and Arnold."
3 See Ellmann, *Consciousness*, appendix, pp. 99, 121.
4 See Sullivan, *Jesuits*, pp. 156–58.
5 Joyce, *Critical Writings*, p. 26. It is difficult to know precisely which of Arnold's texts Joyce is alluding to, but in the preface to *Culture and Anarchy*, Arnold does make a point of denigrating the type of mind that stresses machinery and engineering as key elements of cultural progress.
6 Joyce would have read the 1875 second edition, in which Arnold inserted 'the now familiar titles at the heads of the chapters.' See editor's preface and introduction *Culture and Anarchy*, ed. J. Dover Wilson, (London: Cambridge University Press, 1960), p. vii.
7 *Ibid.*, pp. 130, 144.
8 *Ibid.*, p. 141–42.
9 *Collected Letters*, vol. 1, p. 56.
10 See Lionel Trilling, *Matthew Arnold* (New York: Norton & Co., 1939), pp. 59–62, for Thomas Arnold's attitudes toward Jews, pp. 256–57 for Heine's influence on Matthew, pp. 256–57. See also A. P. Stanely, *Life of Thomas Arnold* (London: John Murray, 1904), p. 402. The elder Arnold believed Jews should be barred from citizenship in England. Arnold cites Heine in "Hebraism and Hellenism," only to accuse him of over-emphasizing Hellenism as a model for modern European culture. See Arnold, *Culture and Anarchy*, p. 131.
11 Trilling, *Matthew Arnold*, pp. 256–257. Trilling believes that Heine in turn derived the antithesis from Ludwig Börne, see p. 256.
12 See Ruth apRoberts, *Arnold and God* (Berkeley: University of California Press, 1983), p. 163. apRoberts notes the interest was partially linguistic: "[As] the inheritors of the Judaic Tradition, the present Jews of Europe, elicited accordingly a certain curiosity. . .Higher Criticism at its most elementary level reminded the world that the Bible is a translation, of the Hebrew in the Old Testament."
13 *Ibid.*, p. 166. apRoberts relates that Arnold "enjoyed the domestic circle, and enjoyed the *beau monde* at the Rothschild townhouses. . .[and] Mentmore Towers, the Mayer Amschel Rothschild estate. The company included . . . Disraeli or Gladstone, Thackery, Browning, Tennyson. . ."

14 *Ibid.*, p. 169.
15 *Ibid.*, p. 170. From Arnold's *Letters*, vol. I, pp. 458–59.
16 *Ibid.*, p. 175; From Arnold's *Letters*, vol. II, pp. 1, 26.
17 Cheyette, *Constructions of "the Jew*," p. 22.
18 Arnold, *Culture and Anarchy*, p. 132.
19 *Ibid.*, p. 134.
20 Trilling, *Matthew Arnold*, p. 256.
21 Arnold, *Culture and Anarchy*, pp. 143–44.
22 See Ellmann, *JJII*, pp. 59–60.
23 Arnold, *Culture and Anarchy*, p. 132.
24 See Ellmann, *JJII*, p. 118.
25 Hannah Arendt, *Origins*, p. 23.
26 *JJII*, p. 142.
27 *My Brother's Keeper*, p. 160.
28 See Ellmann, *JJII*, pp. 76, 188, 192. Joyce attempted to learn German on his own so he could read Hauptmann in 1902. He began taking lessons in Trieste in 1905. It appears by the time he left Trieste for Zurich, however, he could read and speak the language to some extent. Throughout this chapter I quote from the Haussmann, Tille, Volz, and Zimmern translations Joyce would have read, and not contemporary translations, such as those of Walter Kaufmann, which Joyce could not have read.
29 Along with other works, *Also Sprake Zarathustra* and *Das Froliche Wissenschaft ("Gay Science" or "Joyful Wisdom")* were commissioned by Nietzsche's German publishers, Naumann of Leipzig, to be translated by Thomas Common and W. A. Haussmann in 1895. See David S. Thatcher, *Nietzsche in England, 1890–1914* (Toronto: University of Toronto Press, 1970), pp. 22–23, (list of translation and publication dates).
30 See Otto Bohlman, *Yeats and Nietzsche: an Exploration of Major Nietzschean Echoes in the Writings of William Butler Yeats* (Ottawa: Barnes & Noble, 1982), p. 1–2. Nietzschean thought influenced Yeats throughout *A Vision* and the later poems. See Ellmann, *The Identity of Yeats* (New York: Oxford University Press, 1964), pp. 91–98.
31 Bohlman, *Yeats and Nietzsche*, p. 126.
32 *Ibid.*, p. 129. The review appeared in *Athenaeum*, March 1903.
33 Nietzsche, *Thus Spoke Zarathustra: a Book for All and None*, translated by Thomas Common (London: T. N. Foulis, 1909), p. 43.
34 *Ibid.*, pp. 107–08. Walter Kaufmann translates the term "rabble" in its use in this line from "On Reading and Writing." See Kaufmann's translation of *Thus Spoke Zarathustra* (New York: Penguin, 1978), p. 40.
35 See Nathan Rotenstreich, *Jews and German Philosophy: the Polemics of Emancipation* (New York: Schocken Books, 1984), for a discussion of the ideas for and against the Jews in the works of Mendelssohn, Kant, Hegel, Schopenhuaer, and Nietzsche.
36 See Kaufmann, *Nietzsche: Philosopher, Psychologist, Antichrist* (New York: Vintage Books, 1968), p. 45.

37 From a letter to his sister and mother, September 19, 1886. Quoted in *The Basic Writings of Nietzsche*, ed. by Kaufmann (New York: Modern Library, 1968), p. 185.

38 Letter to his sister, Christmas, 1887. Quoted in Kaufman, *Nietzsche: Philosopher, Psychologist, Antichrist*, p. 45.

39 Sander Gilman, "Nietzsche, Heine, and the Otherness of the Jew," in *Studies in Nietzsche and the Judeao-Christian Tradition*, eds. James C. O'Flaherty, Timothy F. Sellner, and Robert M. Helm, (Chapel Hill: University of North Carolina Press, 1985), pp. 206–25, quotation, p. 210.

40 Joyce's comments on the Jews were strewn throughout his conversations. Some examples are Joyce likening the Irish temperament to the Jewish, and his opinion that the Jewish rejection of Jesus could be viewed as an heroic act, see Ellmann, *JJII*, p. 395, 375. Another source is *Portraits of the Artist in Exile: Recollections of James Joyce by Europeans*, ed. Willard Potts, (Seattle: University of Washington Press, 1979). In the memoirs of Georges Borach, Joyce repeats his favorite idea from the Talmud: "We Jews are like the olive: we give our best when we are being crushed, when we are collapsing under the burden of our foliage," Potts, *Portraits of the Artist*, p. 71. Such comments have given rise to a mythology about Joyce and the Jews, wherein Joyce becomes a "champion" of the Jews and Bloom becomes unequivocally Jewish. Demystifying this rhetoric is obviously at the core of my research.

41 See *Beyond Good and Evil: Prelude to a Philosophy of the Future*, translated by Helen Zimmern (New York: The Macmillan Co., 1907), section 251, p. 210.

42 See Keith Ansell-Pearson, *An Introduction to Nietzsche as Political Thinker: the Perfect Nihilist* (Cambridge: Cambridge University Press, 1993), p. 95. Ansell-Pearson calls Nietzsche not an anti-Semite, but a "typical gentile."

43 See *Beyond Good and Evil*, section 241, p. 197. Nietzsche explains that nationalism supplants cultural heterogeneity, which brings expansive thinking: "Indeed, I could imagine dull and sluggish races who would require half a century even in our rapidly moving Europe to overcome such atavistic attacks of fatherlandishness and soil addiction and to return to reason, meaning 'good Europeanism.'" Translation taken from Walter Kaufmann in *The Basic Writings*, p. 364.

44 Eric Heller, "The Importance of Nietzsche," in *The Importance of Nietzsche: Ten Essays* (Chicago: University of Chicago Press, 1988), p. 11.

45 Kaufmann, *Nietzsche: Philosopher, Psychologist, Antichrist*, p. 153. The quote is from Nietzsche's notes of his last years, collected in vol. xvi of the Musarion edition of *Gesammelte Werke* (23 vols., 1920–29), no. 373. Nietzsche believed the Greek culture to be superior because of its absorption of Northern cultures; Kaufmann offers for evidence of this "recent scholarship [that includes the] fact that Sparta, where the invaders prohibited intermarriage with the native population, did not develop a great culture of her own," p. 153. Nietzsche himself was of a

mixed German and Polish heritage.

46 *Beyond Good and Evil*, section 251, p. 208.

47 *The Birth of Tragedy or Hellenism and Pessimism*, translated by William Haussmann (London: T. N. Foulis, 1909), section 9, pp. 72–73.

48 *Ibid.*

49 See Reizbaum, *Joyce's Judaic Other: Texts and Contexts*, as well as "Swiss Customs: Zurich's Sources for Joyce's Judaica," pp. 203–18.

50 Between *Die Geburt der Tragodie (The Birth of Tragedy)* and *Menschliches Allzumenschliches (Human, All Too Human)*, Nietzsche wrote and published several articles that were collected into book form and published in 1876 under the title, *Unzeitgemässe Betrachtungen (Untimely Meditations)*.

51 *Human, All Too Human: a Book for Free Spirits*, translated by Zimmern, (New York: Macmillan, 1909), section 475, p. 347.

52 *The Dawn of Day*, translated by Johanna Volz (London: T. Fisher Unwin, 1903), section 84, p. 75.

53 *Ibid.*, section 205, p. 203–04.

54 See Ellmann, *JJII*, p. 360: "Joyce's version of the epic story is a pacifist version. He developed an aspect of the Greek epic which Homer had emphasized less exclusively, namely, that Ulysses was the only good *mind* among the Greek warriors. . .[in Bloom] Homer's Ulysses has been made less athletic, but he retains the primary qualities of prudence, intelligence, sensitivity, and good will."

55 Kaufmann, *Basic Writings*, p. 375, n. 21 to *Beyond Good and Evil*, section 250.

56 *The Joyful Wisdom ("La Gaya Scienza")*, translated by Thomas Common, Paul V. Cohn, and Maude D. Petre (London: T. N. Foulis, 1910), section 135, p. 174.

57 Nietzsche, *A Genealogy of Morals*, trans. William Haussmann and John Gray (New York: The Macmillan Co., 1897), Section 8, p. 32.

58 *Beyond Good and Evil*, section 250, pp. 206–07.

59 *Ibid.*, section 195, p. 117.

60 *Genealogy of Morals*, section 10, pp. 35–36. Nietzsche's use of the French term *ressentiment* was translated to the English "resentment" in the Haussmann version Joyce owned. Walter Kaufmann tells us that the use of the French term represents one of Nietzsche's most profound psychological insights; one which demonstrates as well how he prefigures Freud. Nietzsche probably chose the French because of its connotation "to feel the effects of resentment" (*se ressentir, to feel*) or to feel a hatred toward something or someone. In a Freudian sense, Nietzsche assumes such a disposition includes a significant projection of self-hatred.

61 *Genealogy of Morals*, section 12, p. 107. This "foundation of self-hatred" was first observed in connection to Joyce by Reizbaum, *Joyce's Judaic Other*, pp. 71–8.

62 *Genealogy of Morals*, first essay, section 7, pp. 30–31.

63 See Steven Aschheim, *The Nietzsche Legacy in Germany, 1890–1990* (Berkeley: University of California Press, 1994). Quoted passage from

Jerry Z. Muller's review, *The Times Literary Supplement,* June 17, 1994, p. 29.
64 See Kaufmann, *Nietzsche: Philosopher, Psychologist, Antichrist*, pp. 40, 78, 123 (Baumler); pp. 412, 417, 429(Spengler).
65 *Ibid.*, pp. 179–207; 230–83.
66 Gilman, "Nietzsche, Heine, and the Otherness of the Jew," p. 206.
67 *Ibid.*
68 *Genealogy of Morals*, first essay, section 11, p. 44.

6   *CUNNING*: JEWS AND THE CONTINENT – TEXTS AND SUBTEXTS

1 Nadel includes in his list of Joyce's Zurich Jewish friends: "Simon Levi from Trieste, the Bliznakoff sisters, Vela and Olga, [and] Sigmund Feilbogen (Germany), Stefan Zweig, Felix Beran, and Rudolph Goldschmidt (Austria), Daniel Brody (Hungary), Rene Schivkele and Ivan Goll (Alsace), Paul Ruggerio (Italy/Greece), Paul Phokas (Greece), and a Pole named Czernovic." See *Joyce and the Jews*, p. 220. For more on Joyce's associations in Zurich see Reizbaum, "Swiss Customs: Zurich Sources for Joyce's Judaica," (1989): pp. 203–18.
2 See The Gorman-Gilbert Plan for "Nestor," in Ellmann, *Ulysses on the Liffey* (New York: Oxford University Press, 1972).
3 See Ellmann, *Consciousness*, pp. 97–134, appendix: Joyce's Library in 1920. The other texts include Arnold's *Hebraism and Hellenism* and Renan's *La Vie de Jesus*.
4 See Svevo, "James Joyce," in Livia Veneziani Svevo, *Memoir of Italo Svevo*, translated by Isabel Quigly (Malboro, VT: The Malboro Press, 1990), pp. 171–72.
5 See Ellmann, *JJII*, p. 340. Ellmann informs us that before Joyce left Trieste for Zurich he had in his possession three small pamphlets in German: Freud's *A Childhood Memory of Leonardo Da Vinci*, Ernest Jones' *The Problem of Hamlet and the Oedipus Complex*, and Jung's *The Significance of the Father in the Destiny of the Individual*, all published between 1909 and 1911.
6 In his section on Trieste, Nadel includes an allusion to the argument – made originally by Freud himself – that psychoanalysis issues from what is essentially a "Jewish" method of exegetic reasoning. See *Joyce and the Jews*, pp. 203–07. See also Marthe Robert, *From Oedipus to Moses: Freud's Jewish Identity*, translated by Ralph Manheim, (New York: Doubleday & Co., 1976). See also Susan Handelman, *The Slayers of Moses: the Emergence of Rabbinic Interpretation in Modern Literary Theory* (Albany: State University of New York Press, 1982), pp. 129–52.
7 See Ellmann, *JJII*, p. 395. The only mention of the book that seems to have been Fishberg's was mentioned in an interview between Ellmann and Ottocaro Weiss about these years of Joyce's life.
8 *Selected Letters*, letter of February 28, 1905, p. 56. Curiously enough, Joyce had just mentioned his growing proficiency in German and Danish, as well as his desire to send Georg Brandes a copy of *A Portrait*. It would be

less than a year later that Joyce expressed his astonishment in discovering that Brandes was a Jew (in his reading of Ferrero).

9 Nadel begins *Joyce and the Jews* with a similar discussion. He states: "the overriding historical link between Joyce and the Jews is the exodus, a situation experienced individually by Joyce and universally by Jews – and a stage in Joyce's recognition of text as the supreme element of permanency in an impermanent world," p. 16.

10 Cecil Roth, *History of the Jews of Italy* (Philadelphia: The Jewish Publication Society of America, 1946), p. 337.

11 *Ibid.*, pp. 487–88.

12 A prime example of this Jewish leadership, other than Joyce's acquaintance Teodora Mayer, was Salvatore Barzilli, who was often spoken of as "the Deputy for Trieste," in the Italian Parliament. Appointed to the Senate in the years before the war of 1914, Barzilli helped to convince Italy to leave the Germano-Austrian alliance and join forces with England, France and their allies. See *ibid.*, p. 488.

13 Furbank, *Italo Svevo: the Man and the Writer*, (Berkeley: University of California Press, 1966), p.19.

14 Livia Veneziani Svevo, *Memoir*, pp. 6–10, 65, 75–6.

15 Nadel, *Joyce and the Jews*, p. 202. Nadel obtained this vital statistic from Arthur Rupin, *The Jews in the Modern World* (London: Macmillan, 1934), pp. 318–19.

16 P. N. Furbank, *Italo Svevo*, p. 17. The source of Burton's quotation is: Lady Isabel Burton, *The Life of Sir Richard Burton*, (London, 1893) vol. 1, p. 535.

17 Manganiello, *Joyce's Politics*, p. 43.

18 Italo Svevo, *James Joyce*, translated by Stanislaus Joyce, (San Francisco: City Lights Books, 1969), p. 3.

19 *Selected Letters*, letter of July 12, 1905, p. 64.

20 *Ibid.*, letter of July 29, 1905, p. 71. The landlady was one Signora Moise Canarutto. Her Triestino translates "It's a fine boy, sir."

21 *Ibid.*, Letter of September 24, 1905, p. 76.

22 *Ibid.*, pp. 112, 131, 136, 286.

23 *Ibid.*, p. 58.

24 See the text of *Ahasverus: a Play in One Act*, by Hermann Heijermans, translated by Caroline Heijermans-Houwink and Dr. J. J. Houwink (Boston: Walter H. Baker Co., 1934).

25 Manganiello, *Joyce's Politics*, p. 466–67.

26 Susan L. Humphreys, "Ferrero Etc: James Joyce's Debt to Guglielmo Ferrero," in *JJQ* 16:3 (1979): pp. 239–51. See pp. 239–45 for discussion of "Two Gallants."

27 See Fishberg, *The Jews: A Study of Race and Environment* (London: Walter Scott, 1911), republished (New York: Arno Press, 1975), p. 36 and in-text citing throughout.

28 Manganiello, *Joyce's Politics*, p. 46.

29 *Ibid.*, p. 48.
30 See *Selected Letters*, ed. by Ellmann, letter of November 6, 1906, p. 125.
31 Manganiello, *Joyce's Politics*, p. 49.
32 *Ibid.*, p. 53.
33 *Ibid.*, p. 53. Manganiello's interpretation of Ferrero's words, *L'Europa giovane*, pp. 409–13.
34 Humphreys, "Ferreor Etc," p. 247. Her translation of Ferrero. p. 368.
35 *Ibid.*, pp. 247–48. Ferrero, p. 371.
36 *Ibid.*, p. 248.
37 *Selected Letters*, November 13, 1906, p. 128.
38 Ellmann, *JJII*, p. 784, ns. 42, 43, p. 779, n. 15. Ellmann credits Fogel with the identification of Fishberg as a book Joyce referred to in conversation with Ottocaro Weiss, p. 394.
39 *The James Joyce Archive: Finnegans Wake: a Facsimile of the Buffalo Notebooks* VI, C 7, edited and introduction by Denis Rose (New York: Garland Press, 1978), pp. 265–66.
40 Ellmann, *JJII*, p. 395. In the first edition of his biography, Ellmann called the author "Fisher," and had no reference to the exact book. In 1979, Fogel's article, "James Joyce, the Jews, and *Ulysses*," revealed the probable book and the author's correct name.
41 Stanislaus Joyce, *The Complete Dublin Diary of Stanislaus Joyce*, ed. George H. Healey (Ithaca: Cornell University Press, 1962), p. 114.
42 *Ibid.*, pp. 56, 60.
43 Otto Weininger, *Sex and Character*, authorized translation from the sixth German edition (London: William Heinemann, 1906), pp. 310–11.
44 See Rotenstreich, *Jews and German Philosophy*, pp. 3–7.
45 *Ibid.*, pp. 185–7.
46 Schopenhauer, *Selected Essays of Arthur Schopenhauer*, translated by Ernest Bax (London: George Bell, 1891), pp. 341–42.
47 Gilman, *Jewish Self-Hatred*, p. 244.
48 Weininger, *Sex and Character*, p. 7.
49 *Ibid.*, pp. 186–213.
50 *Ibid.*, p. 286.
51 Ellmann, *JJII*, p. 156.
52 Weininger, *Sex and Character*, pp. 306, 303.
53 *Ibid.*, p. 206.
54 *Ibid.*, p. 312.
55 Ellmann, *JJII*, p. 396.
56 See Nadel, *Joyce and the Jews*, pp. 70–71.
57 Weininger, *Sex and Character*, p. 321.
58 Theodor Herzl, *The Jewish State*, (New York: Dover, 1988), p. 76.
59 Fishberg, *The Jews*, p. vii.
60 *Ibid.*, pp. vii-viii.
61 *Ibid.*, p. 31.
62 *Ibid.*, p. 106.

63 *Ibid.*, 471.
64 See Raleigh, *Chronicle*, pp. 18–19, 77, 98. Molly's background is murky at best and while she says she "looks like a Jewess," she appears to have no Jewish blood in her heritage.
65 *Ibid.*, pp. 7, 110.
66 *Ibid.*, p. 67, figure 20.
67 Herzl, *Jewish State*, p. 76.
68 This idea is not only central to Herzl's belief in the necessity of Zionism, but, of course, later became Sartre's premise in defining the most significant type of Jewish identity in his work *Anti-Semite and Jew*, translated by George Becker (New York: Schocken Books, 1967).
69 Richard Wagner, *Judaism in Music (Das Judenthum in der Musik)*, translated from the German and furnished with explanatory notes and introduction by Edwin Evans, Senior, FRCO, (London: William Reeves, 1910), pp. 12–13.
70 Joyce's words as spoken to Alssandro Bruni in "Joyce Stripped Naked in the Plaza," in *Portraits of the Artist in Exile*, ed. Willard Potts, p. 28.
71 Carlo Cattaneo, *Opere edite inedite di Carlo Catteneo*, ed. by Agostino Bertane (Florence, 1908), vol. IV. The passage appears in Dominic Manganiello, *Joyce's Politics*, p. 55. I am indebted to Professor Manganiello for both this translation and his thoughts on Cattaneo.
72 Weizmann, "Zionism and the Jewish Problem," in *Zionism and the Jewish Future*, ed. H. Sacher (Westport, CT: Hyperion Press, Inc., 1976), pp. 1–11. First published (London: Murray, 1916). Quoted passage appears on p. 10. Nadel points out that versions of this Irish–Jewish analogy appear at two other points in Sacher's text, see *Joyce and the Jews*, pp. 76–78.
73 See Sacher, p. 142. In his article "Agendath Netaim Discovered: Why Bloom Isn't a Zionist," *JJQ* 29:4 (1992): pp. 833–38, Robert Byrnes claims Joyce "must have had [Tolkowsky's essay] open before him as he wrote." Tolkowsky does in fact introduce "the farm of *Kinnereth* on the shoes of Lake Tiberias," which Joyce alters to the more romanticized "the model farm at Kinnereth on the lakeshores of Tiberias" (*U*4.154–55). Byrnes asserts Joyce's parody reveals the author's ridicule of the idea of a Zionist state in Palestine.
74 See Sacher, pp. 216–34.
75 Sokolow, "The New Jew," pp. 216.
76 *Ibid.*, p. 220.

7 *CUNNING*: THE MIRACLE OF LAZARUS TIMES TWO – JOYCE
AND ITALO SVEVO

1 In the preface Svevo wrote for the second Italian edition of *Senilità* (*As a Man Grows Older*), he expressed his gratitude toward Joyce for his role in the former's success: [Joyce had] "been able to renew the miracle of Lazarus...That a writer whose own work weighed upon him so urgently

should spend valuable time on helping his less fortunate brethren is so generous that, I think, it explains his own astounding success, because every other word of his. . .are expressed by that same great soul," see Livia Veneziani Svevo, *Memoir*, p. 104. In *Italo Svevo*, P. N. Furbank entitles his chapter about Svevo's recognition "The Miracle of Lazarus."

2 "Italus the Swabian" or "the Italian-Swabian" which he took in honor of his father's Italian–Hungarian–Austrian heritage.

3 Livia Veneziani Svevo, *Memoir*, p. 67.

4 Joyce came to know individuals such as Teodor Mayer, Roberto Prezioso, and Silvio Benco, all of whom embodied his perception of the politically active journalists. Mayer has often been suggested as another model for Bloom. See John Gatt-Rutter, *Italo Svevo: a Double Life* (Oxford: Clarendon Press, 1988), p. 234.

5 Sigmund Freud, *Jokes and their Relations to the Unconscious*, translated by James Strachey, (New York: W. W. Norton, 1960), pp. 49–51, 111–15.

6 John Gatt-Rutter creates a nice cross section of these similarities: "The twenty year age gap between Bloom and Dedalus matches that between Schmitz and Joyce; Schmitz had married a Catholic and, if only for literary reasons, had changed his name; he had a sense of humor and was well-informed about Jewish custom; he loved both cats and dogs; like Bloom he enjoyed eating offal; also, his father, like Bloom's, originated from Hungary and had earned a living as an itinerant vendor of nick-nacks; and Schmitz too had himself baptized for practical motives." See Gatt-Rutter, *Double Life*, pp. 233–34.

7 See Ellmann, *JJ*, 1959 edition, p. 275.

8 See Stanislaus' introduction to Italo Svevo, *As a Man Grows Older*, translated by Beryl De Zoete (Westport, CT: Greenwood Press, 1977), p. viii. All subsequent citings appear in text.

9 This honor gives the recipient the privilege of beginning the new yearly cycle of the reading of the Torah, and is usually awarded to an active, prominent member.

10 Gatt-Rutter, *Double Life*, p. 52.

11 Furbank, *Italo Svevo*, p. 98.

12 Gatt-Rutter, *Double Life*, p. 50.

13 *Ibid.*, p. 52.

14 As quoted by Naomi Lebowitz, *Italo Svevo* (New Brunswick: Rutgers University Press, 1978), p. 40. Quote originally taken from Sergio Solmi, "Ricordi di Svevo," in "Omaggio a Italo Svevo," *Solaria* (March–April, 1929): p. 71.

15 See Gatt-Rutter, *Double Life*, pp. 144–6.

16 See Furbank, *Italo Svevo*, p. 43.

17 As quoted in Furbank, *Italo Svevo*, pp.50–51; from Marie-Anne Commene, "Italo Svevo," in *Europe*, (1960): p. 114.

18 Livia Veneziani Svevo, *Memoir*, p. 18.

19 Gatt-Rutter, *Double Life*, p. 341. Quote originally taken from G.

Debenedetti, "Lettera a Carocci su 'Svevo e Schmitz,'" *Solaria* 4:3–4 (1929): pp. 28–34.

20 For the attitude toward race, see Joyce's "Ireland, Island of Saints and Sages," in *Critical Writings*, p. 165–66. For the quotation on Mangan, see his 1902 essay on Mangan, "James Clarence Mangan," p. 81.

21 Joyce's remark on this subject appears in my introduction. Joyce claimed that the Irish and the Jews were both "impulsive, given to fantasy, addicted to associative thinking, and wanting in rational discipline." See Ellmann, *JJII*, p. 395.

22 Livia Veneziani Svevo, *Memoir*, p. 52.

23 *Ibid.*, p. 66.

24 See Gatt-Rutter, *Double Life*, p. 235–36. While Stanislaus suggests that Joyce's formality was a sign of respect, Gatt-Rutter cites different reasoning. After the death of Svevo, Joyce declined to write a preface to *As a Man Grows Older* in 1929, stating that Svevo had been rather tight with him on certain occasions. He went on to say that he had never been invited to the Schmitz household as a guest, but only as a teacher, and that Livia wouldn't acknowledge Nora in the street. These accusations, however, may be another example of Joyce's obsession with betrayal, a problem that affected nearly every friendship he ever made when it came to the loaning of money.

25 See Livia Veneziani Svevo, *Memoir*, pp. 21–23.

26 See *Collected Letters*, vol. III, ed. Ellmann, pp. 172–73. Letter from Schmitz to Joyce, dated March 27, 1928.

27 Stanislaus Joyce, introduction to *As a Man Grows Older*, p. xi.

28 The Schmitzes may well have been the first people to ever hear the story read. For the date of Joyce's writing the story see *Selected Letters*, ed. Ellmann, p. 64. For date of the commencement of Joyce's lessons with Svevo, see Furbank, *Italo Svevo*, p. 80.

29 Stanislaus Joyce, introduction to *As a Man Grows Older*, p. vi.

30 *Ibid.*, p. vi.

31 Furbank, *Italo Svevo*, p. 82.

32 *Ibid.*, p. vi.

33 Livia Veneziani Svevo, *Memoir*, p. 67.

34 Introduction to *As a Man Grows Older*, p. vi.

35 Larbaud and Cremieux translated *Zeno* into French. Cremieux was a Jew himself, and his enthusiastic support of the novel may have included a certain undisclosed pride about the protagonist, who by the end of the text appears to be revealed as Jewish.

36 See Thomas F. Staley, "The Search for Leopold Bloom: James Joyce and Italo Svevo," in *JJQ* 1:4 (1964): pp. 59–63. This information about Svevo's visits was told to Staley by Mary Kirn, a maid and nurse in the Joyce household from 1910 to 1911. She also remembered Livia bringing her children to the flat to visit with the Joyces; see p. 60.

37 In *Joyce and the Beginnings of Ulysses*, Owen challenges Hans Gabler's

opinion of which chapters Svevo read in 1909. Gabler based his belief that Joyce had given Svevo chapters I through III and the beginning scenes of chapter IV on Svevo's comment in the letter that he had "already a sample of what would be the change of [Stephen's] mind." Owen believes Svevo only received III, and that his comment was based on Stephen's dream and vomiting at the end of that chapter; see p. 45.

38 The entire text of the letter can be found in Ellmann, *JJII*, p. 273–74.
39 *Ibid.*, p. 274. See also Furbank, *Italo Svevo*, p. 88.
40 *Ibid.*, p. 430. Ellmann states that to those who inquired, Joyce would only identify this photograph as "the model for Leopold Bloom."
41 See Budgen, *Making of Ulysses*, p. 59.
42 See Furbank, *Italo Svevo*, pp. 140–2. See also Livia Veneziani Svevo, *Memoir*, p. 115.
43 Italo Svevo, "James Joyce," in Livia Veneziani Svevo, *Memoir*, essay translated and edited by John Gatt-Rutter, p. 168.
44 See Ellmann, *JJII*, p. 374. The question was asked by Dr. Daniel Brody and told to Ellmann in an interview with Brody in 1954. See above, chapter 7, note no. 46.
45 Furbank, *Italo Svevo*, p. 163.
46 *Ibid.*, p. 68.
47 See Gatt-Rutter, *Double Life*, p. 8.
48 *Ibid.*, p. 68.
49 Schopenhauer, *The World as Will and Representation*, translated by E. F. J. Payne (New York: Dover Press, 1969), vol I, p. 399. See also D. W. Hamlyn, *Schopenhauer* (London: Routledge & Kegan Paul, 1985) pp. 159–61.
50 Schopenhauer, *ibid.*, p. 29.
51 Italo Svevo, *A Life*, translated from the Italian by Archibald Calquhoun (New York: Alfred A. Knopf, 1963), p. 397. All subsequent citing will appear in text.
52 Schopenhauer, *World as Will*, vol. I, p. 398.
53 See Ellmann, *Consciousness*, appendix, pp. 134, 126.
54 *Selected Letters*, letter of September 20, 1928, p. 37.
55 See Freud, "The Resistances to Psycho-Analysis," in *Collected Papers*, translated by Joan Riviere (London: Hogarth, 1952), p. 174. See also *A Psycho-Analytic Dialogue: the Letters of Sigmund Freud and Karl Abraham*, ed. Hilda C. Abraham and Ernest L. Freud, translated by Bernard Marsh and Hilda C. Abraham (New York: Basic Books, 1965), p. 34. Outside of Freud's own circle, the notion of psychoanalysis as a "Jewish science," was much more a product of the 1930s and onward rather than during the period Joyce came to study Freud.
56 See Gatt-Rutter, *Double Life*, p. 246. Originally quoted in *Racconti, saggi e pagine sparse*, ed. Bruno Maier (Milan: Dall'Oglio, 1968), pp. 685, 686.
57 Gatt-Rutter, *Double Life*, p. 341.
58 See Edouard Roditi, "A Note on Svevo," in *As a Man Grows Older*, p. xiii.

See also Gatt-Rutter, *Double Life*, p. 393. The article was reprinted several times, but never translated into English. Two of the more popular versions appeared in *Solaria* 4:3–4 (1929) under the title "Lettera a Carocci su Svevo e Schmitz," and in *Saggi Critici*, 2nd series, (Milan, 1950).

59 Translated by P. N. Furbank, *Italo Svevo*, p. 185. Original source, G. Debenedetti, *Saggi Critici*, new series, 2nd edition (Milan, 1955), p. 86.

60 Furbank, *ibid.*, p. 184; see also Lebowitz, *Italo Svevo*, p. 40.

61 It may seem that the stereotype becomes irrelevant: Bloom is self-doubting not through "racial inferiority" nor as a result of harsh persecution, but through guilt over his own idiosyncratic failures. But he is self-deprecating *as a Jew* as well – not because he is partly Jewish, but because he has internalized the stereotypes of "the Jew" to the point of self-loathing. The stereotype is thus altered through Joyce's insights into the struggle for assimilated Jewish identity.

62 Italo Svevo, *Confessions of Zeno*, translated by Beryl De Zoete (New York: Vintage Books, 1989) p. 387. *Zeno* is the only one of Svevo's three complete novels to actually use the word "Jew." All subsequent citing of this book appears in text.

63 See John Henry Raleigh, *Chronicle*, pp. 274–75. John Joyce once worked for Drimmie and Sons of Dublin: see Ellmann, *JJII*, p. 230.

64 As mentioned in my introduction, Joyce's choice of this name for H. C. Earwicker's contemplative, bookish son in *Finnegans Wake* is based on the Old Testament narrative about Noah's sons, Ham, Shem, and Japhet repopulating the postdeluvian world (Genesis, 10:1). In this chapter, as well as in 11:10 and the Talmudic interpretation of both, Shem becomes the ancestor of the Semites, specifically, the Jews. Thus the "shems" of the world in Joyce's universe are those committed to the study and creation of books.

65 As quoted in Lebowitz, *Italo Svevo*, p. 74. The original source is Svevo's *Profilo Autobiographico*, chapter 3, p. 802.

66 Ellmann, of course, suggested Joyce's love-interest Marthe Fleischmann as another model for Gerty, see *JJII*, p. 449.

67 Lebowitz, *Italo Svevo*, p. 100.

68 See Joyce's essay "William Blake" in *Critical Writings*, p. 217. See also Ellmann, *JJII*, pp. 188–89.

69 See Budgen, *Making of Ulysses*, p. 315. See also Richard Brown, *James Joyce and Sexuality* (Cambridge: Cambridge University Press, 1988), pp. 86–7, 110–11. For Bloom's reference to Sacher-Masoch, see the "Wandering Rocks," *U*10.591–93.

70 Livia Veneziani Svevo, *Memoir*, p. 67.

71 The Italian of this closing paragraph, which Joyce admired so, reads: "*Si! Angliolina pense e piange! Pensa come se le fosse stato spiegato il segreto dell' universo e dell propria esistenza: piange como se nel vasto mondo non avesse piu trovato neppure un* Deo gratias *qualunque.*"

72 The quoted words are Ellmann on *Senilità*, *JJII*, p. 271.

73 Marilyn Reizbaum made similar observations in *Joyce's Judaic Other*; she designates "Circe" as the locus of Joyce's inversion of Weininger's ideas, see pp. 107–35.

8 ULYSSES

1 See *Selected Letters*, letter of September 21, 1920 to Carlo Linati, pp. 270–71. The translation reads: "It is the epic of two races (Israel–Ireland) and at the same time the cycle of the human body as well as a little story of a day (life)."

2 Karen Lawrence agrees: "it is Bloom's rather than Stephen's sensibility that dominates the kind of book *Ulysses* will become," See *The Odyssey of Style in* Ulysses, (Princeton: Princeton University Press, 1981), p. 48.

3 See, for example, David Hayman's *Ulysses: the Mechanics of Meaning* (Englewood Cliffs: Prentice Hall, Inc., 1970); Hugh Kenner's *Joyce's Voices* (Berkeley: University of California Press, 1978); Anthony Burgess, *Joysprick: an Introduction to the Language of James Joyce* (New York: Harcourt, Brace, Jovanovich, 1973); Marilyn French, *The Book as World: James Joyce Ulysses* (Cambridge, MA: Harvard University Press, 1976). Joyce himself believed *Ulysses* to be on some level a realist novel. His admiration for eighteenth-century realists such as Defoe suggests he respected the strictures of the genre. More revealing are his comments about the preciseness of realism, such as in his criticism of a George Moore character in *The Untilled Field* who looks up a train schedule in her home town of Dublin where trains had run on the hour for many years, or his comment to Arthur Power that "in realism you are down to facts on which the world is based: that sudden reality which smashes romanticism into a pulp." See Power, *Conversations with James Joyce*, ed. Clive Hart (Chicago: University of Chicago Press, 1974), p. 98. For the first comment see Ellmann, *JJII*, p. 193.

4 See Lawrence, *Odyssey of Style*, p. 38.

5 Joyce, *Giacomo Joyce*, p. 15.

6 *Ibid.*, Introduction, pp. xi–xv.

7 Few notes and manuscripts survive from Joyce's work on the *Telemachia*. By October of 1916, Joyce had completed the *Telemachia* and done some work on chapters he was then calling "Wanderings," and "Nostos" (*Collected Letters*, vol. II, p. 387). In 1917, When Ezra Pound became the European editor of the *Little Review*, progressive chapters of the novel were serialized. It was at this time that Joyce began copying and documenting all his work, including his notes and corrected typescripts. See James Joyce, *Ulysses: Notes & 'Telemachus' – 'Scylla and Charybdis': a Facsimile of Notes for the Book & Manuscripts & Type-scripts for Episodes 1–9*, prefaced and arranged by Michael Groden (New York: Garland, 1978).

8 See Ellmann, *Ulysses on the Liffey*, pp. 188–89.

9 I am indebted to Hugh Kenner for this observation. See Kenner, *Ulysses*

(London: George Allen & Unwin, 1980), pp. 34–5.

10 For a discussion of the book's allusions to, and arguments about, the Boer War, See Barbara Temple-Thurston, "The Reader as Absentminded Beggar: Recovering South Africa in *Ulysses*," in *JJQ* 28:1 (1990): pp. 247–56.

11 See Colin Holmes, *Anti-Semitism in British Society*, pp. 64–68. Liberal opposition to the war was often expressed through anti-Semitic allusions. *Clarion* regularly referred to the capital city as "Jewhannesburg." See *Clarion*, February 24, 1900, as quoted in Holmes, p. 67.

12 See Benstock, "Telemachus" in *James Joyce's Ulysses: Critical Essays*, eds. Hart and Hyman (Berkeley: University of California Press, 1977), p. 9.

13 See Deane, "'Masked with Matthew Arnold's Face,'" pp. 18–20, and Cheyette, *Constructions of "the Jew,"* pp. 208–10.

14 See A. M. Klein, "Shout in the Street: an Analysis of the Second Chapter of Joyce's *Ulysses*," in *New Directions* 13 (1951): pp. 327–45.

15 R. M. Adams demonstrates how much of the "history" Deasy presents has its facts wrong; see his *Surface and Symbol*, pp. 18–26.

16 See Cheyette, *Constructions of "the Jew,"* p. 209. In the statement Cheyette is paraphrasing an element of the theory of history found in Jeffrey Perl, *The Tradition of Return: the Implicit History of Modern Literature* (Princeton: Princeton University Press, 1984).

17 Ellmann, *Ulysses on the Liffey*, p. 11.

18 See James Joyce, *Ulysses: Notes & 'Telemachus'* Buffalo manuscript V.B.I, p. 237.

19 Ellmann, *Ulysses on the Liffey*, p. 188.

20 Arius was also one of the five heresiarchs Stephen recalled in "Telemachus." The allusion to Arius' theory and death here are quite accurate.

21 Egan's character was based on the actual Joseph Casey, who as a nationalist during Davitt's heydey was involved with several land agitations in the 1860s and 1870s. Joyce met and caroused with Casey during his stay in Paris. See Ellmann, *JJII*, pp. 125–26.

22 See chapter 4 of this study. See also Marvin Magalaner, *Time of Apprenticeship*, pp. 50–71.

23 Adams suggests Joyce never saw this popular pantomime of the 1870s; instead, he probably attended the 1892 run of *Sinbad the Sailor*, merely substituting the details of that play into *Ulysses*' "Turko." See Adams, *Surface and Symbol*, pp. 76–82.

24 See Said, *Orientalism*, p. 303. Al-Raschid's caliphate included the influential Jewish community of Baghdad.

25 See Gilbert, *James Joyce's* Ulysses (New York: Vintage Books, 1956), pp. 125–26.

26 Three-fourths of Bloom's blood-line may be Hungarian–Jewish. His father was born in Hungary of two Jewish parents. His mother was born in Ireland, the offspring of an immigrant named Julius Higgins (neé Karoly) and a born Irishwoman, named Fanny Hegarty. Raleigh

suspects that Joyce intended Bloom's maternal grandfather, Higgins, to have come from Hungarian–Jewish stock. It is not a poor assumption considering that most Hungarian immigrants to Dublin would more than likely be Jews. See Raleigh, *Chronicle*, pp. 16–18.

27 See Joseph V. O'Brien, *"Dear Dirty Dublin": a City in Distress, 1899–1916* (Berkeley: University of California Press, 1982), pp. 302–03.

28 *Ibid.*, p. 303. See also Judith Barisonzi, "'Who Eats Pig's Cheeks'" Food and Class in 'Araby,'" in *JJQ* 28:2 (1991): pp. 518–19. Bloom also thinks of "pig's cheeks and cabbage" in "Sirens" (*U*11.1230).

29 See Louis Hyman, *Jews of Ireland*, pp. 184–85. See also Nadel, *Joyce and the Jews*, pp. 70–73.

30 Louis Hyman, *Jews of Ireland*, p. 184.

31 *Ibid.*, p. 339, n. 194. The correct Hebrew should read "Agudeth Netaim," translated as "Our Company of Planters." This misnomer appears to be the only incorrect Hebrew or Yiddish reference stemming from an error on Joyce's part and not from Bloom's ignorance of Judaism or Hebrew. Joyce based the advertisement on information from Sachar's *Zionism and the Jewish Future*. In the piece "The Jews and the Economic Development of Palestine," by S. Tolkowsky, Joyce read of several agricultural colonies in Palestine, including those situated around Lake Kinnereth. See Sacher, *Zionism*, pp. 138–70. See also Robert Byrnes, "Agendeth Netaim Discovered: Why Bloom isn't a Zionist," in *JJQ* 29:34 (1992): pp. 833–38. Because the German street "Bleibtreustrasse" translates "stay true street," Joyce may have also selected the advertisement and the street from different Zionist journals he obtained from his Jewish friends' homes.

32 It is difficult to know exactly what attitude Bloom intends by calling Dlugacz an "enthusiast," but one would assume the same as in the more common "fanatic." Offering a biographical analogue, Louis Hyman suggests that Bloom's comment follows Joyce's to Padriac Colum about the Irish revival: "I dislike all enthusiasms." See Ellmann, *JJQ*, p. 135; Hyman, *Jews of Ireland*, p. 184.

33 Citron, Moisel, and Mastiansky are the surnames of actual Jews who lived in Dublin in Joyce's day. See Louis Hyman, *Jews of Ireland*, p. 329. Joyce obtained all three from *Thom's Directory* for 1905.

34 Joyce penciled in this line about the cat as "kosher" in a 1921 page proof. See *Ulysses: 'Telemachus,' 'Nestor,' 'Proteus,' 'Calypso,' 'Lotus Eaters,' & 'Hades': a Facsimile of Page Proofs for Episodes 1–6*, prefaced and arranged by Michael Groden (New York: Garland, 1978), p. 179: Buffalo manuscripts V.C. 1 to 4a.

35 Joyce, *Joyce's Ulysses Notesheets in the British Museum*, ed. Philip F. Herring (Charlottesville: University of Virginia Press, 1972), p. 82.53.

36 The play represents one of several interpretations of Solomon Herman von Mosenthal's play, *Deborah* (Budapest, 1849, 6th edition, 1890). The play was performed in America and London as *Leah, the Forsaken* from

1904–16. For a discussion of the play's themes paralleled in *Ulysses* see Joseph A. Prescott, "Mosenthal's *Deborah* and Joyce's *Ulysses*," in *Modern Language Notes*, 47 (May, 1952): pp. 334–36. See also, Ralph Joly, *The Jewish Element in James Joyce's Ulysses*, pp. 108–11.

37 See Raleigh, *Chronicle*, pp. 70–75.

38 *Ibid.*, pp. 70–71.

39 See Steinberg, "James Joyce and the Critics Notwithstanding," p. 29.

40 This observation finds support in Joyce's own pacifism. He often described himself to Frank Budgen as "not a bloodyminded man." See Budgen, *Making of Ulysses*, p. 256.

41 Stephen in fact mentions the case of Elizabeth's court physician, Roderigo Lopez, who was executed for treason in 1594: "Shylock chimes with the jewbaiting that followed the hanging and quartering of the queen's leech Lopez, his jew's heart being plucked forth while the sheeny was yet alive. . ." (*U*9.749–51).

42 Martin Cunningham's character is based on John Joyce's friend Matthew Kane, who was apparently an extremely amiable person, but had no special relations to Jews or things Jewish; See Ellmann, *JJII* p. 133. John Wyse Nolan's character is based on the actual John Wyse Power, a friend of Joyce's at University College who conducted research pertaining to Jewish matters, and had an active interest in Irish Jewry. In 1909 he gave a lecture entitled "The Jews of Ireland in the Middle Ages" to the Jewish Literary and Social Club on Lombard Street. See Louis Hyman, *Jews of Ireland*, pp. 183–86.

43 This interpretation of ethnicity parallels Joyce's attitude. Joyce was preoccupied with "Irishness" as discovered in the creative ends of the culture including songs, idioms, clothes, places, expressions, art, literature, etc. Those parts of "Irishness" that suggested violence, racism, bravado, and constraint – the Church's dominance, nationalist terrorism, the Literary Revival – Joyce summarily rejected.

44 Hugh Kenner takes a step further in such an assessment of Bloom: "If Nationalist rhetoric meant anything save empty exhortation to take heart, it meant that the ideal citizen of the New Ireland would be a Jew: someone like the Irish in many belauded ways, but also not a boozer, not a squanderer, not a brawler." See Kenner, *A Colder Eye: the Modern Irish Writers* (New York: Alfred A. Knopf, 1983), pp. 194–45.

45 Stanislaus confirms this when he writes "When a sufficient number of men and women have attained [my brother's] attitude of calm, supreme contempt for violence. . .there will be no more fear on earth that civilization can be wiped out. . .Men can begin to cultivate that attitude in peacetime by quietly breaking wind from behind, as Mr. Leopold Bloom does, when they listen to patriotic speeches. . .and [when] rational beings convert themselves into funny, goose-stepping, uniformed robots – things that never failed to provoke my brother's derisive comments." See *Brother's Keeper*, p. 219.

46 Bernard Benstock was the first to count the number (twenty two) of interruptions made by the second voice – which David Hayman had first called "the arranger" – on the "*Nameless One's*" recounting of the events in Kiernan's. See Benstock, *James Joyce* (New York: Ungar, 1985). For an explanation of "the arranger's" role, see Hayman, *Ulysses: the Mechanics of Meaning.*

47 Griffith's "Hungarian" model for a dual monarchy in Ireland has a history with *Ulysses.* Here in "Cyclops" Nolan and Cunningham suggest that Bloom himself had given this idea to Griffith in passing (*U*12.1623, 1636), and Joyce does appear to have drawn on Griffith's pamphlet, *The Resurrection of Hungary*, in constructing "Circe." Dominic Manganiello believes that "Joyce, on the whole, deemed the Hungarian parallel for Ireland to be a political absurdity," see *Joyce's Politics*, pp. 119–22. See also Robert Tracy, "Leopold Bloom Fourfold: a Hungarian-Hebraic-Hellenic-Hibernian Hero," in the *Massachusetts Review* 6 (1965): pp. 523–38, and Bernard Benstock, "Arthur Griffith in *Ulysses*: the Explosion of a Myth," in *English Language Notes* 4 (1966–67): pp. 123–28.

48 David Hyman believes that Joyce combined his opinion of Cusack with his reading of Flaubert's citizen Regimbart in *A Sentimental Education* to form the citizen. See Hyman's "Cyclops" in *Critical Essays*, pp. 243–75.

49 Marcus de Búrca, *Michael Cusack and the GAA* (Dublin: Anvil Books, 1989), p. 59.

50 *Ibid.*, p. 37.

51 See Ellmann. *JJII*, p. 61. The introduction occurred by way of Joyce's friendship with George Clancy, who was an avid athlete and friend of Cusack. In *A Portrait*, Stephen recalls that his friend Davin, Clancy's fictional counterpart, had "sat at the feet of Michael Cusack, the Gael . . . repelling the terror of soul of a starving Irish village in which the curfew was still a nightly fear." See *A Portrait*, p. 180.

52 *Letters*, ed. Ellmann, vol. II, pp. 209–10. Joyce asks here in passing if Stanislaus had seen where "old Cusack had died."

53 See David Greene, "Michael Cusack and the Rise of the G.A.A.," in O'Brien, *Shaping of Modern Ireland*, pp. 74–85.

54 *Ibid.*, p. 77, 82.

55 O'Brien, *Shaping of Modern Ireland*, introduction, p. 16.

56 More frightening is Joyce's labeling of the "sense or meaning" of the chapter as "The Egocidal Terror." See Linati Schema for "Cyclops" in Ellmann's *Ulysses on the Liffey*, appendix. Still more uncanny is Joyce's designation of "Cyclops" as "holocaust" in the list of Bloom's "Jewish day" in "Ithaca," line 2051.

57 See Terrence de Vere White, "Arthur Griffith," in O'Brien, *Shaping of Modern Ireland*, p. 64.

58 See Holmes, *Anti-Semitism in British Society*, pp. 66–79, 81–83.

59 The citizen's prejudice is unrelenting: the French: "Set of dancing masters. . .They were never worth a roasted fart to Ireland'; the English:

"Their syphilization, you mean"; and the Germans: "haven't we had enough of those sausageeating bastards on the throne from George down to. . .the flatulent old bitch that's dead" (1384, 1197, 1391).

60 Joe Brady was one of the "Invincibles" who murdered Lord Frederick Cavendish and T. H. Burke in Phoenix Park on May 6, 1882. The narrator may be implying that such a "brave man" would be virile even in death.

61 This suggests the medieval legend of the *Foetor Judaicus*, which Joyce may have learned from Fishberg's *The Jews*, pp. 314–15. He may have also encountered allusions to it during his religious training. In "Circe," Joyce uses the term itself when Dr. Punch Costello claims that in Bloom's presence "the foetor judaicus is most perceptible" (*U*15.1795).

62 "The friends we love are by our side. . ." is an allusion to a line of Thomas Moore's song "Where is the slave": "the friends we've tried / Are by our side / And the foe we hate before us." See Thornton, *Allusions in Ulysses*, p. 269. Moore's *Irish Melodies* (1807–34) was a staple in the Joyce home as it was in every other patriotic Irish home. The episode is as well strewn with other allusions to nationalistic enthusiasm such as a reference to the quasi-military group the *Slaugh Na H-Eireann* ("the People of Ireland"), p. 859; a parody of the dock-speech and hanging of Robert Emmett, pp. 524–678; Thomas Davis' *A Nation Once Again*, and much much more. It is important to notice that these references lessen as the citizen becomes enraged with Bloom as an "untrustworthy Jew."

63 Linati Schema in Ellmann, *Ulysses on the Liffey*, appendix. Ellmann also relates in his biography of Joyce that the entire discussion of nationhood derives from a conversation Joyce had with Ottocaro Weiss in 1919, in which Joyce finally decided that one person standing on a chair had the right to call himself a nation. It is noteworthy to observe that this discussion was post-war, and that Weiss was a non-religious Jew. See Ellmann, *JJII*, p. 463.

64 This fact can be drawn from a close reading of *Ulysses*, but is more readily accessible in Raleigh, *Chronicle*, pp. 11–21.

65 Phillip Herring suspects the citizen doesn't know that "Kaffir" in South African is a pejorative word for blacks, and in Arabic means "infidel." But racist notions about the similarities between Jews and blacks may be behind his use of the term. See *Joyce's Notes and Early Drafts for Ulysses: Selections from the Buffalo Collection* (Charlottesville: University of Virginia Press, 1977), p. 141. The term "authentic Jew" was of course made popular by Sartre in *Anti-Semite and Jew*.

66 Saverio Mercadante was not Jewish by birth or conversion. Bernard Benstock recognized that Bloom mistakenly names Mercadante when he probably means to include Meyerbeer in his list. He had confused the two composers and their compositions early in the day (*U*5.403; *U*11.1275). Both instances, moreover, allude to the composer of "Seven Last Words," who Thorton claims is neither Mercadante nor Meyerbeer.

See Benstock, *James Joyce*, p. 134.

67 Bloom thinks of Spinoza's philosophy quite often, and on several occasions appears to have attempted to explain aspects of the philosophy to Molly (*U*11.1058; *U*18.1115). Bloom owns a copy of *Thoughts from Spinoza* (*U*17. 1372).

68 See *Ulysses: 'Sirens,' 'Cyclops,' 'Nausicaä,' & 'Oxen of the Sun': a Facsimile of Placards for Episodes 11–14*, p. 224; Harvard collection.

69 The list can also be viewed as a parallel to Stephen's litany of heresiarchs in "Telemachus," which in no way makes Stephen a "non-Catholic."

70 This description of the citizen – "a lunatic has-been" – is David Hayman's. See his essay "Cyclops," in *Critical Essays*, p. 247.

71 Joyce mentioned to Budgen the connection between Bloom and the cuckold hero of the French play *Le Cocu Magnifique*, see Budgen, *Making of Ulysses*, p. 315. Joyce knew the term "cuckoo," as a common euphemism for a cuckold.

72 This event occurred when Bloom was sixteen. See Raleigh, *Chronicle*, p. 49.

73 O'Molloy had also mentioned the Mosaic Code in the closing speech of Seymore Bushe in the Childs murder case in "Aeolus" (*U*7.757).

74 Ironically, Bloom's Gaelic is correct, but his Hebrew is a bastardization. He has combined the opening line of a sabbath prayer "Mah-Tovu Oholecha Yaacov" (how goodly are thy tents, O Jacob – Numbers, 24:5) and the phase often applied to David – Melek Yisrael – 'king of Israel."

75 Leslie Fielder points out that Bloom's last two words in this declaration, "Meshuggah Talith" humorously translates "Crazy prayer shall." See Fiedler, "Joyce and Jewish Consciousness, *Fiedler on the Roof*, p. 53.

76 As Meredith was one of the young Joyce's favorite authors, it is more than likely that he read *The Tragic Comedians* at some point. In his 1981 article, "James Joyce and the Critics Notwithstanding," Erwin Steinberg claims Bloom's mention of Lassalle in "Circe" is further proof of his non-Jewish status because Lassalle had privately denounced Jews and his own Jewishness (p. 35). Steinberg fails to realize that Joyce's image of Lassalle was in all probability dominated by the fictionalized version of him in Meredith's work. As the character Alvan, the thinly disguised Lassalle expresses admiration for the Jews and his own Jewishness throughout the novel.

77 See above, (*U*12. 452–53), n. 64.

78 For a less nihilistic reading of Stephen's reception of "Philip Drunk and Philip Sober" see Theoharis, *Joyce's Ulysses*, pp. 150–54.

79 See Peter Alexander, *Svengali: George du Maurier's Trilby* (London: W. H. Allen, 1982), introduction. Svengali modernized the medieval myth of the Jewish necromancer just as Dickens' Fagin had reified stereotypes of Jewish thievery for his Victorian audience. "Past master" designates a mason who has served as the master of his lodge. There is no special hand sign for a master or past master. There is, however, a secret handshake for all thirty-second degree masons.

80 Joyce drew most of these names from *Thom's Directory* for 1904. See Louis Hyman, *The Jews of Ireland*, pp. 168–71. One of the mourners, Minnie Watchman, was in fact the great-aunt of Hyman himself. See p. 349, n. 9.

81 The Yiddish word *"mensch,"* meaning literally "a human being," primarily connotes the humanistic aspect of the phrase, as in a moral, compassionate, and tactful person. The term to some extent has entered modern American vernacular. Bloom's Samaritan act can be viewed as unrelated to "Jewishness," but in the context of my study and Bloom's own visions in "Circe," especially that of Rudy, it appears he himself views it as central to his "Jewishness."

82 See Kenner "Cyclops," in *Critical Essays*, p. 345–47.

83 The "white-lambkin" peeking from Rudy's pocket could be a symbol of the *Agnus Dei*, Bloom's *"Chad Gadya"* resurfacing, or the sweater Molly had been knitting for Rudy before he was born. For this last possibility see *U*18. 1448–50. Rudy's kiss could be argued as a Catholic rite rather than a Jewish one. However, only the priest kisses the Bible in the mass, whereas all Jews kiss the siddur at least once during many holiday services, as well as on the occasion of dropping or damaging the prayer book in some manner.

84 See *Ulysses: 'Circe' & 'Eumaeus': a Facsimile of the Placards for Episodes 15–16*, p. 234; Harvard collection.

85 *Ibid.*, p. 331; Buffalo collection, V.C. 1–36a.

86 *Ibid.*, p. 340; Texas Collection.

87 Apparently, the last identity here to Joyce was of the highest rank. See his statement quoted at the beginning of the first chapter of this study. Moreover, one could suggest that each of these attributes are essentials of Jewish manhood as prescribed by the Torah and elaborated on by the Talmud. Corresponding Jewish precepts to Bloom's "Jewishness" here would include Tzedakah, (charitable actions and offerings), Shalom Bayit (the peaceful, nurturing home), the Pirkei Avot (The Ethics of the Fathers), and more.

88 See Gerald Burns, "Eumaeus," in *Critical Essays*, pp. 363–83.

89 See Thornton, *Allusions in Ulysses*, p. 445. The Latin is from the Vulgate, Romans 9:5, "and of their race, according to their flesh, is Christ."

90 *Ibid.*, p. 446. For a discussion of the success of the Jewish community in London after their readmittance facilitated by Oliver Cromwell, see Howard Morley Sachar, *The Course of Modern Jewish History* (New York: Delta Publications, 1963), pp. 44–45; see also Alan Edelstein, *An Unacknowledged Harmony: Philo-Semitism and the Survival of European Jewry* (Westport: Greenwood Press, 1982), pp. 141–45. For a discussion of the economic situation of post-inquisition Spain, see Cecil Roth, *History of the Jews*, pp. 213–32; see also Don Salvador de Madriga, *Spain and the Jews*, (London: Jewish Historical Society of England, 1946), pp. 8–14.

91 This is reminiscent of Hillel's famous one phrase exegesis of the Torah: "Whatever is hateful unto thee do it not unto thy fellow – This is the

whole of the Torah, the rest is explanation." See *Pentateuch and Haftorahs: Text, Translation, and Commentary*, ed. Dr. J. H. Hertz (London: Soncino Press, 1970), pp. 502, 563. Bloom's speech, quixotic and muddled as it may be, rests on the same principle.

92 See *Ulysses: 'Eumaeus,' 'Ithaca,' & 'Penelope': a Facsimile of Page Proofs for Episodes 16–18*, p. 155; Gathering 40, Texas collection.

93 For a discussion of the "Jewish gaze" as depicted in the stereotypes of the era, see Sander Gilman, *Jew's Body*, p. 67–69.

94 See R. F. Forster, *Modern Ireland: 1600–1972*, pp. 40–44. Geoffrey Keatings' *Foras Feasa ar Eirinn* (1630s?) was the first modern Irish history written in Gaelic to incorporate these legends. Figured as preliterate occurrences, the legends helped bolster the image of Irish nationalism as divinely inspired through Hebraic origins.

95 Joyce added Lassalle's name in penciled form on a printer's placard in 1922. Lassalle rounds out the scope of Jewish-assimilationist accomplishment here: musical composition (Mendelssohn), philosophy (Spinoza), athletics (Mendoza), and politics (Lassalle). See *Ulysses: 'Ithaca,' & 'Penelope': a Facsimile of Placards for Episodes 17–18*, p. 57; Placard II, Harvard Collection.

Daniel Mendoza (1763–1836) was the English boxing champion from 1792–95. Along with his rival, Richard Humphreys, the two remade boxing as a sport based on agility rather than size and strength. Joyce may have read the *Memoirs of the Life of Daniel Mendoza* (London: G. Hayden, 1816). Although a pugilist by trade, Mendoza was a tactful and gentlemanly person. With his altered sense of the masculine, Bloom thus now does not shy from acknowledging boxing as a viable form of athletics, as he had in "Cyclops." Mendoza, like the rest of the names on the list, became acculturated to the extent of reshaping a staple of his culture, yet always retained a sense of himself as a Jew.

96 Joyce's phonetic translation of the Hebrew here is a bit off. It should read: *Kol ode balevav penima/nefesh yehudi homia*. Joyce originally wrote the question here "What anthem did Bloom chant partially in anticipation of that consummation." In a typescript revision of the episode, he penciled in the words "multiple ethnically irreducible" between "that" and "consummation." It appears he did not want the reader confused as to the exact channel of Bloom's and Stephen's possible connection. See, *Ulysses: 'Ithaca' & 'Penelope': a Facsimile of Manuscripts & Typescripts for Episodes 17–18*, p. 70; Texas collection, TSS V.B.15.c–9.

97 The ballad is based on the medieval English folk piece, *Sir Hugh, or The Jew's Daughter*. See chapter 1 of this study, ns. 6 and 9.

98 The other score can be found in the "Scylla and Charybdis" episode, between lines 499 and 500. This allusion – the first bar of *"Gloria in Excelsus Deo"* – however, is much less conspicuous than its counterpart in "Ithaca."

99 See Sachar, *Modern Jewish History*, pp. 254–55. The case attracted media

attention across the continent and Joyce surely knew of it.
100 For a detailed account of the Hebraic allusions here and their correspondence to Bloom's activities, see Joly, *Jewish Element in Ulysses*.
101 See Raleigh, *Chronicle*, pp. 18–19, 77, 98.
102 Herring, *Uncertainty Principle*, pp. 126–40.

9 CONCLUSION

1 Ellmann, *JJII*, p. 736.
2 *Ibid.*, p. 737.
3 See *Letters of James Joyce*, ed. Stuart Gilbert (New York: The Viking Press, 1957–66), p. 424. Letter of November 23, 1940, to Louis Gilet.
4 Zweig, *World of Yesterday*, p. 1.

Select Bibliography

Abbott. B. H. *Gladstone and Disraeli*. London: Collins New Advanced History
    Series, 1972.
Adams, Robert M. *Surface and Symbol: the Consistency of James Joyce's* Ulysses.
    New York: Oxford University Press, 1962.
Adorno, Theodor. *The Jargon of Authenticity*. Trans. Knut Tarnowski and
    Frederic Will. Evanston: Northwestern University Press, 1973.
    "Reconciliation Under Duress." *Aesthetics and Politics*. Ed. Ronald Taylor.
    London: NLB, 1977, pp. 140–65.
    "The Position of the Narrator in the Contemporary Novel," *Notes to
    Literature*. Translated by Sherry Weber Nicholsen. New York: Columbia
    University Press, 1991, vol. 1, pp. 30–36.
Amiran, Eyal. "Bloom and Disraeli: on the Side of the Angels." Language
    Notes 27:3 (1990): pp. 53–57.
Anderson, Chester G. *James Joyce and his World*. London: Thames & Hudson,
    1968.
    Introduction. *The Seventh of Joyce*. Ed. Bernard Benstock. Bloomington:
    Indiana University Press, 1982.
    "Leopold Bloom as Dr. Sigmund Freud." *Mosaic* 6 (1972): pp. 23–43.
Anderson, George K. *The Legend of the Wandering Jew*. Providence: Brown
    University Press, 1965.
apRoberts, Ruth. *Arnold and God*. Berkeley: University of California Press, 1983.
Arendt, Hannah. *Men in Dark Times*. New York: Harcourt, Brace, & World,
    1968.
    The Origins of Totalitarianism. New York: Harcourt, Brace, Jovanovich, 1973.
Arnold, Matthew. *Culture and Anarchy: an Essay in Political and Social Criticism*.
    Ed. J. Dover Wilson. London: Cambridge UP, 1986.
Aschheim, Steven. *The Nietzsche Legacy in Germany, 1890–1990*. Berkeley:
    University of California Press, 1994.
Bailey, Albert E. *The Gospel in Art*. Boston: The Pilgrim Press, 1931.
Bakhtin, M. M. *The Dialogic Imagination*. Translated by Caryl Emerson and
    Michael Holquist. Austin: University of Texas Press, 1981.
Bangert, William V, SJ. *A History of the Society of Jesus*. St. Louis: Institute of

Jesuit Sources, 1972.

Beach, Sylvia. Shakespeare and Company. New York: Harcourt, Brace, 1959.

Beckett, J. C. *A Short History of Ireland*. London: Hutchinson University Library, 1973.

Benstock, Bernard. *James Joyce*. New York: Ungar, 1985.

"Leopold Bloom and the Mason Connection." *James Joyce Quarterly* 15 (1977–78): pp. 259–62.

Narrative Con/Texts in Ulysses. Chicago: Illinois University Press, 1991.

Benstock, Bernard, ed. *The Seventh of Joyce*. Bloomington: Indiana University Press, 1982.

Benstock, Shari. "Is He a Jew or a Gentile or a Holy Roman." *James Joyce Quarterly* 16 (1978): pp. 493–97.

Bernal, Martin. *The Black Athena: the Afroasiatic Roots of Classical Civilization*. 2 vols. New Brunswick: Rutgers University Press, 1989.

Bishop, Claire Huchet. *How Catholics Look at Jews: an Inquiry into Spanish, French, and Italian Teaching Materials*. New York: Paulist Press, 1974.

Blamires, Harry. *The Bloomsday Book: a Guide Through Joyce's* Ulysses. London: Methuen Press, 1966.

Blanshard, Paul. *The Irish and Catholic Power: an American Interpretation*. Boston: The Beacon Press, 1954.

Bloom, Harold. Introduction. *James Joyce's* Ulysses. Ed. Harold Bloom. New York: Chelsea House, 1987.

"A Speculation Upon American Jewish Culture." *Judaism* 31 (1982): pp. 266–73.

Bluefarb, Samuel. "Leopold Bloom's Jewishness." *Modern British Literature* 2 (1978): pp. 493–97.

Bohlman, Otto. *Yeats and Nietzsche: an Exploration of Major Nietzschean Echoes in the Writings of William Butler Yeats*. Ottawa: Barnes & Noble, 1982.

Boone, Joseph. "New Approaches to Bloom as 'Womanly Man': the Mixed Middling's Progress in *Ulysses*. *James Joyce Quarterly* 20 (1982): pp. 67–85.

Bowman, John, and Ronan O'Donoghue, eds. *Portraits: Belvedere College, Dublin, 1832–1982*. Dublin: Gill and Macmillan, 1982.

Boyle, Robert, SJ "A Note on Reuben J. Dodd as a 'dirty Jew.'" *James Joyce Quarterly* 3 (1965): pp. 64–66.

Bradbury, Malcolm, and James McFarlane, eds. *Modernism*. New York: Penguin Press, 1976.

Bradford, Sarah. *Disraeli*. New York: Stein and Day, 1983.

Bradley, Bruce, SJ *James Joyce's School Days*. New York: St. Martin's Press, 1982.

Brandes, George. *Ferdinand Lassalle*. New York: Bergman Publications, 1968.

Bredin, Jean-Denis. *The Affair: the Case of Alfred Dreyfus*. Translated by Jeffrey Mehlmen. New York: George Baziller, Inc., 1986.

Brivic, Sheldon R. *Joyce Between Freud and Jung*. London: Kennikat Press, 1980.

Brown, Richard. *James Joyce and Sexuality*. Cambridge: Cambridge University Press, 1985.

Brown, Stephen J. M. *The Press in Ireland: a Survey and Guide*. New York:

Lemma Publications, 1971.

Buber, Martin. *On Judaism.* Translated by Eva Joseph, ed. Nahum N. Glatzner. New York: Schocken Books, 1972.

Two Types of Faith: a Study of the Interpretation of Judaism and Christianity. Translated by Norman Goldhawk. New York: Harper, 1961.

Budgen, Frank. *James Joyce and the Making of* Ulysses. Bloomington: Indiana University Press, 1960.

Burgess, Anthony. *Joysprick: an Introduction to the Language of James Joyce.* New York: Harcourt, Brace, Jovanovich, 1973.

Burns, J. F. Shop Windows to the World: the History of the Masonic Boys' School, Dublin. Dublin: published under the authority of the Board of Governors of the Masonic Boys' School, no date.

Byrne, John Francis. *Silent Years: an Autobiography with Memoirs of James Joyce and Our Ireland.* New York: Farrar, Straus, and Young, 1953.

Byrnes, Robert. "Agendeth Netaim Discovered: Why Bloom isn't a Zionist." *James Joyce Quarterly* 29:34 (1992): pp. 833–38.

"Bloom's Sexual Tropes: Stigmata of the Degenerate Jew." *James Joyce Quarterly* 27:2 (Winter, 1990): pp. 303–23.

Cahill, Edward, SJ *The Framework of a Christian State.* Dublin: Gill and Sons, Ltd., 1932.

Carroll, Joseph. *The Cultural Theory of Matthew Arnold.* Berkeley: University of California Press, 1982.

Cheyette, Bryan. *Constructions of "the Jew" in English Literature and Society: Racial Representations, 1875–1945.* Cambridge: Cambridge University Press, 1993.

"'Jewgreek is greekjew': the Disturbing Ambivalence of Joyce's Semitic Discourse in *Ulysses.*" *1992 Joyce Studies Annual.* Ed. Thomas Staley. Austin: Texas University Press, 1992, pp. 32–56.

Child, Francis, J., ed. *The English and Scottish Popular Ballads*, vol. III. New York: Folklore Press, 1956.

Cixous, Hélène. *The Exile of James Joyce.* Translated by Sally A. J. Purcell. New York: David Lewis, 1972.

Cohen, Norman. *Warrant for Genocide: the Myth of the Jewish World Conspiracy and the Protocols of the Elders of Zion.* New York: Harper & Row, 1966.

Colum, Mary, and Padraic. *Our Friend James Joyce.* New York: Doubleday & Co., 1958.

Corcoran, T., SJ, ed. *The Clongowes Record: 1814–1932.* Dublin: Browne and Nolan, Ltd., 1935.

Costello, Peter. *James Joyce: the Years of Growth, 1882–1915.* New York: Pantheon Books, 1992.

Cuddihy, John M. *The Ordeal of Civility: Frued, Marx, Lévi-Strauss and the Jewish Struggle with Modernity.* New York: Basic Books, 1974.

Curran, Constantine P. *James Joyce Remembered.* New York: Oxford University Press, 1968.

Curtis, Perry L. *Apes and Angels: the Irishman in Victorian Caricature.* New York:

George Braziller, Inc., 1971.

Daiches, David. "James Joyce's Jew." *Jewish Chronicle Quarterly Supplement* 25 (1959): pp. 1–3.

Davitt, Michael. *Within the Pale: the True Story of Anti-Semitic Persecutions in Russia*. London: Hurst and Blackett, 1903. Republished New York: Arno Press, 1975.

Deane, Seamus. "'Masked with Matthew Arnold's Face': Joyce and Liberalism." *James Joyce: The Centennial Symposium*. Eds. Moris Beja, Phillip Herring, Maurice Harmon, David Norris. Chicago: University of Illinois Press, 1986, pp. 9–20.

de Búrca, Michael. *Michael Cusack and the GAA*. Dublin: Anvil Books, 1989.

de Gobineau, Arthur. *The Moral and Intellectual Diversity of Races*. New York: Garland Publications, Inc., 1984.

de Madriga, Don Salvador. *Spain and the Jews*. London: Jewish Historical Society of England, 1946.

Debenedetti, G. "Lettera a Carocci su 'Svevo e Schmitz.'" *Solanci* 4:3–4: pp. 28–34.

Demming, Robert H., ed. *James Joyce: the Critical Heritage*. 2 vols. New York: Barnes & Noble, Inc., 1970.

A Bibliography of James Joyce Studies. Lawrence, KS: University of Kansas Library, 1964.

Deutscher, Isaac. *The Non-Jewish Jew and Other Essays*. Ed. Tamara Deutscher. London: Oxford University Press, 1968.

Disraeli, Benjamin. *Coningsby or The New Generation*. New York: Oxford University Press, 1982.

du Maurier, George. *Trilby*. Introduction by Peter Alexander. London: W. H. Allen, 1982.

Edelstein, Alan. *An Unacknowledged Harmony: Philo-Semitism and the Survival of European Jewry*. Westport: Greenwood Press, 1982.

Eliot, George. *Daniel Deronda*. New York: Penguin Books, 1988.

Ellenbogen, Eileen. "Leopold Bloom – Jew." *Changing World* 3 (1947): pp. 79–86.

Ellmann, Richard. *James Joyce*. London: Oxford University Press, 1959; revised edition, 1982.

The Consciousness of James Joyce. London: Faber & Faber, 1977.

The Identity of Yeats. New York: Oxford University Press, 1964.

Ulysses on the Liffey. New York: Oxford University Press, 1972.

Epstein, Edmund. "Joyce and Judaism." *The Seventh of Joyce*. Ed. Bernard Benstock. Bloomington: Indiana University Press, 1982. pp. 221–24.

Fallis, Richard. *The Irish Renaissance*. Syracuse: Syracuse University Press, 1977.

Ferrero, Guglielmo. *L'Europa giovanne*. Milan, 1897.

Feshbach, Sydney. "A Merchant, Stephen Said." *James Joyce Quarterly* 19:3 1982: pp. 349–50.

Fiedler, Leslie. "Bloom on Joyce; or, Jokey for Jacob." *New Light on Joyce from the Dublin Symposium, 1969*. Ed. Fritz Zenn. Bloomington: Indiana

University Press, 1972, pp. 195–208.

Fiedler on the Roof: Essays on Literature and Jewish Identity. Boston: David R. Godine, Publications, 1991.

Fishberg, Maurice. *The Jews: a Study of Race and Environment.* New York: Arno Press, 1911, 1975.

Fisher, Eugene J., A. James Rudin, and March H. Tanenbaum, eds. *Twenty Years of Jewish–Catholic Relations.* New York: Paulist Press, 1986.

Fogel, Daniel M. "James Joyce, the Jews, and *Ulysses.*" *James Joyce Quarterly* 16 (1979): pp. 498–501.

Foster, R. F. *Modern Ireland: 1600–1972.* New York: Penguin Books, 1989.

Foucault, Michel. *The History of Sexuality.* 3 vols. Translated by Robert Hurley. New York: Vintage Books, 1990.

The Order of Things: an Archaeology of the Human Sciences. New York: Random House, 1970.

Frederich, Carl J., ed. *The Philosophy of Hegel: Selected Writings.* New York: The Modern Library, 1954.

French, Marilyn. *The Book as World: James Joyce Ulysses.* Cambridge, MA: Harvard University Press, 1976.

Freeman's Journal, Dublin, 1880–1906.

Freud, Sigmund. *Beyond the Pleasure Principle.* Translated by James Strachey. New York: W. W. Norton, 1966.

Jokes and their Relation to the Unconscious: Tanslated by James Stackey. New York: W. W. Norton, 1967.

The Standard Edition of the Complete Psychological Works. Translated by and eds., James Stratchey and Alan Tyson. 24 vols. London: Hogarth Press, 1953–74.

Furbank, P. N. *Italo Svevo: the Man and the Writer.* Berkeley: University of California Press, 1966.

Gallagher, Sister Anthony Marie, OSF *Education in Ireland.* Dissertation, Catholic University of America, Washington, DC: Catholic University of America Press, 1948.

Gatt-Rutter, John. *Italo Svevo: a Double Life.* Oxford: Clarendon Press, 1988.

Gay, Peter. *Freud, Jews, and Other Germans: Masters and Victims in Modernist Culture.* New York: Oxford University Press, 1978.

Gifford, Don. *Joyce Annotated: Notes for* Dubliners *and* A Portrait of the Artist as a Young Man. Berkeley: University of California Press, 1982.

Gilbert, Stuart. *James Joyce's* Ulysses. New York: Vintage Books, 1956.

Gilman, Sander L. *Jewish Self-Hatred: Anti-Semitism and the Hidden Language of the Jews.* Baltimore: Johns Hopkins University Press, 1986.

The Jew's Body. London: Routledge, 1991.

Gobinet, Revd. Charles, DD *Instruction of Youth in Christian Piety: Taken out of the Sacred Scriptures and Holy Fathers.* Boston: Patrick Donahoe [1878?].

Gogarty, Oliver St. John. *As I Was Going Down Sackville Street.* New York: Harcourt, Brace & World, Inc., 1937.

"They Think They Know James Joyce." *Saturday Review of Literature* 18

(1950): pp. 22–36.

Goldberg, S. L. *The Classical Temper*. London: Chatto & Windus, 1961.

Gorman, Herbert. *James Joyce*. New York: Farrar & Rinehart, 1939.

Gross, Harvey. "From Barabas to Bloom: Notes on the Figure of the Jew." *Western Humanities Review* 11 (1957): pp. 149–56.

Hamlyn, D. W. *Schopenhauer*. London: Routledge & Kegan Paul, 1985.

Handelman, Susan. *The Slayers of Moses: the Emergence of Rabbinic Interpretation in Modern Literary Theory*. Albany: State University of New York Press, 1982.

Hart, Clive, and David Hayman, eds. *James Joyce's* Ulysses: *Critical Essays*. Berkeley: University of California Press, 1977.

Hawthorn, Jeremy. "*Ulysses*, Modernism, and Marxist Criticism." *James Joyce and Modern Literature*. Eds. W. J. McCormack and Alistair Stead. London: Routledge & Kegan Paul, 1982.

Hayman, David. Ulysses: *the Mechanics of Meaning*. Englewood Cliffs, NJ: Prentice Hall, Inc., 1970.

Heijermans, Hermann. *Ahasverus: a Play in One Act*. Translated by Caroline Heijermans-Houwink and Dr. J. J. Houwink. Boston: Walter H. Baker Co., Publications, 1934.

Heller, Erich. *The Importance of Nietzsche*. Chicago: University of Chicago Press, 1988.

Herring, Phillip F. *Joyce's Notes and Early Drafts for* Ulysses: *Selections from the Buffalo Collection*. Charlottesville: University Press of Virginia, 1977.

   Joyce's Uncertainty Principle. Princeton: Princeton University Press, 1987.

Herr, Cheryl. *Joyce's Anatomy of Culture*. Chicago: University of Illinois Press, 1986.

Herzl, Theodor. *The Jewish State*. Translated by Jacob M. Alkow. New York: Dover Publications, 1988.

Holmes, Colin. *Anti-Semitism in British Society: 1876–1939*. New York: Holmes & Meier Publications, Inc., 1979.

Humphreys, Susan L. "Ferrero Etc: James Joyce's Debt to Guglielmo Ferrero." *James Joyce Quarterly* 16:3 (1979): pp. 239–51.

Hyman, Louis. *The Jews of Ireland: from Earliest Times to the Year 1910*. Shannon: Irish University Press, 1972.

Hyman, Paula. *From Dreyfus to Vichy: the Remaking of French Jewry, 1906–1939*. New York: Columbia University Press, 1979.

Irish Times, Dublin, 1897–1900.

Jameson, Fredric. "*Ulysses* in History." *James Joyce and Modern Literature*. Eds., W. J. McCormick and Alistair Stead. London: Routledge & Kegan Paul, Ltd., 1982.

Jeffares, Norman A. *Yeats the European*. London: Colin Smythe, 1989.

Jewish Chronicle, 1888–96.

Johnson, Edgar. *Sir Walter Scott: the Great Unknown*. New York: Macmillan, 1970.

Joly, Ralph Robert. "Chauvinist Brew and Leopold Bloom: The Weininger

Legacy." *James Joyce Quarterly* 19 (1981–82): pp. 194–98.

The Jewish Element in James Joyce's Ulysses. Dissertation, Chapel Hill, 1973. Ann Arbor: UMI, 1973, pp. 74–5931.

Joyce, James. *A Portrait of the Artist as a Young Man: Text, Criticism, and Notes.* Ed. Chester G. Anderson. New York: The Viking Critical Library, 1968.

Dubliners: Text, Criticism, and Notes. Eds. Robert Scholes and A. Walton Litz. New York: The Viking Critical Library, 1976.

Giacomo Joyce. New York: The Viking Press, 1968.

Letters of James Joyce, vol. I. Ed. Stuart Gilbert. New York: The Viking Press, 1957.

Letters of James Joyce, vols. II–III. Ed. Richard Ellmann. New York: Viking, 1966.

The Critical Writings. Eds. Ellsworth Mason and Richard Ellmann. Ithaca: Cornell University Press, 1989.

The Portable James Joyce. Ed. Harry Levin. New York: The Viking Press, 1947.

Selected Letters of James Joyce. Ed. Richard Ellmann. New York: The Viking Press, 1966.

Stephen Hero. Edited from the Harvard College Library manuscript by Theodore Spencer, John J. Slocum and Herbert Cahoon. New York: New Directions, 1963.

Ulysses. New York: Random House, 1961.

Ulysses: Notes & 'Telemachus' – 'Scylla and Charybolis': a Facsimile of Notes for the Book & Manuscripts & Type-scripts for Episodes 1–9. Prefaced and arranged by Michael Groden. New York: Garland, 1978.

Ulysses: The Corrected Text. Eds. Hans Walter Gabler, Wolfhard Steppe, and Claus Melchor. New York: Random House, 1986.

Joyce, Stanislaus. *The Complete Dublin Diary of Stanislaus Joyce.* Ed. George Harris Healy. Ithaca: Cornell University Press, 1962.

My Brother's Keeper. New York: The Viking Press, 1958.

Reflections of James Joyce by his Brother Stanislaus Joyce. Translated from Italian by Ellsworth Mason. New York: The James Joyce Society, 1950.

Kain, Richard. *Fabulous Voyager.* Chicago: University of Chicago Press, 1959.

"Motif as Meaning: the Case of Leopold Bloom." *Approaches to* Ulysses: *Ten Essays.* Eds. Thomas Staley and Bernard Benstock. Pittsburgh: University of Pittsburgh Press, 1970. pp. 61–101.

Katz, Jacob. *From Prejudice to Destruction: Anti-Semitism, 1700–1933.* Cambridge, MA: Harvard University Press, 1980.

Kaufmann, Walter. *Nietzsche: Philosopher, Psychologist, Antichrist.* New York: Vintage Books, 1968.

Keating, Geoffrey. *The History of Ireland.* Kansas City: Irish Genealogical Foundation, 1983. Originally translated by David Comyn and Patrick Dineen. London: Irish Texts Society, 1902–14.

Kenner, Hugh. *A Colder Eye: the Modern Irish Writers.* New York: Alfred A. Knopf, 1983.

Dublin's Joyce. Bloomington: Indiana University Press, 1956.

Mazes. San Francisco: North Point Press, 1989.

Joyce's Voices. Berkeley: University of California Press, 1978.

Ulysses. London: George Allen & Unwin, 1980.

Killen, W. D., DD. *The Ecclesiastical History of Ireland.* 2 vols. London: Macmillian, 1875.

Kimball, Jean. "Family Romance and the Hero Myth: a Psychoanalytic Context for the Paternity Theme in *Ulysses.*" *James Joyce Quarterly* 20 (1983): pp. 161–73.

"Freud, Leonardo, and Joyce: the Dimensions of a Childhood Memory." *James Joyce Quarterly* 17 (1980): pp. 165–82.

Kleebatt, Norman L., ed. *The Dreyfus Affair: Art, Truth, and Justice.* Berkeley: University of California Press, 1987.

Klein, A. M. "Shout in the Street: an Analysis of the Second Chapter of Joyce's *Ulysses.*" *New Directions* 13 (1951): pp. 327–45.

La Libre Parole, Paris, 1898–1902.

Lapide, Pinchas E. *Three Popes and the Jews.* New York: Hawthorn Books, Inc., 1967.

Larkin, Emmet J. *The Consolidation of the Roman Catholic Church in Ireland, 1860–1870.* Chapel Hill, NC: University of North Carolina Press, 1987.

Lassen, Christian. *Indische Alterthumskunde.* Bonn, 1847.

Lawrence, Karen. *The Odyssey of Style in* Ulysses. Princeton: Princeton University Press, 1981.

Lebowitz, Naomi. *Italo Svevo.* New Brunswick: Rutgers University Press, 1978.

Leventhal, A. J. "An Irish Comment on *Ulysses,*" *Claxon* (Winter, 1923–24): pp. 14–20.

"The Jew Errant." *The Dubliner* 2:1 (1963): pp. 11–24.

Levitt, Morton P. "A Hero for Our Time: Leopold Bloom and the Myth of *Ulysses.*"

Fifty Years: Ulysses. Ed. Thomas Staley. Bloomington: Indiana University Press, 1972, pp. 132–46.

"The Family of Bloom." *New Light on Joyce from the Dublin Symposium, 1969.* Ed. Fritz Zenn. Bloomington: Indiana University Press, 1972, pp. 141–48.

"The Humanity of Bloom, the Jewishness of Joyce." *The Seventh of Joyce.* Ed. Bernard Benstock. Bloomington: Indiana University Press, 1982, pp. 225–28

"The New Midrash: *Finnegans Wake.*" *1992 Joyce Studies Annual.* Ed. Thomas Staley. Austin: Texas University Press, 1992, pp. 57–70.

L'intransigeant, Paris, 1898–1902.

Litz, A. Walton. *The Art of James Joyce: Method and Design in* Ulysses *and* Finnegans Wake. London: Oxford University Press, 1961.

Lukàcs, Georg. *The Historical Novel.* Translated by Hannah and Stanley Mitchell. Lincoln: University of Nebraska Press, 1983.

"Realism in the Balance." *Aesthetics and Politics.* Ed. Ronald Taylor. London: NLB, 1977, pp. 35–62.

Writer and Critic, and Other Essays. Translated by and ed., Arthur D. Kahn. New York: Grosset & Dunlap, 1971.

Lyons, F. S. L. *Ireland Since the Famine.* New York: Scribner, 1971.

Lyons, J. B. *Oliver St. John Gogarty: the Man of Many Talents.* Dublin: Blackwater Press, 1980.

MacManus, Seamus. *The Story of the Irish Race.* New York: Devin-Adair Co., 1945.

Magalaner, Marvin. "The Anti-Semitic Limerick Incidents in Joyce's Bloomsday." *PMLA* 68 (1953): pp. 1219–23.

Time of Apprenticeship: the Fiction of the Young James Joyce. New York: Abelard-Schuman, 1959.

Magalaner, Martin and Richard Kain. *Joyce: The Man, the Work, the Reputation.* New York: Collier Books, 1965.

Mahaffey, Viki. "*Giacomo Joyce.*" *A Companion to Joyce Studies.* Eds. Zack Bowen and James F. Carens. Westport, CT: Greenwood Press, 1984, pp. 387–420.

Reauthorizing Joyce. Cambridge: Cambridge University Press, 1988.

Manganiello, Dominic. *Joyce's Politics.* London: Routledge & Kegan Paul, 1980.

Marrus, Michael R. *The Politics of Assimilation: a Study of the French Jewish Community at the Time of the Dreyfus Affair.* Oxford: Clarendon Press, 1971.

McCarthy, Patrick. "The Case of Reuben J. Dodd." *James Joyce Quarterly* 21 (Winter, 1984): pp. 169–75.

Ulysses: *Portals of Discovery.* Boston: Twayne Publications, 1990.

McCormick, Stephen J. *The Pope and Ireland – Concerning Newly Discovered Historical Facts Concerning the Forged Bulls Attributed to Pope Adrian IV and Alexander III, etc.* San Francisco: Waldteful, 1889.

McKenna, Revd. Lambert, SJ *The Life and Work of Rev. James Aloysius Cullen.* London: Longmans, Green, and Co., 1924.

McRedmond, Louis. *To The Greater Glory of God: a History of the Irish Jesuits.* Dublin: Gill and Macmillan, 1991.

Miller, Liam. *The Noble Drama of W. B. Yeats.* Dublin: The Dolman Press, 1977.

Mitchell, David. *The Jesuits: a History.* New York: Franklin Watts, 1981.

Modder, Montagu. *The Jew in the Literature of England.* Philadelphia: The Jewish Publication Society of America, 1944.

Mosse, George L. *The Crisis of Ideology: Intellectual Origins of the Third Reich.* New York: Grosset & Dunlap, 1964.

Murphy, Ignatius. *A History of Irish Catholicism*, vol. v: *Catholic Education.* Dublin: Gill and McMillan, 1971.

Murphy, William M. *The Parnell Myth and Irish Politics, 1891–1956.* New York: Peter Lang, 1986.

Nadel, Ira B. *Joyce and the Jews.* Iowa City: University of Iowa Press, 1989.

Nietzsche, Friedrich. *A Genealogy of Morals.* Translated by William Haussmann and John Gray. New York: The Macmillan Co., 1897.

Beyond Good and Evil: Prelude to a Philosophy of the Future. Translated by Helen Zimmern. New York: The Macmillan Co., 1907.

The Basic Writings of Nietzsche. Ed. Walter Kaufmann. New York: Modern Library, 1968.

The Birth of Tragedy or Hellenism and Pessimism. Translated by William Haussmann. London: T. N. Foulis, 1909.

The Dawn of Day. Translated by Johanna Volz. London: T. Fisher Unwin, 1903.

Human, All Too Human: a Book for Free Spirits. Translated by Helen Zimmern. New York: Macmillan, 1903.

The Joyful Wisdom. Translated by Thomas Common, Paul V. Cohn, and Maude D. Petre. London: T. N. Foulis, 1910.

Thus Spake Zarathustra: a Book for All and None. Translated by Thomas Common. London: T. N. Foulis, 1909.

The Works of Friedrich Nietzsche. Translated by and ed., Alexander Tille. New York: The Macmillan Co., 1897.

Noon, William T., SJ *Joyce and Aquinas.* New Haven: Yale University Press, 1957.

Norman, Edward. *A History of Modern Ireland 1800–1969.* Baltimore: Penguin Books, 1973.

O'Brien, Conor Cruise. *Parnell and His Party, 1880–1890.* Oxford: Clarendon Press, 1964.

O'Brien, Conor Cruise, ed. *The Shaping of Modern Ireland.* Toronto: University of Toronto Press, 1960.

O'Brien, Joseph V. *Dear Dirty Dublin: a City in Distress, 1889–1916.* Berkeley: University of California Press, 1982.

O'Donnell, F. H. *A History of the Irish Parliamentary Party.* 2 vols. London: Kennikat Press, 1970.

O'Flaherty, James, Timothy Sellner, and Robert Helm, eds. *Studies in Nietzsche and the Judaeo-Christian Tradition.* Chapel Hill: University of North Carolina Press, 1985.

Ofri-Scheps, Dorith. "Is Bloom as Jew?" *Cithera* 16 (1977): pp. 3–32.

Oram, Hugh. *The Newspaper Book: a History of Newspapers in Ireland, 1649–1983.* Dublin: MO Books, 1988.

Orwell, George. "Anti-Semitism in Britain." *England, Your England and Other Essays.* London: Secker & Warburg, 1953, pp. 68–80.

Owen, Rodney Wilson. *James Joyce and the Beginnings of Ulysses.* Ann Arbor: UMI Research Press, 1983.

Poliakov, Léon. *The History of Anti-Semitism.* 3 vols. Translated by Miriam Kochan. New York: The Vanguard Press, Inc., 1975.

Potts, Willard, ed. *Portraits of the Artist in Exile: Recollections of James Joyce by Europeans.* Seattle: University of Washington Press, 1979.

Power, Arthur. *Conversations with James Joyce.* Ed. Clive Hart. Chicago: University of Chicago Press, 1974.

Prescott, Joseph A. "Mosenthal's *Deborah* and Joyce's *Ulysses.*" *Modern*

Language Notes 47 (May, 1952): pp. 334–36.

Raleigh, John Henry. *The Chronicle of Leopold and Molly Bloom: Ulysses as Narrative.* Berkeley: University of California Press, 1977.

Reites, James W., SJ *St. Ignatius of Loyola and the Jews.* Unpublished dissertation, Gregorian University, Rome. Excerpts published in *Studies in the Spirituality of Jesuits* 13:4 (September, 1981): pp. 1–47.

Reizbaum, Marilyn. *James Joyce's Judaic Other: Text and Contexts.* Dissertation, Wisconsin-Madison, 1985. Ann Arbor: UMI, 1985.

"Swiss Customs: Zurich's Sources for Joyce's Judaica." *James Joyce Quarterly* 27:2 (1988): pp. 203–18.

Rosenberg, Edgar. *From Shylock to Svengali: Jewish Stereotypes in English Fiction.* Stanford: Stanford University Press, 1960.

Rotenstreich, Nathan. *Jews and German Philosophy: the Polemics of Emancipation.* New York: Schocken Books, 1984.

Roth, Cecil. *Benjamin Disraeli: Earl of Beaconsfield.* New York: The Philosophical Library, Inc., 1952.

The History of the Jews: From Earliest Times to the Six Day War. New York: Schocken Books, 1961.

History of the Jews of England. London: Oxford University Press, 1964.

The History of the Jews of Italy. Philadelphia: The Jewish Publication Society of America, 1946.

Sacher, H., ed. *Zionism and the Jewish Future.* Westport, CT: Hyperion Press, Inc., 1976.

Sacher, Howard Morley. *The Course of Modern Jewish History.* New York: Delta Publications, 1963.

Said, Edward W. *Orientalism.* New York: Vintage Books, 1979.

Sartre, Jean-Paul. *Anti-Semite and Jew.* Translated by George Becker. New York: Schocken Books, 1967.

Scholem, Gershom. *On Jews and Judaism in Crisis: Selected Essays.* New York: Schocken Books, 1976.

Scholes, Robert, and Richard Kain, eds. *The Workshop of Daedalus: James Joyce and the Raw Materials for* A Portrait of the Artist as a Young Man. Evanston, IL: Northwestern University Press, 1965.

Schopenhauer, Arthur. *Essays of Schopenhauer.* Translated by T. Bailey Saunders. New York: Willey Book Co., no date given.

Selected Essays of Arthur Schopenhauer. Translated by Ernest Bax. London: George Bell, 1991.

The World as Will and Representation. Translated by E. F. J. Payne. New York: Dover Press, 1969.

Schwickerath, Robert, SJ *Jesuit Education: its History and Principles.* St. Louis: B. Herder, 1904.

Scott, Sir Walter. *Ivanhoe.* Signet Classic, 1962.

Seccombe, Thomas, "Ivanhoe." *Times Literary Supplement* December 18, 1919.

Shechner, Mark. *Joyce in Nighttown: a Psychoanalytic Inquiry into Ulysses.* Berkeley: University of California Press, 1974.

Shillman, Bernard. *A Short History of the Jews in Ireland*. Dublin: Cahill, 1945.
Staley, Thomas F., ed. *Essays on Italo Svevo*. Tulsa: University of Tulsa Press, 1969.
Steinberg, Erwin. "James Joyce and the Critics Notwithstanding, Leopold Bloom is Not Jewish." *Journal of Modern Literature* 9:1 (1981): pp. 27–49.
"Leopold Bloom and the Nineteenth-Century Fictional Stereotype of the Jew." *Cithera* 22 (1983): pp. 48–61.
"Persecuted...sold...in Morocco Like Slaves." *James Joyce Quarterly* 29:3 (1992): pp. 615–22.
"Reading Leopold Bloom/1904 in 1989." *James Joyce Quarterly* 26:13 (1989): pp. 397–416.
Sullivan, Kevin. *Joyce Among the Jesuits*. New York: Columbia University Press, 1958.
Sultan, Stanley. *The Argument of* Ulysses. Columbus: Ohio State University Press, 1965.
"'What the hell is he? says Ned': Why Joyce Answers the Question with a Question." *James Joyce Quarterly* 23:2 (1986): pp. 217–23.
Svevo, Italo. *A Life*. Translated by Archibald Calquhoun. New York: Alfred A. Knopf, 1963.
As a Man Grows Older. Translated by Beryl De Zoete. Introduction by Stanislaus Joyce. Westport, CT: Greenwood Press, 1977.
Confessions of Zeno. Translated by Beryl de Zoete. New York: Vintage Books, 1989.
Svevo, Livia Veneziani. *Memoir of Italo Svevo*. Translated by Isabel Quigly. Marlboro, VT: The Marlboro Press, 1990.
Szeleky, Andras. *Mihály Munkácsy*. St. Paul: Control Data Arts, 1981.
Tama, Diogene. *Transactions of the Paris Sandhedrim*. London, 1807.
Thatcher, David S. *Nietzsche in England, 1890–1914*. Toronto: University of Toronto Press, 1970.
The Times, London, 1890–1905.
Theoharis, Constantine Theoharis. *Joyce's Ulysses: an Anatomy of Soul*. Chapel Hill: University of North Carolina Press, 1988.
Thorton, Weldon. *Allusions in* Ulysses: *an Annotated List*. Chapel Hill: University of North Carolina Press, 1968.
Tindall, William York. *A Readers' Guide to James Joyce*. New York: Farrar, Straus & Giroux, 1964.
Trachtenberg, Joshua. *The Devil and The Jews: the Medieval Conception of the Jew and its Relation to Modern AntiSemitism*. New York: Meridian Books, 1961.
Tracy, Robert. "Leopold Bloom Four-Fold: a Hungarian-Hebraic-Hellenic-Hibernian Hero." *Massachusetts Review* 6 (1965): pp. 523–38.
Trilling, Lionel. *Matthew Arnold*. New York: W. W. Norton & Co., 1939.
Tucker, Lindsey. *Stephen and Bloom at Life's Feast: Alimentary Symbolism and the Creative Process in James Joyce's* Ulysses. Columbus: Ohio State University Press, 1984.

Tucker, Robert C., ed. *The Marx-Engels Reader.* New York: W. W. Norton & Co., 1978.

United Irishman, 1891–1909.

Veeser, Aram H., ed. *The New Historicism.* London: Routledge, 1989.

Vogel, Leon. "Freud and Judaism: An Analysis in Light of his Correspondences." *Judaism* 24 (1977): pp. 181–93.

Wagner, Richard. *Das Judenthum in der Musik (Judaism in Music).* Translated by Edwin Evans, Senior, FRCO. London: William Reeves, 1910.

Whatley, Richard. *Lessons on the Truth of Christianity, Being an Appendix to the Fourth Book of Lessons, For the Use of Schools.* Dublin: published by direction of the Commissioners of National Education, and reprinted by express permission at Montreal by Armor and Ramsay, 1846.

Wilson, Edmund. *Axel's Castle: A Study in the Imaginative Literature of 1870-1930.* New York: W. W. Norton & Co., 1984.

Wilson, Stephen. *Ideology and Experience: Anti-Semitism in France at the Time of the Dreyfus Affair.* London: Associated University Press, 1982.

Weininger, Otto. *Geschlecht und Charakter (Sex and Character).* Authorized translation from sixth German edition. London: William Heinemann, 1906.

Wollman, Maurice. "Jewish Interest in James Joyce's *Ulysses.*" *Jewish Chronicle Supplement* 176 (1937): pp. 3–4.

Yeats, W. B. *Autobiographies.* London: Macmillan & Co., 1956.

Collected Plays of W. B. Yeats. New York: Macmillan & Co., 1953.

Zimmerman. Michael. "Leopold Paula Bloom: The New Womanly Man." *Literature and Psychology* 29 (1979): pp. 176–84.

Zimmermann, Moshe. *Wilhelm Marr: The Patriarch of Anti-Semitism.* New York: Oxford University Press, 1986.

Zweig, Stephen. *The World of Yesterday.* Lincoln: University of Nebraska Press, 1964.

Index

Joyce, James (*cont.*)
    reads anti-Dreyfusard papers in Paris, 90
    reads Arnold's *Culture and Anarchy*, 106, 109
    reads Fishberg's *The Jews*, 139
    reads of Dreyfus in several Dublin papers,
        66, 67, 70, 72
    reads Scott's *Ivanhoe* at Belvedere, 48
    reads Svevo's novels before writing *Ulysses*,
        155
    reads Weininger, 138
    recognizes "Jewishness" of Svevo's
        protagonists, 172
    recognizes dangers of aggressive nationlism,
        119
    relationship with J. F. Byrne, 77
    relationship with Oliver Gogarty, 99
    relationship with Schmitz, 160, 161, 163
    "rescued" by Alfred Hunter, 103, 105
    respects Catholic paternalism at Clongowes,
        45
    returns to Dublin in 1903, 99
    says Bloom's loneliness based on his being a
        Jew, 179
    says he's not a "bloodyminded man," 89
    self-image as a male, 9
    studies Old Testament at Clongowes, 43
    thinks little of GAA, 214
    thinks Schmitz took his own life, 168
    uses Nietzsche's ideas in Dubliners' story, 112
    uses Parnell-as-Irish-Moses allusion, 36
    writes essay on Munkacsy's *Ecce Homo*, 73
    writes *Giacomo Joyce* with Scott's *Rebecca* in
        mind, 50
    writes reviews in Paris for Dublin papers, 88
Joyce, John, 26
    anti-clericism, 39
    childhood in Cork, 27
    Home Rule politics, 17, 29
    involvement in Dublin musical world, 28
    rage at rejection of Parnell by Church, 38
    trip to Cork to sell properties, 57
    uses Parnell-as-Irish-Moses slogans, 35
Joyce, May, 17, 24, 25
Joyce, Stanislaus
    accuses brother of stealing from his diary, 112
    Dublin Diary, 140
    finds Conway's teachings ignorant, 22
    hears brother has been asking about Jews,
        156
    James prefers "people rated as failures," 82
    My Brother's Keeper, 23
    says Schmitz's praise inspired Joyce, 162
Judaism, 6, 127, 202
    apostasy from, 205

as a religion without a true "spirituality," 141
Azazel, 225
Belial, 225
Deuteronomy, 231
Exodus, 221
"Hebraism," 6
Halacha, 1, 4, 9, 204, 218, 236, 237
Hebrew read from right to left, 228
Hebrew written from right to left, 207
Kaddish, 227
Kashrut, 157, 201, 204
Levitical law, 201
Messianism, 221, 225
Old Testament patriarchs, 41
Passover ritual, 207
rite of circumcision, 19, 201, 221
teaches compassion, 207
tephilim, 221
the *Haggadah*, 236
the Judaic God, 189
the *Shema*, 227
the *Talmud*, 235

Kaufmann, Walter, 121
Keating, Geoffrey, 35
Kenner, Hugh, 103, 228
Klein, A. M., 192

L'Instransigeant, 90
La Patrie, 198
Lamb's *Adventures of Ulysses*, 47
Larbaud, Valery, 2, 163
Lassalle, Ferdinand, 138, 224
Lawrence, Karen, 185
Lazare, Bernard, 87
Le Bon, Gustave, 85, 92
Le Juif Errant, 134
Le Juif, French idea and history of, 86
Lebowitz, Naomi, *Italo Svevo*, 170, 178
Leo XII, 18
Leo XIII, 18, 21, 54
Leon, Paul, 128
Lessing, Theodor, *Der Judische Selbtsthass*, 142
Levenston Brothers, 28
Leventhal, A. J., 3, 14, 25
Levitt, Morton, 3
Limerick, anti-Jewish riots in 1904, 37, 102
Lombroso, Ceasar, 136, 138
Lukàcs, Georg, 12, 53

Magalaner, Marvin, 3
Mahaffey, Vicki, 50
Maimonides, Moses, 193, 233
Mangan, James Clarence, 72, 193, 199